With the Royal Engineers in Italy, the Peninsula & France

Captain Charles Boothby R.E.
Born 1786. Died 1846

With the Royal Engineers in Italy, the Peninsula & France

Under England's Flag

A Prisoner of France

Charles Boothby

With the Royal Engineers in Italy, the Peninsula & France
Under England's Flag and *A Prisoner of France*
by Charles Boothby

First published under the titles
Under England's Flag
and
A Prisoner of France

Leonaur is an imprint
of Oakpast Ltd

Copyright in this form © 2011 Oakpast Ltd

ISBN: 978-0-85706-781-4 (hardcover)
ISBN: 978-0-85706-782-1 (softcover)

http://www.leonaur.com

Publisher's Notes

The opinions of the authors represent a view of events in which he was a participant related from his own perspective, as such the text is relevant as an historical document.

The views expressed in this book are not necessarily those of the publisher.

Contents

Under England's Flag 7
A Prisoner of France 195

Volume 7

Under England's Flag

Contents

Introduction   13
Note   15
From Journal Notes   23
Appendix   179

Ubique Quo Fas et Gloria Ducunt

Introduction

Why should I now write my life, or retrace the more adventurous part of it? I have no material to afford instruction or impart knowledge even to the humblest class of readers.

I have been an unobservant and an unintelligent traveller. The exclusive occupation of an arduous profession may indeed excuse this, but cannot obviate its sterilising consequences.

I have no new events, no unknown regions, no wonderful discoveries to unfold. Reader, there are a great many good reasons for not troubling thee with a book, and thou mayest well inquire why I have not attended to them.

The fact is, they have had considerable weight with me, and for these fourteen or fifteen years have served to keep my manuscripts quiet in my desk, and they would have kept them there forever if, by reflection and consideration of the times, I had not conceived a hope that their publication might be useful to my countrymen.

Another motive I have, which I mention last, because it is the most serious, and this is, that I have found much of the writing and style of contemporaneous authors calculated to undervalue religion, to undermine it by sneers and insinuations, and to look down upon it with compassionate airs of superior illumination.

Hundreds who are startled, interested, and attracted by the audacity of assaults upon religion neither know nor care what has been the deliberate conclusion of Newton, of Locke, of Milton, or of Pope. Therefore, let the man who has through life felt religion to be as a guard and shield spread before him, becoming a more ample and secure protection as the exigency became more pressing and severe, let him oppose his sober experience to that of the scoffer, whose works and words give out that he has found some secret of happiness in throwing religion aside as a troublesome, childish, and unfashionable restraint.

Most indolently, most imperfectly have I served my God, but I have never in any part of life forgotten Him, never have ceased to love and fear Him.

The return He has made to me it is that I think worthy of remark.

In the depression before Him of conscious unworthiness, He has enabled me, in spite of my transgressions, to carry my heart serenely and lightly in my breast.

Whether my soul has conceived her danger from the wars of earth or the storms of ocean, the conflict of armies or of elements, if I have had courage, if I have had comfort, if I have had the tranquillity and firmness of a man, I know of no source from which I can have derived them, excepting only the kindness of God speaking to my soul through the promises of religion.

In sickness and in suffering, the friend and the nurse remove every object of external disquiet, and the faults of the strong are forgotten in the sufferings of the sick. But what friend, or what nurse is, or has ever been to me, so kind as the Spirit of God.

Silently then, (removing the far more disquieting subject of internal uneasiness), the mountain of recollected offences, and the anxious cloud of apprehended evils, are melted away before the steadfast beam of Christian hope, like snow before the sun of summer. Does it need, then, much learning or much study to contradict the sneer of the mocker or emancipate the spirit of his victim? I think not, and hope that in the book now offered to the public something like good fruit may be found. The seed indeed is small, but may God give the increase.

Charles Brotherty

Sutterton, Lincolnshire,
1824

Note

Captain Boothby's design of publishing his journals was never carried out in his lifetime, and now, six-and-seventy years after he wrote the above introduction, (as at time of first publication), they are brought out for the first time in book form. Incorporated with them are his letters to the various members of his family, which, having been written without any thought of reproduction, are perhaps even more vivid and natural than the journal itself. These carry on the narrative, and bridge over what might otherwise have been gaps in its continuity.

That branch of the military profession to which I was destined (the Royal Engineers) requires an early dedication to its peculiar studies. We are put under military discipline while we are yet boys, and are in many respects good soldiers before we come to be men. Hence a consequence is derived to this service which I think is favourably felt by its members in after life; and this is, that their companions in arms and in the labours and dangers of war are, for the most part, those with whom they have shared the yoke of education, and the more than redeeming pleasures of youthful fellowship. Much doubt, therefore, in the selection of friends, and much of the disappointment and injury which so often accrue from a bad choice, are hereby spared, since at a period when Nature seldom permits any sustained disguise, each young mind has furnished itself with friends, chosen, as it were, in the castle of truth. Here it has obtained the knowledge of which to seek and which to shun.

Thus, when at the age of seventeen or eighteen I assumed the sword of a British officer, the branch of service into which I entered contained numbers of my chosen friends, whose hearts I knew to the bottom, and who knew mine. A character on both sides was already established which we would have died rather than sully, and certainly the advantages of this emulous friendship did not terminate with the individual, but extended to the service in which they were employed. Of all my early friends, I never knew one who was not eager and importunate to be placed in the front of danger and of enterprise, or who thought even for a moment of sparing any extent of labour, peril, loss of liberty, or life itself in the service of his country; and most of these, in the flower of youth and dawn of military glory, have fallen in battle.

After about a year spent on a home station, in compliance with my earnest request, I was nominated, early in 1805, to proceed with a foreign expedition, going, no one knew whither, under the command of Sir James Craig.

This order plunged me immediately into a new state of existence, wherein every sort of agitation, activity, and conflicting emotion succeeded to the monotony of routine duty. I exulted that I was so early to taste of foreign service, and the note of preparation and outfit was well suited to the stirring propensity of youth; but in the midst of all my satisfaction and ardent hope there did lurk a fear and a dread at the bottom of my heart of something I had first to encounter.

My father and mother had accustomed the hearts of their children to such unbounded tenderness and love as is sure to draw a proportionate return; and in spite of the commonness of such separation, I knew better than anyone else could that the thoughts of my departure would make that home unhappy whose happiness and peace I prized above all other things.

I knew that my incomparable father, whatever he might feel, had no wish to make a home soldier of his son. I knew he would both mourn and approve my departure. But it was a thing which lay in my way and hung at my heart, and my first object on arriving in London was to seek my new commanding officer, and gain his consent to my making a hurried journey to take leave of my friends.

The name of my new chief I had long known, for his fine person and dark flashing eye had been pointed out to me when a boy as belonging to the finest officer in the service, and his manner and conversation were all that a raw boy could hope to find in a young man, of kindness, genius, and experience. My heart beat with the thoughts of serving under such a master, of being trained to actual service under his eye, and (youthful vanity perhaps added) of being made by him as fine and clever a fellow as himself.

He entered at once into the feelings which made me so desirous to make a journey home, and the moment he could ascertain that the time would serve, "Be off then, Boothby," he said, "but make all the haste you can back; and if I have left London, lose not a moment in getting to Portsmouth."

Away I went. The parting scene was more trying even than I anticipated, but *"Time and the hour run through the roughest day,"* and I was soon on my way back to London. I had seen my father's venerable form and manly features shaken with childish weeping as he held me to his breast, and though long the pang of that sight dwelt in my mind—for I have ever since cherished that sacred picture as one of the holiest my memory can retain—I never shall forget the relief and lightness I felt from having got through this sad passage of tears and lamentations. On arriving in London I feared that my chief had left it, so I hastened to that second mother who had spent the short interval of my absence in collecting all the various articles desirable for an officer in the Mediterranean, to which we were supposed to be destined.

I found her in her drawing-room, where every sofa, cabinet, chair, and table was covered with my clothes and linen, which hers and other kind hands were marking. The perpetual consciousness of doing kind and useful acts had made an angelic smile the inseparable companion of her face, and with that loved, that dearly-remembered smile did she now receive me.

To all the stores she had so laboured to procure for me she had added as her own present a complete writing-box and dressing-case combined—a luxury of peculiar value to me, which my own funds would have found it difficult to compass; but finding me uneasy lest I should be left behind or be thought tardy by my commander, "Go," she said, "you shan't wait for your baggage; we will have it all packed up, and I will send my butler with it to Portsmouth, that I may be sure of its reaching you."

Down to Portsmouth then I went on the outside of the Mail, in the highest health and the ardent spirits of youth—spirits that made, I suppose, even my body buoyant and elastic, for the Mail overturned in the night and threw me on the road without giving me so much as a scratch or a bruise. It was about twenty miles from London when we met a team of horses standing in a slant direction on the road, the night very foggy with misting rain, and the lamps not penetrating farther into the mist than the rumps of the wheelers.

The coachman, to avoid the waggon, turned suddenly out of the way and ran up the bank. Finding the coach swaggering, I got up, with my face to the horses, hardly daring to suppose it possible that the Mail could overturn, when the unwieldy monster was on one wheel, and then down it came with a terminal bang. During my descent I had just time to hope that I might escape with the fracture of one or two legs, and then found myself on my two shoulders, very much pleased with the novelty and ease of the journey. I got me up, and spied the monster with his two free wheels whirling with great velocity, but quite compact and still in the body, and as soon as I had shaken my feathers and opened my senses I began to think of the one female and three males in the inside, whom I supposed to be either dead or asleep.

I ran to open the door, when the guard, having thought of the same thing, did it for me, and we then took out the folks one by one, like pickled gherkins, or anything else preserved in a jar, by putting our hands to the bottom. We found that the inmates were only stupefied, though all had bruises of some kind, and one little gentleman complained that he was nipped in the loins by the mighty pressure of his neighbour, who had sat upon him some time after the door was opened, to recollect himself or to give thanks for his escape.

The lady told me "she was terribly hurt indeed," and so, when we got to the supper place, I gave her a kipperkin of boiled port wine with much spice. She agreed it was very nice, and looked more cheery, but the rest of the inside passengers seemed to think that it would not look well to eat after being overturned.

Not one on the outside was hurt in the least degree, and I, being on the top of the coach, had the farthest fly.

I had not been without my fears that on arriving at Portsmouth I should have to hasten on board, and perhaps sail without my baggage; but the wind had changed, all the troops were not yet embarked, and nobody seemed to be thinking of anything but gaiety and amusement, or the not unpleasant business of laying in comforts for the voyage.

Sir James Craig and Lefebure were lodging together, and kindly took me in till I could provide myself better. With Lefebure I had early acquaintance, and since entering the army we had been employed in neighbouring stations, and I knew that under Sir James Craig's command he had come to be reckoned perhaps the best officer of his early standing. He, I found, was to be of our company, as well as Hoste and Lewis, two more of my earlier friends.

Our second in command was Sir John Stuart, whom I saw for the first time. The best and bravest could not have chosen fitter company

THE START

than every one of these. Sir James Craig and Sir John Stuart were of great experience and superior rank. Sir John Stuart had served long at Gibraltar; Sir James Craig everywhere. The rest might be called equals, for in youth, inexperience, and rank they were about equal, but of the whole party I was the junior officer.

Two excellent vessels, a ship and a brig, were appointed for our accommodation, and some of us were allotted to the ship and some to the brig.

Each party now addressed itself to the important task of laying in a comfortable sea stock, and the two ships agreed, as opportunity should occur, that they would interchange fresh meat on the voyage.

For our part we provided several sheep and pigs, a milch goat, and a great many ducks and fowls, with hay and grain for their provender, a prodigious quantity of eggs and potatoes, butter, cheese, and lard, of pickles, sauces, spices, portable soup, white and brown macaroni, vermicelli, and celery seed, with a variety of other stores, but particularly a great stock of bottled porter, a barrel of ale, and a pretty allowance of wine and spirits.

The procuring and embarking of all these various things, animate and inanimate, fell in equal portions to Lewis and myself. It was no light task, but neither was it bad fun. Lewis was a pleasant, lively, and most efficient colleague; many a voyage did we make to Spithead; many an hour did we spend on board to see proper accommodation prepared for our live stock, and to place our stores out of the reach of damage or of breakage.

The general obligation of such provisioning makes the streets of Portsmouth like a rabbit-warren, the scarlet purchasers popping in and out of the shop doors incessantly in long succession.

Between two and three weeks passed over not unpleasantly, for letters and various accidents had extended my acquaintance amongst the staff of the army, and tended to wear off any feeling of strangeness.

The general impression was that Malta was our destination in the first instance, as indeed it was known that we were charged with despatches for that island.

On the 18th of April 1805 we set sail—a numerous fleet of transports under the convoy of the *Queen*, a three-decker, having the Commander of the Forces on board and his staff, and the *Dragon*, a seventy-four, carrying Sir John Stuart, the second in command, and his staff.

The army was supposed to be from 8000 to 10,000 strong, accompanied as well by four companies of artillery, and a prodigal supply of all warlike stores.

Portsmouth, April 17, 1805.

My dearest Father—I can only say we are all going on board, and expect to sail tomorrow, certainly for the Mediterranean. Don't write any more to this place. I am perfectly happy and comfortable. God bless you, and my mother, and Louisa.—
Ever yours, my dearest Dad,
Chas. Boothby.
You must not expect to hear from me anymore, but I will seize every opportunity.

From Journal Notes

Began to blow hard as we made the Scilly Isles, chops of Channel so rough, landsmen on beam ends. In Bay of Biscay, increased to squally gale. One entire day in cabin. Great confusion from violence of motion. Every day afterwards on deck.

April 26, 1805.—Delightful starlight night. Fleet in compact body with lights astern; silence only broken by mellowed sea noises. So happy a time for the feast of thought, that I could not leave deck till after midnight.

April 27.—Voyage ten days old. Wrote to my father.

Off the Coast of Spain,
Between Cape Finisterre and Ortegal,
Sunday, April 27, 1805.

Calm air, bright sun, and a cheerful prospect of land.

With much satisfaction, my ever dearest Father, I sit in the boat astern and turn my pen to a usual and most comfortable employment.

I have been so *very ill* in that Stygian boiling Bay of Biscay, that I would willingly have given something to boot with my commission for a "Burgamy pear" or a "Brown Burer." Nature, I thought, could not stand it! I knew there was nothing in me to comply with those violent requisitions! It began to blow hard just as we made the Scilly Isles, and the winds and waves overcame me in the murky chops of the Channel. But I will not keep you or myself longer upon these disagreeable topics, and so will quit them.

I do not suppose that I shall be able to send you this until we arrive at Gibraltar, but I will add to it from time to time.

Oh, how I long to be roving over those Spanish mountains, and to be relieved from this constant see-saw.

The coast which we see is very romantic. We are about eighteen miles from it, and are under strict orders not to land at any port we may put into, without express permission. So I think it most likely that officers will not be allowed to go on shore at Gibraltar.

Tuesday, April 30.
Land thirty miles distant.

Since I last sat down we have made about 100 miles. On Sunday we were hailed by the *Prince*, the ship in which are our other three comrades—Captain Lefebure (our commandant), Nicholas, and Hoste. They told us on board the *Prince* that the Toulon fleet was out, and being too strong for Sir John Orde, he had put in to Gibraltar, and that they expected we should put in to Lisbon—a slender protection!!

We were more than half inclined to credit this, as we believe that Sir John Orde has not more than five sail, and the French might be reinforced from Ferrol.

Our convoy is, we think, very inadequate, because the loss of this little army would be a sad damper to England, particularly from the nature and quantity of stores, and the six Royal Engineers attached to it!!!—only the "*Queen*," the "*Dragon*" and a "*Bomb*."

A breeze springing up last night had been preceded by the appearance of a shoal of porpoises, which took a westerly direction, and whose novel gambols and beastly black appearances amused us much.

The *Queen* made signal to bring up and lay to, which we did all the night. We supposed that she was waiting for the *Dragon*, who had left us at midday to reconnoitre, and we began to consider how we should like a French prison.

This morning the *Dragon* returned, and we suppose all clear, as we are now on our voyage with a smart breeze.

We see the coast of Portugal very plain, and can distinguish with the naked eye the buildings immediately on the beach, and with a glass we discover further into the country, which appears beautiful.

We have met shoals of Portuguese fishing boats, and today we have been much amused with the sight of a sea-monster of immense size. He frequently gave us very good views of his grand tail, and he was attended by a foreign suite, inhabitants of the surmounting element. His tail was forked, and on one side he displayed a jetty brightness, and on the other a dazzling white. He gave us glimpses of other parts of his body, which increased our respect for him. He was, I should think, two miles distant, and yet we saw him perfectly distinct.

Off Lisbon Rock, May 5, 1805.
We have had blowing weather from the south, but I stood it seaman-like this time. The weather now quite calm. The Ordnance agent is on board. He confirms late reports of the Toulon fleet of twenty-one sail being out, and that Lord Nelson is after them, but not, as we thought, off Cadiz, in which case we expected to put into Lisbon. What they may do I fear! Lord Nelson has but ten. Is he to strive with impossibilities and get the better of them?

The Admiral sending despatches to England, I seize the opportunity.

God for ever with his blessings surround us in one happy circle. ... *Adieu.* We soon shall meet again.

Charles Boothby.

May 7.—Put in to the port of Lisbon.

The orders issued to the troops are to be ready to land at a moment's notice with artillery and every preparation of war in case of emergency, but no one allowed to go on shore on any account whatever.

Hence we conceive that some attempt from the French fleet (said to be at Cadiz) is thought possible; and should it approach the Tagus, the commander-in-chief had determined to land his forces and seize the batteries commanding the river, and this, we conceived, would be excellent fun. Meantime, however the orange groves might tempt us with their fragrance and their verdure, no one was allowed to land. The Portuguese boats, though, brought us off plenty of oranges still attached to their green branches, which tickled the imagination to heighten their zest, and to quench our salt-sea thirst after fruit and freshness.

The *Orpheus* frigate (it is said) sends intelligence into the Tagus that Lord Nelson blockades Cadiz with such a force as the combined fleet dare not encounter. Whatever the intelligence was, however, it produced orders to sail.

We hear that General Junot blustered a good deal at a British armament entering the Tagus, and declared that the first man that set foot on shore should be the signal for his departure. He was spared the trouble, however, for this afternoon we set sail, having received orders to be on the alert to repel any attack from gunboats as we approached the gut of Gibraltar. Good amusement in drilling all hands on board to the service of the great guns and small arms.

May 12.—A beautiful breeze brought us off Cadiz, where we passed through great Nelson's fleet, lying to, and, as we imagined, blockading the combined fleet, who had by this time got to the West Indies. We were now at the point where precaution was necessary.

As junior I took the first watch. A most beautiful moonlight night showed to admiration the coast of Barbary, terminated by Ape's Hill, and on the other hand the not less sublime outline of the Spanish land.

The moon with her immeasurable column on the waters, silvering the prominent points in the dark grandeur of these newly seen and far-famed shores, while the fleets in quiet approached it with swift wings, and the keel-ploughed deep seemed kindling with diamonds and with fire—a sight never, never to be forgotten! Nor do I know the price that (after experience of its sublimity) could have bought this watch from me.

I felt sure that if any attempt were made on us, we should distinguish ourselves, but the blessed wind was too fair and strong, and the whole fleet glided along in silent and unspeakable triumph, the elements that had opposed now inviting to accelerate our speed, the sparkling waves pursuing but to push us forward, and the winds never drawing breath from our full canvas, transparent with the peerless moon. Lewis took the second watch, and in four hours I was again to relieve him, but before they had elapsed he came into the cabin and told me I need not disturb myself, as we were close under the Rock. But we had scarcely composed ourselves before a desperate cannonading began. Up we both jumped, and being nearly dressed, ran on deck cursing the gunboats. But it was only the Spanish batteries saluting the dawn of the birthday of the Prince of Peace!!!

However, the wonderful and beautiful Rock would not let us leave the deck until broad daylight had unfolded all its features. To be so first seen, uprising like the very wall of heaven, and tracing its giant outline upon the dark blue of night, while mortals in their little ships are bounding upon the liquid diamond that bathes its foot, was fortunate, for of all the shows and sights I have ever seen, none so transfixed me with delight and splendid novelty as this glorious Pinnacle of Rock. Close to it we seemed, its peopled and fortified steep rising above us high up into heaven, light above light moving upon the rich darkness of his umbered face, so that to see where his long uneven ridge ended in the sky, the spectator's head must hang back between the shoulder-blades.

After a short sleep, curiosity called us early on deck, and it is impossible to conceive a scene more busy, beautiful, and variously attractive to an inexperienced eye than the Bay of Gibraltar at this time presented. In the first place, even to the most sedate mind, there is a sort of magnificent personality in the form and situation of the Rock fortress itself, difficult indeed to describe, but impossible not irresistibly to feel. There he rears himself proudly out of the blue water into the blue sky, while all around within the sweep of his thunder lies in uniform subjection. Vast mountains and bold shores shut in the horizon, but they approach not him; in the heart of a great kingdom, in the midst of enemies, within his own circuit he is unapproachably supreme. The moment friendly ships come within his shadow, the foe ceases to pursue, and retires in acknowledgment of his power.

On the other side of the Bay, the Spanish port and depot of Algeciras, about seven miles distant, furnishes, in time of war, objects of continual interest. Swarms of gunboats are assembled there, as well as in the African fortress of Ceuta, fifteen miles distant (other side of Gut), and in unfavourable winds infest, damage, and sometimes carry off the merchant vessels as their prey in the very sight of the impregnable fortress, whose garrison, from their parades and quarters, can quietly behold every vicissitude of their running contests, exhibited on a scene beautiful beyond all description. The two fortresses, as daylight ceases and again returns, hear each other's warning gun, and know that either keeps its watch, while vessels constantly approaching from east and west bring produce and intelligence from every part of the world, and every ship that arrives or passes through the Straits is subject to the inspection of every individual. No need to look into the arrivals—all passes under review, and each inhabitant has a place on that high theatre from which to contemplate the spectacle at his own pleasure.

Thus when our friends informed us when the combined fleet had gone up or down, and how long after Lord Nelson had followed (*viz.* a month), they told us not what they had heard, but what each officer had seen for himself, and had counted as the number of each fleet.

In good time some very old and early friends come off, to invite us to the shore, and, to our inexpressible joy, leave is given us to land. We are not, however, to sleep on shore, and receive the most exact caution to be ready at a moment's notice, as the greatest expedition will be made to proceed. My excellent little friend Archer, with whom I had been educated, was one of those who came alongside our ship to welcome his old friend and playfellow and to do the honours of Gibraltar.

It was now we were made acquainted with every point and chronicle of the Rock—where formerly endangered, where subsequently strengthened, whence terribly remembered by the enemy. These were subjects involved in a labyrinth which the practised eye of our commandant could unravel at a glance, and in two days he knew more thoroughly the strength and power of this fortress than many a brave officer resident upon it for half his life.

Some fear subsists that we shall be detained some time at Gibraltar. We are still obliged to sleep on board, and to use precautions in case of attack from the gunboats. If the expedition is broken up, some of us may be ordered to remain. Should I like it or no?

It is a great local confinement, and often entails spare sea diet, but there are garrison amusements, balls, private theatricals, and the most delectable library I ever saw for a not learned man; the apartment splendid, the prospect beautiful, the arrangement admirable, the decorous stillness of those who enter most auspicious, and the terms

GIBRALTER—NORTH VIEW

very easy and encouraging—a trifling half-yearly contribution and entrance of three days' pay conferring a perpetual share. Bathing in extreme luxury. Also the corps to which I belong have a most gentlemanlike and well-regulated mess, and handsome quarters most enviably situated. So that however disappointed I should be in ulterior views, I determined to think I might be worse pleased than by being ordered to remain here. Yet I learn from friends at headquarters that Sir James Craig by no means expects that his army will be dispersed or its ulterior object changed.

June 15.—*In statu quo*, thoroughly tired of the place by this time, and most anxious for despatches to send us on our way.

From this day till June 17th an alarm of preparations amongst the gunboats of Algeciras obliges us to remain on board, and this day it seems we are about to sail. Exceedingly rejoiced at those symptoms of departure, and hoping that the fine western breeze is to take us swiftly up the Mediterranean.

No such thing. We beat about, now the African and now the European coast, in delicious weather, and the going quite close in to these bold shores, so as to contemplate their picturesque beauty, takes off much of the tedium of shipboard. The African side in point of beauty is not comparable to the Spanish—few tracts of coast, indeed, could rival, none exceed it, or the happy, brilliant accidents of night or day, of dawn or sunset, in which we were perpetually viewing it. The object of this cruise was to elude a meditated attack from Algeciras, as so large and spread-out a fleet of ships (not of war) were particularly liable to surprise, damage, and disablement where the enemy is always so near, the night so dark and starlight clear, and weather so serene for sudden operations.

June 25.—The fleet now commences its voyage, and we observe the *Lively* Frigate, having Sir James Craig on board, make all sail, and soon she vanishes from our view.

The voyage is only memorable to me from the unspeakable splendour of the sun's setting and rising, which I chanced often to contemplate trans- fixed with wonder.

Towards the end of three weeks a good breeze, which had brought us off, the island of Gozo, fell from us, and left us nearly becalmed about twenty miles from the harbour of Valetta, giving us full leisure to view the nature of the coast and the face of the country.

Great was our curiosity to see the mode of living on that brown island,[1] of which fame had spoken so much.

When in England we get into a chaise to be driven to some place of note not seen before, we all know there is a sort of interest and stretching of necks as we come near to form some notion of what it will be like. But how much greater the interest when we get into a ship, spread our sails to the wind and our keel to the dark blue water, and set forth to visit some far-famed island long heard and read of as a far-distant thing, and now find ourselves skirting along swiftly by the very shore that girdles in its cities and its wonders; and the more barren, rocky, unadorned, and forbidding the first range of the shore we approached, the more we thirsted to see the high bastion of the capital frowning over the bright blue deep.

July 18.—A light air rose with the morning and wafted us into the harbour of Valetta. Here, as at Gibraltar, some of our comrades come off to welcome us, and though unknown at present, the strong bond of belonging to the same service, wearing the same coat, and hatched, as one might say, in the same military shell, induces them to hold out to us the ready hand of brotherhood and friendship.

Impatient as we were to get on shore and satisfy our curiosity, we had for the present enough to do in remarking the grandeur of the buildings, the spaciousness, security, and many branches of the harbour, and, above all, the stupendous character of the fortifications.

Valetta altogether appeared to me the most magnificent city I had ever beheld. Everything contributed to imbue the scene with traits fit for some splendid picture of growing Carthage; nothing mean or sullied, nothing to stain the clear clean hue of every colour; the sea, the sky, the transparent air, the chiselled stone, the native rock—all seemed as stainless, bright, and *soignée* as a Venetian painting, while the masses of shipping of every description, whose decks displayed a masquerade of divers costumes, brought the image of all nations before us, the *gondolas* and open boats, with gentlemen dressed as if for court, with powdered heads uncovered, under umbrellas of every colour, and wearing silk coats, looking so enviably cool as they touched from ship to ship. All was so curious, so undeniably *abroad*, that we loved to realise all the anticipations of imagination, and might, I doubt not, have been amused during a much longer confinement than it was our lot to encounter.

July 19.—One day was all the trial our patience underwent, as on

---
1 Malta.

the 19th we were permitted to land and regale ourselves, like children, with touching and turning over the forms we had been viewing at a distance. From the point at which we landed, to which the fine streets of the city themselves descend, the ascent to the heart of the city is gained by stairs of vast width and breadth, but each giving a small and imperceptible rise.

The whole street, indeed, is a grand *escalier*, of which the continuous houses of rich merchandise on either hand form the banisters. These stairs appear to be carved out of the native rock, and look as if a carriage and horses might safely descend, though I do not remember that they do.

We were now on shore, mixed up in the quarters of our brother officers, previously established here, and began a very pleasant kind of life, in despite of nightly mosquitoes and daily heat intense, reflected and reproduced from the glaring rock on which it everywhere smote; and this memorandum of the heat remains fixed in my memory—the noble streets of Valetta are extremely regular, and run in broad parallels at right angles with each other—when the sun, therefore, begins to decline, the streets which lie north and south are divided by broad lines of shade and sunshine—down the broad shade then the different parties walk and talk and lounge, with sauntering pace and head uncovered; but when one of the broad crossings must be passed, exposed to the sun's fierce ray, you see every man put on his hat and dart swiftly across the bright space, as if escaping through a fire. Various commanders and married officers helped to furnish our society. Our newfound brethren put all their resources at our command, and mounting us on the beautiful barb or Arabian horses, or the scarce less beautiful ass of Malta, "showed us all the qualities o' the isle."

Stationed at Gozo was Edward Ker, one of my boyish friends, and one of our excursions was to visit him. We were delighted to meet, and though baked and broiled by sea and land in exploring curiosities, whatever we saw seemed to compensate our labour.

What pleased me most was a large steep rock, called the Fungus Rock, because it produces a fungus famous for its styptic power, and which the Grand Master (of the Knights of St. John) formerly distributed to the potentates of Europe. Though not for the fungus did I admire the rock, but for its stupendous eminence over a blue deep bay that lies still and unfathomable below. You pass from one rock to another at a terrific height in a basket sliding on a rope; and as I hung in the air and eyed the sapphire mirror below, I conceived an eager thirst to plunge into the cooling water; my companions consented to wait until I had descended and gratified my desire. When sporting about in this delicious bath, a good swimmer cannot conceive how people can sink in that salt sea, for the water seems so solid and buoyant it requires a great effort to keep below.

These rocks form almost such a cave as Virgil describes with such a thrilling stillness of words:—

Est in secessu longo locus: insula portum
Efficit objectu laterum; quibus omnis ab alto
Frangitur, inque sinus scindit sese unda reductos;
Hinc atque hinc vastae rupes, geminique minantur
In caelum scopuli: quorum sub vertice late
Aequora tuta silent.—Aen, 1. 163.

It was like the place—nay, perhaps it was the place—whose inviolable stillness and stupendous barriers Virgil so divinely describes; and when- ever those still words, "*Aequora tuta silent*" recur to my memory, so does this scene.

This is "*secessu longo locus.*"

A fleet from England declared to be in the offing was a subject of great interest at Malta. We used to repair immediately to the leads of the palace, whose great height, carrying the sight clear over every obstruction of tower, church, and fortress, displayed the wide ocean to our view, covered with the expected ships, their swelling sails as white as wool, and the sea and sky more blue and bright than all comparisons.

Pleasant and full of expectation it was to watch them successively steering into the narrow port; some stately and huge, plumed with the pennant of command, displayed the broad and chequered sides of battle; others more humble, but innumerable; all in gallant trim and guided seamanlike.

Then eager for the mail! the image of home imprisons the truant soul, and brings it back to its first tenderness; the sight of the well-known but long-suspended hand, the endearing accents which distance has made so infrequent; that day, at least, is sacred to home; and if the tidings have been cheering, though the eye may glisten and the cheek of the young soldier may flush with unwonted tenderness, yet is his heart neither solitary nor sad; his friends partake of some reflection of the kindness that his soul is inwardly pouring out to his parents and his brothers.

It is time to close the chapter on Malta, but before leaving I wrote home to my mother.

La Valetta, Malta, August 15, 1805.

Dearest Dona Rafela—I believe this will be brought to England by an officer who has obtained leave. I do not know him. Nothing at all remarkable has happened since I wrote last. We made an excursion to the island of Gozo, which is much better-looking than that of Malta. There is more green and romanticity, but all prospect here is in the sublime, for you see grateful coincidence of rock, sea, and sky, which can stretch the mind to great capacity. But where, my dear mother, are the flowery meads, the green pastures, the murmuring streams that may soothe the mind into content with itself and charity to all around? Hot stone houses, hot brown ground—hot, hot, all hot.

"*England, with all thy sullen skies, I love thee still, my country!*" Dear, dear England, dearest Edwinstowe! What is objected to it? The cold? Why the cold produces that very thing which gives to England the greatest superiority over other countries—a fireside!

Now stir the fire and close the shutters fast,
And while the bubbling and loud hissing urn
Upsends a steaming column, etc., etc.

Wretched people under a burning sun, what do you know of this? or of

The important budget ushered in,
With such heart-shaking musick, etc. etc.

I often think of my dearest father sitting in his little summerhouse by the river, and wish myself beside him.

We have no sight of futurity—Russia, Naples; beat the French; a wound, a medal, and arm in a sling.

My health is uniform, and so are my spirits; only sometimes I sigh for England, for Edwinstowe, and for you. God bless you, my dearest mother.—With great love, your most affectionate and dutiful son,

Charles Boothby.

I cannot tell what the affairs of the continent tend to. We get no news, as the French detain the good, and the Neapolitans the bad. It was verging towards winter before Sir James Craig's expedition actually embarked. I had permission to dine and sleep ashore the day of embarkation. In the night I was seized with cholera—often in that country so fatal. No assistance and no remedy of any kind was to hand. It took its course, and in the morning I felt weak and languid, but, thanks to youth and great strength of constitution, I was well.

At daylight I went on board with a feeling of exhaustion, but no remains of disease.

In a few hours afterwards the fleet set sail, and the weather became almost immediately murky and unpropitious. We made our course round the western point of the island of Sicily without any precise knowledge of our destination. For three weeks in that Cerulean sea did we struggle with weather as moist and murky and with an atmosphere as thick as ever shrouded the chops of the British Channel. But at length the wind moderated and inclined abaft the beam, the sky and sea resumed their blue, and the classic shores of Italy beautified by degrees the farthest horizon. Soon, as evening fell, we were gliding between the fairy isles of Ischia and Capri with a smooth and steady course into the Bay of Naples.

How we watched, how we strained our eyes and wearied our arms with poising the telescope to pry into the beauteous recesses of those approaching shores! But now the night had fallen, and a dark and spangled curtain threw its veil over the beauties we were gazing at, and when we came to an anchor it was too profoundly dark for even the imagination to take hints from surrounding forms. So we went to bed and wished for day—for a day without clouds.

The next morning our dreams were realised.

Vesuvius stood close before us, solemnly breathing upwards his pillar of smoke.

Woods, with young plantations and viny hillocks, spread widely round him. To the right a fair town stood on the brink of the sea, while immediately behind it the steep mountains pushed their wooded peaks into the sky. Far to the left, and out of sight, or indistinctly discerned, lay Naples.

Soon a great number of Neapolitan boats came to the fleet to sell such things as they who have been cooped up at sea buy greedily—bread, fruit, game, and fish. Perhaps the parley thus obtained with these interesting foreigners, and the opportunity to take small flights in our grammar Italian, and to observe their dress, language, and grotesque extravagance of sound and gesticulation, were more acceptable to our curiosity than those dainties to our animal appetites.

We saw distinctly some parts of the great road to Naples, and it was quite a natural pantomime to witness a conversation between parties on the shore, perhaps discussing the object of our appearance and the probability of our movements—far too distant to overhear any sound, or see any minor hints of countenance or gesture. English folks, so seen at a distance, might have hardly been distinguished from statues or from trees. But the Italian's body is a telegraph to the distant observer while his tongue and countenance are reasoning with his neighbour; now the orator, approaching his friend closely, with face and hands concentring towards his breast, seizes his collar or buttons, and shakes his arguments into his ears and mind with a gentle tremulation, as one coaxes gooseberries into a bottle, and again, all of a sudden, retrogrades from him, with head and hands and arms thrown back to mark the irreconcilable extremity of his contradiction.

The day following, one of my brother officers repaired to our chief's ship, and they went on shore together.

On his return in the evening he excited our utmost envy, wonder, and curiosity by giving us an account of his adventures.

In exploring the country they had come to a vine-clad hill, whose farthest side ended in a precipitous bank scarped away by the hand of labour; and spread out below, proceeding out of the bowels of the hill on which they stood, they discovered an ancient Roman town in all its unruined dimensions of streets and squares, theatres and barracks, not gray with the hoar of antiquity, but with all its plastering and painting fresh from the hands of the workmen. The painted borders of the dwelling-rooms, the appropriate pictures of the ladies' bath, the soldiers' names engraven rudely on the walls of their barracks, the ruts worn by the Roman wheels, were all fresh despatched to us from former ages.

Of this inestimable present Pliny had described the packing up, by an eruption of Vesuvius, to which he was witness. It was only now half unpacked, and we might yet be at the unpacking of the remainder.

I was ready to jump out of the ship to see with my own eyes these incredible wonders, and when I could go, when I stood in these streets and called, without knocking, upon one ancient Roman after another (though it seemed hardly delicate to explore unbidden the private chambers, whose painting and fresh preservation seemed to infer an occupancy so recent) anticipation was beggared by the trance which that reality imposed.

They show one such things in the Museum of Portici, that the idea of imposture steals involuntarily upon the mind, but yet imposture is out of the question. The king is the showman, and asks nothing for his pains, nor is there any temptation to fabricate the commonest articles of every-day use into the semblance of antiquity in the midst of such a crowd of self-evident realities. Else, when I was shown an egg with a part of the yolk oozing from the crack, looking exactly as if boiled and cracked yesterday, a loaf of bread burnt to a cinder, and a quantity of grain in the same condition, and was told that these things had been baked by the hot ashes of Vesuvius and buried under them for 1700 years, my belief, I must confess, was a little shy. Yet I know not that it is more wonderful with respect to an egg, a loaf, and a heap of corn than with respect to the innumerable rolls of burnt manuscript which we found Mr. Hayter so busy in unrolling with infinite patience and ingenuity, the characters upon the charred papyrus being still perfectly legible.

With respect to other things, vast quantities of tools and kitchen utensils of every description, fit enough for modern use, also very well wrought golden ornaments and elegant glass vessels of all shapes—in these the interest was equally great, and the belief more easy.

To me Herculaneum, the Museum of Portici, and above all Pompeii, were objects of renewed visitation and inexhaustible interest; but far beyond all these artificial curiosities my mind was absorbed by that unutterable wonder of Nature whose irresistible devastations covered and formed the country all around. Indeed the recent destructive torrent yet bore upon its surface the shells of houses and habitations whose inhabitants had been expelled or destroyed.

It seems strange that after all the ruin which this terrible mountain has wrought with subterraneous thunder and ejected fire, the monuments of which endure through ages to tell the people what he has done, yet that all should be insufficient to frighten them away from his foot, while with smoke and fire and inward groans he threatens them daily with still further destruction. Nevertheless they hew the black vomit of his entrails into building stones, and over the spot where the house and its master were buried in a grave of fire do they build another dwelling for another inhabitant.

A curiosity, partaking of religious awe, led me to its summit. I had expected a peep into the mouth of the inferno, a visible shaft, plumb down into the fiery bowels of the earth, but no mysterious, unfathomable gulf or chimney of the infernal foundry was to be seen. Cracks, indeed, red and white with fire, burnt a good pair of Hoby's boots off my feet, as they crossed the region of the crater in every direction, and with their sulphurous vapour nearly stifled us all.

November 20.—At this time there was in the environs of Naples a corps of Russians, understood to be 18,000 strong, but what the allies might have hoped to achieve by uniting an Anglo- Russian force of 25,000 or 30,000 men with the native Neapolitan forces, which altogether might pass perhaps in round numbers for an army of 50,000 or 60,000, it is no part of my present object to retrace. The rapid progress of French victory on the Continent would naturally make the hopes under which the expedition left England perfectly inapplicable to the present period. We had intended to assume grand operations in upper Italy in conjunction with the main armies of Austria and Russia. But now it seemed to be the general opinion that if the Anglo-Russian corps could enable the Neapolitan army to protect the frontier of its Sovereign's dimensions, more could not be expected.

On the 30th November (and let it be remembered that this was two days only before the overwhelming blow of the battle of Austerlitz) His Neapolitan Majesty reviewed the British forces on a plain between Castel-à-Mare and Naples. Many Russian officers were also on the ground. The king, the hereditary prince, and Prince Leopold (then about ten years old) arrived on horseback, the queen in her carriage, bringing with her old Cardinal Ruffo, who, presently descending, showed us his red stockings. Old Ferdinand appeared in great glee, dressed in a white uniform, with a large cocked hat, and his hair tied in a thick queue. "*Avançons, avançons, mon Général,*" he said to Sir John Stuart, who was leading him down the line. "Your troops are magnificent! your army is as fine as your navy! Body of Bacchus, what an imposing front!" cried the old monarch as he rode up to the queen.

That elegant ruin, standing up in her carriage and addressing Sir John Stuart, cried, "*C'est superbe! magnifique! mon Général. Ce sont des soldats dignes des Anglais, dignes de nos dieux tutelaires.*"

She was now old and hazed, but her figure was erect and her mien princely and graceful. Her form had not yet lost all its original brightness, nor appeared less than a queen in ruins.

The line now broke into column, and passed the king and queen in reviewing order. All on the ground, even the Russian officers, were loud in praise of the appearance of our troops, and certainly 3000 soldiers never formed a more complete and warlike line. I was much amused with the juvenile Prince Leopold, who, dressed like a little field-marshal, and mounted on a superb little charger, richly caparisoned, as often as the officers saluted his royal parent, lifted the cocked hat from his flaxen head (displaying a queue thicker than his father's) with a grace the most measured and majestic. Before the royal party left the ground the wintry sun approached the western wave and blazed upon the brass plates and steely muskets of the soldiers, which Coleridge, who dined with us afterwards, called "a beautiful accident," and clothed in poetic phrase.

We were a good deal struck with the royal equipage. It was an old shabby carriage drawn by six miserable horses, tied together with ropes, very ill representing, to our English eyes, the eight proud cream-coloured Hanoverians and the gilded trappings which attach them to the splendid vehicle of our own sovereign.

December 10.—Early in December the restriction which kept us from visiting the capital was removed. Whether the motive had been to prevent our collision with our Russian confederates quartered in its environs, or whether French employees were still to be temporised with, I neither knew nor inquired. The army began its march to the frontier, and we who had duties still to perform in the neighbourhood of Naples freely satisfied our curiosity by frequent excursions to that interesting place.

Many paternal admonitions did we younger ones receive from the well-versed poet Coleridge to beware of the temptations of Naples, to beware the

Nods and becks and wreathed smiles,
Quips and pranks and wanton wiles,

which would beckon us in every street, and chiefly to beware of the duchesses and princesses, for, said he, "The higher the rank the greater the danger." But I think a youth who has learned to pass unharmed through the streets of London may be trusted in any town in Europe, for all the world is honest to the honest.

One day I went to the Theatre of St. Carlos, and while yet in the lobby my ears were imprisoned by a strain that seemed vocal indeed, but like no human voice which I had ever heard, too potent for woman, too clear and silvery for man.

On coming in sight of the stage the appearance of the divine songster corresponded to the perplexity of his voice—most fair and graceful to behold, but yet neither manly nor effeminate. This was that very

Velluti, amongst the triumphs of whose unequalled talents it is not the least that they have prevailed upon the rugged Londoners to acknowledge the wondrous beauty of his celestial melody.

Before leaving Naples I saw there a great many of the things which ought to be seen, and can say truly that *I saw them*, and to be able to say this, is, I believe, the commonest reason for going to see them.

December 22.—We were now on the march to Sepia, whither the army had gone to assume a defensive position. I had procured a handsome and excellent horse at Naples, whose round and well-fed back exactly fitted my English caparisons, and which soon acquired the name of Napolitanno; never man had a gentler or a better steed, and it redoubled the animation with which I looked to be immediately committed in actual service with the enemy to find myself mounted on so comely and spirited an animal.

Active service, however, for the present was not to be our lot, for before our duties near Naples permitted us to reach the army on march to the frontier, our commanding officer,[2] rejoined us in haste, and set all hands at work to delineate the position of Castel-à-Mare, and to produce so exact a military plan of that bold promontory as would enable him to show fully to the commander-in-chief in what way it might be best occupied to cover the embarkation of the troops in presence of an enemy.

As one of the first objects of Napoleon after the Battle of Austerlitz was the extinction of the Bourbon Crown of Naples and the occupation of the kingdom, no doubt it was become necessary for a British commander, committed upon the soil of that kingdom, to secure a position behind him, under cover of which he might in any event command his embarkation.

Sir James Craig, however, subsequently resolved (and indeed the well-known state of the Continent left him no alternative) not to wait till his little army came in contact with the overwhelming legions of France, but to embark without delay.

The royal family also resolved not to trust themselves too near to an irritated foe, but to transfer the Court of Ferdinand to Palermo.

The great and ready skill therefore with which the wild and noble features of Castel-à-Mare had been applied to the purposes of military defence, and the zealous and unwearied pains with which we had portrayed and mapped out the fastnesses of these rugged mountains, were

---

2. Captain Lefebure, R.E.

of no avail beyond that of scientific practice, as the Anglo-Russian army, long before the proximity of the enemy could communicate any hurry to its operations, quietly embarked where it had landed, and sailed for Sicily.

December 30.—A great many horses which had been purchased for the field equipage of the army were left at Castel-à-Mare for want of means of transport, and for lack of some better arrangement they were successively turned loose into a large enclosure belonging to the dockyard. A scene took place among them very painful to witness, but yet highly picturesque. They were of both sexes, and consequently the most fierce and disastrous contests began amongst the males, whilst their iron heels armed them against each other with more than natural power, and soon these noble animals were disfigured by painful wounds, disabled limbs, and blood.

To have shot them as was done at Corunna would have been much more humane.

December 31.—It was evening at the very close of the year 1805 when we set sail, and night when we beheld the volcanic blaze of Stromboli flash across the dark sea and disclose by fits the isles of Lipari.

Morning unveiled to us the features of those neighbouring shores, now narrowing more and more the gulf into which we were sailing, until they form that narrow and rapid sea that parts Calabria from the Trinacrian coast.

The view of Sicily apparent at this time, though not without beauty, is kept in complete subjection to the rich and lofty magnificence of the Italian shore, whose mountains, topped with cliff and clothed with wood and vine, come steep from sky to sea, with nought between but a border of golden sand, interrupted here and there by peaks and masses of rock for ever washed by the sapphire sea.

On one of these sandy bays, and quite at the foot of these rich and lofty mountains, lies the little town of Scylla and its boat-covered beach, then the main promontory flings a longer slope towards the sea, terminating the beach of Scylla and suddenly forming itself into the abrupt, naked, and primeval rock on which the castle of Scylla is erected.

This is the Scylla on which ships might run that would too anxiously avoid the whirlpool of Charybdis.

After passing the Faro of Messina, whereof Scylla forms one of the confines, the Sicilian shore assumes a bolder and richer form, till at length the romantic seat of Messina itself rivals the grandeur of the opposite scenery, and grafts upon the beauties of Nature somewhat of the proud aspect of metropolitan magnificence. I say this while surveying Messina from the azure bosom of her river-like sea, for her real magnificence has passed away, and her streets of palaces stand in ruins to this hour.

But for the painter's object no harm is done. The rich facades of elaborate architecture are standing entire, and their want of substance on the other side is concealed by the dense town behind, and the castle-crowned heights above, tier above tier of church or convent, each showing its firm footing upon the natural and luxuriant earth; the whole background is finished and filled up by mountains richly clothed with the verdure of dwarf wood and perennial flowers, the heavenly atmosphere ever glistening above and over all things. Nothing on this earth, I should say, can exceed the outward beauty of Messina.

1806.—It must have been about the middle of January when we entered the harbour, an immense round basin, enclosed by a curved tongue of level land jutting out from the line of coast like the blade of a sickle, from which it is said the town derives its name; the point of the sickle, terminating when at a short distance from the main shore, leaves only a narrow entrance into the harbour, which is defended by a fort established on the sickle point.

From every wind and every sea this harbour is perfectly sheltered and secure, but as the narrowness of its entrance makes it sometimes operose for vessels to go in and out, the ships of war and those which expect to be soon for sea anchor in the road outside.

The transports were moored close to each other, the ships of war anchored in the roadstead. The troops were kept on board, but the officers after a time were allowed to go on shore and look about them.

A few days afterwards the troops were disembarked, and we were soon established in the Convent of St. Francisco di Paolo.

The legend which conveys the tradition of this convent's foundation is in various situations rudely represented on the walls, and consists of a man sailing across a narrow sea, with no other vessel, sail, or mast than such as his *capote* and walking-staff would furnish. This was St. Francisco di Paolo, who in that miraculous manner is said to have passed over from Scylla to the spot whereon this convent was erected.

Our accommodations here were not splendid, but such as we could enjoy after the confinement of shipboard. The monks were civil and obliging though poor, and the abbot presented us with some rich Calabrian wine that might have passed for cherry brandy.

It was now immediately the business of our commandant,[3] to place the city of Messina in a respectable state of defence, for as it was certain that the other side of the Straits would soon be occupied by the legions of Napoleon, Messina, which was to be the grand depot and headquarters of the British army, must be placed beyond the apprehension of surprise.

The military position of Messina is by nature extremely defective, and though the existing defences were not in all points the most judicious that could have been devised, yet were they of sufficient importance to incline our chief to adopt the principle of improving what already existed, rather than that of substituting new ones. These works at Messina, extending to forts occupying the heights adjacent to the town, and overlooking the eddies of Charybdis and the castle and rock of Scylla, tended to bring me again and again, and for hours and hours, in contact with the lovely environs of Messina, whose charms are more indelibly imprinted on my memory than those of any other place in the world. We soon moved from the convent into the town, where we occupied a good house opposite to the quarters of the commander-in-chief.

March.—This change of quarters gave me a commodious opportunity of seeing the reception of old King Ferdinand by his Messinese subjects. He had come from Palermo to Melazzo by sea, and from Melazzo (by advice of his Minister) had made his progress on horseback, so that he arrived at Messina miserably fatigued and covered with the dust and soil of travel. Yet the reception he met with from these loyal Sicilians was enough to revive him. In the mid-tide of the dense flood of bareheaded people, he and his horse were borne along

---

3. Captain Lefebure, R.E.

down the principal street; on one side was Sir James Craig bowing in his balcony, and under the windows the vast crowd concentred their faces towards the King, so that in front of him they moved backwards and behind him they moved forwards, facing him on either side. And never in all my life of twenty years did I behold so touching an exhibition of the passion of loyalty.

The good-natured and kindly-mannered but wearied and worn old man, in the midst of his thanks and nods and brief salutations, was begging in some degree for quarter as they thronged about him, and while anxious to gratify their desire of touching him by extending his hands and suffering their pressure on his legs and knees, kept begging they would let him move on, that he might come to a place of rest.

Meantime they rent the air with their "*Vivas*," and ever as he passed, a new concourse of knees was seen to bend, and picturesque and eager heads were bowed around him, pressing devout and reverent kisses on his legs or hands, the skirts of his coat, or the housings of his charger.

Never shall I forget the scene. In vain they might have talked to me of the weakness and tyranny of his reign, or of his misrule and neglect of these very subjects. He was their old and lawful king, now seen for the first time in the pressure of misfortune and in the weariness of that journey he had made to inquire of their disposition towards him. And this was their beautiful answer. They received him with embraces, with loud benedictions, with kisses and genuflexions, which plainly told him they remembered nothing but the sacred bond between him and them, endeared to them the more by his age and evil fortune and his struggle for independence.

At length, though to all appearance (and as I was afterwards credibly informed) deeply touched by this perhaps unexpected scene, he was glad enough to be got into his quarters, opposite to which a magnificent facade of a triumphal temple had been erected for the scaffolding of fireworks to be displayed before him.

At night forth he came bareheaded into the balcony which fronted the street, and after saluting the immense concourse of his shouting subjects, he discharged a rocket, which was guided by a wire-conductor into the centre of that gorgeous temple, and immediately it was living all about with quivering fire. No description can paint the succession of glorious shapes which, amid the clear darkness of an Italian night, animated that palace of fire, and at length, like the finale of grand concerts, every part became such a volcano of fiery gems, and fountains of burning spray, and whirlpools of dazzling stars, that I could not refrain from joining in the shouts of ecstasy.

In honour also of the king's arrival, the most celebrated and costly of all their religious processions was anticipated. This was the procession of the *Anima* (or soul, as I understood) of the Virgin Mary; but as I know nothing of its origin and but little of its symbolical intention, I will not attempt any description.

April 1806.—In this climate it is essential to the expeditious progress of works to take the earliest advantage of daylight, while the air is for several hours cool and the sun still low and feeble. Accordingly we had to be up and dressed before five o'clock.

It happened one morning about this time, when I was buckling on my sword and about to sally forth, that the floor began to shake under my feet. A violent rattling of doors and windows was heard all over the house, and bits of plaister began to shower from the ceiling. I was presently sensible that we were experiencing the shock of an earthquake; and as it seemed to increase in violence and to be accompanied by violent cries of human distress, I opened my door in some haste, and immediately beheld some Sicilian inmates of the house, just as they had sprung from their slumbers, scouring along the passages and making for the stairs. I followed, and beheld the issuing from every room of persons of every age and sex, who were racing down the stairs, with no thought but of present danger, and seemingly unconscious of the exposure of themselves and of each other.

Signor Scamporaccio, the *padrone* di Casa, partaking at first of the general terror, and having sprung downstairs like a wild cat and secured himself under a strong archway that issued into the street, of which shelter he urged me to partake, then began to grin at the preposterous figures of his descending lodgers, and especially pointed my attention to the unadorned dismay of a fat old lady, a relation of his wife, whom he sportively called "*La Baronessa.*" She was of immense breadth and weight, and yet came howling downstairs full trot. On looking into the street, the general terror was too real and too energetic to be ludicrous. The people fell upon their knees wherever they happened to be, some prostrate and laying their foreheads in the dust, some, with frantic hands and uplifted voices, addressing heaven with the frenzied cry of hasty deprecation.

From that posture and from that earnest importunity no creature rose or desisted until the earth had ceased to shake and her houses to rend and groan.

So violent a shock had not been felt for years. The upper part of the spire of the Madre Chiesa was thrown down, and some other buildings materially injured. Every ship at anchor, and some sailing in the mid strait, felt the violence of the shock, but happily there was no injury to human life.

A slighter shock in the course of the day frightened the soldiers from their work on the heights, and still more some Sicilian overseers from the duties of superintendence.

Looking at the ruins with which Messina is surrounded, and knowing them to be the fruits of a dreadful earthquake that caused the loss of thousands of lives, it is impossible not to sympathise with the undissembled terror of these poor Sicilians whenever the tremulous earth reminds them of her instability, for they conceive it to be the angry hand of God shaking over them with menaces of vengeance, and their cries are no less vehement and abrupt than the cries and entreaties of a child at the uplifted rod of a parent.

April 1806.—Sir James Craig now published a farewell order to the army. The new Minister of War (of Mr. Fox's Administration) had written most flatteringly to him, assuring him that all had been in perfect accordance with their views, and now that the army was in security and comfort, he could resign the command with less regret.

He had long borne up against the pressure of severe disease, in the honourable hope of directing the courage of his men and witnessing their victories, but now he was sensible that he owed it to them to make way for a commander whose zeal might be equal to his own, and whose activity sickness had not impaired. He gave much praise to the quality of the troops, whose discipline had certainly been much advanced by his personal exertions.

The necessity of this resignation had long been painfully obvious to the army, not by any faults of discipline, but by the ghastly and suffering appearance of our revered commander, who was much respected and regretted by every branch of the army.

Towards the end of April our commandant was sent to ascertain the strength of the places on this side of the island, giving particular attention to Augusta and Syracuse, and about four days afterwards I was ordered to follow him.

One of my brother-officers good-naturedly lent me a beautiful donkey he had brought from Valetta to carry my servant and *malle*.

My pride at starting, mounted on the sleek and spirited Napolitanno, and preceding Il Bruto Domenico and the ass, was somewhat quenched by the drenching rain in which we set forward, and soon received another fall in the person of Domenico, seen sprawling in the mire, and the donkey at large.

The ass, however, was of infinitely more importance to me than his rider, so I left Domenico and pursued the animal myself.

After this little *fracas* the long-eared rebel was more amenable, and Domenico dare only curse him under his breath, for fear he should repeat the somersault, so that my meditations were no longer interrupted either by the pranks of the four-legged or the deep execrations of the two-legged brute. Furthermore, the day cleared, and the sea and sky and fertile land were lighted up, and re- awakened the sanguine glance of youthful expectation which the rain had in some degree depressed. The road is impassable for wheels; its situation is invariably by the seaside, with mountains on the other hand, which sometimes barely leave room for the road. In other places the wintry torrents have formed, as it were, the opening jaws of a deep and rugged ravine, called in this country *Fiumara*.

Again the bold heights approach the very border of the ocean, and sometimes a rocky promontory obstructs the level beach, and plants a firm broad foot in the midst of the waves. In this case it has been necessary to pass over or to cut through the obstruction. The rocky point of Scaletta traverses the beach as with a wall, and the road ascends into the gorge of the natural rock, which rises like a watchtower on either side, affording such a post of observance and defence as, if properly used, might check a mighty army.

I proposed halting for the night at Taormina, thirty or forty miles from Messina, and soon viewed it in the distance, seated in the clouds on the table of a lofty mountain between two enormous peaks of rock, on the highest of which is a dark old castle.

On arriving at the foot of this mountain, a sentinel stopped me where the gate of the town is constructed, and on finding I was an English officer on duty, directed me to the convent of the Capuchins.

I had permitted Domenico to take up his quarters at a miserable hut on the beach, where he was fortunate enough to find provender, partly to spare the donkey the pain of carrying him and my portmanteau up so toilsome an ascent, and also in the hope that my baggage might gain a little advance in the morning's march, and thus I began to ascend into the clouds alone, worn with heat and travel, and oppressed with a growing and, I fear, somewhat puerile sadness.

After a long and wearisome ascent, I had left the brightness and interest of the world behind me, and had entered an atmosphere which enveloped every object in a thick gray mist.

On reaching the convent of Capuchins, a dead man might have given me a more cheering welcome than I received from the spiritless and hair-clothed superior.

One of his bleak eyes looked full upon me and into me, while the other seemed employed in looking round me and beyond me.

On learning my object he assented with a slow scowl of sullen indifference, and without any pause or gesture indicating the smallest courtesy, he briefly told one of his subordinates to show me a vacant cell. I believe the rules of this order bind them to wretchedness, and they extend them to the stranger that is within their gates, for they offered me no refreshment, and mentioned no refectory. The cell appointed me was naked, windowless, bedless, a bedding of straw being all it afforded.

Never before or since have I felt the heart within me oppressed and borne down by so dense and palpable a gloom—unmanly, to be sure, I felt it to be. "What ails me?" said I; "what is the grievance? Shelter is here tonight, tomorrow there lies the way, and food can be procured. *Why art thou cast down, O my soul, and why art thou disquieted within me?*"

No answer could be given, but the questions were not asked in vain. I began to turn my displeasure from the monks to myself, and presently recovered a more hardy tone of mind. I left the convent and went into the little square of the town. The mountain cloud had dispersed, and a party of Sicilian loungers attracted me to the shop of a little fruiterer, where I bespoke some dinner, and learned with joy they could accommodate me with a bed, which I greatly preferred to returning to the convent.

Whilst dinner was getting ready I walked out to look about me and to summon a *cicerone* to my aid, that I might see the remarkable Roman antiquities for which this place is famous. I then, though very tired, placed myself in the hands of the voluble cicerone, who took me to the large ancient theatre, finely situated in a basin or natural crater formed in the summit of the mountain.

A hasty view would at that moment have satisfied me, for I was weary and wanted food, but when I would have gone away the cicerone forcibly detained me, and placing me in the remotest ring of the vast auditory, proceeded leisurely to the stage and began a long oration, ridiculous in itself, but illustrating how well the situation was calculated to carry the voice of the actor to the remotest spectator. Reluctant as I was to interrupt so remarkable and novel an exhibition as a Sicilian peasant spouting to my solitary self in the midst of the lonely mountains from the ruins of a Roman stage, it lasted so long that I was compelled to cut it short, telling him I could have fancied him a shade of the Roman Roscius, a name he appeared well acquainted with, and with a low bow attributed the comparison to my Excellency's goodness.

On returning to my little hotel I found dinner ready, after which I went to the convent stables to see to my horse; and the bed that I made for him not a little astonished the friar who admitted me, and from curiosity, I suppose, observed, and to a certain extent assisted, my operations. "Such a bed," he informed me, "was something too luxurious even for a good Christian." He said no more, but his look added, what must it be for a heretic's horse.

Napolitanno, however, who was grinding his provender with great animation, and making his eloquent ears thank me for my present attention to his couch, seemed to have no fault to find with my handiwork, and to promise me a fresh horse for tomorrow.

My bed also was clean and comfortable, and I slept intensely, rose early, and mounting the gay and gentle Napolitanno, descended slowly towards the sea, through the hanging orchards and gardens of Taormina, my mind and body equally refreshed, and forgetful of yesterday's depression.

On morning wings how active springs the mind.
And leaves the load of yesterday behind.

Soon after traversing the beach which extends from the foot of Taormina, the road has to make its way (and badly enough it makes it) over the rugged skirts of Mount Etna, or as the natives call it, more euphoniously, Monzebello.

These extreme skirts of the mountain consist of various eddies and whirlpools of different dates of lava, whose black, rough substance is scantily covered by the slowly accumulating soil, seldom sufficient to ensure a clothing of vegetation, the black and naked rock forming a vivid contrast to the brightest verdure.

The pretty town of Jaci, by its elegant and regular structure and air of opulence, takes the traveller by surprise after the unpromising waste he has traversed. It seems built almost entirely of the dark and durable material which the mountain furnishes as a poor compensation for his wide wasting destruction.

And now after a long and weary ride the clustering domes and spires of Catania rise upon our track, with a promise of splendour and magnificence for which the pretty and prosperous Jaci was but little preparation.

I was astonished at the grandeur of design and costly style of building.

The principal street, of vast width, seems to have one extremity in the ocean, and the other lost in the ascent of the stupendous mountain, whose fiery summit it seems to approach with an avenue of temples and palaces.

What an effect have place and scene upon the sensitive spirits of youth! At Taormina I felt abandoned and cast out from the beauties of the civilised world, whereas here in beautiful Catania I felt as if everything were my own, and that the sky was bright, the sea blue, the mountain awful, and the city splendid—all for me; and in good and grateful part did I accept of it.

No king could be happier than I, when, having seen my horse comfortably served, I ascended into the best parlour of the Golden Lion, and with my eyes upon the noble buildings of the square, sat down to a well-cooked dinner and a flask of the rich white wine of Etna. After dinner, leaving this fair city with regret, I pursued my journey towards Augusta. On this side the mountain throws a mantle of sloping woods, and becomes more and more level and in the nature of open pasture as it approaches the deep and rapid Giarreta, which we pass in a ferry, and over which few Sicilians would believe it possible to construct a bridge.[4]

Augusta enjoys the advantages of Mediterranean sea and sky, but, *au reste*, not Hartlepool nor Skegness are less indebted to soil or surface. The town, though regular, is meanly built, and occupies a peninsula fortified towards the land.

The bay, however, is of noble extent, and by its firm anchorage and easy access affords a fine rendezvous for large fleets employed in these seas. Here Lord Nelson watered previous to the battle of the Nile. I slept in the large convent of the Augustines, close to the seaside, where

---

4. The sight of our Westminster Bridge greatly astonished one of the Sicilian servants on our return to England. "*Cospetto*," he exclaimed, "and they pretend they could not make a bridge over the Giarreta!"

the prior and monks assured me it was their greatest pride to have entertained the great Nelson within their walls, of whose glory they were perfectly enamoured.

The cheerful urbanity and comforting welcome of these good Augustines made me forget the Capuchins of Taormina, and I must say in all the many convents in which I have taken up my quarters I never experienced but that one unpleasant reception.

The governor of Augusta, on whom I necessarily waited with my credentials, was very polite, spoke of Captain Lefebure in the style sublime, and finding I must start in the morning for Syracuse, insisted that I should come that evening to his conversazione.

A good many people of both sexes and the higher officers of his garrison were assembled to stare at the Giovane Inglese, and for an hour or two it answered my purpose very well. I had no objection to be looked at, but liked looking at others still better, always taking a greater interest in people than in lifeless things.

I slept comfortably at the convent, and was on horseback early in the morning.

The ride to Syracuse is not particularly interesting along the shores of the Bay of Augusta, and after ascending the promontory which bounds the bay to the south, the road no longer finds accommodation by the seaside, but makes its way more deviously over hill and dell until it approaches the obverse side of that dilated rock which shelters Syracuse and its harbour from the blustering north. Upon an extended table of this ridge lie the ruins of the ancient city of Syracuse, and as the road ascends, the naked rock is tracked in deep ruts by the carriages which trafficked with the ancient Syracusans, just as ruts are deeply worn in the more frequented streets of Pompeii.

The present town and harbour of Syracuse, with its lovely vale stretching far into the west, are finely seen from the heights over which you approach it.

The peninsula on which the town stands divides the harbour into two compartments.

The grand harbour to the south and west is one of the most beautiful in the world. The other is of little importance except in a military point of view.

The fortifications, houses, and churches of Syracuse are all formed of the beautiful stone [5] of which its great northern screen consists, and in consequence of these vast quarries and excavations, ancient and

---

5. Not unlike the Portland stone.

modern, nothing can be more abruptly broken and scarped than the environs of this fortress.

The land front is finely and elaborately executed with magnificent gateways; the town is dense and unequal; the cathedral an ancient temple (I believe of Minerva), whose Christian front acts as a garish mask to its ancient heathen sides.

I presently found my friend Lefebure, who received me with joy, and after giving me some account of his proceedings, took me to the good old governor. "I know not whom this governor takes me for," said Lefebure, "but he really overwhelms me with honours; his coach is always dodging me wherever I go, and when I consent to take a little tour into the country, he mounts upon the box, with all the decorations of his rank and symbols of his power, and drives me himself. I am half dead with the variety and quantity he makes me eat, and bewildered with the daily company of barons and princes, baronesses and princesses, with their dark eyes and soft accents, so articulate and intelligible, and yet to which I dare hardly attempt to reply."

"Well," I replied, "this does not sound to me so distressing as you represent. I am glad I am come to your relief. This noble governor shall stuff *me* now with good things and drive *me* in his coach, and *I* will now listen to the soft accents of the dark-eyed *principessas*, and expose myself to their smiles at my blundering answers. So *have* with you, Lefebure; take me to the governor; we shall be in time for his dinner."

"Oh," he rejoined, "don't distress yourself. We are both engaged already to dine with him to meet a hundred people. But it will be taken well if I present you to him first." So away we went. The governor, a good, solicitous old soul, was of course charmed with the Bravo Giovinetto, and offered everything within and without his power both to me and to Lefebure.

The number of the people at dinner could only, I think, be exceeded by the number of the dishes, and when I found the order of proceeding, I no longer wondered at the surfeit complained of by the temperate Lefebure, for the governor, having relaxed his girdle and tied a napkin under his chin, surrounded by laughing beauties ready to applaud every word he spoke and every morsel he distributed, sent in succession for every dish, and having divided it absolutely and unsparingly into portions, it was carried round, and if any one failed to taste, the wail and lament of apprehended sickness was raised around him, and some sweet princess with bewitching eyes loaded his plate with her own fair hands.

I am not aware that English people can quite realise the ease and good-humour and incessant but not unpolished mirth with which this great dinner from beginning to end was accomplished. And but for that, I hardly believe the economy of man would be able to dispose of such sudden and copious supplies as were then thrown into his system.

Well it was the governor, after dinner, took us in his carriage to show us his points of vantage without the town, for to walk would have been very inconvenient!

The worthy governor of Syracuse was not the only person prodigal of attention and kindness to the two English officers.

There then lived upon a beautiful farm in the midst of the vale an English gentleman of considerable genius and learning, whose energy of character and acuteness of judgement, and the application of English skill to a Sicilian soil, had given him a very powerful ascendency over the population within his reach. Equally a master of the language, from the Tuscan tongue to the dissonant jargon of the Sicilian peasant, his tall, athletic, but not ungraceful figure, and his intelligent and finely-featured head made him no ill representative, among foreigners, of the personal predominance of an Englishman.

I had met him at Valetta, where he had opened an acquaintance with me by accusing me of some resemblance to Lady Hamilton. He immediately remembered the circumstance, and perhaps even so slight a thread acted as a bond of old acquaintance. Yet there is a stronger bond than that which draws one to a countryman in a foreign land.

My Anglo-Sicilian friend showed Lefebure and me how truly he felt this by the unbounded kindness and grateful hospitality he extended to us, and his handsome, noble-hearted wife received us with a smile of welcome that was redolent of home.

Our fare was studiously English, and to our delighted eyes appeared the effect of magic.

There was the burnished brown of the small fillet of veal, the small smoked ham, cauliflower, potatoes, and melted butter; the household loaf of barm-raised bread as white as snow; the ample slice of fresh-churned butter, not lard of goat's milk, but yellow butter, from the breathy cow. And then the bubbling and loud-hissing urn, the presiding lady, plates of real bread-and-butter, and genuine tea, attempered with thick cream!

No one untried in travel can imagine with how keen a zest a robust English appetite returns to these wholesome and ordinary provisions of his country in lands where he has no hope of meeting with them.

On our return to Messina we simply retraced our steps, and met with nothing remarkable, so I give no account of our journey of 120 miles.

It was about the second week in May when Lefebure and I arrived at Messina, and on the 25th of that month our force received a valuable acquisition by the arrival of the 78th Regiment of Highlanders, a beautiful regiment, 900 strong, whose picturesque national dress made a great impression upon the Sicilians, though the women, indeed, seemed to think it due to modesty to say the dress was very ugly. "*La Baronessa*" also maintained "It was an ugly dress, and a very curious dress, and a very curious thing that such a dress should be approved of in England, which she thought was a cold country." The arrival of this regiment gave us the more satisfaction, as rumours were afloat that Sir John Stuart would take advantage of his interregnum to do some dashing thing.

A great sensation was created by the resolute defence which the old Prince of Hesse Philipstahl continued to make at Gaeta.

Our Gilespie had been sent to his assistance, and was well qualified by his knowledge of the language, his military science, and his daring constancy of character both to assist the brave prince in his defence, and to give true information and sagacious comments to the British general.

Sir Sidney Smith, the naval commander-in-chief, came to Messina immediately from the scene of action. He had brought with him a plan of Gaeta and of the French approaches, which he wished to have copied, and being well acquainted with the commanding engineer, requested his assistance for that purpose. Our commandant brought the plan to me to copy, and said, "When you've finished the plan, Boothby, you will like an opportunity of becoming acquainted with the hero of Acre. You will admire him of all things, but be sure when you see him, he will take you to Acre."

Accordingly I copied the plan with my best skill and despatch, and then carried it on board. I had to wait a considerable time. At length I was summoned into the admiral's presence. He held the plan in his hand, and good-humouredly said, "So, sir, you are the young officer who has had the goodness to copy this for me. Well now, sir, just look here. They pretend to tell me that this place is indefensible—*me*, who know pretty well what determined hearts can do behind very simple barriers—who have seen a handful of men behind the angle of a wall bid defiance to the bravest troops led on by the first general in the world—I mean Mr. Bonaparte at Acre. Tally-ho! said I."

I was really in pain lest a smile should be detected on my features, which would have seemed to belie my sincere admiration for the gallant spirit in whose presence I stood, and that anxiety gave me an air of deeper attention to the inferences of strength and capability of Gaeta which he drew from the defence of Acre.

And it is well known that the brave old Prince of Hesse fully justified these inferences by the spirit and duration of his resistance.

The gallant Sir Sidney then repaired to the Court of Palermo, into which the defence of Gaeta and the mountain spirit of the Calabrese were infusing vain hopes, vain aims, and inordinate desires.

Old Ferdinand, who had entrusted Sir John Stuart with the defence of the east coast of Sicily from Milazzo to Cape Passaro, now invested Sir Sidney Smith with viceregal power by land and sea in the territory of Naples, and the whole persuasive power of the court, and I suppose of the chivalrous viceroy, was then addressed to excite the British general to hazardous enterprise, but probably the natural ambition of his own brave breast was the strongest advocate.

The floating viceroy adroitly disarmed any jealousy which his powers might have excited in the breast of the land commander by saying, "This appointment would have been more suitable for you, but I made no difficulty about it, thinking it a great object that *one* of us should have it, and the whole powers of the commission are quite as much at your disposal as if your name had been placed in it instead of mine."

The phrase ran, "How nicely Sir Sidney had got himself made viceroy," but I can easily believe, remembering their worship of Nelson, that it was a much easier thing for the king and queen to give such a commission to a renowned naval officer, whom they might view as Nelson's successor, than to a British general.

Sir John Stuart, however, had too much sense to care a straw about it. He saw here an opportunity of glory, and however circumstances might fail of their promise, he saw at all events a justification of the hazard, and he was no more to be daunted by the sense of responsibility than of danger.

I was in great terror lest I should not be included in this heart-stirring expedition, but I was soon put out of suspense.

All the arrangements being complete and the fleet ready to sail, Sir John Stuart, in order to gain the advance of it, drove with one A.D.C. in his barouche to the point of Faro, and then embarked in a ship of war on the evening of the 30th of June 1806. We were watching him from our quarters opposite when he stepped into his *barouche*. Never man, I thought, seemed better pleased with what he was about, or looked more to personate the spirit of enterprise. A nice military figure, he jumped gaily into his carriage, laughing with his *aide-de-camp*, and nodding kindly, drolly, and significantly to the *vivaing* Messinese, who, notwithstanding the profoundest secrecy, had a pretty good guess what he was after, drove rapidly off.

June 30.—We then embarked when the fleet was already getting under way.

No happiness is greater to a young soldier than the high expectation attending an expedition of this kind. The great things he looks forward to are close at hand; there is no prospect of protracted toil and uncertain pursuit, but in the full vigour and freshness of his strength he moves quietly and swiftly to his object on the silent waters, expecting every moment to fall like a thunderbolt on the astonished foe. Several hours during this interesting night, big with expectation and imagining the eventful future, did I walk the deck, contrasting the present fair heaven, refreshing sea, and noiseless vessels with the dire principles of destruction and slaughter within them. Wistfully I looked toward the bold outline of the Italian shore, on which the condensing fleet was bearing with unflagging wing, and wondered how soon the hour of action and of glory could begin.

About midnight on the 30th June we came to an anchor in the Bay of St. Eufemia, and an order was immediately passed through the fleet that the troops should land at two in the morning.

A heavy surf upon an open beach made this operation difficult, but it was effected without loss and without opposition. A vast plain with much cover of brushwood extended from the beach to the receding mountains.

It began to be believed that no enemy was near, but upon the Light Infantry running forward a firing commenced, which continued in a sort of bush-fight the greater part of the morning. The enemy consisted of about 300 Polish sharpshooters scattered about in a very thick brushwood. They did their duty well, retiring as we advanced. No fox-hunters after a long frost could appear to enjoy their sport more keenly than our soldiers as they ran at the enemy with shouts and cries of delight. The event of the day was some 20 of the enemy wounded, 2 officers and 100 men taken prisoners. We had only one man wounded.

The army now took up a position on the high ground in advance of the place of landing, one flank upon the town of Nicastro, the other below the village of St. Eufemia, whilst at the same time it was thought prudent to throw up an entrenchment on the beach, under cover of which an embarkation might be effected, should the pressure of superior numbers or unforeseen disasters render a retreat to our ships desirable. Sir John Stuart expressed surprise at the celerity with which this service was performed.

During the whole of this long day, and part of the next, the reports concerning the enemy were various. One prisoner (a Gascon) answered gaily to the question of number, "Oh, a trifle; some 27,000 or 30,000." But towards evening on the 2nd of July it was discovered that an enemy's force had occupied the heights overlooking the plains of Maida. The lights of the enemy exhibited at night extended along a considerable front, and a rumour prevailed that he intended battle.

On the 3rd some information was obtained of the strength of the enemy, and it was rated so low as between 2000 and 3000. At night the order of march was given to commence at two o'clock, our general being probably anxious to come to blows before the enemy should have collected his full strength; but whilst the order of march was forming, an important reinforcement of several thousand (as we have since learned) arrived in the enemy's lines.

If this reinforcement had not arrived, the opposing forces would have been nearly equal. As it was. Sir John Stuart, at daybreak on the 4th of July, with about 4000 men, found himself in presence of 7500 of the best troops of France.

To my eternal regret, I was not present at the battle. My mind was in a state of curiosity and high expectation, and when I received the order to remain behind, though aware of its necessity and justice, my disappointment was childish and excessive.

An entrenchment which we had thrown up on the beach required still to be completed, and our chief was very anxious to strengthen it by an inundation, for which the mouth of a small rivulet offered great facilities. He felt it necessary to entrust an officer with the execution of his intentions, and as junior officer (in that spirit of perfect fairness with which he always treats us) he selected me, and sent me strict orders not to leave the spot until duly relieved. There was a high square tower at a short distance from our entrenchment, which was occupied by four companies of Watteville's regiment under Major Fischer, who had remained to protect the point of debarkation.

By the time some sound of cannon announced the approaching conflict of the two armies, my inundation wanted little of completion, and my men were well under the observance of this tower.

From hence, therefore, with the veteran Major Fischer, I saw the general movements of the battle, near enough to be filled with the most terrible interest, to see the masses descend from the heights, tracked by smoke and fire, to see opposing bodies approaching to collision, and by the rapidity of motion to distinguish horse from foot, and where approaching columns had been lost to sight, to recognise their conflict from the sudden smoke of the volleys. But though near enough for this, I was too distant to pretend to give the description of an eye-witness, not indeed being able to distinguish one regiment from another, or indeed the enemy from ourselves, except from the direction in which each was moving.

What anxious moments did we pass, near enough to see where the battle raged, but not in what way it was decided. However, it was more like victory than defeat, we thought, as no runaways came to spread bad tidings, and the whole system of sights and sounds seemed rather more distant than more near.

At length I descried a brother-officer riding alone towards us. I flew to meet him.

"Well, Theso, you have been fighting all morning. What have you done? We are half dead with anxiety."

"Oh," said the good-natured fellow, "would you had been with us! Never was anything more complete. They are all but destroyed."

"Now, God be praised!" said I, running to seize Theso's hand. "God Almighty be praised! This is grand news indeed."

"I came to tell you," said he, "that you need stay no longer here. We don't think of entrenchments now."

"Then I may ride to the field, where I can better understand all you have been doing."

So saying I mounted my horse, Theso giving some directions as to the right track, and away I cantered.

This might have been a scene harrowing to the last degree, for I might have found it full of suffering I had no power to mitigate, and have paid dearly in agony of mind for the gratification of a natural and overwhelming curiosity. But the noble compassion and prompt activity of the victors, aided by our generous sailors, had already removed from the field, without distinction of friend or foe, all who stood in need of the offices of humanity.

Still it was a field of battle smoking with recent carnage, peopled with prostrate warriors distorted with the death agony, harnessed for battle in gay colours, feathers, and gold, but stained and bathed in their own life-blood, having on that gory bed suddenly closed all the sanguine, joyous hopes of life.

A sight so disfigured, what heart of rock could long dry-eyed behold!

The events of the battle were in some sort told by the mute and motionless, but sad and appalling forms with which the ground was covered; all indeed were still and silent, but all bore the attitude of struggle, of fearful flight, or eager chase.

A picture of a battle represents but one instant; no figure can move, yet all seems stirring and tumultuous.

So, in some sort, is the actual field of glory. The chieftain's hand is lifted to strike; his lips have not closed since the shout of victory or mandate of battle has passed through them. The passions, too, in the midst of death remain strongly impressed upon each warrior's features. The daring courage, the bitterness of anger or revenge, and the thrilling agony of mortal pain—all speak distinctly in the countenance of the dead.

The route of the flying enemy was thickly tracked through the straggling course of the shallow Amato and up the heights beyond by slaughtered bodies of the 1st Regiment of French Light Infantry, which had ventured to charge ours with the bayonet. All lay in one direction, in the attitude of headlong desperate flight.

I forget the number of this regiment buried on the field, but a skeleton of it only could have escaped.

Amid all the disfigurements of wounds and scenes of human agony, nothing so powerfully inclined my heart to pity and compassion as the letters which lay near each unburied soldier, representing the last remains of the affections and softer feelings, as the body represented his warlike powers. Many of these, in female characters, were expressed with all the tender beauties of the French tongue, and, with an absence of reserve taught by the Revolution, showed by their intenseness of feeling how bitterly living hearts were to be grieved with the tidings of the scene before me.

No one can tell from description how wretched is the feeling, when standing over the body of a youthful soldier, to read in a fair female hand such expressions as these:—

Oh, preserve thy life! Venture not too much for the sake of thy poor Adèle, who has never ceased to deplore thy absence, but who will think the first moment of thy return an ample compensation for all her sufferings.

Return! shall that prostrate bloodstained figure ever return to the poor Adèle? The beauty of youth indeed has not yet left him, but by tomorrow the form even of humanity will be gone! Many of the letters were from all degrees of kindred—mother, wife, sister, daughter. It was impossible to read unmoved.

Poor Harry Paulet was dreadfully wounded in the thigh, and our commandant had a beautiful horse killed under him.

Having been unable to be actually present at the Battle of Maida, I write the following account from subsequent observation and inquiry, by which I satisfied my natural thirst to know all the events of this memorable day.

Battle of Maida

July 4, 1806.—The position of the enemy was at right angles with the trend of the beach, and so distant from it as to admit of operations between the sea and his left flank, which was weak from the nature of the ground, an inconvenience the enemy could not avoid from our being masters of the water, upon which was Sir Sidney Smith with a line-of-battle ship and three frigates. The British marched with extended flanks and a heavy column in the centre, the right flank covered by the sea, the left flank exposed, so that during the approach of the English the left flank of each army was more particularly exposed to the operations of the other.

General Regnier, thinking with some reason that the impetus of assault has much influence over the fate of battles, determined not to wait for our attack. He descended from his position, crossing the river Amato, which bathed its foot, and rushed upon the daring foe that was advancing to attack him.

It happened that the Light Infantry Corps, under Colonel Kempt, in advance of our right, was opposed to the *Premier Regiment de L'Infanterie Légère*, one of the most distinguished regiments in Napoleon's service. After these two regiments had exchanged some well-directed volleys, the French corps rushed forward at the *pas de charge*, their commander exclaiming furiously as they advanced, "*Ne tirez pas! ne tirez pas! A la bayonnette! a la bayonnette!*"[6]

"*Steady, Light Infantry!*" shouted Kempt. "*Wait for the word! Let them come close, let them come close! Now fire! Charge bayonets! March!*"

All this passed in a moment, but duly as ordered each deed was done. When the French were very near they received a murderous volley from their steadfast-hearted opponents, who then, as one man, rushed forward to the charge. Just as that thing, which it is said has never happened, *viz.* the equal shock of opposing lines of troops, seemed inevitable, just as the two regiments seemed in the very act of contact, the French Light Infantry, as one man, turned round and fled. They were driven across the river and up the heights, and a horrible slaughter took place of this beautiful regiment, which was almost totally destroyed.

Other regiments now volleyed and charged, as is usual in battles, and the enemy's left being totally routed, Regnier redoubled his efforts to make an impression with his right, but with no better success. Neither cavalry nor infantry could make the smallest impression in front.

The cavalry now made a rapid movement to turn our left flank, which was unprotected; but at this critical moment the 20th Regiment, which had just landed, led by the gallant Colonel Ross, advanced in such a manner, and so skilfully availing itself of the advantages of cover which the ground afforded, that the cavalry were compelled to go to the right-about under a galling fire.

The victory was now decided, the enemy flying with the utmost precipitation. But as we had no cavalry, he was enabled, with those regiments which had less entirely committed themselves, to preserve some order in his retreat.

The slaughter on the side of the enemy was immense, indeed hardly credible when compared to the smallness of our loss. In killed, wounded, and taken, the French loss has been estimated at more than 3000, while our total loss exactly amounts to as many hundreds, our killed amounting to 40 privates and 1 officer, while 700 Frenchmen were buried on the field. A French general (Compère), severely wounded, is amongst the prisoners. He led the enemy on to the charge with an *acharnement* that seemed like individual hate, and on being taken he rode with his shattered arm through our ranks, menacing with the ac-

---

6. "Don't fire! don't fire! With the bayonet! with the bayonet!"

tion of his other arm, and cursing and swearing with the most voluble bitterness.

Another prisoner said, "*Ma foi!* they told us the English were fish that could only fight by sea, and knew nothing of the matter by land."

An officer asked him "What he thought now?"

"Oh, now," said he, "it's quite another thing."

Surely this must be considered a brilliant victory when the disparity of numbers is taken into account, and it is the more gratifying to us because Regnier stands so high in reputation, and also because one of these French fellows had formerly spoken very slightingly of the talents of our gallant little general.

After having advanced some miles in pursuit of the enemy, our army resumed the position of the morning.

The action began at half-past eight, and the firing ceased at eleven on the 4th of July.

July 5.—The army after so severe an exertion formed a sort of camp of rest about a mile from the field of battle, and near the sea, so as to have an easy communication with the fleet.[7]

Tents were established for the convenience of the officers, and all the wounded were comfortably accommodated on board, while whatever could contribute to the comfort of the troops was brought to them on shore.

After a short refreshment of this kind, the army advanced to Maida, and there took possession of some French stores.

Having increased its distance from the sea, all the comforts of camp equipage were abandoned, and we now bivouacked in the open fields, and shared in all respects the fare of the private soldiers. Our mess of raw meat was delivered to us in the same proportion as theirs; our camp kettle hung gipsy-like over a fire of sticks, and each officer's cloak and blanket spread upon the ground served him for a bed and his valise for a pillow, where he lay with his sword by his side and his spurs on his heels, while his horse was picketed close at hand. In the morning I went to some rivulet or spring with shaving tackle and brush in my pocket, and sat down beside it, to lather and brush and scrape uncomfortably enough.

This was a fine climate and a fine season, and that mode of lodging on the bare ground had nothing in it really formidable to youthful

---

[7] Yesterday I met Sir Sidney Smith upon the field, and he asked me to dinner on board.

strength and spirits, but I never thought it agreeable; and by far the worst night I spent was one in which we had all endeavoured to be a little more comfortable by making huts of branches of trees, and beds of the new-cut corn. An unhandy Sicilian, who acted as my squire of the body, had undertaken to make "my Excellency" a superb "*camera frondosa.*" Nothing could be worse. A few ill-arranged and ill-supported branches to shade my head only, and over these a loose thatch of wheat. I had made my own bed of golden flax, but he assured me this generated a malaria, and made me change it for bearded wheat. I no sooner lay down than every bearded ear, as if endued with life and motion, began to work itself into my pantaloons, which for coolness were of the dark blue Sicilian web silk, then worn by all our officers. Soon the discomfort this occasioned was increased by the changeful night.

My Dominico, the unhandy, had made the mouth of my little canopy to face the seaward wind, which now blew rudely upon me, drifting in all insects of nocturnal wing, especially the large, cold, chaffy locusts, with which the country was so covered that your horse kicked them up like dust under his feet. Awkward, ill- guided creatures, as big as one's thumb, that when they got upon one did not know how to get away again.

My under-lip, like that of all the officers, was almost cleft in two by the effect of sun and night air, so that to laugh or smile brought tears into one's eyes, and every time the wind dashed a locust against my face I gave myself a slap on the chops that stung my poor lip to distraction. Then it began to rain like the deuce, and soon giving weight to the wheat at top, the branches could no longer support it, so down it all came, wet bearded corn, branches and insects, all at once on my face.

I was extremely glad when this memorable night was over, and ere earliest dawn the signal for awaking sounded through the leafy roofs under which the army had that night reposed. At two o'clock I was busy in preparing my horse for his march, caring little now for the ill construction of my hut or all the disasters of the night.

The enemy, who had advanced to meet us from the south, having immediately after the battle retreated northwards to Catanzaro, instead of attempting to cover the country whence he came, it was plain that he no longer thought of defending Lower Calabria, which province with its garrisons he thus abandoned to his victorious adversary. Sir John Stuart was strongly minded to pursue these extraordinary advantages, and with his small unassisted army (for there was no indication of a national rising) to drive the French still further to the north, and increase the extent of his footing in the kingdom of Naples.

There was certainly more gallantry than prudence about this idea; for when the interests which depend on this little army are considered, the importance of the Island of Sicily at this moment, and our trifling numbers for territorial occupation, there can be no doubt that those about the general, who prevailed with him to be satisfied with the conquest of the province,[8] almost touching this important island, with whose safety he was entrusted, did better service by their counsels than they could at that time have rendered by their swords.

Of this number, I believe, was his quarter-master-general, a young man of great acquirement and high military promise; and certainly not the least influential of them was our own commandant [9] of the Royal Engineers, whose vigorous and strong professional opinion certainly had great influence, for the quartermaster-general in reference to it used these emphatic words, "It has succeeded." It was in conformity with the decision produced by these counsels that the headquarters had moved to Monte Leone, and the general was now disposed to content himself with placing the province of Lower Calabria upon such a footing of military occupation as would delay its reoccupation even by a very superior force, and ensure to us for a considerable time both shores of the Straits of Messina.

Most of the ports to the southward of Monte Leone were so inconsiderable as to surrender on the first appearance of a military force or of a ship of war. But the port which by its position was by far the most important (*viz.* the castle, strongly built upon the rock of Scylla) was in a good state of defence, impregnable to assault, fully garrisoned, and commanded by the chief engineer of Regnier's army; so as might have been expected, the commandant had treated the admiral's summons to surrender with contempt. It was necessary, therefore, to march against the place. And when the commander of the brigade which sat down before it gave a more serious summons, the Frenchman answered that before he could surrender he must at least see the means by which he could be reduced, meaning without doubt *heavy artillery, so placed as to batter him in breach.*

It became necessary therefore to attack this castle by a regular siege, and the army on the 12th of July began its march at four o'clock in

---

8. Calabria.
9. Captain Lefebure, R.E.

the morning. It had not proceeded many miles before I, being then about fifty miles distant, received an order from my commandant to repair to the siege also. So I set forward alone.

The road lies over bold mountains, and is so intricate and devious that I lost my way and greatly lengthened my ride; but having traversed the promontory of Tropea, the route is then more certain and confirmed—keeping still indeed over mountains, but having the near-sounding sea as a general guide, sometimes showing itself through the cleft of two mountain peaks, and sending up the report of every gun fired on its surface multiplied by the muffled echoes of the mountains.

After riding about fifty miles, the incessant sound of guns advertised me of my approach to the scene of action, and soon, by one of those dangerous paths whereon a horse moves with difficulty, and a stumble would precipitate both horse and rider many hundred feet, I descended to the small marine town of Scylla (bounded to the south by the peninsular rock on which the besieged castle stood), and saw on its highest tower (in spite of its investment by sea and land) the tricolour flag flying.

The rock on which the castle stands seems, as it were, shoved out a considerable way into the sea by the low and narrow isthmus which ties it to the shore, and from this isthmus it rears itself suddenly in the midst of the waves.

Before the castle was built this spot was probably an inaccessible peak of naked rock; the top, however, has been blown away to afford space for military occupation, leaving height enough to afford a formidable scarp of natural rock towards the land as the basement of the artificial rampart; towards the sea, an abrupt precipitous cliff, inaccessible to man, descends perpendicularly into the deep water.

The fort constructed upon the table of this peninsular rock was, up to a certain point, admirably adapted for security and strength. But that abrupt and lonely precipitousness of inaccessible circuit, which to the unlearned eye presented so imposing a picture of invulnerable strength, was in fact the radical defect of the position, which made it impossible to secure it against the means and measures of modern war. The great strength of modern fortification consists certainly in the glacis, or in that smoothly sloping mound which conceals and covers the rampart to the very chin, yet is severed from it by a deep and impassable ditch, screening it from every injury, even by the heaviest and most numerous ordnance, whilst its own gradual slope is swept by a rain and hail of cannon-balls, grape shot, and musketry, both from its own parapet and that of the superior rampart. But to construct this, ample space is necessary, and consequently for a rocky peak like Scylla, joined to the land by a narrowing isthmus, this work, so indispensable to durable strength, was totally unattainable.

The strength, then, of the Castle of Scylla lay briefly in this, that its reduction required the bringing against it of heavy artillery, capable of beating down the rampart that fronted the land.

So much for the castle which I now beheld, and which, surrounded with enemies by sea and land, and cut off from all connection with any friendly force, stood up boldly in the midst of that sapphire sea and unfurled the three-coloured flag of national defiance.

I shall now briefly describe the circumstances and things by which it was at this time surrounded, not so much on account of any historical importance attaching to this little siege, as because the classic associations and natural beauties of the scene consecrate it to memory, and its local form subjected all these operations to the eye, like some warlike spectacle in the theatre of the gods.

If we can fancy ourselves within the castle and looking over the isthmus in the direction of the land, behind us and almost all round us is the sea. On the left hand is the beach and town of Scylla. On the right the bold and mountainous shore takes a gradual sweep, till over a space of sea it looks down upon our right flank. Here Sir Sidney Smith has established a battery and hoisted the English colours.

Immediately in front, from the base of the isthmus, rises a steep cliff, whose brow, divided into several distinct hills, overlooks the castle at the distance of some five or six hundred yards. These heights have a surface very spacious, rising very gradually from the cliff towards the steeps of the Superior Mountains. Farms, vineyards, gardens, and country houses occupy and intersect this sloping headland. But the head of each hill or cliff looking upon the castle has been kept bare, probably with a view to defence, though unfortunately the same precaution had not been observed with respect to the ground nearer the foot of the cliff, and looking very close upon the main rampart; for there, for marine convenience, a little suburb had been suffered to rise, and it was behind the mask of one of these houses that the breaching battery was at last erected.

Beyond that vine-clad *esplanade* or level district which rose very gradually from the brow of the cliff, the heights, still clothed with cultivation, ascended more steeply towards the summit of that vast range of mountains, which makes this trend of coast so bold, imperious, and pre-eminently beautiful.

It was partly upon, and partly still above, these steeper slopes that the besieging army bivouacked, as the nearer ground would have made them liable to annoyance from the guns of the castle.

All the necessary communication with the army from Sicily and from the sea was by a rugged mountain path formed upon the side of an awful ravine, whose embouchure opened upon the beach between the town and castle.

The road which this ravine afforded was not only difficult but likely to cause frightful accidents; for when I ascended by it the first time, to join the besiegers' army, I saw where a sumpter horse heavily laden had fallen the day before with its load, and the poor animal was still visible lying on its back some hundred feet below.

To supply the requisites for a siege by such a road, it may well be believed, was difficult in the extreme, and would have been impossible but for our all-conquering sailors, who with their tackling and their "yo-hee-ho" hauled the guns and carriages up the rocks at the points nearest to the ground chosen for their position. Yet it was some days after my arrival before operations could be commenced, and much of those days I passed in a lofty observatory built of branches, in so elevated a position that I looked down upon the castle and the sea.

On one side I saw the Neapolitan gunboats, and on the other Sir Sidney Smith's battery, cannonading the castle, and the castle occasionally making a shrewd shot at the gunboats, which also, oftener than the castle, were startled by the plunging fire of our naval battery. On the arrival of my commandant all these futile operations died away. The general and the admiral equally relied upon the resources of his science and the natural energy of his powerful mind, and after some loss from irregular experiments, no one was suffered to interfere with his plan of operations.

He went with us to the embouchure of the ravine to have a good view of the castle from head to foot; and whilst he stood with his uplifted telescope carefully examining the nature of its defences, a cannon-ball very nearly struck him, and covered him with sand; but he never even lowered his telescope or remitted his attentive speculation, and only showed that he was aware of the fact by saying, as he continued to look through his glass, "What asses, to fire in that way at an individual!"

It seemed to my inexperience that this was standing fire tolerably well—brave and invincible Lefebure! It was as he stood just so, with his eagle glance bent on the foe, the last to quit a ruined fort he was ordered to evacuate, that in after years a cannon-ball struck his breast, and severed his brave spirit from his noble form.[10]

That there might be no disappointment in the stores expected from Messina, I was desired to cross the Faro, superintend their embarkation, and return with them. For this purpose I took one of the Calabrese boats which lay on the beach.

The warders of the castle seeing a British officer put off in a boat, honoured us with a shot or two, to the great and undissembled terror of the boatmen, while I was doing all I could to imitate the cool indifference of our commandant on the preceding day; but we soon got out of their range, and they ceased to fire, which made me wonder the more to see that the boatmen were going a devious course, sometimes one way, sometimes another. "What now," said I, "body of Pluto! what ails the rogues?"

"*Zitto! zitto! cellenza!*" they whispered, and with their eloquent hands at once motioned me to be quiet, and to come forward to the prow. There on the very peak one of the men, having thrown off his jacket and shirt, stood up, as straight as a *mast*, with his flat hands pressed together on his breast, and looking down intensely upon the sea. Following the direction of his eyes, I perceived at a great depth, in the bright blue sea, rowing itself contentedly along, a turtle of a size uncommon in these waters. With great dexterity they so managed the boat as to follow closely the course of the turtle; and when they had brought the prow of the boat nearly over him, the man who stood there, lifting his joined hands above his head, turned himself over, and went head foremost like an arrow into the sea.

In a moment up he came again, bearing the dripping, gasping turtle on its back, in his two hands, clear above the water, flapping its oary legs, and gasping with its hawk's beak; the man treading the water, panting and laughing at his exploit, and his delighted companions, as they relieved him of his load, all applauding him at once, helping him in, and saying, "*Bravo, Signor, bravissimo! La Maestro! da capo! et viva!*"

I thought I never saw a neater bit of fishing. A small silver coin served to make the turtle my own, and I determined to take him back with me to see what we could make of him.

But to return to Scylla. Before heavy guns could be got up, it was thought advisable to make such use of the Light Artillery as could

---

10. Captain Lefebure was killed at the assault on Matagorda, near Cadiz, in 1810.

destroy as much as possible the defences or fire of the enemy.

The most anxious night I ever passed was in erecting a breastwork for two 12-pounders within half musket-shot of the place, as everything depended upon its being completed before the light should discover us to the enemy. And though I explained to the men their danger if they should be discovered, it did not appear to create in them any extraordinary vigour. On the contrary, if my back was an instant turned, I found half of them asleep or sitting down, and it was difficult to detect them owing to the darkness of the night. Only by the most violent means could I extort a tolerable portion of labour, though I knew that if we were not covered before dawn, the spot was so exposed that at least half the party would be sacrificed.

By perfect silence, however, we avoided discovery during the night, favoured by the enemy being himself employed, as we could distinctly hear by every move, which, at cautious intervals, interrupted the silence of the night. The radiance of the stars faintly delineated the features of the gloomy horizon, and when the light of day discovered us to the enemy, he opened upon us a very brisk fire of musketry without intermission for an hour and a half, which, after being partially silenced by a howitzer, continued at intervals until the battery was finished. We were so well covered, and so little remained to be done on the outside, that only one man was wounded.

Nothing could be prettier than the siege to a person out of fire. The ruddy evenings gave the most tranquil warmth to the scene, which was bounded in front by the Lipari Islands, with Scylla on the left, and the beautiful Calabrian promontory on the right, and the only thing wrong was that the volcano should (quite contrary to usual practice) choose to remain in perfect repose.

When I left Scylla, the two 12-pounders had destroyed a part of the fort which hitherto had given us considerable annoyance, and in two days it was expected that we should open a battery of four 24-pounders within 150 yards of the castle, which could not fail in a few hours to knock it to pieces. The result was that Scylla surrendered on the 23rd July 1806.

Now for myself. I was ordered to put myself under the command of Lieut.-Colonel M'Leod, who with his regiment (78th) was to proceed on a reconnaissance on the eastern coast of Calabria; and here I am, installed on board the *London* transport, and probably after a month's cruising we shall come back and settle quietly in Messina.

London Transport (off Calabria),
July 20, 1806.

My dearest Father—I seize the only advantage immediately resulting from being cooped on board, *viz.* the opportunity to address one's friends leisurely and comfortably; and as the duty on which I am now going is not likely to be at all dangerous, I have no fears of alarming you by giving as much account of myself as will be comfortable to you and me.

H.M.S. *Amphion,* July 24, 1806.

My situation has been considerably amended as to comfort since coming on board this ship, which is commanded by the brother of my friend Hoste, R.E., whom I never spoke to until my arrival in the Bay of St. Eufemia. Yet with the most gratifying attention, he has rescued me from the miserable transport, where I was destitute even of those comforts which usually palliate the sufferings of a transport imprisonment, and taken me into his own cabin, which is like most other cabins of men-of-war—a compact assemblage of convenience and comfort. It was besides in some ways better that I should be here with Colonel M'Leod, who came the moment we fell in with the frigate, which, with the vessels and boats under the command of Captain Hoste, is to co-operate with the troops under Colonel M'Leod.

Very important despatches were intercepted yesterday; they were from King Joseph to General Regnier, containing a positive order to retire to Cassano, which is completely out of Calabria.

The king is afflicted and yet more astonished at the conduct of the troops, which rendered nugatory the good arrangements of General Regnier. He would have the 1st Regiment of Light Infantry reminded that they never before had any fear of the English, but always made them fly before them; and the rest of the troops—that they have, until this unfortunate moment of panic-struck terror (for which His Majesty is unable to account), been uniformly victorious.

But above all, they are desired to remember *that they are Frenchmen.* and also to be assured that the emperor shall be ignorant of their conduct until some fresh intelligence convinces H.N.M. that it is really a body of French troops of which General Regnier has the command.[11]

We are every moment receiving on board the leaders of the Patriot Mountaineers, who are the most striking, barbarous-looking fellows.

6th August.—I send these sheets as they are. I have no time to revise, and add the conclusion of my expedition, as though I am at present on board the *Amphion*, yet not much time will elapse before I tread the firm ground of Messina.

The march of the enemy from Catanzaro towards Naples was very much harassed by the frigate, which threw her shot with admirable precision, insomuch that the column, dispersed and flying for cover, with the utmost precipitation, presented a favourable moment for the Mountaineers, which, alas! they let escape them.

This system of annoyance on our part was followed up on the enemy's camp, north of Cotrone, from whence they marched in the night, leaving a garrison in the fortress which surrendered to our summons.

When we went on shore we were joyously received by the poor oppressed inhabitants, and the nobility of the town vied with each other in attention to us.

Being chief engineer I was attached to Captain Hoste and Colonel M'Leod, so that my situation was as pleasant as possible; for neither of the commanders treating me with the least *Big-wig*, we carried on the war like three jolly fellows.

A carriage waited each day at the marina for our coming on shore, and a good dinner was prepared for all the officers.

The first day we dined at the house of a baron whose family had during the stay of the French been in the most terrible alarm, as the house was just in the range of fire between the vessels and the fortress.

One daughter was very beautiful, and I asked her if she was glad that the French were gone; she looked pensive and pale, and answered *"Ma quanto."*

There was something gratifying though melancholy to me in the way these people clung to us in all their fears—for the French being gone, their alarm as to the depredations of the native masses was equally oppressive.

---

11. I saw these despatches.—Charles Boothby.

During dinner, some of the savage chiefs entered upon business with Colonel M'Leod, and this young creature showing evident signs of inquietude, I asked if she were afraid? "*Con voi*—no," with much softness of expression, replied the beautiful Italian.

The British authorities, however, with very laudable solicitude, by threats and promises ensured to the town tranquillity, and quite calmed the fears of the inhabitants.

Yet I was shocked at some of the misery which I saw; alas! human misery can attain a very high pitch.

Colonel M'Leod desired me to give him a report upon Cotrone.

Now, reports are very ticklish sort of things, it being no difficult matter to get the wrong side, and then you are subscribed a fool in black and white to the end of your days—and this was the first time I had been called upon to act by myself. I obeyed orders with much trepidation, but as I afterwards found that Colonel M'Leod, in a despatch to Sir T. Stuart, called my paper "an able report, the ideas in which coincide with his own," I am well satisfied, and indeed I have had a most pleasant expedition.

Messina (2 hours later),

I find that General Moore has arrived. I hope I was recommended to him.—Ever your dutiful son,

C.B.

Messina, August 13, 1806,
and August 28.

My dearest Mother—I am just returned from a most unexpected cruise in the Gulf of Taranto (mouth of the Adriatic), where I was despatched at a very short notice to reconnoitre Gallipoli and Tarentum, port towns in the Gulf, and I this day carried in my report to H.E. General Fox, who is a man of pleasant manners and sensible appearance.

I was sent out in H.M.S. *Wizard*, a very fast-sailing brig. Captain Palmer commander, and as he could not take me into the harbour of Tarentum in the brig, owing to the batteries on an island at the mouth—from which they gave us a hint or two—he lowered his boat, and we advanced unmolested, very near the walls of the town, which imprudence nearly cost us our liberty. For the enemy on the watch let us come on as far as we would, and the moment we turned, sent out a boat full of soldiers with a huge sail. We attempted for some time to sail before them, but finding they gained on us very fast, the sail was *downed*, and we threw ourselves upon hard rowing for escape, which at one time neither the captain nor myself had any hopes of; and I felt no small degree of exultation to find myself on board H.M.S., as I was far from wishing to be captured in so silly a manner.

They tell us of peace, but I will not believe it. No minister can, no minister dare make peace in the present position. Nothing, in my opinion, but this island being an acknowledged British colony, could justify our admitting Joseph's title to Naples, and we cannot do this without providing for this king, and if he be provided for, somebody else must be robbed. No, no, it won't do.—*Adieu*, my dearest mother, ever your affectionate son,

Charles.

September 1.

Today I wish my dearest father much good sport, and you a good appetite to enjoy his success.

I am ashamed, my ever dearest lady mother, to send you so dirty a letter, but I trust you will excuse it, as I was hurried by the idea of the vessel sailing.

Sir John Stuart carries the mail in which are these letters. I hope the country will receive him as the daring nature of his exploits and the fullness of his victory warrant and demand.

Messina, October 10, 1806.

My dearest Father—I have seen but little of General Moore. When I meet him he treats me in the most agreeable way possible. I dined with him the other day. He came very close to my heart talking of you in a very friendly manner. Not indeed that he said much, but when he mentioned you, he had a sort of friendly satisfaction very agreeable. He told me I was not such a slim fellow as you, and asked about your shooting, etc.

I feel it a sort of comfort to have some interest with a man who may possibly prevent my being left in holes and corners when I should be elsewhere.

General Sherbrooke is here. I do not know him, but hear he is a first-rate officer.

We are extremely anxious for the packet. We expect to hear by the next arrivals what our countrymen think of the Battle of Maida.—Your dutiful and affectionate son, C. B.

Catania, Feb. 21, 1807.

My ever dearest Father—I did not remember until I dated this letter that probably in the course of this day I should come across your recollection. I beg your blessing, and that of my dearest mother, and I pray God to bless you both, that you may long be able to give it me on the return of this day.

My change of place prevents my writing so often as formerly, from not being in the way of opportunities.

The packet of January has arrived, and possessed us of very late papers.

It is believed here that the French, having crossed the Vistula, have been beaten by the Russians, and any reverse with so large a river in their rear would be incalculable. It is likewise believed that Buonaparte is at Paris, endeavouring to reinforce his army, in spite of a general ferment throughout France.

An expedition is expected to leave Sicily every hour, generally supposed to be destined for Alexandria; but it is difficult to conceive why we should wish to garrison Alexandria (the Porte having defied us). As Turkey will do for the enemy as well as Egypt in respect to India, to seize Constantinople would seem more desirable, for I think there is no doubt but that Napoleon will occupy the states of his ally as far as he thinks expedient; and thus we should anticipate Buonaparte and preserve the passage of the Dardanelles.

If this expedition is going to Egypt, I am glad I remain here, but if Constantinople, I shall much regret that I was not ordered to join it. There is still, I believe, some doubt about its going at all, but I trust our dear old sturdy State will still be superior to the continental commotion. She never saw the time more calculated to try whether she be a solid fabric or no. For in this dearth of political talents, and of all talents (for there are no great men as yet visible), she must go almost by herself.

I am now quartered in this most beautiful town (Catania) upon Mount Etna, which I shall ascend when the fine weather comes, if I am still here.

I am rather inclined to believe that the war is near its close; but

I cannot discern the end.—Ever, my dearest father, your very affectionate and dutiful son, Charles.

Augusta, May 25, 1807.

My dearest Mother—I make an effort to save this packet, because you will perhaps be anxious about Egypt, of which you will now learn such unpleasant intelligence. There is at present no prospect of my going there, although I expected it some days ago, for I should think that the first advices from England will lead to the evacuation of that precarious possession. By what I can learn. General Fox designs to maintain Alexandria until he can receive new instructions.

Captain Lefebure, to my great vexation, has at his own desire been relieved from his command by Major Bryce. He wrote me a long and very kind letter upon the subject, and I transcribe a paragraph which occurs at the latter end, because I know it will give old Dad pleasure:—

> Dear Boothby, praise from me is superfluous, but I must yield to my feelings, and give you my hearty thanks for your unremitted, zealous, and useful professional support since we have been on the same service.

I am here under the command of Colonel Campbell, who, I suppose, is one of those men than whom there cannot be a better. I never knew him before.

Augusta is on a peninsula between Syracuse and Catania. The party of Guards with whom I live is the pleasantest society that can be, and I sometimes go over to Syracuse, where I see Lord Fred Bentinck, who is a capital fellow.

General Fox comes here today. He came here some time ago, but was suddenly called to Messina by the Egyptian despatches. Being obliged to go away early in the morning, he desired me to walk home with him after dinner to show him a plan of the works, in which walk he talked a great deal about Minorca and your family. My kindest love to all.—Ever your truly affectionate son, Charles.

The packet is gone, but a friend of mine goes to England under convoy of the *Intrepid*, which will sail immediately with General Fox, leaving General Moore in chief.

Copy of Letter from Sir John Moore to Lieutenant Boothby, R.E., Augusta:—

Messina, August 18, 1807.

My dear Boothby—I had the pleasure of receiving your letter of the 22nd July, on my return from Palermo, two days ago. All I shall say at present is, that I have a strong wish to serve and to oblige you.

I shall speak both to Major Bryce and to General Oakes on the subject of your wishes, and when an opportunity offers, if the situation is thought eligible for you and can be managed, you shall have my interest.—I have the honour to remain with great regards, very faithfully, John Moore.

Augusta, Sept. 14, 1807.

My ever dearest Father—The arrival of the packet at Malta has relieved very strong apprehensions for her safety. If, as I hope, there are a great many letters for me, I shall not get them until they are delivered at Messina, and sent from thence hither. It always happens in this manner that my answers are never able to reach the return mail, but on this occasion I am determined to answer by anticipation.

I can at least assure you that I am perfectly well, which is all in the present press that I have time to do.

The heat of the summer caused an epidemic of fever, which has now, however, almost entirely subsided. It plagued me for about a week, since which I have been rudely well, though the weather has been hot to a most irksome degree, and I have been obliged to brave the sun at the peril of no other inconvenience than the prickly heat—if you know what that is. I have indeed been harassed more by anxiety than labour: the former, however, is nearly at an end now.

When I found my fever gone and my appetite returned, and nothing left but depression of spirits and a little languor, I puts me into a boat at night by a beautiful moon, more lovely than the sun, and starts me for Syracuse for the next day's races, where I had a horse to run, and I knew there would be jollity.

I arrived much fatigued and slept a most excellent night, and breakfasted late next morning—no sooner finished, than the sporting gentlemen entered, and roused me up with a long pole, and the quicksilver mounted directly; for these were people that I much affect.

But first of all, for fear you should suppose that there is much extravagance in this affair, I must tell you how it goes.

The races have been generally about once in six weeks, subscribers pay a guinea, and each subscriber may, if he pleases, enter a Sicilian horse. The guineas thus collected are divided into four parts or three, according to the number of horses, which are also arranged in classes according to their merits. The winner of each class gets one of the divisions of the money, and then all the winners run for the last division. They are weighted by handicaps.

In this manner my horse has won for me upwards of twenty guineas. I should always subscribe whether I had a horse or not, because the meeting is more pleasant than anything in this horrid country, and I can afford it. With a little care I keep my head very well above water.

Well, on the race day I was very merry, and dined in the evening with the Jockey Club, which was entertained by a man by everybody loved and esteemed for his excellence of all sorts, and who was by me additionally regarded, because we were made acquainted by a letter from poor Gould,[12] who was his first cousin. Finding myself *de buon appetito*, I drank lots of champagne well iced, and since have enjoyed robustness of health.

I do not see where will be the sense in talking to you about what you will see in the papers. They now say that the seven islands are all strictly blockaded; and it appears, by a letter from our Consul at Corfu to Colonel Campbell, that Caesar Berthier with 1500 men had taken possession of Corfu, and felt himself critically situated with so small a force in case of attack from us.

I fancy Zanti and the other islands are not yet occupied by the French. We are all in a bustle to put the fortresses in a good state of defence, and indeed, now the French have nothing else to do, it behoves us to be very much on our guard if we are to keep the island.

But I imagine that the immediate preparation was against any attempt that might be meditated from Corfu—the very island which now appears to have been in equal fuss on our account.

As I have been some time resident here upon other business, I

---

12. Lieutenant Edward Gould, a great friend.

was desired to draw up a full memoir upon the defences of the place,[13] which I set about reluctantly and fearfully, unwilling to write myself ass, and not knowing that it would so soon come in question.

The thing gave much anxiety and trouble, but it seems that I have not come very wide of the mark, as I am threatened with an order to execute most of my proposals. This is very pleasantly terminated, as I wrote to recommend that an older officer should be sent down (which some would call spiritless, *but we call honest*); and now I find that the captain whom I particularly wished to have, is ordered to come here immediately.

September 27.—Since I last wrote I have been highly delighted with a visit to the crater of Mount Etna, which is not only more sublimely terrific and more dreadfully beautiful than anything else I ever beheld, but much more than my imagination had ever pictured. I had been so much occupied since my residence in this island, as to be prevented from joining any of the numerous parties of last year. Thus I began to be very apprehensive that I might labour under the reproach of residing near two years in Sicily without beholding one of the most stupendous objects of nature—the greatest of volcanoes. But the history of my ascent to Mount Etna must be suspended *sine die.*

We were fortunate in finding the crater in an incessant state of fiery eruption—tremendous indeed! It threw out red stones very near us. The guide was alarmed. Hereafter I may relate more at length an excursion strongly impressed upon my mind.

An expedition is on the eve of departure from Sicily. It will have about 7000 men, commanded by General Moore and General Paget—the Guards and Moore's own regiment (52nd),—in short, the flower of the army.

I wrote to go, and was gratified to find that I was in the arrangement. I am told that it is intended to place me on the staff. At any rate I am delighted to go.

Nobody can guess our destination. All parts of the world have been conjectured, England and Ireland not excepted.

I have been very lucky never to be ill on these occasions, and am much pleased at being remembered, though in this out-of-

---

13. Augusta, on the east coast of Sicily.

the-way place, and being placed immovably on the list.

I long to see General Moore wave his hat, and hope we are to trim the real French—and no auxiliaries nor Turks.

Burgoyne is Commanding Engineer, and almost all my friends and people to whom I am attached are going, which gives much huzza to my feelings. I should certainly have hanged myself had I been left in this hole after the Guards had left it, and when all my world had gone forth. Perhaps my being on the expedition may much expedite my return to God's dearest blessings, which I prize so far above all other earthly goods. It is fortunate for a man's piety when the objects of his gratitude are so undeniably great as to fill his heart and make him know how good God has been to him. I have come to that state when I would be thought truly pious—I had always a hankering after it,—as I find that nothing encourages half so much the gladness of the heart or the sublimity of the mind.

With infinite love, your truly affectionate

Charles.

October 17.—At the time the above was written the fleet was getting under way, and was to rendezvous at Syracuse, where it was to be joined by the troops from Egypt, who were already at Messina. Colonel Campbell had no idea of the destination of the expedition. An order has since gone out for its recall to Sicily.

Elizabeth Transport, Mediterranean Sea,
240 miles from Gibraltar. Foul wind, fresh.
November 29, 1807. 30 days at sea.

My dearest Louisa—I know nothing more efficacious in my present misery than writing to you, by which for the moment I may lose the consciousness of it. Do not be alarmed; they are only the miseries of this restless element and stinking prison to which I allude.

On leaving Sicily someone persuaded me that our undoubted destination was Palermo. When that was passed, we all thought Lisbon the mark. Now we learn by the *Minstrel* (which spoke the *Queen* about ten days ago) that the Prince Regent of Portugal has declared against us; and I am inclined to think that this event may make the object of this army a secret to Sir John Moore himself; but Brazil is the general speculation. For my part I think our return more likely, as it appears of increasing importance to rivet Sicily as our perpetual colony—a measure which I am persuaded would be unattended with difficulty in the execution, and, as far as I can judge, filled with advantage in the end.

But leave we this to the wise, while we content ourselves with ourselves.

I find complaints about not writing so unavailing that I am quite puzzled how to act. I will have no letter that can be written in a day; I will have a journal! a compilation! Why do I see others—Colonel Campbell, for instance—receive packet upon packet copiously filled? Do you think that because he is a great man his friends write to him about state affairs, which are better treated in the papers—or philosophy, or history perhaps? No, no; they write to him those heaps of gossip which are interesting only to him, but which of course delight him a thousand times more than any other subjects. Those incidents, dear Lou, which you think too trivial to send two thousand miles, never considering that domestic anecdotes so many thousand miles as they travel are so many thousand times more valuable to a man of affections than if sent to him a trifling distance, which you would not scruple to do.

It surprises me the more that you, my dearest lass, are silent, who write with such apparent facility and impress your expressions with the graces of your nature—the true secret to make correspondence delightful—when that which I have long loved in yourself breathes through your letters and gives them the air of your conversation.

I therefore recommend that you would keep a regular journal, enough to make me an immense letter once a month; and don't be particular about a subject, so as you talk about what is actually going on amongst you. If "Molly Morley be brave to what she war," it is very interesting to hear so, and if you still keep your taste for barley sugar! which I doubt not! But Brookes' exploits must always be productive, with his badgers and things, and I thank you again for those anecdotes. I wrote the lad a letter some time ago. How I long to see him! Nobody makes me laugh half so much as he does, and I love a hearty laugh.

But my home letters feel always so skinny between the finger and thumb that I am always sure there cannot be much in them, and every line I read I grudge, for fear of coming to the end.

When once I do get home what a zest will my absence give to every blessing; for wherever I go or whatever I see, I may say with the feeling Goldsmith—

My heart, untraveled, fondly turns to thee,
Still wanders o'er the peaceful scenes I love.
And drags a lengthening chain at each remove.

I long incessantly to return to the bosom of that family to which may be applied the words of a less celebrated poet—

Nor last, tho' noticed last by me.
Appears that happy family.
No pen can do strict justice by.
And mine should be the last to try—
Wher'ever going—there approved
And only known to be beloved.
                                    Couch, *canto* ii.

This letter will probably be concluded from Gibraltar, where I may have a better idea of my destination. At present I am tired out with this tedious passage and tossing about from one side of the cabin to the other. The soup in my lap! and my fist in the pudding. Oh dear! Oh dear! But now, please Neptune, we may have a fair wind, and may run into Gibraltar in two or three days. The only amusement on board ship is light reading and making verses. It is quite impossible to bore.
Since I came on board I have read with a good deal of attention for the first time Dryden's *Virgil* and Pope's *Homer*, from which in themselves I did not derive half so much pleasure as the conviction of Milton's decided superiority to both.
A man reading a translation cannot of course judge of the language or numbers of the original, but these I believe are not of the first consequence, and Pope is generally esteemed a greater master of both than Milton (though I am myself quite of a contrary opinion); but it is in the thoughts that Milton so astonishingly surpasses, I think, both *Homer* and *Virgil*; for surely nobody who reads *Paradise Lost*, and the *Iliad* by Pope, can doubt how cumbersome rhyme is to an epic poem, or how much it relaxes the energy of the verse, or how much grander a translation of Homer Milton could have furnished than that for which we are so greatly obliged to Pope. I prefer the *Odyssey* to the *Iliad*,

and the *Georgics* to the *Æneid*, for the latter is something like a servile imitation of the Greek.

By the way, if you have never read Boswell's *Life of Johnson*, let me recommend you to a most delicious entertainment. Although the biographer portrays himself an inconceivable goose, I never met with anything so interesting as his book, nor so wonderful as the conversation and universal wisdom of Johnson, whom he will never believe to be a coward, though it were proved in fifty thousand courts—and this indissoluble attachment is with me called rectitude of heart.

Gibraltar, December 4, 1807.

After a most unpleasant passage of thirty-six days, we arrived here on the 1st inst. We have received no intelligence of any sort. Sir John Moore has sailed alone to the westward, and it is supposed that his object is to concert what may be best, by what he may find to have happened at Lisbon. All thoughts of South America seem to have subsided; and if in the end we do return, our advance and enterprise do not seem to be yet quashed, from the orders which the general gives us.

I have been much gratified by a letter from the mother of my friend,[14] promising that the epitaph I sent should be placed on his tomb, and professing to have derived much comfort from my sympathy, and from the affectionate tribute paid to her son's memory. It has in a manner set my heart at rest on this melancholy subject, for there is a great mental satisfaction, if no solid sense, in the consideration that I have performed the last sad duty to his ashes, by establishing a little register of his virtues and our friendship, which otherwise would have sunk with me and those who loved him into oblivion, the idea of which is horrible.

5th December.—The mail closes tomorrow and I have no time to alter or peruse anything—so take it as it is—it's just a talk.—

Yours,   Charles.

Isle of Wight,
St. Helens, December 29, 1807.

Ever dearest Father—If you have not been prepared for it, my arrival in England will be to you an agreeable surprise, as in fact it is almost to me.

---

14. Lieutenant Edward Gould, R.E.

We had a favourable passage of thirteen days, and came to anchor last night. When I have seen Sir John Moore in Portsmouth and General Morse in London, I shall be better able to fix my movements; at present my thoughts are to stay here two or three days, then to London, and so meet you at Sudbury before the 9th.

Hereafter I shall probably wish to adhere to General Moore, who has intimated a disposition entirely friendly to me. But I cannot help hoping to spend the greater part of the winter with you—a hope, however, too flattering to be implicitly trusted. I heard, by means of Colonel Campbell, the valuable intelligence that you were all well on the 12th November. As I trust we shall meet very soon I need not lengthen this letter, farther than to say how much I am, my dearest Dad,

your ever most affectionate   Charles.

P.S.—There is not such an air of happiness in this letter as my situation may be supposed to inspire. The fact is, I fear giving myself too much up to certainty which may possibly forerun disappointment.—*Adieu.*

LETTER FROM LIEUT. CHARLES BOOTHBY TO SIR JOHN MOORE

Sudbury, March 1808.

Dear Sir—I did myself the honour to wait upon you in London, and trust that you will allow me to say by letter what I would have expressed in conversation.

I experienced with much regret the breaking up of that army in which I felt so fortunately situated and befriended by you. But I do not despair of being again under your command, which is my first wish, and have only to fear the being sent out of the way before anything should occur.

As your kindness on that head, as on all others, left me nothing to desire, I am anxious to state that my wish to belong to an army of which you have the command is entirely independent of any hopes I might suffer to arise in consequence of your late disposition to indulge my wishes and promote my advantage, and that I shall ever esteem myself sufficiently fortunate to meet with active practice in my own particular profession under your auspices in any part of the world. I found my father and family here on a visit to Lord Vernon. I delivered your message, which gave him much pleasure, and he is highly gratified to find himself remembered by your kindness to me.—I have the honour to be, dear sir, with great respect, your very obedient, obliged, and humble servant, Charles Boothby.

I had not long to wait before this letter was answered by a summons to join the expedition to Sweden, under Sir John Moore, and by the 15th April I was in London preparing for departure.

Blenheim Hotel, Bond Street, London,
April 27, 1808.

Ever dearest Dad—I feel conscious from your letter that you have not much spirits to spare. Whatever hurts you, goes to the quick with me also. But God did not mean us to be perfectly happy here, and I hope that we jog on towards the next place with as comfortable prospects as our neighbours.

If from any want of efficiency on my part, it were your business to prescribe my motions, you would (however disagreeable to your affections) direct me as I am now going. The rage that pervades the youth of blood to go with General Moore exceeds anything I ever heard of, and many suicides are expected in consequence of rejected applications.

I pray God to bless you all, and me, in such a return as lately gladdened my heart.—

Your ever most affectionate Charles.

Blenheim Hotel, Bond Street, London,
April 29, 1808.

Ever dearest Dad—I hope it will not be a great disappointment to you not to find me in London, as I was peremptorily obliged to leave on the 30th.

I would have done anything to save you a disappointment. But for myself, I should have had no pleasure in the meeting unless you were merry, and much pain at parting if you were sad.

Your remittance was very convenient and sufficient, and I am not in want of anything.—Ever dearest Dad, yours, C.

Sheerness, May 6, 1808.

The ships are under way and bound for Yarmouth. Thence I suppose to Gothenburg. Perhaps I shall see Sir Brooke in my rambles.

Yarmouth, May 9, 1808.

We arrived in the roads this morning, and I have just come on shore for an hour to get a few things that are wanting, as a fine fair breeze is to be taken advantage of immediately, and I hope to see Gothenburg in less than a week. General Moore is on board the *Mars*, and not an officer is to be seen on shore, as the Fleet is to sail at three o'clock.

Amity Brig, May 10.

Got under way at 4 o'clock p.m. Wind blowing towards evening with rain, and threatened a gale; moderated again, and the moon rose in unclouded majesty.

Fine clear night. List of men-of-war of the convoy. *Mars* 74, *Audacious* 74, *Tigress* 16, —— 16, and *Piercer*.

Friday 13.—All last night hazy weather, moderate breezes; in the morning thick fog—so thick that not a ship in the Fleet could be discovered except at intervals, although the voices of the people aboard could be distinguished.

The faint form of the ships, at times in the fog, had rather a sublime appearance. The commodore was on our starboard beam, which we knew by his occasionally firing guns of guidance; the sound was very near, but the flash could not be perceived. About twelve o'clock he made a signal to alter the course, and at two o'clock he made another signal, and we had some anxiety lest a mistake should make us lose the Fleet.

At about three o'clock, however, the fog cleared away, and discovered the commodore close on our larboard-quarter, steaming the same course with us, some thirty or forty miles from the coast of Jutland.

These Baltic fogs are extremely unpleasant, and lie chiefly on the shoal called Jutland Reef. The vessel was obliged to be constantly beating drums and ringing bells, lest some other ship should come upon her unknowingly, from the perfect obscurity in which we were involved.

Tuesday, May 17.—Wind blowing very fresh and a heavy sea. At a quarter before three had Gothenburg on the lee beam. At half-past three pilot came on board, at four anchored near Elfsborg Castle; experienced much pleasure from the force of contrast—coming at once from very rough sea-weather into harbour, and leaving the waves in the lurch.

Aspect of Gothenburg Harbour very wild and bleak.

Wednesday 18.—May go on shore, but not to sleep. Mr. Hindmarsh takes us in his boat and we land at Tod's Quay.

After entering the gates of Gothenburg, we went into a shop to inquire for an inn, and found a very pretty boy translating English into Swedish. His book was entitled *Village Dialogues*. He spoke English very well, and also French and German, and was exceedingly modest and well-behaved. His father stood by, and contemplated the acuteness of his son with delight, pleased to find that he could make Englishmen understand him.

We proceed, meet a gentleman, and ask for an inn where a dinner might be got.

"'Twas a shocking place," he said, but told us of an hotel. I then asked where I could hear of foreigners who might be in Gothenburg. "Did not know. Who did I want?"

"Sir Brooke Boothby."[15]

Had seen him that morning; showed me where he lived—"*Not at home*." Go to dine at Eryxon's and find party of officers. After dinner go again to call on my uncle (Sir Brooke Boothby), whom I had not seen for nine years. We were delighted to see each other; had tea, walked to Tod's Quay, embarked at nine, and was on board at ii p.m.

General Stewart is the kindest creature in the world. He went the other day to ask the general (Sir John Moore) to appoint me his *aide-de-camp*, as the brigadier-generals were to be allowed them; but General Moore's answer was, that he intended me for himself.

If the general has an opportunity of putting his intentions into execution, I shall have the situation which I wish for more than any other in the army. But my mind misgives me that we shall come home without achieving or seeing anything.

My uncle has introduced me to the best society here. We went to a ball on board the *Victory* the other day, and the prettiest lady said to me in very pretty broken English, "Wan I dance wid you, sair, I will assure you dat I wish we dance de whole long of de sheep"; and when the two dances were over, she said, "Sair, I tank you; I will assure you it is de plaisantess dance I dance today." Seeing me smile she added, "You not belief it. Ah! it is true!"

I went simpering up to another lady and said, "What a very fine day, ma'am, for our party." She curtseyed, and uttered from her throat with a smile, "*Bakkelseg Morgon Vakka Thikka Pukk*," and so I simper-

---

15. It may interest the reader to know that the Sir Brooke Boothby here mentioned was the father of Penelope Boothby (whose portrait by Sir Joshua Reynolds is so well known). She was his only child, and died when six years old, in the year 1791.

PENELOPE BOOTHBY.
Born 1785. Died 1791.
Only Child of Sir Brooke Boothby, Bart.

ing replied as if I understood her, "*Yaw, yaw, Pukk*," bowed and went away.

June 14, 1808.—Agree with Wilmot, Sandham, and Foster to go to Trollhattan, and on Friday, 17th, at 5 a.m. start in two gigs with two horses each, arriving at half-past one, after a pleasant journey of fifty-two miles, stopping an hour on the road. The waterfall fell below my expectations, although it be terrible to stand close beside an enormous body of water in motion so rapid; but the view from below is much less grand and astonishing than I can conceive a cataract to be, nor do I think my ideas of the tremendous much invigorated or more defined than they were before, and as a proof that the cataract did not fill or satisfy the mind, I observed, that on beholding it, I ever cast my eyes to the lofty precipice on the right, saying to myself, "Oh, that it came tumbling over that!" The canal was just what I expected, and a most laudable work.

June 19.—Start for Ström at four. This road offers to the eye of the traveller much picturesque beauty. A great part of it lies as if through a beautiful English park, and from the excellence and trimness of the road and culture of the verdure you imagine yourself in some studied approach to a great man's house, while the beautiful gleams of the romantic Gotha, seen through the trees, make you exclaim, "Happy he whose eye is frequent on such a prospect." The Gotha is an exquisitely beautiful river: its waves are true silver and azure; its banks are green, enamelled with flowers, embossed with dwellings, and feathered with woods; and its stately windings are frequently caught through an irregular perspective colonnade of the trunks of trees, while their beautiful foliage embowers you above, and calms and attunes your mind to the beauties of the farther prospect. Its vessels never overpower it (I mean as landscape), that is to say, you never think of a crowd of masts, of coals, of bawlings, of canals, and all the horrors of navigation.

A graceful sail now and then glides swiftly through the trees, or dimples the silver surface, the here-and-there cascade having eminent beauty, deserving of notice; and the cultivated fields enwrapping the hills.

The skirts of the vast cataracts at Trollhättan, and indeed at Edet, are applied to the sawing of timber; and in various parts of Sweden the sledge-hammer is raised, the borer driven, and the polisher whirled by the same perpetual power.

Thursday, June 30.—Sir John Moore embarked last night. Learn that he had been a prisoner at Stockholm, and had made his escape.

See General Stewart; learn that the point in dispute between the general and the king,[16] had been the attack upon Norway, which His Majesty had stated was impossible, but in a subsequent conversation, being reminded of this statement, he denied it in the most positive terms.

The general said, "Not only I, but Colonel Murray, heard you; but if your Majesty says you did not say so, I must have misunderstood you." The king accuses him of disrespect—in a rage. Sir John, to pacify, concedes so far as to say he will wait for further despatches, but on going home and reflecting, finds his instructions too positive to admit of it, and apprises the king that he must depart from the country.

The king sends to him in the middle of the night to say that he must not leave Stockholm without his permission.

The general immediately despatches a messenger to embark every part of the army, and remonstrates upon the detention. No answer; but the next day a repetition of prohibition arrives.

Sir John takes a drive in the *curricle* of the Secretary of Legation beyond the first stage, where he is taken up in his plain clothes by a messenger, who, with his courier's pass, gets along uninterrupted. He arrived at Gothenburg on Wednesday, 29th June, and pushed off for the *Victory*. Only the admiral knew him.

Saturday, July 2.—The general desires to see Burgoyne and me immediately, and we go on board the *Victory*.

Sir John Moore informs us that the admirals, particularly Keats, are anxious about the little island of Sproe in the Great Belt, upon which during winter the French might establish themselves, and harbour gunboats, to the annoyance of the passage in summer.

The French had designed to possess it, and built a barrack on it, and there is a probability that next winter they may complete their design, which formerly they began too late.

The admirals desire to forestall the enemy, and I must go to see if the nature of the island and our means admit of such a defence being established before the necessary departure of the Fleet. The British have destroyed the barrack made by the French, so that barracks, storehouses, etc., for the troops must be established, as well as fortifications.

Sunday, July 3.—Get up at 3 a.m.; pack. At four pilot comes on board. Fleet gets under way. At seven admiral sends on board and takes

---

16. Gustavus IV.

me away.

Go on board the *Superb*. No instruments, no colours. Apply to be sent on board the *Victory* to see Sir John Moore. Sir John comes up himself to take me to the admiral's breakfast. General Stewart brings instructions; admiral very civil.

Sail with a convoy of merchantmen and the *Etna* towards the Belt. The army leaves for England.

July 5.—Heavy foggy weather with rain; coast of Jutland in sight.

July 6.—Came in sight of Sproe. Next morning I go on shore with surveying implements, half survey it, and next day complete survey. *Superb* in sight. As I go on shore in the afternoon, I receive a note from Admiral Keats to breakfast with him, and come again on board the *Superb*. Takes me altogether into the cabin. I enlarge my scale of plan, and prepare it for the field.

Sunday, July 10.—*Victory*, *Edgar*, and *Cruizer* in sight, entering the Belt. Admiral Keats takes me a *divil* of a row to meet the *Superb*,' Captain Graves dines there, and begs the boys to go on shore. Joey Easterbrook prefers it to the admiral's dinner. Poor FitzClarence left behind. "It was a cruel thing," he said. After dinner ye admiral, Captain Graves, and myself, go on shore. Boys shoved off ere our arrival. Admiral snuffs the green air; walk over the ground, gather wild spinach, return on board. The youngsters were in dismay! The captain's Newfoundland dog Tigress having run down a sheep, which had taken refuge in the sea, they feared it would be laid to them, but they had neatly skinned it, and hoped their mess would benefit by it. Little rascals! The admiral, from prudential motives, took particular care that they should not taste it.

Dear little Georges begged the officer on deck to let him put me on board the *Brunswick*. This began our friendship. He put me on board, I having agreed with Admiral Keats that, as I should finish with the island tomorrow, I should again come on board the *Superb*.

Tuesday, July 12.—This day drew up my report. Ships weigh, and anchor again.

July 19.—Desired by Sir James to travel in plain clothes. Make necessary change. Signal made, "Send Mr. Boothby on board the *Swan* cutter immediately. Make haste." [17]

---

17. This hasty summons meant that he was to proceed at once *via* Ystad and Helsingborg to England to rejoin Sir John Moore.

Sit down in the cabin with a party of particular friends. Georges in the chair. Lord Bury on my right hand, little Johnny Russell over against me. Boat ready; cutter waiting. Take an affectionate leave of my friends, Georges, Lord Bury, and Johnny, and part from Admiral Keats in the kindest manner; indeed, his behaviour and friendly conduct had quite attached me to him.

When taking leave of the wardroom officers I am entreated below to wine, steadily refuse, but Captain Jackson being gone with the Admiral, Mr. Crowe, the first lieutenant, orders me to be carried below, upon which officers, youngsters, and marines surround me, and spite of a strenuous resistance, carry me bodily by neck and heels into the ward-room, where I drink *adieu*.

Sent on board the *Admiral* to receive more despatches. Get on board the cutter; nasty odious little thing. Pass close under the *Superb's* stern. All hands crowd the poop, and actively wave me many farewells.

Wind foul; go to bed.

July 20.—Wind still fouler. Change our tack, and at length conceive hopes of arriving at Ystad, a pretty-looking town as seen from the distance; but nothing can be more park-like and beautiful than the shores of the Great Belt.

Get on shore about 5 p.m. Sailors take up my baggage. Go to the inn. Mr. Lucas brings Mr. Strom (clerk to an Ystad merchant), who undertakes my passports, horses, etc. Asking about Swedish travelling, it appears that robbing or breach of trust are species of dishonesty unknown to the Swedes. Send my baggage off at ten, start at eleven. No moon, good horses. As I go along, astonished to see the sea on my right hand. "How the devil," said I, "can this be?"

The sea, in or out of sight, must be to the left hand. But still I saw the sea approaching even to the edge of the road, broken by beautiful ports, isles, and rocks. "*Diable*," said I, "what call you dat?" pointing to a fine harbour, embossed with islands and romantic shores. The driver looked, but returned no answer, for he saw nothing but the white mist arising from the face of the earth. The deception was complete. A bank on the left of the road obstructed my view, but on the right it commanded an extensive tract of country.

The thick, white, shining mists lying in the low grounds gave them the exact appearance of water at that dusk time of night, while mountains in their range sketched out the harbours and islands which I had discovered.[18]

Overtake my baggage, and arrive.

July 21 .—At Everslip by half-past one. Dispatch the *holker* for horses. Go into a room in the house, like an oven; no light, but merely darkness visible; lie on a sofa; see a black many-legged reptile glide across the wall; start up and go out to meet my baggage.

Men impatient for payment. "What will you have?"

"For my two horses, five dollars."

"Rascal! I will give you one and a half, which I know to be right, and a half for yourself."

"Very right, tanka," said he.

Baggage arrives—relieved.

Daylight now, as with a mantle, robed our world, and bade fictitious seas and white mists yield the deceptive mask. And now I took the reins.

Crick, crack, the horses fly,
At every click more swift they hie.

Sudden each blade of grass, each feathered shrub, gleamed golden bright, and turning to the east, the glorious orb above the hills exalted half his disk.

This morn his crimson robe he chose, translucent,
That sheds its glowing tints on every mound,
And spreads its warm refulgence o'er the ground.

Arrive at Regerberg much tired, and roost. Wait for horses; start at half-past twelve, and arrive at Glumslouf. View beautiful—wooded banks of Zealand, Copenhagen spires. Meet divers Swedish nobles; they are diverted at the manner in which I expedite the hostler. "*Holker*," said I, and he looking back, I shake a bag of halfpence at him, and he runs like blazes.

Arrive at Helsingborg at five; much delighted as I approach with the view of Zealand.

The *Orion* and *Vanguard* and *Calypso* in the Sound, and beautiful Cronberg Castle beyond them.

Drive to Mr. Fenwick, the British Consul, and deliver letters. He, a gentlemanlike young man, actively obliging, procures me a room, and invites me to his house. Covered with dust and sweat, I plunge

---

18. The editor has seen precisely the same effect before sunrise in Scotland, over the Ochils near Crieff.

delightedly, and lave my limbs, then I robe myself afresh, and freed from all my dirt, sally forth and drink tea at the consul's. The boat announced, we proceed on board the *Orion*, and I deliver my despatches. As Admiral Bertie is not on board, I reclaim them, and pursue him to the *Vanguard*, Return on shore, sup with Mr. Fenwick, who gives me a snuff-box. Go to bed at twelve.

July 22, Friday.—Get up half-past 2 a.m., open the window, to find a midshipman looking for me, so I dress quick and send baggage to boat.

Admiral had said at daylight the *Calypso's* instructions should be perfectly ready. Get on board about four—delightful brig. Captain goes on board the *Orion*; no despatches yet. Fine breeze, which would shoot us by Cronberg Castle and the swarming gunboats, blowing to waste. At 2 p.m. calm.

Signal made by telegraph: "Come on board; bring the engineer." So we go on board, and *Calypso* weighs; as the breeze rises away we go; there is no firing, and we dart along.

July 25, Monday.—Fall in with a Dutch fishing-boat and board her, and get ten or a dozen very large cod. Fish ourselves; catch numerous mackerel in a light breeze—beautiful dying—green, blue, red, and rose. Becalmed. Plumb for cod; catch plenty, very large codfish and ling, also a dogfish. Cabinetmaker begs the skin to finish off his work. This evening the sun set in unusual splendour; he sank down into a thick indigo bank, whose edges he tinged with colours dipt in heaven. Sky tinctured green, and all above was yellow golden radiance, richly fretted in vapours, which blended off to the wilder clouds in the richest roseate glow. The sea was glassy smooth, but heaved gently with majesty, in her borrowed robe of gold refulgent, while in the east a perfect bow shone in full colours, striding over heaven, an arch superb, which the reflecting waves joined underneath again, making the round complete:—

> *The horizon round was dim, sublime,*
> *And wild, warm clouds mingled with ocean line.*

Rain,—imperceptible breeze; slip through at four knots. 140 miles from Yarmouth.

July 28, Thursday, 4 a.m.—Fair wind, going nine miles per hour. Board a suspicious vessel like a French privateer and find her a Greenland schooner. Heavy rain, dirty weather, close to Norfolk coast. Anchor for the night.

July 29, Friday, 4 a.m.—As we were getting up anchor the fog came on very thick. And though the wind at length relents, the envious fog still obscures the entrance to port; as it clears away we weigh anchor about 1 p.m., at which time I land, having preceded in the gig with Captain Bradby.

I wait upon Admiral Douglas, and hear that Sir J. Moore is at Portsmouth and expected to sail hourly. After this very fretful. Go on board again to make distribution of bag, but return immediately and get on shore half an hour before the mail starts. Take my place. In the mail are two men in coarse jackets and trousers, just escaped from France, having broken their parole. The joy of having escaped seemed entirely to fly away with all compunction, if indeed they had any conscience. They had undergone great hardships, so I smothered the severity of my disapprobation.

July 30.—Go to the Blenheim Hotel, Bond Street. Find that General Moore has taken care that I shall follow him. The General invites me to breakfast to talk of my report. See Sir R. Milnes. Call on Mrs. Meynell.

July 31.—Breakfast with General Moore. Office tomorrow. No tidings of baggage. Write letters home.

Blenheim Hotel, New Bond Street,
July 31, 1808.

My Louisa—First let me tell you that I am going tomorrow to Portsmouth to join or follow Sir John Moore, so hope not to see me just yet.

Having completed my services in the Baltic, I arrived at Yarmouth yesterday, and hearing that Sir J. Moore only waited for a wind, I was upon tenterhooks until in London, so half an hour after I landed I put myself into the mail, and arrived here at nine o'clock this morning. "Keep moving" has been for some time my motto.

Now, my own lass, have I much to discourse with thee about. There is my journey to Trollhättan and my peregrinations in the Baltic, my travels again through Sweden, all which, as I kept a circumstantial journal, you shall be sure to have. The civility and kindness of Admiral Keats, with whom I lived, made my stay quite delightful. After I had been on board three days it was necessary to transfer me to another line-of-battle ship, and when I was going he told me he should be back in a few days: "And then, if you please, you shall take up your quarters with me." This pleased me much, and when he did return he took me into his cabin, and I was as happy as the day was long, although very hard worked.

He is by all the Navy esteemed now the first character in it, and all his officers, although they dislike him, absolutely swear by him in a professional point of view, and acknowledge that they believe a better or more tender-hearted man does not exist, but still he is disagreeable on duty. He, as Captain Keats, commanded the *Superb* in Admiral Saumarcy's action off Algeciras, dashed in between two Spanish three-deckers, and, giving each a broadside, passed clear in the smoke and engaged another ship of equal force, which he sank. Meanwhile the two Spaniards continued by mistake to fight each other in the smoke until they both blew up; thus by such conduct he destroyed three line-of-battle ships.

All the great folks send their sons under his charge, and admirably kind and masterly he is with them. A son of the Duke of Clarence is with him, a fine lad. I never saw such delightful boys. The admiral makes them write sham letters to him every Saturday. My favourite, little Georges, gave an account of a sea-fight. "My Lords," he says, "I enclose a copy of my letter to Admiral Easterbrooke (another monkey just like himself), and in an event of this importance I have thought it necessary to send my first lieutenant, Hawkins (another), to whom I refer your Lordships for any further, etc., and beg to recommend him, etc., as an officer of distinguished merit, etc.," and so on.

The admiral has a favourite little dog and a favourite cow. "I think it very odd, Mr. Georges," said he, "that none of you youngsters have had the civility to write to my dog or cow; it would do just as well to exercise you; besides, you might take a sly fling at the admiral."

So next time young Georges writes:—"Dear Madam Cow," begging her to bestow a little of her great bag of milk on the youngsters—a pretty broad hint to the admiral. But what prattle is this! I delivered my papers to the chief engineer this morning, the originals of which are sent, I fancy, to Lord Castlereagh and the Admiralty. My chief received me very graciously. I learned from him with great joy that General Moore had applied to Lord Chatham to have me follow him, and that his Lordship had acceded; but as General Moore does not command in chief, I have no staff hopes, for the present at least.

The people in this house speak in raptures of dearest old Dad.... Do you write by return of post, and I shall write tomorrow, and in the meantime, my dearest Lou, Heaven have thee in its holy keeping. Charles.

I breakfast with my chief tomorrow, and only wait my baggage from Yarmouth.

I think after a Spanish or Portuguese campaign I may rest a bit, and perhaps a peace will bless the world and fetter Buonaparte, for unfettered the rascal cannot be left.

August 2.—Wretchedly fidgety about my baggage. Get a letter from Bradby telling me where to find it, as it has been delayed by the Custom House officers.

August 4, 5 o'clock a.m.—Start on the stage for Portsmouth, having sent my baggage on before.

Penelope Transport (P.S.),
August 9, 1808.

Dearest Louisa—Here I am embarked, and your letters in future had better be addressed to me with the expedition under Sir Harry Burrard and sent to the engineers' office.—

Ever yours, Charles.

August 9, Tuesday.—N.E. Bustle aboard the *Penelope* brig. Get on board at twelve. Get under way.

N.W. Tossing ten at night. God send a good passage. Forty-two sail, including the convoy.

August 10, Wednesday.—Off. St. Albans barely in sight. Foul wind. At the old work—toss, tack, toss, toss, tack toss, toss tack. Stercoraceous smells under my berth; porter used to be stored there; a chance fracture stains the straw and accounts for it.

August 12.—A very numerous fleet under the land, sailing up Channel. Breeze freshens. Cool dry weather. An Italian tailor told me today that the English have good pay, but that in five weeks in London he spent all he had gained in the rest of the year. When mirth sat in the heart and money lay in the pocket he could not resist it, he said; and what with dances, coaches, dresses, and feasts, guineas flew out like dust, and he was forced to come to sea again!

Breeze increased at about 11 p.m.; blew very hard; short high sea; signal to veer, and sail on starboard tack.

August 13, Saturday, 2 a.m.—A gale S.W. very high. Suppose at daylight he will run for Plymouth. Rendezvous signal. Plymouth Sound. Anchor outside the Drake Islands at 8 p.m.

August 14, Sunday.—Weigh and get within the bight. Write letters.

Plymouth Sound,
Penelope Brig, August 14.

Sweet Sister—Encountering a S.W. gale has led us a sad rakish life. We were glad to put in here tonight, an operation which the thickness of the weather rendered very bothering.

As the wind may blow contrary some time, write to me here, directed Army under Sir H. Burrard, Plymouth, or elsewhere.

Chickens all well, but Jack and I cannot get the ducks to eat now; they waddle about and crack their toes. Jack's great delight (Jack is the cabin boy, my only companion) is my solicitude about the ducks, and I thought he never would have done laughing when I told him to clean away some tar from the coop because it made them sneeze; and when we turned them out to exercise the other day, one tried to quack and could not, so Jack said, "He's speechless, sir." We anchored at eight o'clock—sad, sad work. Should have been half way to Lisbon.—

Ever yours,   Charles.

August 15, Monday.—French prize brought in yesterday, a fine brig of war of eighteen guns. She was in company with a *corvette* and another brig of equal force. They gave chase to an English twenty-gun-ship, which disguised herself and stopped her way. The brig that was taken out-sailed the other and began to engage the Englishman, upon which the *corvette* and other brig crowded sail and made off, while their more honourable companion, after fighting thirty-five minutes, was taken.

August 19, Friday.—Wind fresh, six knots, smooth water. At evening a bird flying like a duck met the ship, and lighted on the foretop-sail yard, where he began looking up and down and all about, peering, as it were, with his long flexible neck and long beak. When it became dark, Antonio, a cunning, merry Italian, went aloft to try to catch him, at which everybody cried, "Fool!"—As he perched with his face aft, the man got on the foreside the sail (they wondered how the devil he managed it), and we could see his hands glide under the yard until they laid hold of the animal, which he brought down with him upon deck, the enraged creature snapping at him all the time with great dexterity.

He was very savage and the size and colour of a large goshawk, but a much slimmer-bodied bird; his pinions, plumage, tail, and standing position of his body like a hawk; his head but very slightly deviating from the bulk of his neck; sleek appearance; his long beak hooked at the end of the upper limb; his eyes, light blue, yet wild, ardent, and piercing, were placed close to the sit of the beak; his legs short and thick, of a black colour; his feet large, long, and triangular, the webs white, and claws at the ends of the toes.

Unfortunately and thoughtlessly Antonio's wish to have his wing cut was complied with, and he would not eat.

August 20, Saturday.—At 6 p.m. land discovered well on the larboard bow; supposed neighbourhood of Cape Ortegal. Blowing exceeding hard, heavy sea, eight knots. Bird won't eat.

August 21, Sunday.—3 a.m. wind drops. Eight o'clock thick fog; not yet weathered Cape Finisterre. Having seen the land at no great distance, and the strange bird refusing all food, I proposed to liberate him, thinking that of two chances for his life that was the least desperate, namely, his being able to row to some land where he might seek his food unassisted by flight. Accordingly the string was taken from his leg and he was left at large. After walking about a bit, he came in sight of the water through the door of the gangway that had been opened for him. He immediately perched upon the edge of the vessel, looking earnestly about as if to discover land, tried his wings, seemed sensible of the defect, but at last he stooped and soon reached the water.

We had endeavoured to palliate the injury by cutting the other wing exactly in the same manner as the first, not pinioned, merely the ends of the feathers taken off. When he reached the water he rowed from the ship with amazing swiftness and began to wash himself and play with infinite delight, plunging his head into the water, and seeming in complete enjoyment. The ship was stealing on about a mile and a half an hour, and we had lost sight of the bird, when, to our great surprise, he hove again in sight, and seemed pulling after the ship as hard as he could. There was a very heavy swell, and we could see him dive up hill and down, and gain upon the ship astonishingly fast.

We still could hardly think he wished to come on board again, until he came close alongside, and kept close to the gangway (where he had gone from the ship), looking up with anxiety. A man was then let down to the water's edge, when, instead of pulling off, the bird came to him with open mouth, clapping its wings, and showed the utmost impatience to be taken up. When he came on board he was much fatigued and his plumage was wet. He still refused to eat, but a little fish and water was put down his beak, which he swallowed. He seems weak and ill, and I fear will die before we are able to relieve him.

He is become tame, however, and has his liberty about the deck, and he knows he may go when he likes, which I hope comforts him. I would give two guineas at this moment (and I have but six) to restore him those bits of feathers of which he was robbed; but, at any rate, he is no longer disgusted with the nastiness of the ducks, with whom we put him at first, in hopes they might get acquainted and induce him to take pot-luck with them; but he treated them with the most scorning contempt, and seemed to think them most filthy companions, and the devotion and animation with which he cleansed himself from their filth when he got into the water was quite beautiful to see. At twelve it cleared up so as we could see the land—Cape Finisterre. Light breeze. Fog gone.

August 22, Monday,—This morning the strange bird at four o'clock leapt again from the side and pulled from the ship with a swift and steady course until out of sight. He kept up his looks amazingly well, and probably the fish and water stuffed down his throat sustained him, and, as if aware that he had exhausted himself before, he never stayed to wash or amuse himself. Fare him well.

August 24, Wednesday.—Fogs, foul wind, good breeze towards evening. Land ahead. Signal made for Mondego, and bear away accordingly.

August 25, Thursday.—A nice breeze at 12 a.m. and very clear. Sandy shore, sand hills, north of Mondego. Lay to for three ships astern.

August 26, Friday.—Breeze blowing right out of harbour. Very angry at the wind; expect not to get in today. At half-past nine boat alongside. Onions, pears, apples, apricots, bread. Learn from them that the great fleet is gone to Lisbon, and am then sure that we shall follow. Soon after signal to steer W.S.W.

August 27.—Dead calm, fog, rain, heavy sea.
Foul breeze.
Sad work.

August 31, Wednesday.—At 5 a.m. Rock of Lisbon in sight. Pass through Sir Harry Burrard's fleet on their way to England. When we come abreast of the Rock, seven o'clock, we soon hear from the agent that the army had made a bad business of the landing, which took place on the Maer, many lives being lost. It was supposed that we were either to land in the same place, should the wind favour, or return to Mondego.

An action had taken place, in which Sir H. Burrard was in person. 5000 French taken, 800 British lost. The British forces said to consist of Sir A. Wellesley's expedition. Stand in at ten o'clock for the Rock of Lisbon. Come in sight of the Tagus blockading fleet, under command of Sir Charles Cotton. Bring to, then go on the starboard tack, and God knows when or where we shall land. *Eurydice* leaves us for Halifax.

September 1.—Still tacking for Lisbon. I go on board—the commander of the convoy, Captain Mayne—*Primrose* brig sloop.

Tell him that, being astray, I was just now particularly anxious to get to the army, as I supposed the Engineers might possibly be actively employed. He then told me that the game was up, that Junot was allowed to return to France with his troops and plunder, but that the English had told the Russian Admiral that he must either surrender or fight; that Sir J. M. and Sir A. W. were raving at Sir H. D.[19] and Sir H. B. on account of the terms allowed to General Junot, and that we should go in today or tomorrow. Stand out till twelve. Wind blowing very hard.

September 2, Friday.—Signal to anchor. Beat up towards an anchorage near the Rock of Lisbon, where the *African* and convoy had brought up last night. At nine o'clock see a Russian flag of truce go to the British Admiral.

Come to an anchor off Cascaes at two o'clock. Go on shore. See Captain M'Leod of the *Barfleur*. Find on inquiry that it is not known where the army was. It had been at Mafia, but it appeared that it was moving. The 42nd Regiment, commanded by Colonel Stirling, had taken port at Cascaes. The colonel despaired of getting important despatches to Sir Henry, so I determined not to set out for the army until their situation is known. Write home.

Off Cascaes, Sept. 3, 1808.

My Louisa—After the most tedious and provoking passage we came to an anchor yesterday noon off the fortified town named in the date, at the entrance to the Tagus. Things are in this situation, General Junot having lost a battle, much to the glory of Sir A. Wellesley and his army, in which the enemy were nearly two to one. Sir Henry Dalrymple, by terms which at the first view appear unaccountably favourable to the French, has induced him to capitulate, and he, with his troops, are to be sent in our transport to Rochefort, and the Russian fleet on the Tagus, we hear, is to be taken to England under Russian colours, to await the event of negotiations with the autocrat.

In pursuance of this treaty. Fort Sao Juliao, and all the works

---

19. Sir Henry Dalrymple.

and places more remote from Lisbon, are already under English colours, and it is expected that today or tomorrow the embarkation of the French will take place. Sir Harry Burrard, they say, arrived himself just before the action commenced, having landed at Mondego, but left Sir A. Wellesley to carry through the plan of battle, which was fully designed. The event was that the enemy were amazingly beaten.

Just as the French had fallen back on their entrenchments, it is said that intelligence was brought of Sir J. Moore having arrived with 14,000 men, which new situation of things and proportion of armies relatively convinced Sir Harry Burrard that the enemy must capitulate, and although (it is said) Sir A. Wellesley did all but *kneel*, saying that unless he was permitted to follow up the glory of the day that of the army would be tarnished, Sir H. B. persisted in putting a stop to hostilities, and a capitulation has been finally entered into by which the main point is carried, but in which the pride of the army and the wishes of the Portuguese do hardly appear to have been sufficiently considered. The enemy was at our feet, and after very hard fighting the army had a right to conquest, and after being ground by their oppressors, the Portuguese should have been allowed the natural triumph of seeing the objects of their abhorrence humbled. I went yesterday to Cascaes, with intent to join the army, but the commanding officer (colonel of the 42nd) knew not where it was, and could not forward despatches of importance to the General. Today I shall go to the Fort Sao Juliao and make a stout attempt to get to them, but all fighting is over here. Farewell, own lass.   Charles.

September 3, Saturday.—*Penelope's* boat lands us at Fort Sao Juliao at one o'clock. Go to Colonel Blunt (commanding 3rd Buffs). Very civil man. Sends his orderly with us to Ociras to point out the road to Cintra, where the army is. At Ociras, a mile from Fort Sao Juliao, get animals. Arrive at the palace of Cintra, occupied by Sir Henry Dalrymple. Get an excellent bed, the inn kept by an Irishwoman. A romantic spot. The mountains of Cintra part of the range of the Rock of Lisbon.

September 4, Sunday.—See Squire, Lord W. Bentinck, and Burgos. Walk with Burgos towards English camp. Meet mules. Return with him and ascend the mountains of Cintra. Meet General Moore—*bon!*

Reach the top, crowned with a convent, continuing the very highest peak of the Rock. Noble view from thence. Take many angles with a righted compass. Go west over the mountains to a reputed curiosity, which Mulcaster calls the convent of cork. Find it lined with cork—cork door and cork ceiling, etc., to keep out damp. Go into refectory; drink and eat. Table hewn out of the top of an enormous pebble, whose bottom formed the ceiling of the church. Find Williams and Drevil at the inn, having come from Sir A. W.'s army. Williams and I sleep at the inn. In the morning army to move towards Fort Sao Juliao.

September 6.—Dine with General Moore—*bon!* Ordered to hold myself in readiness for Elvas.

September 10.—Buy two horses at 18 guineas each. Dine with Squire. Fletcher arrives and tells me I march at four o'clock the following day.

September 11 .—Pack up till two. Row servant. Send artificer off with baggage and start myself. Arrive at General Moore's quarters. Go to Lisbon to embark the horses.

September 13 .—March with regiment and arrive at Vendas Novas, passing through uninteresting country. Here is a palace belonging to the prince capable of containing 10,000 men, stables for 500 horses, adequate kitchens and water. Beastly contrived, great staring barrack rather than palace, and the French had torn down wainscoting and false doors in search of treasure.

Proceed over like country until within five miles of Montemor o Novo, when it becomes more rich and wooded; indeed, all along the beautiful foliage of the cork trees greatly relieved the sandy sterility of the way.

Arrive at Montemor o Novo. Regiment camps out. Get good billet. Wall round the castle. Examine the position. Sup and sleep excellently. Silver ewers and covers.

September 14.—Re-examine position. Nuns of the castle send to say glad to see us. Breakfast—tea, coffee, bread, butter, honey, eggs, sweetmeats, oranges—latter sent by the nuns. The Prioress from St. Domingo—the colour of gold. Eat cakes and see the ravages of the French in search of money.

Regiment marched through this morning at five o'clock.
Start for Arrayolos, distance twelve miles.

September 15.—Arrive at Venda do Dogue, apparently a poor farmhouse, and we found that the farmer was a captain. I observed that the captain was a sensible man, preferring to gain bread by open honest industry to starving his wife and family by a strained support of gentility; and on asking whether we might not venture to offer some sort of compensation for what we were supplied with, my servant told me they were the richest people in the country; that this was their place of retirement from their palace in the city! We had a sumptuous breakfast, with sweetmeats. Started at twelve and reached Estremoz at four—a walled town with a citadel. Here we find the regiment. Get a billet on Adjutant Gaze and find that the Spaniards are before Elvas. Propose to Colonel R. to go forward to reconnoitre. Regiment encamp a league beyond the town.

September 16.—At six o'clock start for the camp, and find I had better not go forward, as Cockburn, who was gone to Lisbon, had brought intelligence that the Frenchmen had required an officer from Junot to authenticate the orders of surrender, and a suspension had been entered into between all parties for six days; also the fort had made a convention with the town—one not firing, the other not supplying or admitting the Spaniards. Therefore he thought the appearance of an engineer might excite jealousy, etc.

Get permission to go on.

Bring Elvas and Fort La Lippe in view. Arrive at the first post of cavalry in rear of the Spanish camp. Sent from one camp to the other, till at last, about two o'clock, we reach the colonel's tent off Badajoz. We step into the tent and join the colonel and other officers at dinner—a most excellent mess of rice and salt fish, in a camp kettle, and first-rate sausages. We get on most merrily. I give the health of Fernando Septimo. The jolly colonel roars. Replies the thundering tent, and the whole camp resounds. *Bon!*

Conducted to the general. He doubts our errand, and bids us wait the return of a British officer from Badajoz. This was O'Brien, who had been sent on before with a communication to the fort.

We said no; if the general would not give us permission to see the batteries, we would go to Elvas.

The general's *aide-de-camp* said that we could not go to Elvas because of the convention.

I asked if there was a Spanish guard over the gates.

"No."

"Then pass us through your camp."

An officer conducted us through the greater part, and pointed out the road to Elvas and left us.

We were brought up by the advanced posts, commanded by a colonel of cavalry—true Spanish face. He made some difficulty, but passed us at length, and we arrived at half-past four at the gates of Elvas, where we sent in for permission to enter the town.

While we were waiting in the sun, sufficiently vexed at our occupation, up came two Spanish dragoons and said that by order of their colonel we must go back with them.

Finding that we were two armed to two, we refused compliance with their arbitrary message; but soon four more arrived, and intimated that they were prepared to enforce it. I then desired that we might wait the answer from within the town, Bernardo damning them into compliance. The gates at length opened, and a Portuguese officer and guard appeared, when we were admitted in pomp, and the poor dragoons refused a hearing. We said we were far from wishing them to enter, and Bernardo set up a loud laugh. We then went to the general, who took us to the bishop—a good man, trembling at the critical situation of his town.

I explained what had happened, and he rather wished our return. I said we could go there tomorrow on our way home.

He then offered us his country house, and we were taken to the *junta*, of which the bishop is the head, and it was resolved there that we should stay. The bishop told them what I had told him, that there was no doubt of the French surrendering the town, because the whole French army was in our power, and it would ruin them if the convention was broken. Lodge at the house of a jolly, hospitable Major de bon Coeur.

September 17.—Start for the Spanish camp at nine o'clock, having procured credentials from the Judge. Visit the cavalrymen's tent. Nothing passes about yesterday. Rains excessively hard. Conducted to the general; find O'Brien there. Now well received. Get permission to see the batteries—four 24-pounders and 6 guns,—and am set down to a ham, the finest I ever tasted.

Return to Estremoz. I, a Christian, talk much by the way to O'Brien, a sceptic. Agree on poetry. Lose our way five times. Pass through Borba, the prettiest Portuguese place yet seen. Arrive at Estremoz, and get some dinner at Colonel R.'s.

September 18, Sunday.—Seek for breakfast. Find in a coffee-house a nauseous party of Portuguese officers, who gamed and drank and smoked and stank. The dignified commander of cavalry—a yellow individual covered with dirt and stars—undertook to ask for what we wanted, as he spoke French. I told him we wanted bread, honey, coffee, and boiled eggs. I watched his interpretation to the women. He said these gentlemen want "bread, honey, coffee, and eggs, all boiled together," to explain which he made a motion with his hand to stir it about. The woman looked petrified, and we roared, and the cavalier was confounded. Swallow our breakfast. Get another billet.

Colonel R. has a field day in the square, to show the people how to do it, which went off admirably.

September 19.—Colbourn returns at 5 a.m. with a French officer, a nice little fellow with a red face, much tired by attending Colbourn's rapid steps from Lisbon. We arrived at the camp, and at the general's found some difficulties—no admittance to the fort without communicating with Badajoz. A messenger was despatched, and we said we would go to Elvas. That could not be permitted. They begged we would remain with the general until the return of the messenger, which would be at six o'clock. Colbourn said first of all, "Very well"; but upon consulting, we agreed it would be better to go to a village about a league off and return at six. We communicated this to the A.D.C., who seemed much troubled, and said his general understood we should remain, and would be much better pleased if we did.

"But we have changed our minds."

"Ah! but I don't know whether the general will permit it."

"What! would he keep us prisoners here?"

"Oh, no."

Upon which he ran to the general and returned with answer, "That we must do as we pleased."

We then went to a house about a league off, ate some bread and fruit, and returned at 6 p.m. to find the messenger not returned, nor post horses from Elvas arrived.

The having the French officer with us in the Spanish camp, where everyone was ready to cut his throat, gave us some uneasiness, for we witnessed in the Spanish, officers and all, a hatred not to be overcome for a moment. The adjutant-general came to me and whispered, "Is that an Englishman?"

"No," said I, "French." He started away, and the effect it had on him immediately called to my mind the case of a man with hydrophobia at the sight of water. They would offer him nothing to eat, although they saw him sinking for want of refreshment and rest. So whatever they gave us we offered to him before we would touch it. Even the old cook who filled my glass with a smiling face settled his countenance into a solemn gloom as he transferred the mouth of the bottle to the Frenchman's cup.

This sort of thing made us determine to decline the entreaty of the general and to sleep in a small town called Bersim, in which Colbourn knew a house where our charge would be secure.

"*Et me voilà à cheval encore,*" said he as we left the camp. Our kind demeanour to him contrasted with the Spanish scowl; our jokes, loud laughter, and general merriment seemed to give him the utmost confidence in our protection. He was about seventeen years old, with a florid countenance and slight form; a page to Napoleon and a lieutenant in the 1st Regiment of Dragoons.

When we arrived at our house about ten o'clock the master received us very well, and immediately began talking of the French, asked if they were all embarked, and hoped we would send them to the bottom. At this the little Frenchman cocked his ears, and bursting with laughter, asked if he did not tell us to send 'em to the bottom. This afforded us much amusement a great part of the night. We put the Frenchman in the middle, that they might have the less chance of finding him.

September 20.—O'Brien and I, getting up, could not perceive the head of the Frenchman, so we removed softly the cloak to see whether it was on all safe. Our host coming in about six, I asked him how he did, saying, "England forever! no Frenchmen!" which made our little friend laugh right heartily. The old man again hoped we should send them to the bottom.

"Why?" said the Frenchman.

"*Because they are good-for-nothing fellows,*" said the host. At last he began to suspect, by our laughter, the difference of uniform, and the two different languages, which he perceived we spoke among us, that all was not right, and I being dressed in blue and the Frenchman in green, he set us both down for Frenchmen; and though I assured him I was English, all the household looked at me with a very doubting civility afterwards.

At ten o'clock we started again for the camp, and arrived there about twelve. The answer had arrived, and the Spanish general Galazo admitted of our communication with the fort, but sent thither at the same time some ridiculous proposals of his own. We set out for the fort accompanied by a Spanish *aide-de-camp*. The commander of the fort was General Novellard. After settling our business, the Spanish *aide-de-camp* proposed from his general that the French should evacuate the fort in twenty-four hours and lay down their arms on the glacis.

The Frenchman, instead of reply, gave him a most severe rowing upon the little attention paid by the Spaniards to the laws of war. The officers, he said, had neither probity nor honour.

"If," said he, "you recommence the fire, I shall destroy Elvas, while all the harm you can do to me will be the loss of ten or fifteen Frenchmen; the harm you do to the fort will injure your friends and allies the English, whose possession it now is. I had hoped that this business would have been ended in a manner worthy of civilised soldiers, and that all our rancour, our hatred, and our courage would have been reserved for another field of battle. I will have no communication with you. If you send a flag of truce I shall fire upon it; so you have served mine. There are forty Spaniards (besides two, my prisoners, who have broken their parole) offered for three French prisoners in your hands. I have made this offer twenty-five times unanswered! I consider this fort is an English possession, and in the execution of a treaty under the sanctity of the French word we will all perish. *Messieurs Anglais*, come to your fort; its guns shall protect your approach; here you shall be lodged, but I cannot march out my garrison until the Spaniards have decamped, for they are not soldiers, and in spite of all treaties, would assassinate my people in the road."

So spake General Novellard, a keen, cool, sensible Frenchman with a hawk's eye.

In reminding the Spaniards that the Convention of Lisbon allowed them to show themselves again on the Spanish frontier, as well as in the drift of his whole speech, he showed a cunning desire to set us together by the ears.

But although the Spaniards had provoked us, and we enjoyed the whole thing, we refused even a smile, or motion of assent or approbation.

The Spaniard was greatly agitated, and spoke bad French. He said he had no plans.

We then went to Elvas without asking leave of the Spaniards. Got post-horses there, O'Brien and I leaving our own horses. While taking our coffee we talked much with a Spanish brigadier-general, who complained of our convention. "We were sending 20,000 men (whose throats they had fondly hoped to cut), with their arms in their hands, upon the Spanish frontier. These men," he said, "had committed such enormities, that even though a different conduct on the part of our General had caused the erasure of Lisbon and the death of half its population, it would have been witnessed with shouts of joy, so long as the French themselves were included in the crash."

"Well, but," said I, "we have just brought you 10,000 Spaniards from Denmark."

He smiled and said, "He had heard it."

"And," I added, "if you will let us assist you, our greatest desire is to go with you into Spain and help you to drive out the French, whom we long to fight again. We honour the Spanish nation, and desire to be friends with it forever." He seemed highly pleased, and made some apology for the dress of their army before Elvas.

I said, "It was no uncommon thing to see soldiers all dressed alike, but when we saw a Spanish army in the dress of peasants, it reminded us of the glorious exertions made by the whole body of the Spanish people, and we honoured them ten times more."

He seemed delighted, and said that "the Spanish people were the noblest in the world, that the Government had wished to clothe them, but with one voice they replied, ' In the dress of peasants we have rescued our country and beat the French in Spain; in the dress of peasants we will utterly destroy them." This Spanish general then reprobated the conduct of Galazo, who, he said, had sent his troops before Elvas in consequence of the convention made by the English.

We were now ready to return to the Spanish camp, so we called at the fort for the French officer, and all started together.

O'Brien's horse and the Frenchman's soon knocking up, the former takes him under convoy, and Colbourn and I ride on.

This was the first of my acquaintance with Colbourn, a sound, well-judging, good man, having also great refinement of feeling, and I hope to know more of him.

Colonel Ross sends Colbourn back to get some written extracts of what the Spanish general proposed. I sleep at the inn.

September 21.—Colbourn returns about 2 p.m. and sets off with the French officer to Lisbon.

September 23.—Regiment marches at 4 a.m. We start at nine, I leading my horse. Wills and O'Brien theirs, and Bernardo the mule, because of sore backs. Arrive at Borba, six miles, at half-past ten.

I meet a man on the road to Elvas who tells me he is the richest person hereabouts, and insists that we shall come to his house, and the ladies run to us crying *viva!* and embracing our knees. We repose on a couch while breakfast prepares, consisting of chocolate, eggs, bread, pears, peaches, apricots, angelica, melon, biscuits and macaroons, and a couple of boiled fowls, with excellent wine.

Arrive at Villavicosa at two. Dine with Colonel Ross. Immense sweetmeats sent by the nuns. A marquis sends two bottles of pink champagne, one of white, and one of claret, all excellent.

September 24.—Colonel Campbell, with two more companies of the 20th Regiment, march in at 6 a.m.

September 27.—Ride with O'Brien towards Jeramenha, where the French are pouring into Spain. Portuguese treasure disgorging at Lisbon.

September 28.—Regiment marches at four for Elvas. I ride through the park and overtake the regiment before Villaboim. Ride on before it to Elvas. Find Colonel Ross, Major Colbourn, O'Brien, and Q.M.G. at breakfast with the bishop; a very chaste breakfast and quiet attendance. *Monseigneur* gives us a billet upon his *provisore.* The whole town in a frenzy of joy, a many-tongued "*Viva!*" I go out with Colonel Ross to meet the regiment at the gate. At the corner of a narrow street a wild-looking Carthusian presented himself, shouting with all his might, and trembling with agitation, "*Viva los nostras amicos Ingleses,*" which he continued to repeat incessantly, accompanied by the most frantic and terrific gestures.

The bishop invited all the officers to dinner at three o'clock. Very pleasant dinner, excellently cooked. Sat between old Byron and Wade, and enjoyed it much. The bishop gave several loyal toasts, and a filial Frenchman (come to seek a wounded father) stood up and bowed with the rest. He had narrowly escaped assassination two or three times in his search.

This afternoon I went with Colbourn to see the garrison from Santa Lucia march to La Lippe, and we perhaps prevented some stragglers on the road from sharing the same fate. Afterwards I go to my *provisore*, an old asthmatic pastor, who understands French, and has in his library Voltaire, Racine, Molière, and many other interesting books, also the *Paradise Lost* of Milton in Portuguese prose. A capital house, with a charming view into Spain, far over Badajoz.

September 29.—The next day I walk to Fort La Lippe, and the French Engineers show me all over the fort, one of them a modest and agreeable sort of Frenchman, who says, "*Cela coutera cher, mais on le prendra.*"

Before leaving I come across an Irish rebel, who having been sent to Prussia and taken by the French, now wishes to serve King George. He had almost forgotten to speak English.

September 30.—Bishop's conversazione in the evening.

It appears that the *junta* of Seville did not authorise the interference of their foolish General Galazo in the affairs of Portugal, and it has now given him orders to join the Patriot Castanos immediately, so in obedience the Spaniards have decamped, and we are no longer obstructed in the performance of our treaties.

There is something quite curdling in the fell spirit of revenge which has taken possession of the minds of the Portuguese. No desire of freeing their country, no ardent patriotic zeal can now actuate them in their thirst for blood, for their oppressors are quelled, the game is up, and they only desire to get out of the country; and yet if a poor way-worn French soldier were to lie down and sleep under a hedge, that the first Portuguese who saw him would cut his throat and insult his corpse is as indisputable as that an Englishman under such circumstances would spare and protect him.

Last night as I was going into my room an old gray-headed woman called to me, and Bernardo (my Italian servant) interpreting, I found she accused another female of favouring the French.

I took a stick, walked into the kitchen, and jestingly shook it at the accused, whom, on turning, I perceived to be a very pretty, pensive-looking lady (for ladies here snuggle round the only fire in the kitchen), who entered on her defence very gently and persuasively, saying "that she hated the French as much as any Portuguese ought to do, but could not enter into the general triumph the other day when the mob murdered a solitary French officer, who possibly had not committed the smallest fault against them; nor could she think otherwise than with horror of those beastly women who ran and plunged their knives into the bleeding body."

I laid my fingers on her arm, and then carried them to my lips, in token of approbation, and shook my stick at the old dame.

The bishop gave a grand dinner two days ago to all the officers. A

French officer had come with a flag of truce into the town to see the good man, as his father had been well-nigh assassinated and severely wounded, but he succeeded in getting him under the protection of the English surgeon.

The bishop, who is an excellent man, had him to dinner, because he dare not trust him in the hands of the people; and we all, by civility and conversation, endeavoured to assure and comfort him, which gave great umbrage to the Portuguese.

I shall now for some time be very much occupied, as I am instructed, after examining Elvas, to inspect the nature of the frontier towards Spain, an occupation which is unlimited as to time.

October 5.—French march at six o'clock—1400 men.

I ride on the Estremoz road to the head of the march, and take leave of General Novellard.

Go to the fort to hunt for plans, and find that Wills has them.

October 12.—Ordered to Badajoz, and on to make a reconnaissance. Write home.

Elvas, October 12, 1808.

My Louisa—I am now in much higher mind than when I last wrote, for by far the greater part of the army on this Peninsula has been placed under Sir John Moore's command, and is shortly to march into Spain, where the glorious, virtuous enthusiasm is the admiration of all foreigners.

We find that the Spaniards are now disposed to send to the devil all diffidence of the English, and will be delighted to receive us, and to profit by our assistance. I am just ordered a good jaunt on the frontier, to the Tagus at Alcantara, to get some local information preparatory to the passage of the army into Spain. Afterwards I am to join General Paget, at which I am much pleased.

No time to say more.—Yours,   Charles.

October 12.—Arrive at Badajoz, and the day following get half a league onwards. Meet some peasants on the road to Merida, who ask for our passports. Show them English ones from General Hope, and continue our way, but they pursue and carry Bernardo and myself back to Badajoz. I told them that an English passport was good enough, and one fellow said that it might be in England or Portugal, but not in Spain. I congratulate myself that it occurred so near Badajoz. Get a passport from D'Arcy and start again.

Six bitter long leagues to Albuquerque; thirty miles at least of most uninteresting country.

On arriving at the town I find Colbourn, who has been very near shot for a Frenchman several times, and thinks I shall be also. He was going to Salamanca tomorrow.

October 14.—Start for Salorino, scale a great wood, and find in the midst a castle. I stop here, and dine with the keeper of these woods and domains regal, and he promises to give information, and also to accompany me in finding a road passable for carriages.

He is to take me to Cartillano, but loses his way, and takes me across the mountains of Piedrabuena to Herreruela over an immense plain.

A very civil good man, and a nice little wife. He told me at parting "these were neither roads nor times to go without an escort," and strongly pressed me to apply for one to the *alcalde*.

We arrive at last at Herreruela, twenty-four miles from Albuquerque. The *alcalde* is a dirty artisan.

All the town come into my room and smoke and spit and make me show them my maps.

A miserable town, and I was glad to leave my abominable host the next day and start for Alcantara, the carriage road leading us by Villa del Rey and Cartillano.

October 16.—All the people marvel at the wonders of my toilette. My comb, my brush, my tooth-brush and nail-brush, my shaving-brush and soap were all as much objects of wonder to these peasants as the comb and watch of Gulliver to the people of Lilliput.

I start from the Cam di Cartillano at eight o'clock, and arrive at Alcantara at half-past two.

The Tagus here flows between two great mountains, and the bridge is about 120 feet high.

At the house where I am billeted they are dancing the *ballora*—very curious. A handsome youth and lively girl, and another couple, then the old gentleman joins, others singing and playing the guitar. One pretty girl, looking half ill-natured, half—I do not know how—bewitching, sang, and I gazed and tried to find out her lover. As I sit at dinner the *alcalde* (mayor), dressed excellently with a scarlet cloak, says he is come to fetch me to his house, sends for wine, cheese, etc., and invites me to breakfast tomorrow. They all treat Bernardo as a gentleman.

Visited the bridge before dinner; go down a mountain to it, and up one from it.

October 17.—Take chocolate and biscuit with the *alcalde* (mayor) and start for Salvatierra, pass the bridge over Tagus and ascend the Estremadura mountains. Go to Zarza la Mayor, a large town on the high road to Ciudad Rodrigo, turn westward and go to Salvatierra, a small Portuguese village, and then on to Segura, a miserable place, but lodged comfortably in an old priest's house. On the road we met a man who said, "Is that an Englishman? I'm very glad of it. I wanted to see the face of one, for they are fine fellows." Yesterday, at Alcantara, the *alcalde*, hearing me speak Italian to Bernardo, took me for an Italian.

"I am an Englishman."

"Aye, aye, your passport tells me so. Yes, yes, English."

I hope I shall get a good dinner, not having eaten since eight, when I took a thimbleful of chocolate and a biscuit. It is now six. Bernardo bought a partridge on the road, and plucked it as he rode along, saying it was to gain time. He Has bought another here. Both now on the fire, besides cabbage, pork steaks, and fried eggs. The acorns of the cork trees make this country famous for pork. Bernardo a capital cook. The priest pulls a partridge to pieces with his fingers!!

October 13.—Get up at five. Arrive at Rosmaninhal and proceed to Monforte, four leagues farther, and a prettier place. Start before four o'clock for Lentiseves, and the guide, as it grows dark, declares he has lost the road, and does not know which of the two to take. We take the right, and are so long in finding the place that we are sure of being wrong. Arrive at Lentiseves by half-past six. The judge in his hovel issues his billet and leads us to a miserable cot. I ask for a better house. There is none. Go with the horses to an excellent stable, full of wheat straw, and in the house find a good man and woman and a blazing fire, with fried eggs and bacon and a roast chicken. Sleep in the corn chamber.

October 19.—Leave Lentiseves and traverse four tiresome leagues to Villa Velha, an inconsiderable town, situated curiously on the side of a lofty mountain, traversing in range the Tagus. In winter it must roar through them properly, to be sure. There is a mine near, made by a Moorish king to get to the Queen of Portugal, where she used to grin at him from the other side.

We go over the mountainous country about two leagues and arrive at Niza. The Judge, an old fool, and the people where I am quartered in this large walled town are plaguing me a good deal, so shut up shop.

October 20.—Start from Niza at three o'clock. Arrive at Alpalhao, and on to Portalegre, sixteen miles, having passed several villages in the way. Here we meet Mr. Parr, Commissary, who tells me that General Moore is gone towards the frontier. General Hope still at Elvas; General Paget at Estremoz. General Crawford commands.

Leave Portalegre, one of the best and most beautifully situated towns of Portugal. At midday overtake a native of Osamar saying his "*Ave Marias.*" Pass a great wood, twelve miles wide, and arrive at Osamar, a pretty town. Lodge in a beastly house. A priest visits me, a gentlemanlike man, who speaks French very well. We are now twenty-eight miles from Elvas.

October 21.—Start from Osamar and ride three leagues through a wood and breakfast at Sta. Olaya. Pass through other villages and *kintas* and arrive at Elvas. Go to Squire's quarters. Get letters. Dine at General Hope's. Get a billet. Call at the bishop's, and sit up writing till three o'clock. Woodchafers tumble upon and bite me. Go to bed under the table.

October 22.—Get up at seven. Write and give in my report of roads. Dine with the general, and ordered tomorrow to Aliseda, *via* Albuquerque. Pack up.

October 24.—Start at seven on post-horses to Campo Mayor and arrive at Albuquerque at two. The *corregidor* not at home. Go to the secretary, who gives me a billet; but they won't take me in.

Another *ditto*; another *ditto*. At last I go to *corregidor's* wife to upbraid, and she, inviting me into the house when the *corregidor* comes home, I get him to press three beasts for me in the morning. While at dinner I hear Bernardo frantic with rage, and on asking what was the matter, he said, "*Bella cosa*, the governor has commanded this man to bring his mules tomorrow to carry sugar from Elvas for his consumption." When the old deaf *corregidor* heard it he was quite raving, danced about and stamped, his jaws toothless with age.

The man at last said he would not go without the governor's permission. The *alcalde* said he would commit him to prison.

The fellow judged well enough, for he told the governor that the

alcalde had bound him in twenty dollars penalty. "And I bind you," said the governor, "in thirty and a month's imprisonment," so the muleteer kept to the strongest side, which in these warlike times was the military governor. This being the case, I saw that any trial of strength between the two governors would inevitably keep me here until the decision, so I told Bernardo to bring me my hat and sword. "*E dove dudate*," said he.

"To the governor's," said I, "and mind that you repeat my words to him word for word without a single addition of your own."

So I went to the governor, and told him that I understood he had pressed my beasts, and that if I found myself impeded in the execution of my mission I should complain direct to my general, who would carry it to the central *junta* at Madrid.

The governor then said that the *corregidor* had only a divided authority, and could not press beasts without his permission. Luckily I caught the scope of what he said, and saw that the business was over, for Bernardo began to enter into the argument with much spirit, and I, with a certain amount of vehemence, desired him to interpret and not converse, which made the immense fat lady die a-laughing.

When I heard where the shoe pinched I said I had nothing to do with the disputes of governors and *corregidors*, but that these were my passports, and I was sure that a military governor would not be behindhand with a civil one to facilitate the performance of his duty to a British officer. This had the desired effect, and the fat lady seemed delighted.

As we went away Bernardo applauded my moderation, and told me it was a plot of the ladies to draw the Englishman to their house.

October 25.—Rise and find that the muleteer had made his escape at midnight. Go to the governor's. "In bed." Send up to say "that I will despatch a complaint to the general at Elvas."

"Not his fault," he says; "the *corregidor* should have obtained his permission to impress the beasts." I return to my *corregidor's* house, desire him to provide a man, and write a complaint to the general. While writing it the governor's approach is announced.

"Don Jose Gonsalaz di Madrigal."

I attended with much interest the collision of these two dignified bodies, and it was a fine scene. They put their heads close together and vociferated their claims of superiority.

The governor was certainly wrong, and the rage of the old *corregidor* reasonable enough.

To me, however, the governor knocked under, and told me he would punish the man for making' off; so I did not report him, but got one horse from the governor and two from the *corregidor*.

The wife of the latter seemed rather to fancy me, as she begged me to return that way, and if I knocked up the horses she would indeed be angry. She tried to be handsome, but a complaint in her eyes was a most formidable adversary.

Start, and in the course of the journey tell the guide he was more stupid than his mule.

"What!" says he, "did you say I was more stupid than my mule?"

"Yes," said I, and he turned away and laughed as if he could not restrain it. We arrive at four o'clock at Aliseda, six long leagues from Albuquerque.

October 26.—Leave Aliseda for Arroyo del Puerco, a large good-looking town. Return to Aliseda, and then on to Zagala upon asses.

As the sun sets we get into the park of Zagala, thinly covered with large cork trees and under-spread with smooth pasture. Here, having the best animal, I, given up to my own thoughts, insensibly ran ahead of my servant and guide, but the road turning suddenly to the right and descending to the bed of the river, reminded me of the imprudence of parting with my servants and baggage, who might take another road. I therefore pulled up in the midst of the stream, and casting my eyes upward and around, beheld one of the most beautiful nights that ever etherealised the human mind. The woods were not breathed on, all was still; the half moon rode high in heaven, frequently passed over by the light blushing clouds with which the sky was chequered. The solemnity of the scene was such as is not to be described.

I had talked some time ago with a sceptic, and been bothered with his subtleties; how did they now all fly before the sublime soarings of my spirit at this moment! Does this airy transport tend to nothing, 'and must this mind with such an ardent curiosity to explore the heavens, and such a celestial gratitude for the refinement it feels in itself, perish with the body? Could I have made the sceptic take my feelings as the best argument I could offer, he had been soon converted.

A sceptic should by analogy be of a sordid mind, but this man was intelligent.

Having passed the river, we soon began to ascend through a thick wood to the castle of Zagala, crowning the very summit of a rock-gnarled mount.

When we were half up the hill my donkey started at the appearance of an animal half as big again as itself, which advanced with a majestic, deliberate step, and on going close up to it I found it was a beautiful red stag that very politely came and kissed my hand—beautiful, elegant creature.

On arriving at the gate of the old mouldering castle we thundered for entrance, but for some time all was still. At length we thought we heard the steps of someone dimly sounding through the echoes of the castle, and ere long a hoarse voice demanded, "Who's there?"

"An English officer with his servant and guide."

"What do you want?"

"Shelter for the night."

The steps were then heard to retire, and all was still. Soon after, they were again heard approaching, and the voice again asked, "How many are you?"

"Three."

At last the grating gate was slowly opened, and we beheld a snug village within, and at the end of the street a fine-looking hall door with lamps, etc.

They took us to this house, and going upstairs the steward of the estate of Zagala, belonging to the Marquis of Portachio, received me with great cordiality and politeness. I was comforted to find a most capital house with curtains, etc., the picture of cleanliness and convenience, but how much more delighted when his most beautiful wife entered the room, with long black mantilla, brilliant rolling eyes, Roman nose, sweet mouth, jet black hair in short graceful curls upon her neck, tall, polite, retired, conversable. Could not take my eyes off her during supper, and feared the administrator would cut my throat. There was an old priest who disputed with me concerning Popery.

Adventures romantic at first they told, as they had just killed a large wolf, whose skin was brought in to show us. They then took me into a nice little ante-room with a clean-looking bed, where I slept delightfully.

Surely no man can live more happily than my host. This is his castle. He is alike fearless of the wolves or thieves, for his peasants form an ample garrison and he has plenty of arms. He lives in modest luxury, a beautiful wife and fine children, what would he more? The man himself was a fine black animated Spaniard.

October 27.—Rise, and when dawn began, the view of the mountains was grand, the rocky peaks tossing their wild forms above the foggy clouds.

Start for Villa del Key and soon arrive, as the beast provided for me was a good little animal. Go on to Campo Mayor and arrive at Elvas at four o'clock.

Find the general, and soon discover that I have left Squire's map at Villa del Rey. Borrow twenty dollars from Colonel Ross to enable me to purchase the little horse that brought me from Villa del Rey, and pay forty-three dollars for the same.

Army entering Spain ordered to wear red cockades.

October 28.—Bernardo starts at seven o'clock for Villa del Rey to retrieve Squire's map.

Write my report upon the Aliseda road, which I take to the general when he has dined. Confess my sins to Squire, who laughs and receives the mortifying news with good-natured philosophy.

October 29.—Breakfast with the general, who starts with his suite for Badajoz at seven. I arrive at Estremoz at eleven and General Paget in the afternoon. I begin to fret about Bernardo.

October 30.—Sunday. Breakfast at the general's. No Bernardo. Write the general a copy of last report, and after dinner, to my great satisfaction, Bernardo is announced, for the fellow has become extremely useful to me, and I depend on his fidelity. On journeys, also, as I ride before and he behind, he entertains me exceedingly with the drollery of his anecdotes and remarks, which are extremely acute. He has withal a very good judgment, is unobtrusive, and can bear a rub. Thus, though I allow him to talk and laugh, he is not sulky when told to hold his tongue. Then his cookery and *providonata* is so good and his honesty undoubted, he is a perfect interpreter, and up to their manners. I was glad of his return.

October 31.—To march tomorrow to Arronches; only hear of it when I go to dinner. Get a pair of velvet overalls.

November 1.—On arriving at Arronches, seven leagues from Estremoz, find Major Gilmore, who gives me soup. Sleep in the justice house. Little Kickery[20] comes on well. Buy a blanket, of, I think, a rogue.

November 2.—Start for Albuquerque and overtake the 95th Regiment, having first passed the Spanish boundary and taken out the Portuguese cockade. On arriving at Albuquerque we find the deaf *corregidor* disputing with the general's staff in a great rage; they receive me with smiles, to the astonishment of the others, and insist on my being quartered there. At least fifty officers come in about quarters. They make no hand of the deaf *corregidor*, but I explain the matter to the lady, and she soon arranges it, for she is, in fact, a very good *corregidor*. Find the 20th Regiment here, and Colonel Ross quartered at the house of my friend the governor.

November 3.—Colonel Ross comes to induce the old *corregidor* to swear in the paymaster. The wife achieves it, otherwise the old man would have first inspected the regimental accounts!!

N.B.—The man who ran off with his mules before has never returned. I am badly off here now, for the great room that I had before is occupied, and I am in the family.

November 4.—Start in the morning with the 20th Regiment for Aliseda. Ready at three. No mule. Colonel Ross starts. The *corregidor* in a fury. I start at four, leave the column in the dark, and take a doubtful road. Hear a dog bark, and ferret out a peasant, who rights us; but soon after we were again *presque au désespoir*, when a dear dog not far off began to bark. We made for the noise, holloaing, and at length a peasant rights us. It now begins to rain like the devil. Lose my way again in a great wood, but retrieve it, and arrive at Aliseda, wet and tired, at eleven o'clock. Regiment arrives at two, after a wet, painful march.

November 5.—Fine fair day, and after breakfast we leave for Brozas.

November 6.—Start again at daylight in excessive rain, and arrive at Alcantara at nine, perfectly wet. Quartered on my old friend the *alcalde*

---
20. The horse recently purchased.

(mayor), who receives me with the greatest *bon cœur*. The general is quartered at the Benedictine convent, the richest order in Spain, and the prior, who is chaplain to Charles IV., undertook to prepare dinner for the general, his baggage not having arrived. So one was rather disposed to expect something sumptuous, and at half- past four go up to the convent to dinner; dismayed to see a little *tabletto* with one glass and a pint of wine. For dinner there was a soup made of bread, water, beans, and salt in a flat plate, and a light leg and shoulder of goat—execrable; silver plates, and a few grapes after dinner.

Coming home we hear the *fandango* playing and singing. Go to the door, which is immediately shut. Complain to the *alcalde*.

"Do you wish to see it?" said he quickly.

"Yes."

"*Vamos.*"

And away we went, and were now highly received among the dancing peasants. I think it exceedingly pretty, the girls seem so glorified, dizened out in all their finest costume, and preserving such a gravity of modest dignity, that awes the boors into distance and respect. They, on the contrary, with their hats on, and in all their working dirt, dance with the fair, but never touch them, both snapping their fingers all the time, and raising their heads alternately with a graceful motion. When it was over we retired to the *alcalde's* house, and entered into conversation, in the midst of which he was called out to quell a disturbance in the street. I asked what it was.

"Nothing," they said; but from the looks of the women, who wished to detain me in the house, I suspected some English were concerned, so I went out, and Bernardo followed me, and, directed by the noise to a neighbouring house, we found two English officers—Tilford and Falls—in a small room, bayed by about fifty Spaniards with swords and fixed bayonets. I was going to inquire very quietly what was the matter, and prevent mischief as skilfully as I could, when that fool Bernardo, like a horse taking fright on the brink of a precipice, darted on one of the peasants, dragging him away, and calling him all the devils in hell, and cuffing him with all his might.

This immediately, as I foresaw, raised the fury of this disorderly patrole to ungovernable bounds. They heeded neither corporal nor *alcalde*. They entirely threw off all authority, and seemed prepared, with drawn daggers and swords and fixed bayonets, to take the most plenary revenge. I seized Bernardo, stamped and bawled to him to be quiet, but still the fool with his damned tongue and violent gestures inflamed them so much, that, losing all distinction, having seized him, they hemmed us in,. and drove us backward into the room.

Seeing Bernardo pinioned, with a parcel of swords clashing about and twenty bayonets ready, I expected fully every instant to see him fall with fifty stabs, and pushed forward to the Spaniards, saying, "*Prighonera, prighonera,*" meaning that they should take him prisoner and not kill him. And perhaps this hint saved him, for they repeated, "Yes, yes, prisoners; all of you prisoners." Just then Bernardo broke loose, and rushed to us within the room.

Immediately, with loud shouts and execrations, the mob from behind, pushing the mob in front, came tumultuously and blackly towards us, their bayonets thrusting open the door.

I entreated Falls and Tilford to be perfectly quiet and to use no gestures nor loud words, and told Bernardo, with an angry frown, he would be answerable for our lives. He seemed to have found his senses, and to see the madness of his conduct. I then went quietly up to the first rank (we were unarmed) and asked, "What do you want? To murder your friends? Are we not your friends? What do you want?"

Immediately reason seemed to strike one of them, and he pulled off his hat and said, "Yes, sir, we are friends, and we only want you to stay here until the governor settles the dispute."

This was breath and blue sky, and I employed the interval in conciliating them as much as possible, and, going close among them, told them we were friends come to help them, that we had the same cause, etc., and how silly it was to make ill blood owing to some foolish mistake.

Still the storm clamoured from without, and through the windows I perceived the street full of furious faces and glistening arms.

At length, however, the calm which I had obtained near me gradually pervaded the others, and we entered into quiet conversation. Still, however, they were bitter against Bernardo, and Tilford wished for the Grenadiers of the 20th, if he could get them.

In the beginning of the fray our excellent little *alcalde* (mayor) had been very active and bold, and pushed the fellows out of the room with many a crack; but when Bernardo put them in such a fury, he was fairly jostled to the outside, and could not get to us again until the calm reached him from within.

He then settled the matter by taking Tilford, against whom the offence was, into his own house. Bernardo made very handsome apologies, which were accepted with good heart, and I went home very thankful that the thing had ended as it did, and gave Mr. Bernardo very cogent hints respecting the gallant fire he had so perniciously displayed.

The cause of the foolish affair was the spite of the beastly master of the house because Tilford had come to join Falls in his billet, and he had lyingly persuaded the patrole that he had insulted his wife.

November 7.—I find that last night when Bernardo had followed me the dangerous fellow had concealed the *alcalde's* long *toledo* under his cloak, and made a thrust at one man, but the sword luckily only passed through his coat.

The general after breakfast complains to the assembled authorities of the town that the men are not received with sufficient friendship, and that it may have a bad effect on the minds of the soldiers. The 20th Regiment marches to Zarza, and Colonel Beckwith with the 95th marches in.

The Benedictine church is extremely fine inside; the bare stone in Gothic arches extremely grand. We view the bridge. Nothing can exceed it. Its venerable air, as well as the inscription over the triumphal arch, declare its structure of antiquity. It was built by the Emperor Trajan, and is about 150 feet high, stretching from mountain to mountain. The stones are immense, and of nearly equal size, with all the roundness of time's rubbing. Standing on the bed of the river and catching the wild mountains through the enormous arches, it appears like the Bridge of Sin and Death striding over chaos. The piers seem to have been exceedingly well clamped, and there is a triumphal arch in the centre of the bridge.

I should think it as fine and perfect a Roman relique as any that exists, and being in this country it involves a number of inferences very interesting to the antiquary and historian. I wish some of them could see it. There is a striking grandeur of rude yet elegant simplicity in this structure which must always have rendered it most imposing; but that very venerable air that the whole has acquired, from each great stone being mouldered by time, until there are wide joints between them, and the whole inexpressible shade cast over it by a thousand years, give it an impression on the mind (while the light clouds dance over the top of the arch) that is not to be described.

Alcantara, November 5, 1808.

My ever dearest Dad—The advanced division of the Army under General Paget is now moving onwards by the shortest route

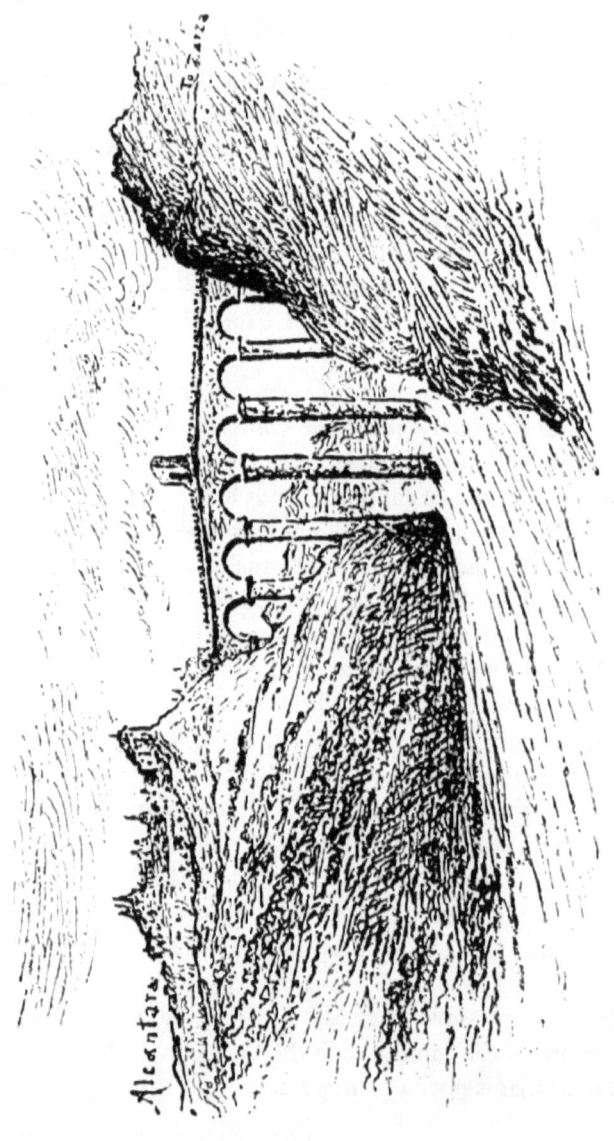

Bridge of Alcantara

towards Burgos from the Alemtejo. The roads along the frontier into the north of Spain by Alcantara, Ciudad Rodrigo, etc., are so bad that all the artillery on the south side or left bank of the Tagus is moving on by the high road to Madrid. The rest will go from Lisbon to Almeida, and so on.

There has been a very irksome interval between the knowledge of our destined entry into Spain and the commencement of the march.

The rainy season appears to have commenced, but I devoutly hope that its effects will not be great before the arrival of this division at Ciudad Rodrigo, from which place I believe the roads are not liable to be broken up by bad weather.

If we get in time upon the theatre of war, the British Army has every reason to be sanguine. I believe there is no man in the army who is not confident in Sir John Moore. He has under him as generals as fine ardent fellows as ever breathed, and I believe his particular attached friends. Then the troops are the best quality of British troops, which is as much praise as can be given. So if Buonaparte himself with 50,000 Frenchmen of his best bands will please to oppose himself to the British corps of the Allied Army, we can wish no more. I shall take care that you get a line from me as often as is possible.

I rambled a good deal about this part of the country before the division moved, and had some curious adventures. I have been fortunate enough to get an invaluable servant, who is an excellent cook, interpreter, and travelling companion, of tried fidelity and diligence, and more entertaining and conversable on the road than Sancho was with Don Quixote in the same relations and in the same country. I have completed my stud for forty guineas. Two chargers and a baggage pony make my establishment, and in these I have been so fortunate that I would spurn sixty guineas for them, and was offered twenty-five for one that cost me fifteen the other day. However, by the end of the campaign I expect I shall have taken out of them a little of their worth.

It is the greatest comfort to me to be with such a man as General Paget. I consider myself as a part of his suite, and shall be very proud if I gain the esteem of such a noble man.

This morning before we set off from Brozas it was not light, and a man was smoking a little paper cigar in the hall. The general said he should like one of all things, so I asked the man if he had one, and one readymade was produced. There was some embarrassment about which end was to be lighted, and which to be taken into the mouth, so the man seized it very readily to show him the way. I endeavoured to redeem it before it was, as I should have thought, rendered unfit for service by being in the man's mouth, saying with impatience, "He's going to put it in his mouth."

"No, now let him alone; never mind," said the general. "He knows nothing about that sort of thing, you know, and I'd rather do that than offend a fellow."

It was said in such a natural, quiet, unaffected way as to be quite delightful.

Do let me hear often. I received a letter from dearest Mamsey, which gave me great delight. That Mr. Leckie is a very clever, but rather wild gentleman, who treated me very hospitably at Syracuse. I liked him very much. My friend Lefebure, to my great delight, is in Spain, most creditably employed as a missionary on affairs of very particular importance. The higher his employment is, the more I am sure his energetic mind will do him credit. I have had a very long communicative letter from him. I find he has applied to Lord Chatham for me, among a few others, to assist him in his occupation. I shall send this to headquarters by one of General Paget's staff, who happens to be going, and hope that it will tell you very soon that I am well and happy.—

With greatest love, ever, dearest Dad, Charles.

November 8.—Start at nine o'clock for Zarza, and arrive about two.

My host is a Spanish gentleman, very civil, and the lady apologises for giving me a tin wash-hand basin, as all the silver ones are buried in the woods on account of the French.

Wait three hours for dinner, and at eight o'clock in comes cold meat.

November 9.—Get up at half-past four to start for Perales.

Shall be glad when we get to Ciudad Rodrigo and emerge from this miserable part of Spain.

We pass remarkable ridges of mountains and Moorish castles, also through great woods and watery tracts, but no towns, houses, or human beings. Perales six leagues from Zarza.

November 10.—Rise at four; very dark. Straw makes a good torch. The guide of the 20th Regiment takes them the wrong road. Error soon discovered. Violent rain.

General starts without a guide. I return for one, and by threats get an old postillion. The road by the Puerte desalto de Perales goes marvellously over the very summit of an exceeding high mountain, excessively steep, and much injured by great rain. Looking back, while climbing, I find the view most extensive and well wooded, half obscured by a heavy cloud, whose watery skirts, as they lift, reveal more and more of the landscape; then looking forward, I see a convent resting in a bunch of rare trees on the bosom of the mountain.

Here was formed a vast abrupt vale, in which better than ever before I could observe the system of waters as they sever the mountains. Many little runs joining, form a larger one, many of these again join, and amass a larger course, which forms a ravine; these ravines, falling into the same bottom, wear a torrent, these torrents brooks, and brooks rivers, and rivers a great river. All this lay with the most interesting development before the eye; but soon, ascending higher, I reached the clouds, and could see nothing but a circle of two yards round me, the bleak, rocky, wretched road, with a black hill on one side, and a precipice on the other, both lost in the impenetrable clouds, and what one could see of them covered with the stumps of heath, which, having been burnt, were quite black, and this, added to the excessive cold, made me feel as if I were travelling on the bare outside of the world, bordered by the chaotic beginning of things.

Soon after, without descending much, one enters a vast oak wood, which continues even to Penaparda, a miserable village. Wait with the postillion at the *alcalde's* house. The general arrives an hour afterwards. Proceed to Gainaldo, a noble city compared to Penaparda. Get good billets, and a happy family by a kitchen fire make me a welcome guest. Go to bed betimes.

November 11.—Gainaldo; halt today. This place is two leagues from Penaparda, six from Perales. The happy family now sitting at dinner before me by a good fire. Three fine brats have a little table and a little pot of porridge apiece. There is besides a beautiful omelet. The man and his wife and mother at another table.

The right wing of the 20th Regiment marches into the town. Ride my pony, *restivissimo!* Sentence him to an immediate hard gallop, and further to carry his master to Ciudad Rodrigo tomorrow.

November 12.—Breakfast at five; start at seven, I on my pony, which starts very docilely today. The ground about this place is open and cultivated. Slight hills and enclosures. Part of the ride put me in mind of that part of the walk to Ollerton where there is a sandy hollow and a steep bit of the road. Fine morning, but the huge mountains threaten rain, which attacks us a short league from Ciudad Rodrigo, with sufficient spirit to wet us through completely. On our arrival we meet some officers of the 50th and 28th, and Colonel Ronch conducts the general to his quarters.

I get to a priest's house, who makes a good palaver; but on seeing my little dungeon-room I sink under the weight of my afflictions. So after taking a glass of Malaga I sally forth, and get an excellent billet with a watchmaker. I intend to tell the priest that I am very fond of him, but detest his apartments.

Sir John Moore left this morning, without baggage, for Salamanca.

November 13.—Read papers, and see a great many old acquaintances, and on returning to the house find Engineers' horses at my door—Fletcher, Burgoyne, and Mulcaster. We call on General Paget, who asks us all to dinner.

Ciudad Rodrigo, a walled handsome town, standing on the river Agueda, which runs beneath.

November 15.—Go on miserable beasts, with Stewart, to Almeida, within six leagues of this place, and arrive at dark, getting horrid dirty billets.

November 16.—In the morning I go with Wilmot round the hexagonal works of Almeida, and also to Fort Conception. The angles of the flank and the ravelin of one front blown up by the French.

Return to Ciudad Rodrigo and desired to report on the place.

November 17.—Get up at six and start on "Blacky" to examine. Try to ford the river, and fail in several attempts. At last he and I part company; he runs home on one side, and I on the other. Walk the rest, and write my report.

Ordered to set out tomorrow for Salamanca.

November 18.—Start at eight, and *en route* get a volunteer guide for Cuba de Sancho, who runs amazingly fast and long. On arrival get comfortably lodged, and start at dawn for Salamanca, which we reach by five o'clock, being in all eleven leagues.

Here meet Mr. Fletcher, Mulcaster, and Foster, who tell us that the French had pushed on cavalry to Valladolid, and also that an order has been given to the troops at Salamanca to prepare to march at the shortest notice.

November 20, Sunday.—Breakfast with General Paget and write out report upon last roads.

Salamanca merits particular notice and attention. The church magnificent, and the door of the cathedral the richest, most superb thing I ever saw.

November 29.—Anxiety prevails about the Allies, and I receive orders late in the day to accompany Colonel Offeney on an excursion.

November 30.—We start at six, and after passing Tormerellas meet a sickly-looking man on horseback, whom we stop. He appears a good deal frightened, and confesses to have conducted thirty dragoons to Pedroso. He also delivers up certain papers—a requisition for 50,000 rations of bread and 10,000 of forage; a paper from Besseares to the Spanish people; and another, a bulletin from the grand army, announcing the total defeat of Castanos, which, added to that of Blake and La Romano, left nothing of a Spanish army but a small corps in the rear of the enemy under Palafax. Send this fellow with his papers to headquarters.

Start again, and having learned that the enemy had abandoned Pedroso, proceed thither, and find they had left the town two hours before our arrival. It was thought they had merely withdrawn into a wood a mile beyond, into which it was not deemed prudent to penetrate.

It appeared they had come for information, asking after us; and hearing that we had 24,000 in Salamanca, they said, "It was nothing; they had 40,000, and would soon settle us."

December 1.—Enter the wood with some precaution, and strike off to the left, crossing the stagnant Guareña to some houses, and are induced to believe that the French have gone back to Fresno.

Strike to the right to Villa Fuente, a short league distant. Then return to Pitiegua, and sleep at the house of the excellent *curé*, having made a hideous dinner upon nothing.

December 2.—Start for Mollorido, a mill on the road to Valladolid, and the next day receive intelligence that 10,000 infantry and 2000 cavalry have marched towards Segovia.

Go again to Tarazona, and meet on the edge of the wood the servant of the Bishop of Coimbra on his way home from Bourdeaux. The bishop was one of the Portuguese grandees sent as hostages to France, and the servant had been to visit him. He told us that he had both seen and spoken to Napoleon at Burgos, and that he was now at Aranda on his way to Madrid, to which the whole attention of the French seemed now turned, in consequence of the defeat or rout of Castanos.

We send this man with a dragoon to headquarters, and proceed to Mollorido, where we meet some people who advise us of a *don* living at Tarazona, a village half a league to the left. Go there, and find Don Jose Mental, who had fled from Rosseda, and here he was in his own farmhouse. We endeavoured to make him a sort of master intelligencer. He promised much, but is actually no great shakes. Leaving him, we return by the sedgy banks of the wild poolly Guareña. I rode ahead with the guide, and whe ever we came to a pool he gave a shuddering look thereon, and looking at me and shaking his head, said it was a terrible place, and whoever went in never came out again. This was his impression, as he could not swim, and had probably never been immersed in his life; to me it was no more than a deep pool.

December 4, Sunday.—General Alton calls, and we ride with him to Bahel Fuenta *via* Villa Ruella.

Set out on return journey, not knowing the road. The guide says he is sure that the wrong road is the right one. We take the wrong, and wander a long, long time in a heavy impenetrable fog, not seeing three feet before us. At length we shoot into a flock of sheep, and I, thinking there must be a shepherd, begin to whistle as hard as I can; and soon, to my great joy, I behold three upright forms advancing towards me, and make one of them put us on the right road for Pitiegua. We had gone more than our distance, and were still five miles off.

December 6.—Take a walk with the curate. He asks me about my birth, parentage, and education, and finding I had a mother, he says, "Ah, how often does she say to herself, 'Oh, if he should be dead, my dear child!'" This throws me into the blue devils.

December 7.—Yesterday General Alton intercepted the imperial mail from Burgos to Madrid. It was carried by a Spanish courier, and guarded by two French officers and a French courier. The party was attacked by about twenty peasants a few leagues from Burgos. One French officer and the French courier were killed. The other Frenchman made his escape, and the Spanish courier set off full speed for the English outposts. The mail had many letters for Napoleon and his dukes and nobles.

Today we set out for Tarazona, but on meeting some people from Cantalapiedra, they tell us such a parcel of stuff that we determine to go there.

We reach Cantalapiedra, five leagues off, and ask for news. A priest, coming up, asks, "Do they seek for news here?"

"Yes."

"Oh," he says, "the Emperor of Russia has sent his ambassador to Buonaparte to Madrid, to say that unless he desists from his projects against Spain, the Muscovite will declare against him."

The Marquis Goraze is here in retirement. He is the *intendente* of Burgos, and made his escape. The people point to an equipage just arriving. 'Tis the Marchioness, drawn in a dung-cart, her daughters and women preceding her on donkeys, and the Marquis himself bringing up the rear.

After a most beautiful sun-bright day and clear night there advances suddenly from the north (between Pedroso and Pitiegua) an overwhelming cloud resting on the earth. I kept before it some time, and could see far before me (though it was night), but behind me not an inch, till at last, meeting a man and talking with him a moment, it got ahead, and I found myself in the thickest pudding of a night, and was obliged to grope my way to Pitiegua.

December 8.—Stay indoors and determine on what to be done.

December 9-11.—Ride north, reconnoitre, make maps and plans.

Frost and excessive cold. Get a letter from Burgoyne,[21] dated Salamanca, about my coat. He tells me that General Hope is with them at Alba, and that the French have attacked Madrid in force, and are reported to be repulsed with loss. Also that Napoleon has declared in Paris—"I am now going at the head of 200,000 men to place a prince of my own family on the throne of Spain, after which I shall proceed to plant the Imperial eagles on the walls of Lisbon."

Napoleon has been at Aranda de Duero some time.

December 14.—Start for headquarters, and find that General Stew-

---

21. Afterwards General Sir John Burgoyne.

art has surprised a valuable convoy of cotton in some town on the Douro, taking thirty-seven prisoners, fine-looking fellows.

Colonel Murray tells me I shall find General Paget at Toro, and that Captain Campbell is going thither. Arrive at Toro. General Paget not there, and I get put up at his old quarters, and am informed that an officer had murdered his landlord, and immediately after, there enters a man with his head all bloody, and people screaming.

My first object was, and always is, with the Spaniards, to make them cease their storm, and then I can redress or excuse their wrongs and talk reason to them. For the passion of the Spaniard rises at the sound of his own voice; he hears it reciting in an angry tone, and his grievances mount to sudden fury and chide the tardy execution of revenge. I take the man to General Beresford.

Noises and knockings at the door all night.

December 15.—In the morning an old woman enters and gives a most humorous description of the night's disturbances.

Start with Captain Bayley for Tiedra, and there find General Paget, who had arrived with the Reserve.

December 17.—Hard frost, march to Villalpando. Met by the people with enthusiastic exclamations.

The generals have a confab, Sir D. Baird having joined.

December 18.—Sunday. I am desired to plan the place.

December 19.—Advance to Valderas and make a sketch. The cavalry pass the bridge, and while on the bank, under-run by the river Cea, I was almost blown away and benumbed by the violence of the wind.

Sir John dines with General Paget,—and Battle is the word!!

(The Journal here is omitted from 19th December to 24th December, the details of the campaign being more clearly related in the letter to his father, dated 24th December.)

Grajal,[22] December 24, 1808.

My ever dearest Father—I see so many foolish letters in the papers respecting the operations of armies and the faults or merits of generals, that however naturally I might be inclined to chat with you and give you in narrative my ideas of our movements, made and required, I have, I believe, pretty generally refrained from entering into the subject more than in a general cursory

---

22. A few miles south of Sanagun.

manner. The enemy was in force at Saldana, and extended to other towns on the river Carrion, which runs from the Asturias through Leon into the Douro. It was determined to beat him here if he would wait, and accordingly by a mutual flank movement right and left, a junction having been formed with Sir David Baird, the whole army advanced towards the Carrion without losing time, taking up at the end of each day's march such lines of cantonment as were the most secure that the situation of the towns and villages would admit of, keeping the cavalry in our front, then the Reserve, behind which, in three divisions, was the main army, having its flanks covered by the cavalry and flank corps of light troops.

As in the advance our patroles fell in with those of the enemy, that superior valour of which the English are so conscious, and which is conspicuous in all descriptions of English warriors in their battles with the enemy, was very strongly and repeatedly displayed by our Hussars. Lord Paget having gained information that 700 of the enemy's cavalry were at Sahagun, conceived it possible to take them by surprise. He therefore moved at midnight with the 10th and 15th. He divided these regiments at a suitable spot, and directing the 10th to move direct into Sahagun, so as to arrive at a stated time, he himself advanced by another road with the 15th, so as to turn the town and prevent the escape of the enemy.

This plan, wise as it was, was frustrated by a neighbouring picquet of the enemy, having been attacked in the first instance, perhaps not wisely, for though some were taken, some (as might be expected at night) got off, and put the others on the *qui vive*, in consequence of which Lord Paget, advancing towards the place with the 15th in a column of division, found the enemy drawn up in line to receive him. He was thus with 400 opposed to 700, and according to all military rules, in a devil of a scrape. His Lordship, however, forming them into line, immediately led them on to the charge.

The French are said at first to have stood like a wall and received the enemy with front give point. The impetuosity of the charge broke them, however, and much single-handed work ensuing, the final result was I don't know how many killed, and 140 taken prisoners, besides which 2 lieutenant-colonels and 20 officers, one of the former being nephew to Josephine and *aide-de-camp* to King Joseph. The 10th came up too late to make the result of this affair more brilliant.

Brigadier-General Stewart with the 18th, both before and since this affair, has been in several instances proportionately dashing and successful, and latterly 30 of the 18th attacked 100 of the enemy's cavalry, killed 20, and took 6 alive.

Our loss has been so trifling that I forgot to give it due place; it does not exceed 3 killed and 6 wounded in all—that is, seriously wounded, and these wounds have evinced (sufficiently, I hope) that the muff Hussar cap is no defence to the head, all the wounds being in consequence of their non-resistance, while our fellows hacked at the brass *casques* of the enemy in vain. As it was found that the chief body of the enemy under Marshal Soult, Duke of Dalmatia, was at Saldana, behind the Carrion, it was resolved to cross this river at the bridge of Carrion, five leagues distant, and to march upon Saldana with the left flank upon the river. Arrangements were accordingly made, in pursuance of which the Reserve under General Paget moved from this place at six o'clock yesterday evening, and was to take its place with respect to the rest of the army at a given time.

The bridge of Carrion was to be forced at daylight, and a subsequent battle was fully expected and ardently desired by all ranks of the army, from Sir John Moore to the junior drummer—at least so I believe, and spite of the severe frost and night cold, with snow upon the ground, the spirits of the troops beat high; they enjoyed the night march, for they thought that at last they had caught this "Duke of Damnation," whom they believed they had been running after from the neighbourhood of Lisbon. No men, they think, did ever go so fast, for they never saw anything of them, and almost despaired of coming up with them.

The Reserve had moved about four miles when an officer met General Paget, and the division was marched back to Grajal, its former cantonment. This is all I know. I suppose the enemy was found to have bolted, and that it will not do for us to play with them in the middle of this continent.

I therefore think that we shall get away as soon as we can. I think our Chief very wise, very brave, and very disinterested.—

  God bless you,   Charles.

December 24, Sunday.—March to headquarters at Mayorga. Make a sketch. A dragoon officer of the 10th begs to be let into our billet. I cannot say no. His horse kicks Lutgins', who rows me like blazes for letting the dragoon in.

December 27.—Ammunition waggons without number, and the tag, rag, and bobtail of all the other divisions here fall to the convoy of General Paget, a tremendous string, which makes the Reserve a baggage guard. He executes this with patience, mastery, and accomplishment. Guns being posted so as to rake the road.

We get no billets at Benavente, but Lutgins perseveres and gets an excellent one, and Lord Paget and Colonel V. dine with us.

December 28.—At ten o'clock Lutgins and I, sitting at breakfast, hear a row in the streets. Ask what is the matter. "Turn out, sir, directly! The French are in the town." Oh what confusion, what screaming and hooting and running and shoving and splashing and dashing! My sword, spurs, and sash mislaid. *Olla!* Mount my horse and ride to General Paget's quarters. Find him just sallying forth. He at once takes up his ground and gets his people under arms. False alarm. Nobody knows the cause of the row, but the people of the house had fled in despair. Unhappy people! Such are the miseries of war, that the unoffending inhabitants, despoiled of the sanctity of their homes, find every social tie jagged to the root, and then enters cold, desponding indifference.

Ride to the bridge, where preparations are making to destroy the same. A very wet, cold night. I am sent with a message to Sir John Moore, and ride back again through devilish rain and numbing wind. A party of the enemy's cavalry come to reconnoitre this operation, and exchange a few shots with our pickets. All the people having withdrawn, the houses on the other side the bridge and piles of timber are set on fire, and make a most superb and interesting appearance in spite of the inclemency of the night; the mounting blaze, bursting

through the crackling roofs, glares sunlike upon the opposite promontories and sub-current waters. The teeth of the cursed saws refuse to do their duties, and hours are spent in sawing the woodwork. I leave the business at 5 a.m.

December 29.—Get to bed at six o'clock, wet, cold, and shivered to death. The Reserve marches at eight. The bridge having blown up, the enemy's cavalry in one part swim, and in another ford the river, and fall in with our pickets under General Stewart. The enemy 500, we 300. A great deal of sharp fighting ensues, in which the enemy are worsted, and seeing other bodies of cavalry coming on them, disperse and re-swim the river with loss both in drowned and killed; but the ground was so excessively heavy that our horses were blown, or their destruction would have been complete.

I post myself on a hill with Captain Eveleigh's troop of horse artillery, and see a large body of cavalry advance towards us from a neighbouring village. We make all dispositions to receive them well, and they appear to design to take our cavalry in flank, edging off towards the river. When they come within reach, and Captain E. is just going to give them a round shot, we find them to be the 15th Dragoons!

Ride to the river, where the enemy attempt to form again on the other side and fire at our *videttes* with their carbines; but the horse artillery soon come up, and give them a few shrapnels, which disperse them and send them up the hill. Result (of the whole engagement) about twenty on each side killed and many badly wounded, about twenty French prisoners of the Imperial Guards, their General, Colonel of the 2nd Imperial Guards, and several officers.

I go on the bridge to see the effect of the explosion, which was complete, then ride in again, and on towards Baneza. Overtake Captain Griffiths, and converse much with him. Get pretty well put up with Lutgins, but the Scotch make inroads upon us.

December 30.—Cavalry arrive at Baneza. Start for Astorga (four leagues). The town excessively full and stinking.

On the road talk with French officers. They say that the Spaniards never fought at all, and that Buonaparte must have been looking at the action yesterday from the heights on the other side the river.

I and Gos billet together and receive orders from headquarters. Major F. Gos and Mul.[23] ordered one way, myself and Foster another.

This night tramp about the town to Q.M.G.'s and C.G.'s, etc., and

---

23. Mulcaster.

am franticated about guides.

Order from Headquarters

Mr. Boothby will be pleased to proceed this night by Castracontrigo, and endeavour to reach Sanabria tomorrow evening, or early on the following morning.

The object is to obtain correct information of any movements of the enemy from Benavente towards Orense, and to transmit the same by the most expeditious and secure route to Sir John Moore. Also to endeavour to induce the Spanish troops now at or near Sanabria to defend the passes as long as possible, and also to defend the fortress of Puebla and that of Monterey, and throw every impediment in the way of the advance of the enemy.

A detachment of the 76th is at Monterey, which must be ordered to retire in time to Orense, where it will find another detachment and wait for further orders.

Should there be any provisions at Monterey, and the Spaniards not be disposed to defend it, they must be, if possible, sent to any place on the road from Orense to Villafranca for the use of the column in that line of march, or else they must be consumed or otherwise destroyed to prevent their falling into the hands of the French.

Headquarters will be at Villafranca till the 3rd, and afterwards towards Lugo.

All intelligence must be also put to the column marching on Orense.

Guides must be procured this night, and whenever wanted, and care taken to get intelligence whether the enemy have pushed any parties of cavalry towards Sanabria.

Geo. Murray, Q.M.G.

Headquarters, Astorga,
December 30.

December 30.—Start at twelve o'clock. December 31, Saturday.—Very cold, leagues infernally long (5 = 7), freezes very hard. Enter the mountains, my horse weak and broken down. Arrive at Castracontrigo at six o'clock, seven long leagues.

Hunt up the *alcalde*, and desire to be taken to the curé's house. He proposes our waiting till daylight.

Knock up the *curé*. Get fire and chocolate, and lie down at seven.

Rise at ten. Breakfast and start again at twelve. Our guides tell us we shall not arrive at La Puebla till midnight.

This is all mountainous, and snow on the ground. Arrive at seven. Taken to the governor's, who secretly places a sentry over us, as I had not shown him my passport.

January 1, 1809, Sunday.—Go out to speak to the governor. He is now very civil and frank, and tells me his intelligence, which I forward to headquarters.

Get a better house belonging to a man, who tells us afterwards that he has devoured at a sitting seventy-two eggs with their corresponding bread and butter.

Colonel Chabot, charged with despatches, arrives.

January 2.—Colonel Douglas, A.Q.M.G., and York and Hutchinson arrive on their way to the army.

I despatch spies to Benavente.

January 3.—Breakfast these people, and they start for Monterey. Go three leagues on the road to Monbuey. Hear a lie, that the French are at Castracontrigo.

Colonel Peacock comes in late, his party halting a league behind at Otero.

January 4.—A Spanish ensign endeavours to turn me out of my quarters. I turn him out instead.

The inhabitants of Otero send to beg the Spanish soldiers may protect them from the plunder of Colonel P.'s stragglers. I write to Colonel P. to apprise him of this.

Mr. Murray, Com. G., arrives.

Commissaries, officers and soldiers, mules and devilment arrive all day. Spies return.

January 5.—Mr. Murray departs. Conceiving my commission to be performed, I determine to start for the army tomorrow, and the governor writes to Marquis Romano and encloses my despatch to Sir John. A colonel of Spanish artillery arrives with the cadets of Segovia in charge. Poor little fellows! he is to take them to Corunna.

Don Alonzo Gonzalis tells the people that the English are going to embark. They do not believe it. "What," says he, "if the English have not so many men as the French that follow them, would you have the poor English stay and be destroyed?"

"God forbid." In the evening I go to the governor's, and find round the brazier many Spanish officers, principally artillery. They talk of the destruction of the bridge of Benavente, and speak theoretically of the line of least resistance, etc., and I am asked if we do not carry with us some new and extraordinary machine of destruction. I cannot make out what they mean for a long time, so they send for the officer who had seen it.

He describes to the wondering circle a terrible machine, in which I recognise the wheel car! Then have we, is it true, an invention for carrying musketry to the distance of round shot? It was incredible. Describe shrapnel shells. A little black fellow starts up and swears it is no new invention. He is scouted and silenced. Take my leave.

January 6, Friday.—Start for Villarviejo. Freezes hard, and the ground is a sheet of ice. As the sun gets up, however, it thaws.

Pass numerous villages, and at three leagues encounter the first Portilla, where the road goes over a high mountain, which is sometimes impassable, and at this time bad and dangerous, not so much on account of the quantity of snow, but because the road, undermined by the run of waters in a thaw, becomes like the worst of rabbit warrens. And besides this, the beaten path is so narrow that two mules meeting could not keep it, and the one that leaves it flounders half buried in the snow. Pass the other Portilla, not in so bad a state, at six leagues, and reach Villarviejo, on the other side, at seven leagues. The general and busy run of waters, as if to their appointed stations, calls forcibly to my mind the description given by Milton of the assemblage of waters at the great command to let dry land appear.

Scenery wild and very high.

Get put up at the *curé's* house, which stinks excessively.

While cooking in the kitchen the whole family assembled round the fire, pop on their knees as the *curé* rises, and say the Rosary aloud. "*Santa Maria! Madre de Dios!*" is chimed out at the beginning of almost every prayer.

Foster and I sleep in the same room with the *curé*, who blows like a whale.

January 7.—Start for Monterey. Excessive, heavy, and continued rain. Overtake Colonel Peacock, in charge of £130,000, about four leagues from Verin, which is at bottom, while Monterey is at top, almost adjoining. Converse a good deal with him. Arrive at Verin completely drenched

These two days' journeys, though each called seven leagues, are at the lowest calculation eight.

About a league from Verin we are on a hill commanding a complete view of it and the Valdi mountains, most beautiful and romantic, a fine winding stream with green meads, and in the midst villages, woods, groves, pastures, houses, gardens—the garden of Eden.

Find Mr. Murray at Verin. Consult. He has learned that the army was at Lugo on the 5th, on which same day the English entered Orense. It is therefore doubtful whether or no the English will be found there when we arrive, the distance being ten leagues.

Get billets on an apothecary and go to bed. Much disturbed. Knocked up. Sick and ill, and what rest soever my illness allowed was snatched away by voracious and innumerable jumpers that bit me in all directions, and where they did not bite they ran and hopped about my feverish body.

January 8, Sunday.

Because I dare not touch them for my life,
Enticing grapes and honey were produced,
And when my parched palate prompts my hand,
My qualmish stomach sends its veto up.
Baboon-faced John projects my certain cure,
And gives me burnt bread sopped in scalding wine.
I go to the Corregidor, and there
Find Murray's information is confirmed.
I write to Colonel Peacock, and resolve
To take the shortest road to Vigo Bay,
Passing the Minho, by a ferry boat. . . .
Engage a mounted guide, and disfatigue
Our weary bodies with two hours' repose.
Then, rising in the dark of night, we go
And wonder how the practised guide can find
The labyrinthine way, how he can tell
The rocks and waters manifold (from snow
Just thawed, and pushing for the lowest place)
With such sure step to evitate at night.

At last a little village we descry, and thunder at a cottage door, but, alas! the inhabitants of this cottage persist in a death-like silence and a dread repose. Thus we remain, we know not where, in a very cold night. At length the guide goes to another house by himself, and gets a Galician with straw torches, which are very pretty and convenient.

The road is very dreary and unpleasant, and still three leagues to Villadita. On arriving we get a woman to show us the way to the *corregidor's*. It was three o'clock in the morning. *Corregidor* looks out of his window and says with a loud voice, "*alguacil*."[24] The old *alguacil* leads to one and another, but we make him give us a smart-looking house with windows to it. The mistress makes a rail, but first the maid comes to the balcony and says, "Good morning, gentlemen."

"A curse, you ugly witch," says Bernardo, "is this a time for the compliments of the morning?" When we get into this house it is so mouldy, forlorn, and faded fine that, late as it is, we try another, where we find a man in bed in every nook and corner. Get very comfortably lodged, and find that we are only nine leagues from Vigo.

January 9, Monday.—Get a most excellent breakfast, and, notwithstanding my increasing malady, I venture to swallow a quart of rich new milk, which I have not tasted for a long time.

The people come and bother and say, "Behold here are two dear Englishmen that don't know what good news we have for them. The English, pursued by the French, have headed round at Betanzos and driven the French before them sixteen leagues, and orders are come to halt the troops at Orense that were going to Vigo."

Although I did not think this account entitled to credit, coming from the Spaniards, who give and take lies with greater assurance and credulity than any other people, I thought that I might so far trust it as to the intelligence which respected Orense, only two and a half leagues distant; and they said the ferry across the Minho was not always passable.

Not feeling safe in the hands of the precarious, headlong Spaniards, I was rather anxious to get to a British column, as the circumstances of the evacuation would not be much longer in spreading, and who could tell the impression it might create.

(A break occurs here in the Journal, but we know that Captain Boothby was now on his way to join Sir John Moore at Corunna via Vigo Bay, and the next tidings we hear from him occur in the letters to his father and brother after the battle of Corunna.)

On Board the *Barfleur*, Jan. 18, 1809.

My ever dearest Father—I am very anxious that you should have a line from me as soon as you will hear of the action of the 16th, the result of which, had it not deprived us of Sir John

---

24. Guard or watchman.

Moore, would have been everything that could be wished. He was killed by a cannon shot early in the action, which tore away his shoulder. He, however, lived till nine o'clock, being perfectly collected, sensible, and great to the last.

The French in attacking us had at last complied with his most earnest wishes, and the battle had the effect which he foresaw, that of ensuring to us an unmolested and complete embarkation, which took place the night of the action and yesterday, the French contenting themselves with throwing a few shot among the shipping, which, operating on the fears of the masters, caused two or three transports to be lost. Otherwise it had the beneficial effect of getting the fleet under way most expeditiously.

The action was very obstinate and warm, and lasted three hours. It is the first I have been in. Our loss in killed and wounded, particularly in officers, has been very severe, considering the number of troops exposed to fire, which was not more than half the army.

I have no more time, as the bag is closed. God bless you,

Charles.

At Sea, 1809.

My dear B.—As my daily adventures just now would be rather disagreeable than interesting, I shall give you some account of the latter operations in Spain. As much as I can vouch for will be included in a relation of my own movements.

When the army arrived at Astorga, Sir John Moore sent me to La Puebla, the capital of Sanabria, a mountainous district in the kingdom of Leon bordering on Portugal. The place is in the direct but worst road from Benavente to Orense, and as it had been determined that a column should take a better though longer road to Vigo, the object of my mission chiefly was to give immediate intelligence to Sir John Moore should the enemy show any disposition (by taking the shorter route from Benavente or elsewhere to Orense) to cut off the retreat of the column marching on Vigo.

I was apprised of the time when our army would reach the different stages of its retreat, that I might judge where to rejoin it, having executed the service for which I was detached. Being satisfied on this head, I set out for Orense, making long journeys and sometimes travelling by night, the roads very bad and mountainous, rendered almost impassable by snow, but the scenery in many parts extremely beautiful and romantic, particularly in the neighbourhood of Monterey, an old mountain castle of, I believe, no military importance.

From the intelligence I procured at Verin, immediately below it, I thought it better to avoid Orense and proceed to Vigo by the shortest road, crossing the river Minho (over which there is a bridge at Orense) by a ferry.

The Minho at this place is a very rapid, turbid stream, carrying down with great velocity huge timbers and fragments torn by the waters from the mountain sides, or hurled from their tops by the fury of the winter blasts. The scenery is extremely rich and beautiful, having an inexpressible charm viewed from the stupendous heights, immediately impending the river, over which the road winds.

The rugged steepness of the roads greatly lengthens the leagues, and the journeys, which one laid down from the experience of other parts of Spain, are obliged to be most teasingly divided in Galicia, particularly irksome to me on account of the uncertainty there was of the light in which our retreat would be viewed by the barbarous, arrogant, and ignorant, though not ungenerous, Spaniards, for few of the most enlightened would be capable of exculpating me in any cause of anger they might imagine against my country. Having performed a hundred miles of this journey, I unexpectedly fell in with the column that marched upon Vigo, and having communicated with General Alton, I was confirmed in my determination to proceed to Vigo, as all communication between him and the main body of the army had for some time ceased.

As it appeared that the enemy had not got scent of this small column, and there was not the smallest probability of anything interesting taking place at the embarkation at Vigo, it became a very earnest object with me to reach Corunna, where it did not seem likely that affairs would have so insipid a complexion. I was therefore very well pleased to find that my friend Burgoyne had been sent to Vigo, and was to wait there until the embarkation was effected. At this time it was pretty confidently believed at headquarters that I had fallen into the hands of the enemy. This left me fully at liberty to proceed with the transports to

Corunna, and Sir Samuel Hood, whom I had formerly known in the Baltic, was so kind as to offer me a passage in the *Barfleur*. It would be needless to describe the anxiety I felt respecting what might be the state of affairs at Corunna, where I was sensible that the army must have been some days. I supposed and hoped that some natural advantages would enable them to repel for so long a time the forces of France, but this might not be the case, and when we arrived that beautiful army might be no more.

I got into the harbour in the *Minerva* frigate on the evening of the 14th January. I went immediately to Sir John Moore, who received me most kindly, and notwithstanding the cruel anxiety he must have suffered, still supported that most engaging exterior so endearing to his friends and so prepossessing to strangers on whom he did not think proper to frown. I then sought out my friends and brother officers, and was greeted by them as one risen from the dead. I, too, felt inexpressible pleasure at getting again amongst my companions, and in feeling satisfied by the tranquillity at Corunna that things were not going on badly; to find my friend Lefebure, too, one of the party, and almost re-established in health (for owing to excessive anxiety and fatigue in his attendance on the army of Blake, he was attacked and nearly carried to the grave by a fever) gave me the highest pleasure.

He spread a mattress for me on the floor, and I slept as undisturbed as if the French had not passed the Pyrenees. I found that the whole effective forces of the British occupied a position about three miles from the walls of Corunna, which they had held since the 12th, and where they had hutted themselves. This position in a military point of view was very bad, for it was immediately opposed to one of greatly superior strength and elevation, which ground the British, being the defensive and smaller force, could not possess, their object being to contract the front presented to the enemy, who had the power to attack with unlimited numbers. They were therefore obliged to relinquish the commanding ground to the enemy, and to make up by their superior firmness and courage the great defects of their position.

I know not if you understand plan drawing well enough to be assisted by a small hasty outline. The position of the British

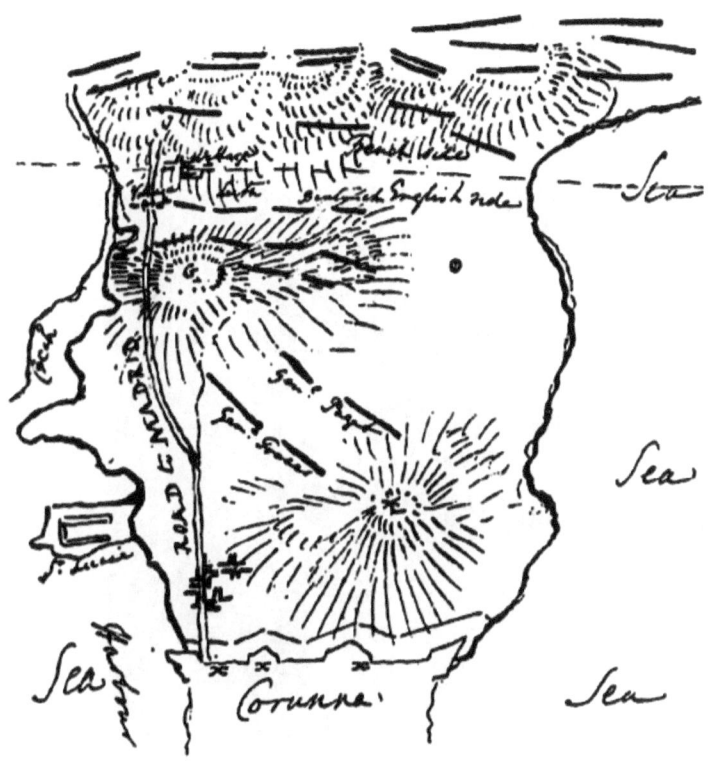

was bad because commanded by that of the enemy, but more especially because the right was liable to be turned—⊕.

The hill itself, G, was very well against assault, because the side was very much intersected by steep banks and fences which, defended by our troops, could not be carried. The sketch I have given you is on the first impression of memory, and without the wish to be accurate, just to help you by a spilt-port-wine drawing to the sort of thing. The fortification of Corunna (xxx) was infinitely better than any entrenchment thrown up occasionally. It was much improved and strengthened by us, and though its being fatally commanded, without bomb proof, and many other faults and disadvantages, natural and incurred, would prevent its pretending to withstand a regular siege, yet as a barrier against assault for a certain time it was as good as could be; 1500 men might stand behind it and defy 20,000.

Nothing, therefore, could be better to cover the tail of an embarkation. The outer position was maintained that the fleet might not be molested, which it might have been, for instance,

VIEW OF THE BRITISH AND FRENCH POSITIONS BEFORE CORUNNA, TAKEN FROM THE CITADEL.

a b British Line.   *c d* French Line.   *e* Magazine blown up 14th Jan. 1809.
f The village of Elvina.   *g g* Heights occupied by the French on the morning of 17th Jan.

From an illustration in "Campaign of Lt.-Gen. Sir John Moore, K.B." (1809).

from St. Lucia, etc., that the first business of the embarkation might be neither looked into nor molested, and that the tranquillity of the town might be as long as possible preserved. And now, after this explanation, I shall continue my narrative.

On the morning of the 15th, after breakfast, upon hearing some popping and that the enemy were making some demonstration, I borrowed Lefebure's horse (having left both my own at Vigo) and rode to the English position.

The enemy were thrusting out their sharpshooters in all directions, a species of warfare or battle which they understand the best. Ours, however, were not backward, and gave them at least shot for shot. A distant cannonade was soon after commenced on both sides, the French firing at our groups of officers, and indeed at individuals, for I was honoured twice in this way, and my friend Lefebure's horse had a narrow escape. They then made a parade of their force and several movements on their heights as if they meant something, but merely meaning, I fancy, to know if we still held our ground and with what force. Sir John Moore was out all day, and I followed in his suite over our whole position. He spoke to all officers as he went along, giving cautions, orders, and instructions, and looked wistfully at the enemy, apparently wishing with painful eagerness for a battle. Those who suppose these wishes were excited by any thought of his own fame, do not know Sir John Moore. He wrote to Sir S. Hood that he was anxious for an engagement, because he thought it would be the only means of securing an unmolested embarkation. The sharpshooting and cannonading continued throughout the day, but the number of killed and wounded on our side was inconsiderable, and probably was no greater on that of the enemy.

On the morning of the 16th no skirmishing was heard from the outposts, and everything wore the face of an understanding on the part of the enemy that it was now their business to fight us. As long as we remained embattled upon our position we thought it was not their business, and feared they waited a more favourable opportunity, which must soon be afforded them. For Sir John Moore was determined, much as he wished to give them a check, not to wait any longer, for every day, while it added to their strength, brought with it the chance of a foul wind, which could not be too much dreaded if it lasted long enough to drive us into the town, and to give time to the French to establish batteries on the margin of the harbour for the destruction of the fleet.

At one o'clock I was charged with the erection of a battery in the town and some other works on the ramparts. At about three o'clock we heard the firing begin, sharpshooting first, and then more general, and so much cannonade as convinced me it must be more serious than on the preceding day. Nothing I could say or do could prevail upon the soldiers to lay aside the air of the last extremity of fatigue which they had assumed. The shovel of earth approached the top of the bank as leisurely as the finger of a clock marches round the dial.

I was therefore a good deal struck with admiration at their behaviour when at four o'clock an order came for them to join their regiments, which were marching to the field. They threw down their tools, jumped to their arms, hallooed and frisked as boys do when loosed from school, these poor, tattered, half-dead-looking devils. I was no less pleased to be left at liberty. An engineer has no appropriate place or defined duty in an open battle, but he is always acceptable in the field if mounted, because he is generally a good sensible smart fellow that looks about him, and is trustworthy in the communication and explanations of orders.

What we generally do, therefore, is to offer our several services as *aides-de-camp* to the several generals whom we may pitch upon or fall in with; and had I been mounted I should have gone straight to General Moore upon finding myself at liberty. But now a horse was my first object. The firing rather increased than slackened. I had never been present at a general action, and I wished painfully for a horse. Thinks I, "I'll walk towards the scene of things, and I may meet a horse that has lost his master." I went a little way and overtook a gunner with a saddle on his back.

"What are you going to do with that?" said I.

"I am taking it to St. Lucia," said he.

"What for?"

"It is there that all the artillery horses are."

"Oh, ho!" A thought struck me, and I followed him. When I arrived I went straight to an officer of gunner drivers and explained to him my situation. The obliging fellow instantly ordered a horse to be saddled, to my great delight. I asked him, "What news from the field?"

"General Baird is killed," said he. I galloped off, and on my way up I overtook an artillery officer, who told me General Moore was dangerously wounded. I know not how it was, but I certainly galloped on with much less count of personal danger. The enemy had so placed two guns that the overshots invariably came whizzing down the road. As they passed one another I leaned on one side, and thought each destined for my head.

The object of my search now was General Hope. I spied a clump of officers standing just behind the two lines engaged. From the situation they had taken up I thought this group most likely to be General Hope and his suite, so I hastened to it, and was not disappointed. He was looking very attentively at the two uninterrupted lines of fire though he said hardly anything, just sent an order in a quiet way now and then, and whenever the fire immediately before him seemed to slacken, he appeared instinctively to potter down to some place where hotter firing was. I was very glad to find myself so little disturbed by the whizzing of balls. The fire was very hot, and several men and horses of our group were struck, but I was thinking more of the novel sight before me, and glorying in the brave obstinacy of our people, who after so furious and long-continued and unabated an attack still refused to yield one inch to the column after column, relieving each other, that assailed them.

When first indeed I reached General Hope's party, I looked up at a clear part of the sky and silently begged of God that should a ball this day despatch me, He would forgive me my sins and take me to heaven, and after that I felt finely settled and elevated and indifferent to the event, while the cheering and volleying of our soldiers warmed my heart.

As it was growing dusk a roar of musketry was volleyed on the left, followed by a roar of huzzas quite as loud. General Hope asked, "What's that?"

"The 59th coming up fresh, sir."

Colonel Graham came up and told him (the firing had almost ceased) that the enemy still possessed a village which was thought too near to us, and asked if it should be taken. General Hope desired that some companies of the 15th might take it, and soon after an officer came up and announced the capture.

The firing had totally ceased. General Hope rode round the position, and then went to Corunna to make such arrangements as might be required. We got to the town about eight o'clock. I rode to Sir John Moore's quarters, and going upstairs met Colonel Graham. He told me Sir John was lying on his mattress dying, that he heard him groan. Perhaps had I gone in, pressed his hand, and got a kind word from him, it would have been a source of pleasure to me now, but then I had no stomach for it. His shoulder and part of his left side were carried away by cannon shot. His great good spirit left his body at nine o'clock.

General Hope's letter[25] is as accurate and chastely true as it is simple, elevated, and beautiful; so great a degree of accuracy one would scarcely have expected, or thought compatible with the elegance of the language, the smoothness and entireness of the narrative. I advise you, if you have forgotten it, or did not know that it was something more than a beautiful piece of writing, to read it again.

Our obstinate battle, the coming in of our wounded, and the melancholy death of our chief had a very great effect upon the feelings of the people of Corunna. "This is for us! this is for us! Poor English, they bleed for us!"

This sort of thing soon worked itself into a transport of generous enthusiasm, which was both beneficial and satisfactory to us.

At about four o'clock on the morning of the 17th, when my companions and I got up, we found that nearly all the army was embarked. The wind was beginning to blow very hard, which made the embarkation very difficult, but, thank God, it blew the right way. On the 16th Sir John Moore had desired Fletcher, chief engineer, to name the number of men he thought necessary to occupy the town line, and to furnish a minute distribution of them upon the different works.

This Fletcher did, and I went round with him and General Beresford (who was entrusted with the forlorn hope), that Fletcher might explain the distribution to him.

Had the French not been so severely cowed and beaten as they were, and had come on to the attack at dawn, Beresford with 1500 men would have held that line while the embarkation was

---

25. Appendix.

completing, and probably at night have withdrawn to the citadel, protecting that and his own embarkation with a small portion of his force. Then these last would have rushed to the boats in waiting, jumped in, and trusted to the gates and ditches to keep out the enemy until they had shoved off from the shore.

But the impressive lesson the French had received rendered these operations unnecessary; and had not General Hope determined by doing things with the leisure he could command, to do them completely, the whole fleet might have been out at sea on the 17th before a Frenchman had ventured to show his nose.

But it was resolved to embark the sick and wounded, to bury General Moore, and therefore to keep the 1500 men upon the line until evening.

I went with Squire (a friend of mine in the Engineers) walking about the line, and at about seven o'clock we fell in with General Hope, and accompanied him all over the peninsula behind the walls of Corunna. He spoke with much satisfaction of the result of the battle. The troops, he said, had been withdrawn without the knowledge or suspicion of the enemy, deceived by their remaining fires.

At about ten o'clock, I think, a few Frenchmen appeared slinking into the houses near the walls of Corunna, and the Spaniards, acting up to the magnitude of their hatred to every Frenchman, banged at each individual with a 32-pounder. They were sharpshooting this way all day long, though at first we could not conceive the cause of such a heavy cannonade.

General Hope asked us to breakfast with him. "Squire, Boothby, will you come and have some chocolate?" were not unacceptable words. I have loved and admired this quiet, modest, superior being ever since I have known him.

I believe the Spaniards were entirely aware of our determination to embark, yet their enthusiastic blaze in the good cause continued to increase. "They would die in the ruins of their walls." It even pervaded the women, who all day long were seen with cartridges and wads upon their heads for the service of the batteries.

They were jealous of our interference on the walls, which they wished to defend themselves, so that orders were given to our people not to appear on the walls, the portion destined for their defence being posted behind the ramparts, which were covered with all sorts and both sexes of Spaniards.

Everybody commanded, everybody fired, everybody hallooed, everybody ordered silence, everybody forbade the fire, everybody thought musketry best, and everybody cannon. In short, you have no notion of the loud misrule which prevailed.

However gratifying to us the display of such a spirit might be, or however beneficial to cover and complete our retreat, I believe a scrupulous care was had neither to promote nor increase it.

It was a spontaneous burst, coming up itself, and impossible to be checked—so much unexpected by us that arrangements were made for the last party to spike all the guns in the place. And while we could not but admire the honesty of their zeal, we lamented that it might increase the calamities of the capture, but this, I am happy to find, has not been the case.

It is said that the governor candidly acknowledged that he should not attempt to stand a siege in so defective a place, but promised that as long as his walls gave protection to an Englishman or an English ship, he would never surrender.

The ground now in possession of the French would enable them to cannonade the shipping which still remained in the harbour as thick as a wood, although for the most part filled with troops.

The general had urged this point with Sir S. Hood, who urged it strongly to the Admiral, De Courcy. It is said that the transports did get the order to proceed to sea the moment they had received their complement of troops.

If so, they, with a degree of idiotic disobedience not unusual nor incompatible with the character of masters of transports, took no heed.

Certain it is that we in the town were rather longing to see a French battery open upon them, which we thought would make them get under way with a signal and beneficial expedition.

But the fact was that we did not despise them half enough, nor know of what extreme cowardice and rascality they were capable.

General Hope determined to be the last man on shore, and desired to have some Engineers remain with him, in which number I was. But at about two o'clock, when the general found that no preparations were making against our line, and that the enemy contented himself with preparing a battery on the top of the height overlooking the shipping, he expressed a wish that we all should embark, as at dusk the boats would be so much occupied that we might find it difficult to get off.

We therefore proceeded together in search of a bit of victuals into the inner town, induced the people to unlock a high tavern, and sat down to a plate of cabbage soup.

It was while thus employed that the French battery opened upon the shipping. It consisted of two field-pieces, which the fears of the French had situated in such a manner as to be as little hurtful as possible.

Instead of going to the top of the hill, had they ventured down to an old stone fort (which we had abandoned) with their guns *à fleur d'eau*, they would probably have hulled some ship or other every shot, but their plunging fire could only touch one spot, and if that spot were not a ship, the ball went innocuously to the bottom. But the end which the caution of the enemy would not permit him to attain was effectually given to him by the cowardice of the masters of the transports. The wind was blowing very strong, and the first shot from the enemy was the signal for them to cut their cables. Thus, being all adrift at once, it is only wonderful that more did not strike upon the leeward rocks. Seven, I believe, struck, three were got off, and four, after being cleared, were burnt by us, and beautifully lighted the last of the embarkation. The transports that were got off had been previously abandoned by the masters.

A midshipman of the *Barfleur* told me that on going alongside of a transport on the rocks, the master threw his trunk into the boat, jumped in after it, and then, before a single soldier was out, he cried, "Shove off, or she'll bilge." He was knocked backwards by a sailor.

We got on board a man-of-war's boat, which put me on board the *Barfleur* to get something I had left there. I was invited to go home in her, which I gladly accepted.

The embarkation being completed, General Beresford came on board at two o'clock in the morning, and when the fleet was collected it sailed for Old England. . . .

After taking the trouble to write this very long letter, my dear B., shall you be able to get through it? I beg at any rate that you will not destroy it, as it completes my Spanish Journal, and I have no copy of this or any other narrative of that period of my proceedings.—Your most affectionate brother,

                                                      Charles.

JOHANNES MOORE
EXERCITÚS BRITANNICI DUX PRÆBIO OCCISUS

Corunna, 1808

On the Burial of Sir John Moore

Not a drum was heard, not a funeral note,
As his corse to the rampart we hurried;
Not a soldier discharged his farewell shot
O'er the grave where our hero was buried.

We buried him darkly at dead of the night,
The sods with our bayonets turning,
By the struggling moonbeams' misty light
And the lantern dimly burning.

No useless coffin enclosed his breast,
Nor in sheet nor in shroud we bound him,
But he lay like a warrior taking his rest,
With his martial cloak around him.

Few and short were the prayers we said,
And we spoke not a word of sorrow;
But we steadfastly gazed on the face of the dead,
And we bitterly thought of the morrow.

Plymouth Dock, January 28, 1808.

Ever dearest Father—You will not be very sorry to hear of my arrival in England in good health, but, on the other hand, I have not a penny that I know of, nor a shirt nearer than Lisbon.

I shall come up to London without delay, find out where you are, and endeavour to spend some time amongst you, to lay down my head, and settle my affairs.

The man I looked up to as a god, and held in the most cordial respect and affection, after devoting his life to the service of his country, is praised by some and blamed by others.

I know the latter to be the ignorant, but consequently the most talkative, and your catchpenny generals come forward and tell you how they could have done better. All this makes me sick, and cools my military ardour. For can the utmost blindness of self-love make me think I can ever equal the virtues or military worth of Moore! And yet, as the result of his laborious services, a doubt comes in every man's mind whether he would now take upon himself that general's reputation. When dying, though perfectly sensible, he had great difficulty at last to articulate. He said gently, however, that he had endeavoured to serve his country diligently and conscientiously, and he hoped it would be satisfied with what he had done. His latest anxiety seemed to be for victory. "Are *they beat? Are they beat?*" he repeatedly asked. He wished to send some message to General Hope, who had succeeded him in the command. "Hope, Hope," he said at intervals, but could not articulate more. His last words were, "Tell my mother." He could no longer speak, and expired. Was not this the death of a hero and a good man? God bless you.—Your   Charles.

The loss of men and money in Spain, I think, are amply compensated for by the acquisition of military fame, but the loss of Sir John Moore at such a time admits of no consolation.

Bath, January 28, 1809.

Dearest Mother—The press on the road, the waters, etc., have made me travel slower, but I set off for London tomorrow, whence you shall hear from me.

We are three Engineers here together, one of whom is my friend Lefebure, the pleasantest and right-thinkingest man in the world. The people here show distinction to our rusty habits, particularly the fair sex, who advance to converse with us, to the astonishment of the well-dressed *beaux*.

I hope soon to embrace you and my Louisa, and all of you. God bless you, dear people.   Charles.

On returning home after the glorious Battle of Corunna, which terminated Moore's celebrated retreat and his life together, I conceived a thorough dislike and hatred of the military service. My patron was dead, and as a reward for services which I thought inestimable, his memory was reviled by his ungrateful countrymen, and tarnished by crafty, self-interested politicians, who, willing to wound, but yet afraid to strike, took the most impalpable means of offending his sacred memory.

All this increased the disgust which the sight of military operations in a devoted country had excited in my mind.

Bilious with these thoughts, I took the sweet medicine of family endearments.

I did not expect a speedy summons to the wars, for the only theatre which seemed to offer us a part in the drama was just closed, and I therefore promised myself some months of sweet repose and enjoyment, as a change rendered most delightful by those fatigues and dangers which entitled me to welcome it without blushing.

The pictures which had been given me of my family's distress between the beginning of those horrid accounts from Spain, and the hearing from me after the Battle of Corunna made me shudder at the thought of renewing such frightful anxiety; for while delighting in my father's affection for his children, I was always frightened at it. The violent expression of grief or the admission of immensurate apprehension in a female are less impressive because more consonant to her softer character; but when the safety of his children was concerned, my father lost this distinction.

The masculine firmness and well-tempered equality of his mind no longer served him, and he, my mother, and my sister, equally giving way to their fears for me, vainly looked to each other for support. And what a task for my brother .... to be obliged to laugh at their fears while smothering his own!

Early in the month of March the whole village circle dined at my father's house—Milnes, Lumley, Cleavers, etc.; happiness prevailed, and I was glad. After dinner my brother, opening the post-bag, drew out a large Government letter for me. My father's eyes followed it

Major Boothby, 51st Regiment.
Afterwards Sir William Boothby, Bart.
Father of Captain Charles Boothby, R.E.

across the table with infinite disquiet,[26] my mother's with dismay, and Louisa paled a little. Under such eyes it was necessary to command my own countenance.

I told my father calmly that it was an order for foreign service.

Nothing could represent such an order to them in a flattering point of view. All their fears, all their anxieties were to be renewed, and perhaps in the end not to be so happily relieved. I there fore made no comments, but professed that the future now opened to me was flattering to my prospects, and I further added that I considered active service in Europe as a safeguard from the more distant and unhealthy colonies.

But in fact I was but ill satisfied with the summons, for the Austrian war was but vaguely-rumoured, and nothing but the *éclat* and spunk of some dashing and prompt expedition could make going abroad agreeable to me. My own regrets, however, I was once again obliged to smother, and my own tastes to kick downstairs that I might communicate some degree of consistency and firmness to my aching family, and in this task my brother was my second self.

The next day the whole party met again at the Lumleys'. It will appear strange when I say that we were in better spirits than I wished, for in spite of all I could say, they would not abandon the hope that some event or other would put off the expedition.

As the post time drew near, my father grew grave, and I could see he dreaded a final summons; and even as he dreaded, a large Government letter, like the one before, was put into my hand. I dare not look at my father. My mother, to be out of the way, ran upstairs.

When I had glanced over it, with what alacrity did I put into my father's hand what I knew would quiet his old heart and illumine his benignant features. It was a simple counter order.

My mother and sister were not long before dancing with joy. It was an harmonious uproar, very delightful to see, and I joined in it with all my heart; to rejoice when they were rejoicing was too natural to my heart to be restrained.

The next day my brother and myself went to spend a night at Welbeck. On returning, the little party met us at the end of the village; they walked slow, and were sorrowful.

The counter order was annulled, and the order for foreign service

---

26. It was by his father's desire that Captain Charles Boothby entered the army instead of preparing for Holy Orders, and this intensified the anguish in parting with his son throughout the war, as was often stated by Captain C. Boothby in later years.

RAFELA, WIFE OF SIR WILLIAM BOOTHBY, BART.
Mother of Captain Charles Boothby, R.E.

in force.

For all that the world holds I would not retrace the bitterness of separation.

My brother drove me to Newark, but I was glad to get rid of him, glad when I had escaped my whole kindred, and was left at liberty to weep without adding to their tears.

To have the business of leave-taking over cheered my spirits. I once more felt free, and turned my thoughts upon my companions, those dear companions with whom for years I had been traversing the seas and the lands of Europe.

The passage to Lisbon was boisterous and disagreeable. We set sail on the 17th March 1809, sprang a leak, were run aboard of in the night, and expected to go down, and, in short, were forced to acknowledge that a transport is full of horror.

We landed at Lisbon on the 2nd April, and found it generally expected that Sir John Craddock would re-embark his army in a very few days. The force under his command was said to amount to 17,000, and Marshal Beresford with his Portuguese was called 25,000.

On the other hand, Soult had taken possession of Oporto with 13,000, or, according to some, 17,000. Victor was menacing the Alemtejo with 40,000, and another movable corps of 10,000 had shown itself in the neighbourhood of Ciudad Rodrigo.

Taking this rumoured state of things for granted, the re-embarkation of the army (to a man that knew the nature of Iberian troops) seemed at the first glance to be the most salutary measure that could be adopted.

Lisbon, 2nd April 1809.

My dearest Lou—After a disagreeable voyage we arrived in the Tagus today at two o'clock. I do not intend this for a letter, but to take the first opportunity to tell you of my safe arrival.

The French have taken Oporto, and we are supposed to be in force on the frontier.

I would make a bet that I see you again before the expiration of the summer, for they dare not stay to come in contact with the French army, at least I think so.

Nothing ever was more dead than this town. Oh, intolerably dead! No news here.

I shall write longer by the next opportunity.

With every best spring of the heart to you all,   Charles.

Lisbon and the Tagus

To one who enters the Tagus in a fine season there is something inexpressibly captivating whereever he turns his eyes.

The magnificent rock or mountain, forming a gigantic portal to the mouth of the river, is remarkable for the richness and variety of colour, the grandeur of its size, and the wildness and taste of its form.

From this feature, towards Lisbon, towns, orange groves, forts, and palaces make every yard a picture, and as he approaches Lisbon the size and style of the buildings advance; the great convents, dazzling white, the activity of the great road, the grinning batteries, the fury of the bar, the whirling of the current, the antique richness and eminent shape of the Tower of Belim, and then the splendid burst of the city, with her thronged quays and mounting palaces, will long prevent the visitor from perceiving that the southern bank of the river has nothing but loftiness to recommend it.

A traveller who has seen Messina from the Straits immediately knows what is wanting to Lisbon, viewed from the Tagus.

Messina presents to his view all that can be beautiful in a superb city, embosomed in all that is luxuriant and romantic in Nature.

At the foot of her fair hills she occupies, with a splendid and uniform length of architecture, the margin of the sea, and is even better seen through the light fretwork of masts and rigging, upon which sailors of all nations and in all costumes busily twine their pliant forms, adding to her inanimate beauties an interesting display of wealth and commerce. The city is backed by hills, clothed with the most various and luxuriant vegetation; some are crowned by forts and covered with the brightest verdure, which Flora has enamelled with a lavish hand; others hang umbrageous woods or many-coloured thickets over their wild precipices. Upon the slopes of these hills, rising above each other in theatric pride and architectural magnificence, grand slashes of palace, convent, and church are nested in this beautiful bed of vegetable profusion.

On the other hand, the Italian mountains, which may be called the other bank of this azure river, display every imaginable charm to snatch his eyes from a successful rival. "Beautiful! thrice beautiful! incomparable Messina!" he exclaims. "Never did mine eyes behold, nor my imagination form, a scene whose laughing charms surpassed, or even equalled, thine."

After this he looks upon Lisbon, towering upon her hills, a vast mass of splendid structures. All is building; a house-seller's shop, a proud and pompous city stretching her sceptre over the red waves of the hasty Tagus.

"Queen of the river with the golden waves," says the courteous traveller, "thy magnificent appearance excites my admiration. Permit me to tread upon thy spacious marts, to enter thy palaces, to contemplate and wonder at thy riches."

He pushes for the shore, where disappointment awaits him, conducts him over all parts of the city, serves him at dinner and prepares his bed, reconducts him to his ship, and with him ascends the side, from whence he will no longer delight in those beauties which he knows to be deceptive.

The streets of Lisbon are generally good, and many of them fine; there are no mean houses, and the greater part are handsome and uniform in height and size. There are but few squares, and those are not remarkable.

The quays are very fine, and some noble streets give upon them through magnificent gates, particularly the Rua Aurta, or Street of the Jewellers and Gold-workers. This street, quite straight, broad, and handsomely built, begins at the principal square and issues through a superb gate upon the quay, where a colossal equestrian statue gives it an imposing termination.

But the shops of this street, though abounding in precious stones and precious metal, are extremely mean and exactly alike, each containing a little working equipage for the jeweller (at which he sits), and the window displays a few clumsy glazed boxes, in which his precious commodities are stored.

But as these shops, though mean, are the best, the buyer, being pressed for the want of a commodity, is obliged to hunt for it. The art of alluring money from the pocket of the passenger by a rich and astonishing display of merchandise which he does not want, carried to its height in London, seems in Lisbon to be totally unknown.

The private houses are, some of them, superbly built and richly furnished, but scarcely any of them are commodious, and there is nothing that can be called the environs of a capital.

A public garden, which, though sheltered and well kept, is small, formal, and uninteresting; and one theatre, which, though formerly supplied with the first Italian performers, would not be admired at a provincial town in England. The equipages, although of course diminished in number, absolutely surprise by their barbarity; a clumsy little body, seated upon two huge leathern straps, enormous wheels, and two noble mules, is the only thing to be seen in the shape of a carriage; and from the melancholy relics of the court, which I had an opportunity of observing, I should doubt if it ever exhibited any elegance or splendour.

The streets are not only (even in this burning weather) covered with dry filth and squalid rags, but are lined with naked beggars and disgusting cripples, who bare and often augment their deformities and afflictions to arouse the dormant compassion of the rich.

But however laughable, it is really dreadful to walk in these streets by night, for your foot slides about in soft things, and the whizzing over head and the splash! splash! splash! that assails your ears make you expect to be covered with refuse every moment, for the city is not lighted at all—a circumstance which must have been formerly as favourable to assassination as it is now to these nightly discharges.

If in the night it is to the last degree shocking to walk the streets of Lisbon, it is not very agreeable during the day. The inequality of the ground fatigues, the importunity of the beggars plagues, and the filth of the streets offends you, while nothing remarkable to the right or left diverts the peevishness of disgust or rewards the diligence of curiosity. There are no hotels, nor inns, at least that can serve a decent man.

I cannot leave Lisbon without noticing the aqueduct, which is one of the most stupendous and striking structures I ever beheld. It stretches right across a deep valley, and without attempting to recollect its dimensions or to speak accurately on the subject, the impression it has left with me is that a first-rate, with royals and studding-sails set, could pass through the principal arch without touching in any part. To stand under this arch is almost stupefying, and the gigantic size of the whole is well illustrated by some houses close to it.

Residence in Lisbon

April 1809.—As my stay is remembered with indifference, it was not marked by any high degree of satisfaction. Although I did not pretend to form a deliberate opinion upon the affairs of the Peninsula, yet my involuntary belief was that there would be no campaign.

I considered Sir John Moore's retreat as a lesson likely to teach caution to the British Government, and that they would not now venture to stake the flower of her army on the fate of Spain against the wishes of the nation, seeing that they could hardly answer for having done so when the popular voice was loud in their favour. I thought that unless the Spaniards themselves demonstrated that, in a military light, they could balance their enemies, and were capable in the line of operations of supporting their character as the main army, (which hitherto they had plainly shown they could not do), any further assistance of British troops would be firmly withheld.

The character of the commander-in-chief at that time confirmed me in this opinion respecting the intentions of the Government. Because he was not a man of known military talents, and it was likely enough that, since the employment of General Whitelock, Sir Henry Dalrymple, and Sir Harry Burrard, the favourite principle with our latter statesmen—"that experience and reputation are not required in a fully instructed general"—had been abandoned.

As I considered the kingdom of Portugal incapable of defence, except by an army nearly equal to the offensive one, so I felt assured that when the crisis of its fate arrived, a British army that sought to protect it would "stand alone."

I was led to believe that so soon as a very superior French army should have leisure to move against Portugal, the British army would withdraw and resign her to a fate which it could not control.

As these ideas, however erroneous and indiscreet, possessed my mind, in spite of the warlike breathings of some that I conversed with, I could not help considering my return to England as neither improbable nor very remote, and instead, therefore, of bracing myself for the field, I considered how I might render the time I passed at Lisbon as agreeable as might be, in which pursuit I expected much assistance from some letters of recommendation of which I was the bearer.

The letters on which I most depended were given me by a dear friend and relation to an Englishman of the first rank and consequence in Lisbon, who was invested with a delegated power, and supreme in his particular department, and as this personage had his family at Lisbon, an introduction to him had a very promising aspect.

My other letter, given me by a military acquaintance, was to an Austrian *chevalier*, also a person of consequence in Lisbon, residing there with his family.

I could not in reason expect any great things from being the bearer of a letter from a person with whom I had no particular intimacy, and of which I was not the particular object, but only mentioned as being so good as to take charge of the letter. I carried both on the same day.

The Austrian *chevalier* was laid up with the gout. I left the letter and a card.

The Englishman was also laid up with the gout. I left a letter for himself and another for his lady, and with each a card, and having thus arranged my lines I returned.

The next morning I received a note from the Austrian, contrived with the most engaging and elegant politeness, the substance of which was, that the *chevalier*, sensible of the honour I had done him in bringing him a letter from his friend and mine, trusted that I would dispense with the ceremony of visiting, in favour of an invalid, and allow him and his family to make an acquaintance from which they promised themselves great pleasure, and that, when he had made my acquaintance, he trusted he should be able to persuade me to give him the pleasure of my company as much as I could, and to be a frequent inmate in his house.

It was not long before I made a second visit, and though the *chevalier* was still in bed, yet his daughters were so good as to receive me, and that in so agreeable and sincere a manner, accompanied by such an honest invitation from their father, that, very much pleased, I was resolved it should not be my fault if I did not reap the full advantages of such engaging conduct.

My story with respect to the Englishman is sooner told. The fate of my letters to him will perhaps never be known, as he took not the slightest notice of them or their carrier.

I was billeted in the house of an obliging Italian in the best street, where the commander-in-chief, the Engineer mess, and everything that it was desirable to be near to, were situated.

The mess was very bad, but the mates (as is almost always the case in the corps to which I have the pleasure to belong) were very good and entertaining. Burgos, Mortimer, and myself formed an indissoluble trio, from which union I cannot express the pride and pleasure I have derived for several years, and which I hope will last me through life.

Besides Burgos and Mortimer were several interesting characters which I shall have occasion to notice as I go along, and among others was little Archer, a friend of my boyhood; Captain Notpat, whom I scarcely knew; and Captain Packman, convivial, festive, and good-natured to a great degree, and several younger men. Our chief, a man of indisputable worth and bland manners, used also to honour us with his society.

I had not dined here many days before my little friend Archer took me into his room and desired me to carry his defiance to Captain Notpat, who had offended him beyond reparation.

Before I inquired into particulars I reviled my little friend for being too warlike in this particular, as it was not the first nor the second time that I had known him in similar circumstances. He defended himself as well as he could, declared himself averse to duelling, and said he should be very glad if the captain would act so as to let the affair end peaceably.

Upon this I declared myself very ready to act in quality of mediator if the affair would admit of adjustment, and he would promise to be ruled by my advice, but, at the same time, I declared my unvarying resolution not to interfere if matters took a hostile turn.

Fully master then of my friend's story, and armed with full powers to treat, I knocked at the captain's door. He was not gone to bed, and seemed preparing for a field-day.

He received me involuntarily as his adversary's second, and ceremoniously begged me to be seated.

My friend, I found, had stated the matter very fairly. The captain had been provoked at table rather by a teasing manner than any tangible offence, and in revenge he had told my friend in broad terms that he asserted an untruth, and that he might consider the accusation in any light he pleased. Now, though the captain is a man whose good qualities do sink his imperfections into insignificance, yet had he some certain simplicity or want of usage of the world unfitting his situation and line of life, and this laid him a little open to quizzing, a game at which my friend was not unskilled and much too apt; but fighting is not the way to oppose quizzing, and it appeared to me that injustice and fairness the captain stood as the unprovoked assailant.

I represented with what force I could the melancholy consequences which might ensue, and which he must be sensible would be laid at his door. "You acknowledge," said I, "that you gave an insult which you knew could not be passed over, but which you were determined should stop the provoking manner which my friend had for some time pointed at you? Is this the only way in which you can oppose the flippancy of a boy? You have given him an insult which obliges him to call you out, for unless you do away the insult, I will never advise him not to do what I would do myself; and have you turned over in your mind what may be the state of things tomorrow evening?

The best that can happen to you, according to my opinion of your feelings, is to receive your adversary's bullet; and in that case have you reflected upon what grounds you think yourself entitled to close the days of your parents in misery, and to cast a lasting grief upon all your relations? Perhaps tomorrow evening that youth against whom you have no enmity, with whom you have lived in friendship, and whom you know to be worthy, will be stretched in the ghastliness of a violent death, and weltering in the blood which you have lightly shed. What will be your feelings on looking at such a spectacle, the entire work of your own hands? It will not be his fault, for if he submits to an insult he will be despised, and he had better die; but by sending me to you he has opened the door to atonement, and I expect the proof of your courage and magnanimity will be to make it with candour, than which nothing is more noble or more suitable to the character of a gentleman and a man of honour."

The captain did my address the honour to open his eyes, and saw that it would be infinitely better to avoid an action. He wrote a candid note, to which my friend returned a friendly answer.

I was thanked by both parties, and retired at 2 o'clock a.m., extremely satisfied with myself to have gained so important and very difficult a victory, for my dispute with the Captain was much longer than boots it to set down.

On the 4th April a fleet of transports, having on board six regiments under the orders of General Hill, entered the Tagus, which force was landed on the 5th, and incorporated with the army of Portugal, and on the 6th the regiments of which it was composed marched by different routes to join the respective brigades to which Sir J. Craddock's arrangements attached them.

The arrival of this force, and still more the rumoured appointment of Sir A. Wellesley to the command in Portugal, turned the train of my ideas; and soon after there followed the general cry of "Forward," and an intimation to us that we had better mount ourselves as fast as possible.

Whether this bold determination were caused by the Austrian War (which was no longer uncertain), and extended to the liberation of Spain, or whether it were supposed that Soult had put himself into a *cul-de-sac,* and the campaign had no further object than to destroy him, I could not judge, because I was ignorant of the amount of the French force actually in Spain, and also ignorant of the nature and extent of the Spanish forces, with which in that country we must of necessity co-operate.

It was, however, pretty certain that knocks were toward, and so it behoved to provide myself with a thick doublet.

The rest of my residence in Lisbon, but a few days, was fully taken up in buying horses and in making travelling arrangements. I was so lucky as to get a wee mulette worth her weight in gold, and I called her Sukey.

When the French entered Oporto by storm, the most important capture they made was two British officers of engineers. Captain Goldfinch and Lieutenant Thompson (a boy). Now Captain Goldfinch left at Lisbon in charge of Captain Packman a fine red-brown stallion, a horse fiery in his gait, gentle in his curvets, soft in his manage, swift in his courses, and no mauler of leather. Thirty pounds was the price that had been paid for him, at which sum he was offered to me, upon condition that in case of the owner's return it should be at his option to reclaim him. I snatched at this offer, for the horse if sold outright would have fetched half as much more. So far, so well, my charger and my baggager were excellent. I now only wanted a second charger, and the devil and Burgos advised me to buy an English mare that was worn to the bones, but might be got into condition and be worth double what was asked.

This was downright gambling, and I lost, as will appear in the sequel.

In the arrangements made by the chief engineer, Burgos and myself were attached to the right column, consisting of a brigade of Guards under General Harry Campbell, and a brigade of Infantry under General A. Campbell, who in the absence of General Sherbrooke commanded the column.

Now General Sherbrooke and General H. Campbell were Nottinghamshire friends, and therefore the Guards were likely to be forward; this, added to the society of Burgos as a campaigning chum, was the very arrangement for which I was disposed to intrigue. It had, however, taken place in consequence of changes in the distribution of the army, for Burgos had gone to another division under a former plan two days ago, but was now to receive orders to join me as soon as possible. Captain Notpat received sudden orders to go to Abrantes in pursuance of an application from the Marshal Beresford. Captain Packman was to move with the Chief, as well as my friend Mortimer, which, with a few others, formed the party *du génie* moving with headquarters.

Now my servant's name was Louis, and he was an Italian. Louis, when I picked him up, looked like a very decayed gentleman, his clothes having the cut gentle, but the thread bare, the assortment incongruous, and the articles ill-adapted to his shape. His Hessian boots came above his knees, and were partly obscured by the eaves of his nankeen pantaloons, that had been washed so often as would perhaps have made a Blackamoor white. The warp and the woof of a blue spotted waistcoat were disunited in the pockets and buttons, and his coat was made for a much larger man. His hat was broken in that part of the brim which meets the hand in salutations. His hair was sandy, lanky, long, and dishevelled.

On a dirty shirt was displayed a large brooch, the *gage d'amour* of some sentimental lass, for he had that sleek, effeminate, sodden, yet bearded visage often thought handsome in pictures by means of regular features, and known to be taking in reality among some of the opposite sex. He was about thirty, had a sepulchral voice, and seemed to have destroyed his constitution; yet was he a wit and an accomplished *beau* in his own circle, and very probably styled "the charming Louis."

He got me my milk and eggs of a morning very carefully, but I saw that he was no Bernardo. When I consulted Louis on the line of march, he informed me with much respect that he was unable to walk from infirmity, and seeing me embarrassed about my mare's sore back, he was so active and obliging as to seek out one who was willing to make a swap with me.

The beast offered in exchange was so rippish that I rejected him, and endeavoured to patch the matter by hiring a beast for Louis the next day, which was to be his care, and so all things were arranged for my departure.

I had taken leave of the Austrian *chevalier*, and performed all due and accustomed rights, nor had I any regret at the thoughts of quitting this celebrated city. I write letters home.

Lisbon, Sunday, April 9.

My dearest Mamsey—We have a report here that Sir Arthur Wellesley is at hand. I have no expectation of any actual service against the French, for their force in this part of the world is so superior to ours (and will, I am convinced, continue so) that I have no doubt of our quitting the country as soon as they turn their attention to us.

But if unexpectedly they should, mistaking our force, or too confident, advance towards us with an equal front, we shall drub them well.

When I come to you again, which I guess will be before winter, I shall stay a long, long time. I have been obliged to lay out an immense sum on horses, which are immoderately dear.

I have managed so, however, as that I shall not lose much, in case of being obliged to leave them behind. Ask Louisa if she would like the prettiest little mulette that ever was?

You must not expect long letters, for I am very busy. And when one's mind is called aside by fifty things at once, one cannot write a gossipy letter.

I have sent B. twenty pages about Spain, and he will send it to you, if you desire. It will complete my journal.

I wrote to General Stewart as soon as I got here, and have a very kind communicative letter from him in return. He is at no great distance, and I think we may meet ere long.

General Sherbrooke, too, I have seen, who appears remarkably well.

I expect to quit Lisbon in a day or two.

Give my immense love to dear old Dad, etc., etc.——Yours, my dearest Mamsey,   Charles.

Departure from Lisbon

April 16, 1809.—About the middle of the month of April I left the capital of Portugal. I was to bear-lead a party of artificers and some mules laden with intrenching tools, and among other *désagréments* Mr. Louis came to me already thoroughly exhausted, and could not for love nor money procure a beast.

"Then walk," said I.

"Pardon me," said he, "'tis wholly out of my power."

"Then stay behind," returned I, chafed at his little control over difficulties.

"'Tis what I shall be reduced to," answered he, with a fallen air, "if my master cannot mount me."

"My good fellow," then said I in another tone, "bring me the villain who offered me that misery in exchange for the mare."

He immediately went off, and soon returned.

I was busied with other matters. I was predetermined on the exchange, which was instantly concluded, and gave the order for the march.

My charger bounded under me with a most curvetted agility,

which, added to a very martial neigh, would have made me as proud as Marshal Ney,[27] himself had it not been that the spectacle of my other nag much dashed and diluted the spirit of my exultation. As for Louis he will certainly go to the devil, for there was not somehow room enough on his back whereon to strap my writing-case, for though it was made on purpose for a man's back, Louis had hung it round his neck, and resembled a Jack that had stolen the locket of a giantess. This embarrassed and bruised his arms, which were both employed to tug at the first bridle he had ever laid hands upon, so that the jade, finding no encouragement to violate her own inclination, would go head foremost into a doorway, the upper part of which she found open, and being buffeted away by the indignant housewife, she would swiftly wheel round, to the infinite terror of Louis, and do the same thing by some other door on the opposite side of the street.

Waiting as I was, to see what sort of a figure my valet cut as he went along, and being confounded at the melancholy state of things—my writing-case banging his breast, and the studied awkwardness which he added to the villainy of the beast—I felt there was but one way to save myself from committing some egregious extravagance. So after assailing him with a deal of bad language and worse Italian, I galloped away, and giving a charge respecting the Italian to my good tall sergeant, resolved never to bestow on him another thought, and, very happy to have escaped, I walked my horse along the banks of the Tagus, giving full range to that cheery meditation inspired by youth and fine weather.

COUNTRY BETWEEN LISBON, VILLA FRANCA, AND THE TAGUS

April 1809.—None of the roads leading into the town of Lisbon announce one's approach to a great capital. They are universally paved, the sides of the road overhung with vines and trees, with awkward country houses, and now and then a tasteless palace.

The road from Cintra to Lisbon by Ociras is the best furnished, and more diversified by the contrivances of wealth than any by which I have approached that metropolis.

By the right bank of the Tagus to Santarem nothing is at all interesting until Sacavem. The banks of the Tagus are very tame here as to scenery, and at Sacavem, or a little above it, fenny islands of considerable breadth divide the river into two main streams, which begin about thirteen leagues from the mouth of the Tagus, and end about

---

27. Said to be the proudest man in France.

seven leagues.

I have never had any opportunity of examining the localities of this part of the river, but its banks are not formidable.

But to return to my ride on the road to Villa Franca, at which place I arrived in the afternoon.

The *Juez de Fuéro* happened to be reviewing his lands bordering the Tagus, and was up to his ears in vegetation. I sent to him, but in vain. He walked from one field to another very composedly, discussing the produce with some other land-learned man, and as my patience began to exhaust. Colonel Perponcher arrived on a very fine black horse.

The colonel is a Dutchman who had long served the British, and when I first knew him commanded in the island of Gozo, in which were no other troops than a battalion of Dillon's, which (when we met at Villa Franca) was still in the Mediterranean, whither he intended to proceed to resume the command.

"Well," said I, "how do you get on. colonel, with your brigade?"

"Wat brigaade? Wo tol you I av a brigaade?"

"I was told that you were appointed to the command of two battalions of Portuguese."

"Well, if I was? You call two battalions brigaade? Pretty brigaade! Ha! ha! ha!"

"Why, some of our brigadiers have no more than two regiments under them. What do you call a brigade?"

"Ah, that is de very thing, by ——, with you. A general is nothing, because you av general for all the two regiments. Why, in the Austrian service! Ha! ha! Brigaade! You call that a brigade?"

It was only now and then that the colonel committed a little agreeable foreignness in speaking English; and as I knew him to be a gentlemanlike, well-informed man, and believed him to be an officer of great merit, I was not discouraged by his crustiness, the cause of which I determined to find out; and therefore letting the matter drop, I told him that if, as I supposed, he wanted the *Juez de Fuéro*, he must go to the river for him, as I had endeavoured to fish him out in vain.

"What," said I, turning to his servant, "why don't Sr. Juez come? Is he a Frenchman?"

Here Colonel Perponcher interrupted me with some warmth, and advised me to be more prudent. "These sort of things," said he wisely, "won't do with them, for —— sake take care; you don t know what you may do."

I could no longer forbear laughing at the subtlety of his ill-humour, which vented itself in this manner under the appearance of *sagesse*, for he had too much discrimination not to perceive that my question was calculated to spur the judge to show by his alacrity in assisting Englishmen that he was not a Frenchman, the very name of which was plague, pestilence, and famine to a Portuguese. The colonel, seeing that I really could not help laughing, began to smile himself, and proposed that we should lodge together, to which I readily assented. The *juez*, having returned up to the breech in wholesome soil, gave us the billet we desired. On leaving him I observed that my charger was dead lame.

The death of a first cousin would in numerous instances be less distressing than the lameness of one's best horse at the moment that his services are indispensable. We were conducted to a large house with fine stables, the groom of which knew perfectly well what ailed my horse, recommended fomentation of hot wine mixed with hog's lard, honey, and cow dung, and assured me it would be of no consequence.

I eagerly believed what he said, because if I had not I should have been unhappy all the evening, and if the fellow lied, tomorrow morning would be time enough to grieve. "Sufficient for the day is the evil thereof." Our host was a wealthy Portuguese, and had some guests of his own nation already in his house, an elderly man with his son, a youth of sixteen, very tall, good-looking, and intelligent, also, what is extremely rare for a Portuguese, speaking French very well.

The master of the house offered us some biscuit and wine, which we declined. He then asked what we would take.

"Some dinner," we replied.

"Aye," said he, "but that can't be ready till night. Won't you take something first—a bit of water melon or some oranges?"

The idea of fooling away a lusty appetite upon marshmallows was equally repugnant to the habits of us both, and so we determined to wait, although I was perfectly up to the management of our host, which was by pulling his own ten o'clock supper a little way back towards nine, and giving our five o'clock dinner a most unfeeling stretch towards the same point to make both ends meet and unite in one meal. As I had been in this predicament some fifty or sixty times before, I summoned my patience and a natural capability I have for fasting, while the colonel saw it grow dark with a mixture of surprise, hunger, and impatience.

Poor Louis, who really believed that it was impossible for him to walk six tedious leagues, or twenty-four miles, arrived completely done, for he had not only surpassed his imagined powers, but had been obliged to bear his part in dragging and heaving that wretched animal that was to have carried him. I found I had been taken in, and determined to make the best of it, and with actual labour the beast was pushed into the stable, where it fell to at the manger with a beastly voracity.

One cause I found of Colonel Perponcher's chagrin was the absence of snuff, and this I was fortunately able to supply, having a large box of Prince's Mixture in my pocket.

We sat together some time talking of the Mediterranean, and of his brother, whom I had met at Gothenburg, and at last he discovered the main cause of his vexation and return to Lisbon nearly as follows:—

"You must understand that in volunteering my services with the Portuguese army, and in determining to meet the very numerous and noisome vexations to which the situation exposed me (implicating my character with the conduct of raw recruits of strange nations and striving to reclaim and organise a mutinous rabble), it is natural to suppose that however well I might wish the righteous cause in which we are assisting these swarths, yet that I should look also for some personal advantage as the attendant of success."

And it was, I suppose, "just this personal advantage" which now seemed more than ever doubtful as time went on.

May 14, 1809.—I heard this morning that Sir Arthur Wellesley has had an action with the enemy.

I was differently and very disagreeably employed, as I went up to Lamego with a British brigade, which was to countenance Beresford and his myrmidons. The enemy came before Lamego, intending, I suppose, to sack and destroy, but finding troops there, they retired. The country is exceedingly strong, and I hoped they would not defend it. It was not my wish to see the Portuguese in action. Let who will take the credit of serving with them, I will not. Accordingly I was very glad to find that the enemy had no intention to dispute the country, either having heard that Soult had been beat, or intending to reinforce him.

Having passed the Douro without halting at Lamego, we stopped at Peizo, and marched the next morning to Amarante.

When about two leagues from our destination it began to rain heavily as if to prepare us for the gloomy, wretched scene that awaited us.

We were thoroughly wet through (I having no baggage) when the beauteous Amarante burst upon our view, the fine-looking houses promising a comfortable rest. What was our aggravated disgust at finding that everything was sacked, burnt, and murdered, not a single house but was completely reduced to its shell wall. Here the venerable master of a mansion lay stretched on his back amid the black ruins of his peaceful habitation, and a ghastly wound disfigured his neck... . . It was a horrid spectacle! ! But I will not go on with the picture, it exceeds description, and swells one's hatred to these ruthless and wanton destroyers.

This place, garrisoned by Portuguese troops under Sylvesan, resisted for two days the French under Loison, (the plague of Portugal), and so this inhuman monster thus revenged himself.

Abrantes, June 18, 1809.

My Louisa—I heard that there had been blows, and wrote to tell you I was out of harm's way.

Nothing can be finer than the passage of the Douro, which in his despatches Sir A. Wellesley makes too little of; in short, it is plain he cannot write, for he did the same at Vimiera. However, he is dashing and able, and if a fair game lies before him, he will not, I hope, be able to cover the fame of his victories by clumsy relations. . . .

Captain Goldfinch of the Engineers, with a fine little Scotch boy (a lieutenant), fell with Oporto into the hands of the French, and made their escape in the late bustle. The respect (they say) which all French who were at Corunna bear to the memory of Moore, and to the English in general, is quite gratifying.

They recite a dispute between a French officer and several others, the former maintaining that the English were victorious, the others, not.

Our advocate read General Hope's letter,[28] asking at every sentence, "*N'est-il pas vrai? N'est-il pas bien dit?*" etc., etc., and when he came to the simile of General Wolfe's death he made a very elegant admiration of it.

I was attached to the brigade of General Tilson, who is my friend, and it was with the Portuguese army. We went to Chaves, and penetrated into Galicia. I took the place of an officer who

---

28. See Appendix.

fell ill, otherwise I belong to the brigade of Guards under Harry Campbell, whom I like greatly.

In addition to my mortification at being out of the way, the first notification I had of General Paget's arrival was accompanied by the news of his having lost a limb, my sorrow for which wholly defeated any attempt to rejoice at our successes. People who did not know him talked a vast deal about the manner in which he bore his sufferings. I say nothing of it, because I know him to be perfect, and know upon what he leans.... It is a comfort to learn that the loss is not likely to affect his constitution, as he is said to recover wonderfully fast.

Devil a bit of nobleness have I about me, my dear Lou. I cannot bear this infernal war, that has killed Moore and maimed Paget, disputing about a country that—— But I won't talk politics. If Austria, though beaten and overrun, can entertain Buonaparte for a season, perhaps Wellesley may do something for the Spaniards.

The French fight us very ill, whether from a want of hatred or courage. If what had happened to Soult had happened to an English general, he would have been disgraced forever, for he was shamefully surprised.

But England, although she has every right to expect worse generals than France, is much more rigid with them in articles of skill and judgment; for if she can by any means attribute a disaster to the error of a general, she is not only savage but sanguinary. And this makes very good generals and very brave men so vastly afraid of responsibility, that when they assume command they appear cowardly and indecisive. . . . Don't let there be a shade of melancholy in your letters; it disquiets me vastly. Why should you be melancholy? God is very good to us, and we must not pine if we are not always all together as if in heaven. Therefore write very comically about friends and home. . . .

Eternal blessings crown my darling Lou, and guardian angels hover over her. Charles.

Coria, July 8, 1809.

It is quite a relief, dearest Lou, to be transferred from the filthy styes of the Portuguese to the clean houses of the Spaniards. And as I am shaking off the dust contracted in Portugal, so I am scraping my tongue of those odious inarticulate sounds which compose their language, and gargling vinegar that my throat may be capable of touching with the true Castilian burr the energetic language of Spain.

Alas! I have lost one of my first comforts, a new blue, patent, silver-mounted, morocco writing-case; all my letter-paper, pens, ink, letters, secrets, verses, etc., etc.; also dear Lady N——'s series of useless boxes—all lost by the rascal Pedro, Bernardo's opposite in everything. The devil take it, though I have lost it a week ago, I cannot recover my temper.

Hitherto I pass my time very pleasantly. I have got a fine young engineer to take care of, whom I row, all the time that he does not sleep, about his vanity; not but that I acknowledge myself to be as vain as he, but that I defy him to have found it out, unless I had told him of it. He is coming into very fine order.

Poor Harry Campbell has been some time unwell, but I hope he is now throwing it off.

General Sherbrooke, to whose division I belong, makes it very pleasant to me. I dine with him mostly, and like him vastly. I think of him very highly as a general. He thinks of Sir John Moore just as I do.

Tomorrow we go to Plaçentia, which is much larger than this very pretty town.

Here there is an old castle and walls inhabited by cranes, which interest me very much, perching on the house-tops and church steeples, and cowering over the town.

That fellow there, I at first thought was standing upon the stalk of a weather-cock, but I found by a spy-glass that they were his own long legs, with his great feet happy upon the stone ball.

The air seems fresher here than in Portugal. Sweet F. E. wrote me such a dear note in Mamsey's letter. I wonder how she could contrive to make it so pleasant and yet so proper. For me, I could do no such thing. Were I to write to her warm, kind, affectionate words, my heart would dictate fluently enough, but I am sure they would not pass the school of decorum.

The mistress would say, "You must scratch out there 'dearest F.' Lop away this 'love' and that 'love'"; and so word by word I should see my poor letter robbed of all its graces, looking like a tobacconist's with "Humble servant to command" at the bottom.

What if I should not fill this sheet! It is very big, and I have to give my letter to General Sherbrooke in a quarter of an hour, and you see I write very close.

My poor chum has just lost a horse, which, though I put on outward signs of condolence, I am not sorry for. As to being bridled, he never could think of such a thing. He would always go when he liked it, and where also. He would look very stupid, to entice the unwary behind him; and then, with both feet and all his might, lunge out, as much as to say, "D—— thee, I have thee now." In the same manner he would most innocently pretend to come and rub his head upon you in a dawdling, sleepy sort of way, and then get your leg or arm in his jaws and try as hard as he could to crack it. For these and many other pretty accomplishments

His master loved him dearly.
And mourns him now sincerely,
While I say, "Poor thing" merely,
But feel at heart quite cheerly.
We'll go as fast, or nearly,
Without, as with him, clearly.

Now to take my leave, and remain, as ever, your   Charles.

Castel Branco, July 1809.

I received dear Mamsey's letter, by which my mind was relieved respecting her anxiety.

The moment I heard there was fighting I wrote, but feared you would not get my letter in time enough to be spared that cruel suspense.

It will at least be some time before you need begin to think of being anxious again.

The French, it is understood, are retiring very fast, and will probably not dispute anything south of the Ebro. A long march is before us . . . we only know as far as Placentia. I miss my poor Bernardo very much, and would give anything to meet with him again, which I think I may do, if we go towards Madrid.

This fine battle of the Danube has cheered us again, perhaps ere you receive this you will know how fallaciously; but I will hope that you are in possession of recent victories for which we are yet to Huzza! [29]

---

29. The continuation of the *Journals of Captain Charles Boothby* will be found in *A Prisoner of France*.

Appendix

Between St. Eufemia and Monte Leone,
July 6, 1806.

My dearest Father—In the first place I give you joy of a most complete victory gained by a body of English troops over a French force very superior in number, another proof that the extraordinary bravery of our countrymen is not solely to be attributed to salt provisions and sea air. This army had been reviled as fugitive in consequence of the wise retreat of Sir J. Craig from Naples.

General Regnier, the old calumniator of British troops, had threatened a speedy invasion of Sicily.

It was generally believed that the Calabrians, a ferocious race, held the French in abhorrence, and Sir J. Stuart's plan, as far as I have been able to make out, was to raise the country—arm it—and then give the people a lesson in the art of war by beating the French. It was presumed that the effect of this would be to render the country uninhabitable to the French, and finally to deliver the territory from the general scourge of continental tranquillity.

Sir John left Messina on the night of the 30th of June, in pursuance of his object, which was then unknown.

At about midnight of the 1st of July the transports were collected in the Bay of St. Eufemia. Orders were then given for the landing at two o'clock. It was not expected that there was any enemy at hand, but upon the Light Infantry running forward, a firing commenced, which continued in bush-fighting the greater part of the morning, the enemy consisting of about three hundred Poles, scattered about in a very thick brushwood, they retiring and the Light Infantry pursuing. . . . They ran at the enemy like lions, and the event of the day was—about twenty of the enemy wounded (some badly), two officers, and about one hundred prisoners.

We had only one man wounded.

The army then took a position, one flank upon the town of Nicastro, and the other below the village of Eufemia. Until the 2nd, the reports concerning the enemy were various.... On the 2nd the enemy was discovered on the heights above the plain of Maida. He exhibited lights at night, and it was reported that he intended battle. In the course of the next day some information was obtained, and the enemy then was supposed to consist of between two and three thousand men. On the night of the 3rd the order of march was given to commence at two o'clock.

The enemy still continuing his lights, sometime after daylight it was suspected that he had withdrawn. His position, however, was at right angles with the beach, and so far from it as to admit of operations on his left flank, which was weak from the nature of the ground. This the enemy could not avoid, from our being masters of the water, upon which was Sir Sidney Smith with a line-of-battle ship and three frigates. The British marched with their flanks in line and centre in column, the right flank on the sea, the left exposed, so that in the approach the corresponding flank of each force was exposed to the operations of the other. The Frenchman, seeing his left threatened, changed his position with admirable order, and formed on the Englishman's left, on which the French cavalry charged.

The 20th regiment, having just landed, immediately advanced in support of this flank to meet the cavalry with fixed bayonets, which forced them to retire, the artillery playing upon their retreat. The French Light Infantry now charged ours, which advanced to meet it. The two regiments were point to point, when at this anxious moment the enemy to a man fled in the utmost confusion, we pursuing. The slaughter of this regiment was dreadful. Other regiments now charged and volleyed, as is usual in battles, and, as I hope will always be the case, the victory fell on us, the enemy flying with the utmost precipitation, and we having no cavalry, he escaped.

The slaughter on the side of the French was immense and almost incredible when compared to ours. In killed, wounded, and taken, it has been estimated at 3000, while ours exactly amounts to so many hundreds. If I were a Frenchman I would tell you what I think of the British troops, but the modesty of an Englishman imposes silence when the merits of his countrymen are the subject. Fighting appears their delight, and they seek the enemy with the ardour of sportsmen; let him, however, drop his arms, and he is safe; let him be wounded, he is pitied and assisted—in short, upon my honour, I think the lion and the lamb are here most strikingly united.

I could recite several interesting anecdotes, such as battles generally give rise to, but I am much hurried. We only lost one officer and forty men killed. The officer's servant had one leg shattered and the other badly wounded, yet his own misery he did not think of. "But my poor master was killed," said he. "I hope, however, the day was ours. Well, then, I die content."

"Here" (said a Highlander) "is this —— brute that has been firing at me and wounded me in so many places."

"Water! water!" cried the wretch. The Highlander revenged himself immediately with his canteen!

A general officer was among the prisoners, severely wounded, and the commander-in-chief was also severely wounded. The French force, from returns taken, is considered to have amounted to upwards of 7,000; ours was 4,500, so that considering the vast superiority and other circumstances in favour of the enemy, the victory was as brilliant as one could wish. . . . An extraordinary coincidence with respect to the armies was observed. General Sir J. Stuart was opposed to General Regnier, a man of acknowledged military eminence, who had called Sir John *a man of no talents*. The two Light Infantries were immediately opposed, as were two regiments of Watteville in the different services. Our Highland Regiment was opposed to their 42nd (to cover embarkation), our 31st to theirs.

After having advanced some miles after the enemy our army marched back to the position it had left in the morning. The action began at half-past eight and the firing ceased at 11 on the 4th of July. On the 5th the army marched to this place near the sea, and about a mile from the field of battle.

I am now sitting on the ground sheltered by a round tent. . . . I write this on my hat. *Adieu*, my dearest father.—Your ever affectionate and dutiful son,　　　　　　　　　　C. Boothby.
July 6, 1806.

Monte Leone, July 11, 1806.

My ever dearest Mother—...The day after I wrote you an account of the battle we advanced some miles beyond the field towards the Adriatic, just under the town of Maida. The enemy had retired to Catanzaro, and it was generally expected that we should seek another battle before he could reinforce himself. It was judged, however, that the coming up with him was precarious, and the advantage of the chance of beating him still more—not adequate to the inconvenience of harassing the victors this burning weather, which reasoning was probably strengthened by the risk of any junction having been formed between two parties of the enemy's force.

No prejudgment would have given victory to five thousand men against eight, supposed to be the best troops in the world, fully prepared for the enterprise against them, having all the local advantages and local knowledge, commanded by a general of the greatest reputation, and particularly for manoeuvring skill.

Our general went into the field under the idea that the force he was to attack was between two and three thousand men.

The fatal error of the French general was that, obstinately blind to experience, he despised his enemy—an enemy which the battles of Egypt should have taught him to consider at least equal to himself. He had suffered prejudice to mislead him until his slaughtered and flying troops and the severe personal wound forced open his eyes; but he opened them too late. In defiance of the general principle to avoid an invading enemy until you have involved him in a country of which he is ignorant, and from your own knowledge are certain to destroy him, General Regnier descended from the advantages of his position to fight front to front in the plain.

With the battle of the 21st of March before his eyes, he tells his troops that those very Egyptian regiments cannot stand the bayonet. The deluded Frenchmen charge with confidence, and, expecting to pursue hares, are met by lions.

The same error which has been so fatal to so many generals was fatal to Menon, and was deservedly still more fatal to Regnier; for Menon could not know us, and Regnier would not.

But I stray from the point.

After staying a day under Maida the troops marched to Monte

Leone, and there the general missed his baggage, which did not turn up until yesterday, when the general's cook gave a very good account of himself. The inhabitants of the country were to be deceived as to the intentions of the retrograde movement, and consequently what conversation could be gleaned from the general's table tended to an advance to Catanzaro.

The troops marched backwards at two in the morning, but the baggage, with a guard of thirty men, not being properly attended to, was not quite so alert, but marched about an hour later towards the enemy, whose outposts (taking this little force for our advanced guard) retired and gave intelligence of the approach of the English army, which, corresponding with the report of our intentions, the enemy left Catanzaro to thirty men commanded by a cook, and retreated with precipitation to the borders of the Adriatic. The quick cook, smelling the rat, squeezed himself into the general's coat and personated the general, until, finding himself neither attacked by the French nor joined by the English, he could retire without disgrace and seek the true situation of his allies.

The design of the march through Calabria was to seize the enemy's garrisons and stores all the way to Reggio, which is just opposite Messina. This has already been done, as Reggio has been taken by a party from Messina, so that we now expect to embark from *Pizzo*, which lies just before this place. But *nothing you know is certain.*

In taking possession of the stores we have seen innumerable papers. One letter from Regnier says,[1] "When I have been with the English I shall come to you. They are only 12,000. I shall very soon finish with them." Somewhere else he says he will take good care that we shall not reach our shipping again. Indeed everything betrays a most ridiculous confidence, arising not only from the consciousness of great merit (which was just), but from a most unreasonable contempt of an enemy which had before shown itself superior. Every prisoner whom I have heard speak upon the subject acknowledges to have been deceived, and condemns the order to charge an unbroken regiment. The French soldiers are generally remarkably fine men.

My dearest mother, I have not written you a very proper letter for a lady, but to make it a little more acceptable it assures you

---

1. Written to a French general at Reggio.

of my perfect health and spirits and constant love and affection to all of you. *Adieu,* my dearest mother.—Your most affectionate and devoted son, C. B.

1808
Expedition to Sweden
Two Letters to Sir Brooke Boothby, Bart., from Captain Charles Boothby[2]

Quite private. Don't speak of this.

July 1, 1808.

My Dear Uncle—We are certainly bound for England. Sir John Moore was made prisoner at Stockholm, and escaped in disguise, having, I suppose, been previously provided with couriers' passes, etc.

I am now going on board the *Victory* to ask Sir John if there will be any objection to your going in this ship, and as no objection can be made, you had better, if it suits you, put yourself afloat as soon as possible, as we shall sail tomorrow.

If you think of any comforts for yourself on the voyage, procure them. We have no tea.

God bless you.

You may as well make use of the boat that brought Jack, bringing him also with you. C. B.

To Sir Brooke Boothby, Bart.,
Seagerlind's Hotel.

2nd July 1808.

My Dear Uncle—The information I sent you yesterday was from the Fountain head, and is indeed perfectly true.

The general found himself, by his instructions, obliged to return to England, but the king wished him to wait for despatches from England. This the general declined, upon which he received a message in the night not to leave Stockholm without the king's consent.

Sir John sent a messenger to embark the army and horses immediately, and then remonstrated through the minister. No attention was paid, until a second remonstrance was made, when the prohibition was repeated.

Sir John then made his escape in his travelling dress. The Secre-

---
2. Written off the coast of Sweden.

tary of Legation drove him beyond the first stage in his curricle, and a messenger was despatched by Mr. Thornton with orders to take him up on the road. This is incredible, but *certainly* true. I went on board the *Victory* yesterday. Sir J. M. was very kind, and went himself to the admiral to get an order for your coming on board this ship (which I carried through its several stages), and she is prepared to receive you, and Mr. Christer will describe her accommodations. If you come you will be sorry to learn that I am not going straight to England, being ordered on board the *Superb*, at the request of Admiral Keats, to *reconnoitre* the little Isle of Sproe in the Belt, after which I shall be sent to England by the first ship of war that goes. Pray, if I do not see you this evening (for I shall not go on board the *Admiral* till tomorrow), communicate this to Edwinstowe. It is an excursion which I am delighted to make, because it is creditable, useful, and agreeable. I hope to see you here this evening. In the meantime believe me ever most affectionately yours, C. B. Your fellow passengers are very pleasant young men—quite young.

Major Cockburn, the general's secretary, arrived today. He reports that on Wednesday the king did not know of Sir John's departure, which took place on Monday. When His Majesty does discover it, he will not unlikely take some very strong, furious measures. Therefore pray do not delay getting off.

1809

Corunna

Before reading the official despatches on the Battle of Corunna it is important to have some idea of the plan adopted by the enemy, and it is with the greatest interest we read that:[3]

> When Buonaparte received intelligence that the British were moving to the Duero," he said, 'Moore is the only general now fit to contend with me; I shall advance against him in person.
>
> Orders were then sent to the Duke of Dalmatia to give way, if attacked, and to decoy the British to Burgos, or as far eastward as possible, and at the same time to push on a corps towards Leon, on their left flank. And should they attempt to retreat,

---

3. Extract from the *Narrative of the Campaign of the British Army in Spain Commanded by His Excellency General Sir John Moore, K.B., etc., etc., etc.* By James Moore, Esq.

he was ordered to impede this by every means in his power. The corps on the road to Badajoz was stopt, and ordered to proceed towards Salamanca, while he himself moved rapidly with all disposable force to Madrid, and the Escurial, directly to Benaventa. Neither Buonaparte nor any of his generals had the least doubt of surrounding the British with between 60 and 70,000 men before they could reach Galicia.

Sir John Moore, as appears both by his letters and his conduct, saw clearly the whole of this plan; he had prepared for the danger, calculated the time, and has acquired the glory of being *the first general who has frustrated Buonaparte.*

LETTER FROM LIEUT.-GEN. SIR DAVID BAIRD TO LORD VISCOUNT CASTLEREAGH, SECRETARY OF STATE.

London Gazette Extraordinary

Downing Street, January 24, 1809.

The Honourable Captain Hope arrived late last night with a Despatch from Lieutenant-General Sir David Baird to Lord Viscount Castlereagh, one of His Majesty's Principal Secretaries of State, of which the following is a copy:—

His Majesty's Ship *Ville de Paris*,
At Sea, January 18, 1809.

My Lord—By the much-lamented death of Lieutenant-General Sir John Moore, who fell in action with the enemy on the 16th instant, it has become my duty to acquaint your Lordship that the French[4] army attacked the British[5] troops in the position they occupied in front of Corunna at about two o'clock in the afternoon of that day.

A severe wound, which compelled me to quit the field a short time previous to the fall of Sir John Moore, obliges me to refer your Lordship for the particulars of the action, which was long and obstinately contested, to the enclosed report of Lieutenant-General Hope, who succeeded to the command of the army, and to whose ability and exertions in direction of the ardent zeal and unconquerable valour of His Majesty's troops is to be at-

---

4. French army over 20,000.
5. British army about 15,000.

tributed, under Providence, the success of the day, which terminated in the complete and entire repulse and defeat of the Enemy at every point of attack.

The honourable Captain Gordon, my *aide-de-camp*, will have the honour of delivering this despatch, and will be able to give your Lordship any further information which may be required.—I have the honour to be, etc.,

D. Baird, Lieut.-Gen.

Right Hon. Lord Viscount Castlereagh.

LETTER FROM LIEUT.-GEN. HOPE TO LIEUT.-GEN. SIR DAVID BAIRD, CONTAINING THE REPORT AFTER THE BATTLE OF CORUNNA, 16TH JANUARY 1809.

His Majesty's Ship *Audacious*
Off Corunna, January 18, 1809.

Sir—In compliance with the desire contained in your communication of yesterday, I avail myself of the first moment I have been able to command to detail to you the occurrences of the action which took place in front of Corunna on the 16th instant.

It will be in your recollection, that about one in the afternoon of that day the enemy, who had in the morning received reinforcements, and who had placed some guns in front of the right and left of his line, was observed to be moving troops towards his left flank, and forming various columns of attack at that extremity of the strong and commanding position which on the morning of the 15th he had taken in our immediate front.

This indication of his intention was immediately succeeded by the rapid and determined attack which he made upon your division, which occupied the right of our position. The events which occurred during that period of the action you are fully acquainted with. The first effort of the enemy was met by the Commander of the Forces, and by yourself, at the head of the 42nd regiment and the brigade under Major-General Lord William Bentinck.

The village on your right became an object of obstinate contest. I lament to say that soon after the severe wound which deprived the army of your services. Lieutenant-General Sir John Moore, who had just directed the most able disposition, fell by a cannon shot. The troops, though not unacquainted with the irreparable loss they had sustained, were not dismayed, but by the most determined bravery not only repelled every attempt of the enemy to gain ground, but actually forced him to retire, although he had brought up fresh troops in support of those originally engaged.

The enemy, finding himself foiled in every attempt to force the right of the position, endeavoured by numbers to turn it. A judicious and well-timed movement which was made by Major-General Paget, with the reserve, which corps had moved out of its cantonments to support the right of the army, by a vigorous attack defeated this intention. The major-general, having pushed forward the 95th (rifle corps) and 1st battalion 52nd regiments, drove the enemy before him; and in his rapid and judicious advance, threatened the left of the enemy's position. This circumstance, with the position of Lieutenant-General Fraser's division (calculated to give still further security to the right of the line), induced the enemy to relax his efforts in that quarter.

They were, however, more forcibly directed towards the centre, where they were again successfully resisted by the brigade under Major-General Manningham, forming the left of your division, and a part of that under Major-General Leith, forming the right of the division under my orders. Upon the left, the Enemy at first contented himself with an attack upon our piquets, which, however, in general maintained their ground. Finding, however, his efforts unavailing on the right and centre, he seemed determined to render the attack upon the left more serious, and had succeeded in obtaining possession of the village through which the great road to Madrid passes, and which was situated in front of that part of the line.

From this post, however, he was soon expelled, with considerable loss, by a gallant attack of some companies of the 2nd battalion 14th regiment, under Lieutenant-Colonel Nicholls. Before five in the evening, we had not only successfully repelled every attack made upon the position, but had gained ground in almost all points, and occupied a more forward line than at the commencement of the action, whilst the Enemy confined his operations to a cannonade, and the fire of his light troops, with a view to draw off his other corps. At six the firing ceased. The different brigades were reassembled on the ground they occupied in the morning, and the piquets and advanced posts resumed their original stations.

Notwithstanding the decided and marked superiority which at this moment the gallantry of the troops had given them over an enemy, who, from his numbers and the commanding advantages of his position, no doubt expected an easy victory, I did not, on reviewing all circumstances, conceive that I should be warranted in departing from what I knew was the fixed and previous determination of the late Commander of the Forces, to withdraw the army on the evening of the 16th for the purpose of embarkation, the previous arrangements for which had already been made by his order, and were in fact far advanced at the commencement of the action.

The troops quitted their position about ten at night with a degree of order that did them credit. The whole of the artillery that remained unembarked, having been withdrawn, the troops followed in the order prescribed, and marched to their respective points of embarkation in the town and neighbourhood of Corunna. The piquets remained at their posts until five on the morning of the 17th, when they were also withdrawn with similar orders, and without the enemy having discovered the movement.

By the unremitted exertions of Captains the Honourable H. Curzon, Gosselin, Boys, Rainier, Serret, Hawkins, Digby, Carden, and Mackenzie of the Royal Navy, who, in pursuance of the orders of Rear-Admiral de Courcy, were entrusted with the service of embarking the army, and in consequence of the arrangements made by Commissioner Bowen, Captains Bowen and Shepherd, and the other agents for transports, the whole of the army was embarked with an expedition which has seldom been equalled. With the exception of the brigades under Major-Generals Hill and Beresford, which were destined to remain on shore until the movements of the enemy should become manifest, the whole was afloat before daylight.

The brigade of Major-General Beresford, which was alternately to form our rearguard, occupied the land front of the town of Corunna; that under Major-General Hill was stationed in reserve on the promontory in rear of the town.

The enemy pushed his light troops towards the town soon after eight o'clock in the morning of the 17th, and shortly after occupied the heights of St. Lucia, which command the harbour. But, notwithstanding this circumstance and the manifold defects of the place, there being no apprehension that the rearguard could be forced, and the disposition of the Spaniards appearing to be good, the embarkation of Major-General Hill's brigade was commenced and completed by three in the afternoon, Major-General Beresford, with that zeal and ability which is so well known to yourself and the whole army, having fully explained, to the satisfaction of the Spanish governor, the nature of our movement, and having made every previous arrangement, withdrew his corps from the land front of the town soon after dark, and was, with all the wounded that had not been previously moved, embarked before one this morning.

Circumstances forbid us to indulge the hope, that the victory with which it has pleased Providence to crown the efforts of the army, can be attended with any very brilliant consequences to Great Britain. It is clouded by the loss of one of her best Soldiers. It has been achieved at the termination of a long and harassing service. The superior numbers and advantageous position of the enemy, not less than the actual situation of this army, did not admit of any advantage being reaped from success. It must be, however, to you, to the army, and to our country, the sweetest reflection, that the lustre of the British arms has been maintained amidst many disadvantageous circumstances.

The army, which had entered Spain amidst the fairest prospects, had no sooner completed its junction, than, owing to the multiplied disasters that dispersed the native armies around us, it was left to its own resources. The advance of the British corps from the Duero afforded the best hope that the south of Spain might be relieved; but this generous effort to save the unfortunate people also afforded the enemy the opportunity of directing every effort of his numerous troops, and concentrating all his principal resources, for the destruction of the only regular force in the north of Spain.

You are well aware with what diligence this system has been pursued.

These circumstances produced the necessity of rapid and harassing marches, which had diminished the numbers, exhausted the strength, and impaired the equipment of the army. Notwithstanding all these disadvantages, and those more immediately attached to a defensive position, which the imperious necessity of covering the harbour of Corunna for a time had rendered indispensable to assume, the native and undaunted valour of British troops was never more conspicuous, and must have exceeded what even your own experience of that invaluable quality, so inherent in them, may have taught you to expect. When everyone that had an opportunity seemed to vie in improving it, it is difficult for me, in making this report, to select particular instances for your approbation.

The corps chiefly engaged were the brigades under Major-Generals Lord William Bentinck and Manningham and Leith, and the brigade of Guards under Major-General Warde.

To these officers, and the troops under their immediate orders, the greatest praise is due.

Major-General Hill and Colonel Catlin Craufurd, with their brigades on the left of the position, ably supported their advanced posts. The brunt of the action fell upon the 4th, 42nd, 50th, and 81st regiments, with parts of the brigade of Guards, and the 26th regiment.

From Lieutenant-Colonel Murray, quartermaster-general, and the officers of the general staff, I received the most marked assistance. I had reason to regret, that the illness of Brigadier-General Clinton, adjutant-general, deprived me of his aid. I was indebted to Brigadier-General Slade during the action, for a zealous offer of his personal services, although the cavalry were embarked.

The greater part of the fleet having gone to sea yesterday evening, the whole being under way, and the corps in the embarkation necessarily much mixed on board, it is impossible at present to lay before you a return of our casualties. I hope the loss in numbers is not so considerable as might have been expected. If I was obliged to form an estimate, I should say, that I believe it did not exceed in killed and wounded from seven to eight hundred; that of the enemy must remain unknown, but many circumstances induce me to rate it at nearly double the above number. We have some prisoners, but I have not been able to obtain an account of the number; it is not, however, considerable.

Several officers of rank have fallen or been wounded, among whom I am only at present enabled to state the names of Lieutenant-Colonel Napier, 92nd regiment. Majors Napier and Stanhope, 50th regiment, killed; Lieutenant-Colonel Winch, 4th regiment, Lieutenant-Colonel Maxwell, 26th regiment, Lieutenant-Colonel Fane, 59th regiment. Lieutenant-Colonel Griffith, Guards, Majors Miller and Williams, 81st regiment, wounded.

To you, who are well acquainted with the excellent qualities of Lieutenant-General Sir John Moore, I need not expatiate on the loss the army and his country have sustained by his death. His fall has deprived me of a valuable friend, to whom long experience of his worth had sincerely attached me. But it is chiefly on public grounds that I must lament the blow. It will be the consolation of everyone who loved or respected his manly character, that, after conducting the army through an arduous retreat with consummate firmness, he has terminated a career of distinguished honour by a death that has given the enemy additional reason to respect the name of a British soldier. Like the immortal Wolfe, he is snatched from his country at an early period of a life spent in her service; like Wolfe, his last moments were gilded by the prospect of success, and cheered by the acclamation of victory; like Wolfe also, his memory will forever remain sacred in that country which he sincerely loved, and which he had so faithfully served.

It remains for me only to express my hope, that you will speedily ht restored to the service of your country, and to lament the unfortunate circumstance that removed you from your station in the field, and threw the momentary command into far less able hands.—I have the honour to be, etc.,

John Hope, Lieut.-Gen.

To Lieutenant-General Sir David Baird, etc., etc., etc.

Last Orders given to the Army of Spain by the Great General, Sir John Moore, K.B.

Headquarters, Coruña,
January 16, 1809.

G. O.—The Commander of the Forces directs that commanding officers of regiments will as soon as possible after they embark make themselves acquainted with what ships the men of their regiments are embarked, both sick and convalescents, and that they will make out the most correct states of their respective corps; that they will state the number of sick present, also those left at different places, and mention at the back of the return where the men returned on command are employed.

His Majesty has been pleased to appoint Lt.-Col. Douglas to be Assist. Qr.-Mr.-General. Appt. to bear date 5th Decr. 1808.

Hon. Capt. James Stanhope, 1st Guards, is appointed extra *aide-de-camp* to the C. of the Forces.

John Moore.

A Prisoner of France

Contents

Introduction	199
Chapter 1	203
Chapter 2	213
Chapter 3	218
Chapter 4	224
Chapter 5	227
Chapter 6	230
Chapter 7	234
Chapter 8	238
Chapter 9	242
Chapter 10	247
Chapter 11	252
Chapter 12	255
Chapter 13	260
Chapter 14	267
Chapter 15	275
Chapter 16	281
Chapter 17	288
Chapter 18	296

Chapter 19	300
Chapter 20	307
Chapter 21	315
Chapter 22	321
Chapter 23	324
Chapter 24	359

Introduction

Charles Boothby, third son of Sir William Boothby, Bart., and Dame Rafela, his wife, was born at Dublin in 1786. After a few years at the well-known school of Uppingham, he was sent to the Royal Military Academy, Woolwich. Having passed the examination there, he joined the Royal Engineers. His first year of service was spent uneventfully on a home station. Early in 1805 his career began in earnest. He was then ordered for foreign service under Sir James Craig, with whom he took part in the campaign at Naples. Next year he served under Sir John Stuart in Calabria, sharing in the Battle of Maida and in other military operations, for which all the officers received the thanks of Parliament—those of the Royal Engineers the especial thanks.

Afterwards, for a short time, Boothby was employed in Sicily. Twice he was sent on services of reconnaissance on the enemy's coast by Major Lefebure, who made written acknowledgment of the young soldier's "zealous, unremitting, and useful professional support." When Sir John Moore commanded in Sicily, Boothby, by that time a Captain, was entrusted with the task of preparing the fortress of Augusta for immediate defence. Towards the end of 1807 he left Sicily, under Captain Burgoyne, with an expedition to Portugal conducted by Sir John Moore. The expedition was too late to accomplish the purpose with which it started, and was back in England in January 1808.

Boothby's inactivity lasted only for a brief space. Early in the spring of the same year he sailed for Sweden, under Captain Squire, with the army of Sir John Moore, and surveyed an island in the Great Belt, which, if necessary, was to be fortified. Home again in July, he followed Sir John Moore to Portugal, put himself under the orders of Lieutenant-Colonel Fletcher at Cintra, and, as he himself wrote, "assisted in the laborious duties of forming topographical documents of the kingdom of Portugal." When Moore advanced into Spain, in the same year, Boothby was attached to the reserve, which was commanded by General Paget, and made journeys in search of information about the roads and the regions over which the army was to pass. He was also employed, in advance, in estimating the enemy's strength and watching his movements. After the retreat he was despatched by the commander-in-chief on confidential service; after which he embarked at Vigo, and rejoined the army at Corunna. At the battle there, on the 16th of January 1809, he assisted in the construction of the works thrown up to cover the embarkation of the troops which was to ensue. In England, at the end of the month, again, with his comrades-in-arms, Boothby received the thanks of Parliament.

Early in March he accompanied lieutenant-Colonel Fletcher to Portugal, in which Sir Arthur Wellesley had assumed the command. In the combined operations upon Oporto he served with a British Brigade under Marshal Beresford, who commanded the native troops. Immediately afterwards he joined the British army at Abrantes, and was attached to General Sherbrooke, second in command.

From that time onwards, in the narrative which follows. Captain Boothby's adventures in war time are told in his own words. In these present days, when it seems not improbable that the century, according to the habit of centuries, will die in flames. Captain Boothby's story of the adversities of war, and of the courtesies of the enemy by which they were mitigated, will be read with lively interest. Boothby himself, unfortunately, when at length he was free to quit the Continent, was no longer able to serve his country on any battlefield; but his disposition was too much towards activity to permit of his being a recluse.

Soon after his return home, still a young man, he entered at St. Mary's Hall, Oxford; took a degree; and was ordained deacon by the Bishop of Salisbury. By and by Lord Liverpool presented him to the Crown living of Sutterton, in Lincolnshire, which he held for nearly thirty years, until his death, in 1846. During that incumbency, through the patronage of Archbishop Venables Vernon Harcourt, he became a Residentiary Canon of Southwell Minster, and that enabled him to hold also the living of Barnoldby-le-Beck. Married to Marianne Catherine Beridge, third daughter of the Rev. Basil B. Beridge, rector of Algarkirk, he left seven children. He was for many years Chairman of Quarter Sessions in the Holland Division of Lincolnshire.

In all his various capacities Boothby was highly esteemed. Perhaps we cannot more fitly close this outline of his career than by quoting the written words of one who had the privilege of being personally acquainted with him.

"I had the pleasure," Lady Bloomfield says, "of knowing the Rev. Charles Boothby very well when I was a girl. He was an intimate friend of my mother, Lady Ravensworth. We always looked forward with pleasure to his visits at Percy's Cross. He had charming manners, and was a remarkably handsome man, with a most benevolent countenance and a sweet smile which was particularly winning to children. He had a cork leg and was rather lame, which used to excite my sympathy; but his gentle manners, unvarying kindness, and warm affection, have left an impression on my mind which the lapse of many years since his lamented death has not obliterated. It is with pleasure that I record the memory of one whom I loved and respected."

Chapter 1

On the 27th July 1809 the division of General Sherbrooke retired across the river Alverche: General Cuesta had withdrawn the Spaniards from the bridge on our right flank. The confidence of the allies seemed now converted into apprehension—I speak in a military sense, not referring to the personal fears of individuals, which in a British army have no place.

The fact of General Wellesley's having determined to entrench himself at Talavera, for which there was no premeditation, indicated that the confidence by which he had been buoyed up was changed into the resolution sometimes imparted by despair, or at least that he considered himself inferior to the enemy.

Soon General Sherbrooke entered the town; and, he having no immediate occasion for my services, I was at liberty to provide quarters for myself and stabling for my horses. One very old woman, Doña Pollonia di Monton, was the only human being left in the house to which the magistracy of the town had directed me. Its other inhabitants, alarmed by the return of the British and their countrymen in arms, had fled to the mountains, leaving this venerable dame as the best protection for their dwelling, she being too old and decrepit to provoke desire or awaken ferocity.

She received me with the civility of fear, spoke of the French officers with respect and praise, and, when I told her I was an Englishman, expressed her disbelief by a wistful smile and an incredulous movement of her head. She was much relieved when convinced of my sincerity, but, still preparing herself for troubles, supplied my wants with an air of distrustful melancholy.

Having desired Pedro, my Italian servant, to prepare dinner, I went out to be in the way of information. The town presented a scene of dislocation and alarm that would be difficult to describe. Reports rose up like exhalations, passing from one to another in rapid succession, extending terror and confusion. At one moment: "The French had possession of the suburbs!" The inhabitants ran through the streets with as much anguish in their faces as if they already felt the bayonets in their bodies. At another: "The British general was in full march to Oropesa!" "*O dios! los Ingleses nos abandonan!*" "*Jesus! Maria! Jose! los Ingleses nos abandonan!*"

As the day waned, the occasional sound of cannon announced our contact with the enemy. Tired of being the sport of idle rumour, I mounted my little mule, and, ordering my batman not to stir with my horses until he heard from me, I rode towards the position occupied by the army. I had no expectation of an action that evening; for it is a rule of war that, except in cases of surprise, it is ill-judged to direct a night attack. I concluded that the skirmishing would cease with the light, and that the French would engage us at daybreak. For that hour, therefore, I wished my chargers to be fresh, expecting to return after dark in time to take the refreshment that I needed.

With these ideas I rode to the field, where everything wore the most hostile appearance. The enemy in our front, having driven in the outposts, had begun a heavy and well-directed cannonade upon our whole line. I immediately sought for General Sherbrooke, who, as but few of his staff were then near him, was glad of my timely arrival, and gave me full employment in making known or in executing his intentions. The cannon of the enemy were spiritedly and effectually answered by ours, although we were contending with heavier metal. This encountering thunder, however, ceased with the light, and an awful pause accompanied the fall of evening.

We peered anxiously through the thick dusk, and could see the French columns, deliberate and silent, approaching the brow of the opposite hill. Noticing the light infantry which we had thrown out in front collected in a body and apparently waiting the enemy's approach, I said to General Sherbrooke that I feared the intention was misunderstood. If, on being pushed, they fell back in a body, they would either be taken for the enemy and destroyed, or break our line and throw it into confusion. The General acquiesced in my observation, and desired me to find out the officer commanding and explain his wishes. Away I went, but found that what I had taken for a body of soldiers was a thicket, and that, in fact, the light infantry were disposed, as the very intelligent and brave officer commanding was sure to dispose them, to the best advantage.

I fell in with Captain Blair, who also had been sent to that officer, and just as we had recognised each other a volleying began from our left. It instantly struck us both that in the confusion of night the fire would spread down the whole line, in which case we should be blown to pieces.

Under this impression, I clapped spurs to my mule, and pushed her to her utmost speed. But the blaze from the left came down with greater speed, and before I could reach the line I found myself galloping up to an uninterrupted sheet of fire.

I had just time enough to think my escape impossible before I was struck in the leg by a musket ball, which brought me to the ground.

As the firing continued, I conceived that the enemy was at hand, and got up; but my leg doubled under me, and I had to creep through the ranks on my hands and knees.

A sergeant who was posted in the rear offered to carry me to a distance if I could get upon his back. I made the attempt; but, exhausted with pain and loss of blood, fell from his shoulders and fainted.

On coming to myself, I seemed as in bed, slowly waking from a deep sleep; but my foot was stagnated and full of pain. Instead of this sensation going off, it increased to a very violent degree; and I was beginning to be very much puzzled, when the firing on both sides, and the wondrous scene on which I opened my eyes, awoke me to a consciousness of the reality. The same sergeant was still standing over me, and I again asked him if he could not remove me. Having his halbert and knapsack, he said there was no other way but by my getting on his back. That I could not do.

Ere long the line was a little advanced; and my friend the sergeant told me that the enemy was driven back, which was on many accounts a consolation, for had the troops behind which I lay (Germans) been overthrown, my fate must have been deplorable.

The firing had now subsided, and only a little irregular sharpshooting was to be heard. An officer rode towards me, and a voice which I knew to be Blair's exclaimed, "O, my dear Boothby, is that you?" I asked him if he could get me a surgeon, and he rode off. I afterwards found that poor Blair was speaking to me from the ground, where he lay wounded, near me, and that the mounted officer must have been some other person. Soon after an officer rode past, whom, to my great comfort, I distinguished to be General Sherbrooke. I called to him; and, turning back, he expressed much sorrow at finding me in that plight, inquired into the nature of my wound, and immediately ordered up from the reserve four men and a bier to carry me to the town of Talavera. The road lay for two miles through a wood which joined the skirts of the town. It was dark; and, being encumbered with their arms. and accoutrements, the men who were to carry me were but barely sufficient for their load. Their irregular motion, grating the bones of my shattered leg, gave me excruciating pain; and I should again have become insensible had not one of them put his canteen of wine to my mouth as he saw me growing faint—thus bestowing, with noble liberality, what at such a time was almost as precious to him as his blood.

I was oppressed with heat, and, to gain a freer respiration, took off my stock and bared my throat to the night air; my hat was left in the field. In our passage through the wood the men were frequently alarmed, and, notwithstanding my entreaties, set me several times on the ground, to go in quest of the bushes or stumps of trees which the night-breeze made vocal, and darkness to the eye of apprehension presented as lurking enemies. This proceeding gave me great disturbance. Whenever they put me down in the middle of that wood, I had no security for their return, especially as they had taken it into their heads that Talavera was in the hands of the French, and that my persisting in being carried thither was very unreasonable. I was also afraid that, being so long without medical assistance, I might bleed to death; and the action of putting me down and again raising me up (unavoidable on their part) tortured me.

Those four soldiers, however, had too much honesty to abandon me; but a misfortune almost as distressing occurred. They lost their way. Of the paths that went through the wood they knew not which to choose. One proposed the left-hand path. Another having assured him that that path led to the enemy's camp, they were proceeding on that to the right, when I desired them to stop. Raising my shoulders above the bier, I roused my languid perceptions, and looked attentively round me. I saw then a strong haze of light over the wood, in the direction of the left-hand path, and told the men that it must come from Talavera; but they all insisted that the light came from the camp of our enemies. Desiring them to be perfectly silent, I strained my ear to catch some guiding sound. Then I could plainly distinguish the chiming of clocks, the barking of dogs, and the buzz of populace, that came from where the light was, in a mingled drowsy hum.

The men were now convinced. Had I not been able to make the effort of putting them right, the consequences of their mistake might have proved melancholy indeed. We fell in with several Spaniards, whom, probably, the shelter of night had tempted to listen to the fears which withdrew them from their ranks. These confirmed us in our road, and reassured my bearers by information that the town remained tranquil and secure.

At the skirts of the town they rested near some reserve guns commanded by an officer of artillery whom I knew. It gave me pleasure to see a friend; but to him, I do believe, the meeting was much less agreeable. I asked for the artillery surgeon, but was told he was in the field. The officer pointed out the way to the general hospital; and soon after we fell in with a straggling Spaniard who conducted us thither. We arrived at nine o'clock—about three hours after I had received my wound. I cannot express the anxiety that was taken off my mind to find myself at last in the hands of the surgeon. I now felt that my part was performed, and resigned myself. Mr. Higgins, Mr. Bell, and other surgeons (then all unknown to me) were busily employed in attending such as had suffered in the destructive cannonade which began the action.

Upon my saying that I had a lodging in the town, they agreed that I had better be carried thither immediately, and Mr. Bell readily offered to accompany me. The further exertion of directing the way to my quarters through the intricate streets of the town was still required of me. Fortunately, I remembered the name of my host, Don Manoel di Monton, and of the street where he lived, Calle de las conchas; by which means the house was ascertained, and I was carried upstairs.

The lively manner in which the old lady (who had in the morning taken me for a Frenchman) was affected has left an indelible impression upon my memory.

"What?" she exclaimed, while the tears ran down her furrowed cheeks. "Can this be the same? This he whose cheeks in the morning were glowing with health?[1] Blessed Virgin, see how white they are now!"

She made haste to prepare a bed. Oh! what a luxury to be laid upon it after the hours of pain and anxiety, almost hopeless, I had undergone!

Mr. Bell cut off my boot, and, having examined the wound, said, "Sir, I fear there is no chance of saving your leg, and the amputation

---

1. *Color de rosa* was the expression of the old woman: the Spaniards are generally so sallow that to them the colour which we ourselves consider as the natural attendant of youth and health is an object of admiration.

must be above the knee."

The idea of losing a leg in the heyday of youth could not but be painful; but it was the less shocking as I had prepared my mind for a more awful separation, for I am far from putting a limb in competition with life; nor, I conceive, can anyone do so who loves and is beloved in the world.

> *For who, to dumb forgetfulness a prey,*
> *This pleasing anxious being e'er resigned,*
> *Left the warm precincts of the cheerful day,*
> *Nor cast one longing, ling'ring look behind?*

I demanded of the surgeon if danger were to be apprehended from delay.

He answered that the sooner the operation was performed the better, but that it could not be until morning; and, upon my expressing a wish to have another opinion as to its necessity, he admitted that to be very natural.

I passed a night of excruciating pain, which no effort of my mind could enable me to bear with patience. My groans were faint, because my body was exhausted.

Poor Mr. Bell, who slept in a bed near to mine, did not, I fear, enjoy uninterrupted rest. I called to him before daylight to know if it was not time to see the surgeons, and gave my unabating torments as an excuse for disturbing him. At dawn he went to the hospital, promising to return with Mr. Higgins. Daylight was ushered in by a roar of cannon so loud, so continuous, so tremendous, that I hardly conceived the wars of all the earth, with united voice, could produce such a wild and illimitable din. Every shot seemed to shake the house with increasing violence; and poor Doña Pollonia, rushing into the room with every gesture of distraction, exclaimed, "They are firing the town! They are firing the town!"

"No, no," said I. "Don't be frightened. Why should they fire the town? Don't you perceive that the firing is more distant and less frequent?"

The poor woman acknowledged that it was; and, seeming surprised at my calmness, when she thought that I had more right to be alarmed than herself, she became less distraught and watched by me with sympathising sorrow. The next-door neighbour, a carpenter named Augustin, had been called in to sit with me. He was himself ill of a fever, and suffering much. Finding the day advancing, my pains

DOÑA POLLONIA.
"Van encender la villa!"

unabating, and no signs of any medical assistance, I tore a leaf from my pocket-book, and with a pencil wrote a note to Mr. Higgins, saying that, as I had been informed no time was to be lost in the amputation, I was naturally anxious that my case should be as soon as possible attended to. Giving this note to Augustin, I desired him to wait at the hospital until Mr. Higgins was ready, and then to show him the way. My messenger soon returned, saying that the surgeon could not possibly leave the hospital.

I sent a second note, and a third; and towards ten o'clock the harassed surgeon made his appearance.

"Captain Boothby," said he, "I am extremely sorry that I could not possibly come here before—still more sorry that I only come now to tell you I cannot serve you. There is but one case of instruments, which it is impossible for me to bring from the hospital while crowds of wounded, both officers and men, are pressing for assistance."

Feeling all the reasonableness of this manly explanation, I said I did but wish to take my turn.

"I hope," added he, "that towards evening the crowd will decrease, and that I shall be able to bring Mr. Gunning with me to consult upon your case and do for you whatever may be thought necessary."

"Will you examine my wound, sir," said I, "and tell me honestly whether you apprehend any danger from the delay thus become necessary?"

He examined my leg, and said, after a pause—"No. I see nothing in this case from which the danger would be increased by waiting five or six hours."

There was nothing for it, therefore, but patience, which is rarely the attendant of violent pain. I taxed my mind to make an effort: I endeavoured to recall the manliness of my previous reflections—to fling myself on beyond the present afflicted hour—and to bethink me how despicable and unimportant pain seems when only the remembrance of it remains. But Pain, far from loosening his fangs at the suggestions of reason, clung fast, and persisted in teaching me that, in spite of mental pride, he is and must be dreadful to the human frame.

When I inquired for my two servants, I found that, guided by some false rumour, or struck with panic fright, they had left the town with my horses the evening before, notwithstanding my injunctions to the contrary.

Aaron, my batman, who was a soldier, finding that he had been deceived, proceeded on the 28th to the field of battle, very naturally supposing that I should be distressed about my horses; but soon, hearing that I was wounded, he made the best of his way to my quarters.

Mr. Higgins, as he had given me to expect, came to me about three o'clock, bringing with him Mr. Gunning and Mr. Bell, and such instruments as they might have occasion for. Mr. Gunning sat down by my bedside, and made a formal exhortation: explained that to save the life it was necessary to part with the limb, and required of me an effort of the mind and a manly resolution. I interrupted him by telling him that whatever the surgeons thought necessary I should abide by; that I placed myself in their hands, being incompetent to exercise a judgment on the matter; and that they might depend upon me—as I could upon myself—as equal to any pain that was unavoidable. Then the surgeons, having examined my wound, went to another part of the room to consult; after which they withdrew—to bring the apparatus, I imagined. Hours passed without bringing their return; and Aaron, having sought Mr. Gunning, was told that he was too much occupied. This after having warned me that there was no time to be lost!

"Go, then," said I, "again into the street, and bring hither the first medical officer you happen to fall in with."

He soon returned, bringing with him Mr. Grasset, surgeon of the 48th Regiment.

I stated to Mr. Grasset the source of my impatience. Upon examining my wound, he declared that he was by no means convinced of the necessity of the amputation, and would on no account undertaken the responsibility of so serious a measure, without consultation.

"But," said I, "I suppose an attempt to save the leg will be attended with great danger?"

"So will the amputation," answered Mr. Grasset; "but we must hope for the best, and I see nothing to make your cure impossible. The bones, to be sure, are much shattered, and the leg is much mangled and swollen; but that may all suppurate and come right, so that I cannot think of amputating without more advice. But have you been bled, sir?" he asked.

"No," said I.

Mr. Grasset conceived bleeding absolutely necessary, and at my request he bled me in the arm.

For some moments the hope of saving my limb, which he had given me, glanced a ray of comfort into my breast; but unrelenting pain soon took from me all consciousness but of misery, all power but that of groaning.

The opinion of Mr. Grasset was the more remarkable, if sincere, because Mr. Gunning's departure (which to me seemed unaccountable) proceeded from his conviction that a gangrene had already begun, and that it would be cruel, as he expressed himself to Mr. Higgins, to disturb my dying moments by a painful and fruitless operation.

As I had taken nothing but vinegar and water since my misfortune, my strength was exhausted, and the operation of bleeding was succeeded by an interval of painful unconsciousness. From this state I was roused in the evening by Captain Craig, General Sherbrooke's *aide-de-camp*, who had himself been slightly wounded in the arm. He came to inquire after me and to bring me comfort, having met Mr. Grasset, who had repeated to him the opinion that he had delivered to me. I told Craig that Mr. Grasset's opinion did not give me much consolation, but that if he could find Fitz-Patrick and send him to me, I should then know my fate, as in him I placed the utmost confidence, both as a surgeon and a friend. "But who," I demanded, "has gained the day?"

The *aide-de-camp* then told me that, after a bloody contest, the French had been completely beaten, and had fled beyond the Alverche, with the loss of three eagles and twenty pieces of cannon.

Spent as I was, the comfort and life this account poured into my breast it is quite impossible for me to describe. For some moments I forgot my suffering in the swell of exultation, and heard of the slaughter and repulse of the confident foe with a smile of vindictive triumph. But many men that I knew had fallen to rise no more! Many also were wounded, and suffering like myself. But if I am capable of charitable sorrow for the suffering of others, I fear I am not insensible to the comfort which arises from participated calamity. That "social sorrow loses half its pain" is a reproach to human nature from which I would willingly withdraw myself; but, whatever I might do with others, I could not deceive myself. I felt it to be just.

When Craig left me I relapsed into that troubled stupor in which consciousness of being is only retained by the violence of bodily pain. From this state I was roused by someone taking hold of my hand. It was FitzPatrick.

Chapter 2

"If I had you in London," said FitzPatrick with a sigh, as he looked at my shattered limb, "I might attempt to save it, but amid the present circumstances it would be hopeless."

"Then be it as it may. Now that I am in your hands, I am content."

"Those who told me of your wound said also that the amputation had been performed; else, ill as I could have been spared, I would have left the field and come to you."

"Do you think you are come too late?" I asked.

He said "No"; but he dissembled. At that time I was under strong symptoms of lock-jaw, which did not disappear until many hours after the amputation.

"Then, when will you operate?"

"Tomorrow morning. We must have daylight."

"Could you not give me something to alleviate my sufferings, which are scarce supportable?"

He took a towel, and, soaking it in vinegar and water, laid it on my wound; which gave me considerable relief.

He stayed with me till late, changing the lotion as often as its cooling properties were mastered by the heat of inflammation.

I passed another dismal night, and hailed the morning beam as bringing the promise of some change—sure that my pains could not be augmented.

FitzPatrick and Miller of the artillery, Higgins and Bell, staff-surgeons, were the gentlemen who at nine o'clock prepared to perform this serious operation upon me. Having laid out the necessary instruments, they put a table in the middle of the room and placed on it a mattress. Then one of the surgeons came to me and exhorted me to summon my fortitude. I told him that he need not be afraid; and

FitzPatrick stopped him, saying that he could answer for me. They then took me to the table and laid me on the mattress. Mr. Miller wished to place a handkerchief over my eyes; but I assured him that it was unnecessary—I would look another way. The tourniquet being adjusted, I saw that the knife was in FitzPatrick's hand; which being as I wished, I averted my head.

As I do not choose to gratify the curious (at the expense of the feeling) reader, I shall not describe an operation the details of which are perhaps even more shocking to reflect upon than to experience. But, as it is a common idea that the most painful part of an amputation lies in sundering the bone, I may rectify an error by declaring that the only part of the process in which the pain comes up to the natural anticipation is the first incision round the limb, by which the skin is divided—the sensation of which is as if a prodigious weight were impelling the severing edge. The sawing of the bone gives no uneasy sensation; or, if any, it is overpowered by others more violent.

"Is it off?" said I, as I felt it separate.

"Yes," said FitzPatrick. "Your sufferings are over."

"Ah, no! You have yet to take up the arteries!"

"It will give you no pain," he said, kindly; and that was true—at least, after what I had undergone, the pain seemed nothing.

I was carried back to my bed, free from pain, but much exhausted. The surgeons complimented me upon my firmness, and I felt gratified that I had gone through what lay before me without flinching, or admitting a thought of cowardly despair. I desired that the amputated limb might be brought to me, that I might examine the wound. This request was opposed with some force by the surgeons; but I persisted, and found a certain satisfaction in observing that the limb wore an appearance to the last degree mangled and hopeless. This moderated my tender sorrow at beholding for the last time that active and invaluable servant.

Now that my body was released from pain, my mind attempted to resume a cheerful tone. Hope returned to my breast, and all the fond scenes with which fancy decorates the prospect of youth began again to gleam through the clouds of misfortune. Much was lost; but when all was going, and the gloomy screen of oblivion seemed ready to fall between me and the world, to have saved so much—to have preserved the possibility of yet being given back to happiness and friendship—silenced my regrets, and awakened thankfulness. Reader, if thou hast a friend who is near to thy heart, and in the hour of sickness and affliction he has held up thy head, watched over, and fed, and tended thee as a father his child, thou wilt know that the balm of such a solace enters the heart with so sweet an infusion of peace, as makes it difficult to regret the calamity which has taught thee such heavenly sensations.

> *Some feelings are to mortals given,*
> *With less of earth in them than heaven.*

I shall dilate no further upon the pleasure I derived from the constant attendance, day and night, of Edmund Mulcaster, for whom my affection had grown with our growth and strengthened with our strength. Adorned with all the qualities that demand praise, and the modesty that shrinks from it, now is not the time to delineate his character, nor is mine the hand that can do it impartially. This officer could scarce be persuaded to leave me even for the shortest intervals. For some time after the operation my dangerous symptoms increased. My stomach refused sustenance, and a constant hiccough was recognised by the surgeons as a fatal prognostic.

This faithful friend never left my bedside to take himself that rest which a constant state of previous fatigue rendered so needful to him. I urged the danger of making indispensable to me a constant attendance which it would not be in his power to give, and assured him that I was more at ease when I knew that he was refreshing himself, more especially as his was an ardent spirit, much too active for a delicate frame.

General Sherbrooke was no longer my general, but an affectionate and sympathising friend, or rather a protecting parent. He came to me often, anticipated all my wants, and evinced the most earnest anxiety for my preservation.

Indeed, the kindness and anxiety expressed by the companions who now surrounded my bed, the exhilaration of victory, and the watchful ministering of my friend, offered a charm of consolation that I cordially wish to any sufferer whose misfortunes may resemble mine; a charm which, I believe, encouraged my wavering powers to rally, and cleared the channels to receive the refluent stream of life.

There had run a report that my campaigning chum, a *sweet-blooded lad*[1] of eighteen, had been cut down by the enemy's cavalry, which had caused me much uneasiness, for I was sincerely attached to him. The

---

1. Dr. Moore, in speaking of his son (afterwards so well known and so widely lamented), was in the habit of saying, "*Jack is a sweet blooded lad.*"

falsehood of this report was evinced to me in a most agreeable manner by his appearance at my bedside, safe and sound. His attendant, a faithful Highlander, really had been cut down. His skilful arm was overcome by numbers, and his master was preserved by the fleetness of his horse.

He softly demanded if there was anything in the world he could do to serve or comfort me.

General Sherbrooke, Richard Stewart, and my kind friend and chief, Colonel Fletcher, had all written to my friends; but, thinking that a few words from myself would be a greater comfort to those loved and afflicted beings, I made my young friend sit down, and dictated a letter to my mother, in which I directed them to hope for the best, and to resign themselves cheerfully to what was irretrievable. I signed the letter myself; and, having made this effort to mitigate their pain, I felt less trouble on their account. The feeling reader will not impute disingenuousness to me when I describe my apprehensions and my regrets as deriving most of their poignancy from the deep affliction and alarm into which I knew my relations would be plunged by the news of my misfortune. A man need not be vain of the love of his father and mother: it is not measured by his merit, nor by the return that he makes to it: it is boundless as the beneficence of Heaven, which flows unchecked upon the unworthiness of mankind.

On the 30th, Pedro, my Italian servant, returned. He ran to me, saying, "O, my master—my dear master!"

My most unfavourable symptom was the refusal of my stomach to retain any sort of nutriment. In the night of the 30th, however, by the perseverance of Mulcaster, I managed to retain some mulled wine, strongly spiced, and in the morning I took two eggs from the same welcome hand. This was the "turn." My unfavourable symptoms subsided, and the flowing stream of life began to replenish by degrees its almost deserted channels. So I had continued to improve until August 2, when some officers, entering my room, said that information had been received of Soult's arrival with a considerable force at Placentia, and that General Wellesley intended to head back and engage him.

Nothing was now heard of but the crushing of Soult between Beresford and Wellesley. To some it seemed a nice thing to have got him into such a trap; but to me it carried a more melancholy reflection. I regarded the British general as outmanoeuvred, and considered our blood as flowing fruitlessly. I felt that I must be left, that I must part with the most precious alleviation to my misfortunes, and become the booty of the enemy. To this reverse, bitter as it was, I immediately began to reconcile my mind. I was in a fair way of recovery. I might have more troubles to encounter; but, after all, the end might possibly be well. General Sherbrooke supplied me with whatever money I desired, and sent me some bottles of port wine and claret, a present of which the benefit was incalculable. He brought with him Colonel M'Kennon of the Guards.

"Boothby," said he, "Colonel M'Kennon is to be left in charge of Talavera. When you are fit to move, he will take you to his quarters, which are those I am quitting. You will be cooler and more comfortable there than you are here."

"If the French come while we are away, Boothby," said Goldfinch, "you must cry out, 'Capitaine Anglais,' and you will be treated well. In the very fury of the storm at Oporto, that tide recommended me to their courtesy and respect."

On August 3 my friends all took leave of me with the most affectionate kindness. It was a blank, rugged moment. I had to part with my friend Mulcaster. He took both my hands. I could not speak. It was wresting from me more than may be told. But the hard hand of adversity is the best teacher of submission, and though patience is powerless to preserve us from affliction, undoubtedly it moderates the pressure.

FitzPatrick stayed till the 4th. In the morning he promised to engage for me the attendance of Mr. Higgins, who was left the senior surgeon; expressed great regret at leaving me behind, and promised to see me again before he left the town; but he was prevented by rumours that the French were approaching, which spread a general panic terror, and induced him to depart suddenly.

Chapter 3

[1]The mass of the people of England is hasty and often unjust in its judgement of military events. Reported success gives them undue exultation, and if any reverse ensue they sink as much as they rose. This indiscretion on the part of the people causes uphill work for the generals of England. Instead of feeling any fondness for her bold sons, who to gain her approbation brave death and give up the luxuries of life—instead of feeling a parental concern for their honour and credit, and a consequent reluctance to see their faults—the people are often ready not only to blame them for disaster, but also to impute success to Fortune, and failure to their want of skill.

The demon of discord also, or, as we name him, Party, extends his baneful influence over the fortunes of our heroes. Often half the nation condemns a general as rash when he advances; the other half reviles him as a coward when he retreats. It follows that it is an indispensable duty for a British general to drive from his heart all expectation of popular applause. Let his own judgement be his perpetual guide, and the good and the glory of his country his perpetual object. Should folly, ignorance, or prejudice deprive him of applause, be his sweetest consolation the certainty of having deserved it.

Such was the conduct of Moore!

News of the Battle of Talavera was announced by the trumpet of victory. The people of England, elated by the sound, expected the emancipation of Spain. In the same measure as they had been raised above the mark were they cast down below it when told that the victors had been obliged to retire and leave their wounded to the mercy

---

1. This chapter was written the year after the Battle of Talavera. The subsequent career of the Duke of Wellington has placed him on an eminence which no blame and no common praise can reach—up to which, indeed, I now look with English sentiments of exultation and gratitude.

of a vanquished enemy. They thought they had been deceived by the earlier report, instead of by their own enthusiasm; and few English citizens will now bear to hear of the victory of Talavera.

Yet never was a victory more decided—never was the amazing preponderance of British valour more splendidly demonstrated. And this is the ground of triumph—let who will deplore the loss of Spain, when she *is* lost. No loss of territory, no disasters in other campaigns, can deprive us of the glory of that battle. That, at least, is our own. Why should we give up what was so hardly earned—what the great and the good deem so precious? The glory of that battle is our own. It shall shame our posterity if they degenerate! It shall warm them if they emulate our valour! The English heart is cold which forgets to glow at the recollection of that day—when the dauntless Englishman beat down the crest of his gigantic foe, tore the scarf from his neck, struck the sword from his hand, and drove him ignominiously from the field.

In passing through Poictiers, my heart exulted not the less because that city now owned the sway of the sovereign of France; neither could the future masters of Talavera have any control over the trophies we carried thence. The hand of the spoiler may fell the fruitful olives that shadow the graves of our fallen heroes; but the laurels he cannot touch. In spite of waste, ruin, and desolation, which follow in the train of tyrants, unfading laurels shall grow and thicken over that hallowed spot where English blood flowed as a barrier against merciless oppression.

But, though no doubt can reasonably be entertained as to the victory, which is matter of fact, in regard to the military skill evinced by the opposing leaders there is certainly room for diversity of opinion, governed by the supposititious results of different measures on one part and the other. If we were to suppose that Lord Wellington (then Sir Arthur Wellesley) knew the amount and condition of the force under Soult, he must be a hardy partisan who would attempt to justify his conduct. In Spain, however, it is often not only impossible to procure correct information, but also extremely difficult to guard against that which is false. The Spaniards are deaf to bad news, and idiotically credulous to all reports that tend to flatter their hopes.

I shall suppose that Lord Wellington's information was in accord with the general report, and stated that the French in Galicia were surrounded by patriot armies which were gradually effecting their destruction. This intelligence was corroborated, as well by the nature of

Soult's retreat from Oporto as by the events which actually followed that ruinous movement. Such, indeed, were the dangers that assailed the French marshals in Galicia, Soult and Ney, that a staff officer assured me that they both at different times merely refrained from laying down their arms because they considered such a measure more terrible than destruction itself.

Besides, the personal hatred subsisting between those chiefs rankled to such a degree as often to prevent their co-operation and to urge them to deceive each other as to their intended movements. Their animosity originated in Prussia, and the troops they commanded were infected with its venom. Some curious facts about those two Frenchmen have come to my knowledge, and I shall make no excuse for introducing them here.

When Soult had effected his retreat from Portugal by passing the Minko at Orense, after a serious struggle with a Spanish force, he moved upon Lugo, where Marshal Ney was maintaining himself against the multiform enemies that goaded him on all sides. On arriving at Lugo, Soult immediately repaired to the quarters of his brother marshal, and was ushered in by the officer who is my informant. From the ante-room that officer could distinctly overhear the altercation produced by their meeting. On entering the room where Ney was, Soult, after the manner of the French, went forward with open arms to embrace him.

"Stand back," said Ney. "I don't know you. Where do you come from? You come flying, like a coward, from the enemies of the Emperor!"

"*Allons donc*," returned Soult. "I come to save Lugo, which you were on the point of losing."

"I neither want assistance," said the other, "nor are you in a condition to give me any. I have met by hundreds your straggling fugitives. They all had abandoned their arms, that they might fly the faster; but their packs, heavy with plunder, were religiously preserved! It is you, *Monsieur le Maréchal*, who have taught them to throw away their muskets in order that they might carry the more booty, when your orderly book gave up such a town as Oporto to a three-days' pillage. Is that the way, sir, you consult your master's interests? To give up the second city of the country, you take in his name to the horrible excesses of your brutal soldiers! You are no longer a Marshal of France. I will no longer acknowledge you as a chief in authority under the Emperor."

Soult, though the senior, still endeavoured to appease Ney by representing the importance of their unanimity; but Ney was inflexible, and became so grossly abusive that Soult, unable any longer to command his temper, retorted some very harsh expressions upon the aggressor; stung by which, that furious marshal, suddenly drawing his sword, said, "Villain, defend thyself"—a mandate which was instantly obeyed.

As both were expert swordsmen, they contended for some time without bloodshed, and General Maurice Mathieu, rushing into the room, found them hotly engaged. Having parted them, he reported that their respective corps were volleying at each other in the great square, thus, as if by sympathy, following the example of their chiefs. This intelligence restored Ney to his senses, and both combatants, galloping into the square, by their personal efforts ended the fray of the soldiery, and quelled a civil broil of an aspect the most menacing and alarming. Some appearance ot harmony was established between the marshals; but it was deceptive.

The abandonment of Galicia having been fixed upon between them, it was agreed that Soult should go before, and keep up a constant communications and co-operation with Ney. No sooner had he, by his reconciliation with that haughty chieftain, reorganised and refitted his corps, than he stole a march upon him—allowing a Spanish force to take possession of a bridge between him and his colleague, by which treacherous conduct Ney was for some time isolated, expecting nothing better than destruction.

In this account, given to me by an intelligent officer, I have not attempted to supply any deficiency of particulars, even by the most probable conjectures as to times and places; this, in order that I might withdraw myself from any stake in its authenticity. I give it from memory, as nearly as I can in the words of my informant, and only add that he could not have the smallest motive to deceive me, and that I am well persuaded he had as little inclination to do so. Perhaps it may be difficult to believe that two officers, high in the trust of their sovereign, should let private hatred so completely take the place of public spirit; yet when the temper of Soult is considered, along with the insult and defiance he met with from his inferior officer, the motives to revenge will not appear trifling; nor is it out of nature that he should go fearful lengths to effect the ruin of his enemy.

Be that as it may, we have seen enough to account for the ideas of Soult's distress, which prevailed so much in the British army as to prevent the intervention of his force from being sufficiently adverted to. It is no wonder that, passing through the mouths of the sanguine Spaniards, probability, grounded on real disasters, should assume the form of fact, and that those who saw the ship strike on a rock should boldly assert that she went to the bottom.

Thus the rashness of Lord Wellington in placing himself between two enemies, the least of whom was equal to himself, may be palliated. His conduct, when he was in the scrape, it seems hardly possible to find fault with. His position was skilfully chosen and bravely defended; and the resolution to head back and attack Soult, leaving the Spaniards to check an army which he himself had routed, was truly that of a soldier-like spirit, and does him honour. He could not control the event which obliged him to relinquish that daring purpose. He had no alternative when General Cuesta abandoned Talavera.

On the other hand, the conduct of the French is not so easily accounted for. One would indeed rather suppose that they were as much deceived as the English respecting the corps under the three marshals, than that they were acting in concert with that force. King Joseph was so sure that his opponent must either retreat before him or be destroyed, that no consideration should have induced him to give battle until he knew that his blows would be seconded in the rear of his enemy; but flying before him when he would follow, and following when he would recede, Joseph should merely have kept himself in contact with the enemy—sure that if the enemy were not to be caught, his retreat and passage of a river, in face of a superior force, must be ruinous in the extreme.

To the power of jealousy between the holders of delegated authority, and to that saucy confidence which has been the stumbling-block of most of the French generals who have contended with us single-handed, may be imputed the folly of Marshal Victor in urging the king to give battle at Talavera. Nor was more skill displayed in executing that determination than judgment in adopting it. When a strong position is defended by brave troops, no good general would think of attacking it in front until every method to turn it had been tried. The French leader did endeavour to turn the British by the left. Thus his opponent frustrated by the sacrifice of a body of cavalry.

Then the Frenchman attacked in front, with such perseverance and with such a weight of superior forces that all the strength of the ground, and all the valour that defended it, were only sufficient to repulse him. He seems to have forgotten that there was a right flank also, which formed the longest part of the line of defence, and was occupied by raw, undisciplined troops, destitute of competent officers and of that experience in war which communicates confidence; that the ground they stood on, though much intersected, was easily assailable; and that this flank was, equally with the other, a key to the position of his enemy. If that night attack which he so unwisely directed upon us had been made upon the Spaniards, while he occupied us by a formidable feint (for which purpose he had abundance of troops), he would have had the forest prospect of success. With the Spaniards the panic fright attending unseen danger would have done much. They are individually brave; but the mass was unknowing, and confusion would have been tantamount to defeat.

I am convinced that the town of Talavera might have been taken by 20,000 men, while 25,000 could have occupied the British in the heights. Thus Lord Wellington must either have changed his position with precipitation, while pressed by a superior force, or have suffered the enemy to cut him off from the Tagus and approach him from the rear. On the other hand, in attacking us fairly in front, the enemy had no right to expect anything but hard knocks. He knew of old that we should fight to the last, and had nothing to hope from ignorance or fear. The actual results he ought to have anticipated. He was so completely routed (I have been behind the scenes) that, had not Soult given us check, we should inevitably have destroyed him. For seven leagues the beaten army fled in confusion. No corps, no regiment, was together. All was disorganised that had been engaged; and the king, taking a large escort from the reserve that had been held back in case of disaster, entered Madrid a despairing fugitive.

To the egregious folly of that *soi-disant* monarch, or of his advisers, Lord Wellington owes the occasion of success, and the army and the nation an inestimable wreath of glory.

SOLDIERS ON THE MARCH

Chapter 4

The repulse and flight of the French restored confidence to the fugitive inhabitants. Leaving the mountains, whither they had repaired for refuge, they began to re-enter the town. Thus the house to which I had been carried had received an addition to its inmates conducing much to my comfort, since both old and young, emulous in their attentions, strove to anticipate my wants and alleviate my sufferings. The Spanish commissary-general was received into the house as an old friend and patron. His lady was careful to supply me with the whitest bread, often coming to take a melancholy look at me, always retiring with a shake of the head and an avowed conviction that I should die.

But the evacuation of the town by the British soon repelled the returning confidence of its inhabitants, and their fears awoke with aggravated force. Don Manoel di Monton, the master of my house, again sought shelter in the mountains; but with perpetual thankfulness let me record that a British officer, wounded and mutilated, was to the women of the house too sacred an object to be abandoned; dreadful indeed as were the thoughts of the French, the fear of them gave way to compassion. They had clung to the hope that at least their countrymen would stay and protect them; but on the 4th, seeing them also file under their Endows in a long receding array, they came to me, beating their breasts and tearing their hair, and demanded of me if I knew what was to become of them. Though I could not avoid being agitated by their distress, as well as by my own situation, I summoned my philosophy and communicated it to them as well as I was able.

"Perhaps," said I, "you are mistaken in the movements of our troops, or, at the worst, if the French come now they will enter the town peaceably and commit no excesses."

The commissary's wife, ready for departure, came up to take leave of me and to bring me a supply of bread, feeling that by and by it might be difficult, perhaps impossible, to procure it. She left the house, still exclaiming, "Ah! your poor young Englishman will die!" Señora Pollonia, having observed that I did not despond, expressed considerable hopes of my recovery.

I had sent Aaron on a message to the officer who had been left commandant by General Wellesley. He returned presently, saying that the colonel was gone, having given orders throughout the town that those in the hospitals who were able to move should set off instantly for Oropesa, as the French were at hand. The sensation this notice produced is beyond all description, I lay perfectly still. I had made up my mind that it would be better to fall into the enemy's hands than attempt to go away. Other men in situations like my own had themselves placed across horses and mules, and fruitlessly attempted to escape. The road to Oropesa was covered with our poor, wounded, limping, bloodless soldiers. On crutches or sticks, with blankets thrown over them, they hobbled woefully along. For the moment panic terror lent them a force inconsistent with their debility, their fresh wounds, and their recent amputations. Some lay down on the road to take their last sleep. The rest, unable to get farther than Oropesa, fell afterwards into the hands of the French, when their troops entered that town.

Such tidings, always painted to the utmost by the apprehensive Aaron, and discoloured by the despair of my Spanish attendants, impaired my tranquillity. I was sensible that, weak and exhausted as I was, my notions and expressions of things had great influence both with the Spanish women and with my own servants, who, I feared, did they discover anything like alarm upon my countenance, might consider the case desperate and consult their own safety. Therefore I explained to Aaron that if the French should come my plight would be a sure recommendation to their respect; that he must know it would be useless to take prisoner one who had lost a leg; and that they would surely leave me my servant, if for no other reason than to save themselves the trouble of providing attendance. In using that method to reassure him, I spoke strictly as I believed; nor had I the smallest idea that I should ever be moved a prisoner from the spot.

Still, my mind was far from being at ease. I thought it possible that some foraging party might plunder me and commit excesses in the house, or on the women, who would run to me for protection (however uselessly); nor could I, I am persuaded (however little able to stir), have lain a passive spectator of any violence that brutality might have offered them.

Besides, the panic terror that had been communicated to the hospitals might, I thought, extend to the surgeons, whose assistance was of more importance to me than any other consideration.

The evening of the 4th, however, closed in quietness uninterrupted by the French; and I had a visit from the senior medical officer, Mr. Higgins, which gave me great comfort, as his conversation taught me to confide in his conduct.

Chapter 5

From the stillness which surrounded Talavera, when the morning of the 5th of August dawned upon her towers, her hills, her fields, and her olive woods, a traveller might have supposed her in profound peace, until, gazing on her gory heights, he saw that they yet streamed with blood and were covered with ghastly slain. Those horrid heaps, and the subdued moan sent forth from her hospitals, would, like the prostrate oaks of the forest, and the distant murmurs of the fallen blast, have carried to his mind some image of the storm.

The interval of tranquillity, short as it was, I employed in laying in a stock of provisions. I had a well-founded anxiety on this head, and more foresight than Pedro, who was astonished at my eagerness and extravagance.

"But, *signore*, the *brencone* asks a dollar a couple for his chickens!"

"Buy! buy! buy!" was all the answer he could get from me.

I laid in wine, eggs, and various other provender, at a rate equally provoking the rage and remonstrance of the little Italian. About the middle of the day, a violent running and crying under my windows announced an alarm. The women rushed into my room, exclaiming, "*Los Franceses! los Franceses!*"

The assistant surgeon of artillery came in.

"Well, Mr. Staniland," said I, "are the French coming?"

"Yes," he answered: "I believe so."

"Where is Mr. Higgins?"

"He is gone out to meet them."

"That's right," said I.

In about an hour, however, Mr. Higgins entered, saying, "I have been out of town above two leagues, and can see nothing of them. If, however, they do come, they will have every reason to treat us with attention; for they will find their own wounded lying alongside of ours, provided with the same comforts, treated with the same care. I have been completely round myself, to see that the treatment of their officers and men was in every respect upon the same footing as our own, so that they will have no possible pretext for complaint; and I can boldly claim their protection and respect. Whenever they come, I shall meet them and solicit the general to visit the hospitals with me."

In the course of this day Mr. Staniland brought me messages of condolence from my friend Captain Taylor of the artillery, who was severely wounded by a grape shot in the groin. His wound was not considered dangerous; but his spirits were miserably depressed at the thought of being left behind. He sent me a project for our joint removal, as soon as we should be well enough to follow our army; and I, though well convinced that the French would very shortly enter the town, willingly allowed myself to be cheated, and my thoughts to be turned in that cheering direction.

The 5th of August closed upon the renovated hopes of the unhappy people of Talavera; their feedings made a rapid transition from despair to security; and they laid down their heads in peace.

On the 6th, reports of the enemy's approach were treated with total disregard. Between eight and nine the galloping of horses was heard in the street. The women ran to the windows, and instantly shrank back, pale as death, with each a finger on her lips in token of silence. "*Los demonios!*" they whispered; and then cautiously watched, on tiptoes and aside, in breathless expectation of some bloody scene.

"They have swords and pistols all ready," said Manoela, trembling.

"How's this?" cried old Pollonia. "Why, they pass the English soldiers, unnoticed! And see there—they go talking and laughing together! Jesus! Maria! what's all this?"

"Jesus!" cries Manoela.

"Maria!" adds Catalina.

"Jose!" concludes old Pepa.

In short, nothing could exceed their astonishment at that display of civilised warfare; and I had scarce yet persuaded them to believe their senses when Mr. Higgins again made his appearance.

He had ridden out to meet the general who commanded the cavalry, and on making the representation he had preconcerted, had found that soldier prodigal of encomiums, assurances, and professions.

"The chance of war," said he to Higgins, "has thrown your unfortunate countrymen into the power of the French, who will be incapable of abusing it. If respect for the bravery of our adversaries and the dictates of humanity could ever be disregarded by us, gratitude for the manner in which now and on every occasion you have treated us, when the same chance of war has thrown us into your power, would make it impossible for us to consider these unhappy Englishmen otherwise than as the most sacred trust to our national generosity. And as for you medical gentlemen, who have been humane and manly enough not to desert your duty to your patients (many of whom are Frenchmen) in the hour of difficulty and distress, and have done us the honour to trust yourselves in our hands, not the smallest constraint will be put upon your motions. Stay amongst us as long as you please; go when you will. You are as free as the air you breathe. And whenever you think proper, our safe-conduct and unfeigned thanks shall attend you to your countrymen."

We had afterwards reason enough to know how much we were indebted to this good beginning arranged by Mr. Higgins. Only their wish to support some appearance of consistency checked their natural disposition to ill-treat us.

Throughout, Mr. Higgins displayed the character of no common man. To be loaded with the charge of such groaning multitudes—almost wholly unprovided with medicines, medical stores, or provisions—would have been regarded by most medical men as a task of no common ardour; and to perform it at the expense of personal liberty and all prospects of advancement was a case of peculiar hardship. But to prepare for the approaching crisis,—determined to ride forth and parley with the enemy, and persuade him that he owes you respect, gratitude,—this is the province of an officer of. the first class; and Mr. Higgins in so acting—in adopting the duties of every station that happened to be vacant, in letting no office stop for want of an officer, but supplying the place of the absent, and encouraging the present—discovered a manly superiority, a dauntless indifference to events, that communicated confidence through every inferior branch and secured to his suffering countrymen the blessings of a perfect medical attendance and the protection and respect of their enemies.

Chapter 6

The party that had first entered the town, having found no resistance, had no sooner established their quarters and disposed of their horses than they addressed themselves to the purposes of plunder; and various reports reached us, sufficient to overset the confidence which Mr. Higgins's account had inspired. Yet when Mr. Staniland came and related several instances of the respect and distinction preserved by those marauders towards British officers, the agitated women began to hope that their dwelling would, on my account, be exempt from the horrors of pillage. Too soon, however, every hope gave place to the consciousness of contiguous danger; for again Mr. Staniland appeared, and again related to us passing events; and this time they were ominously fearful.

Three troopers, he said, had entered the quarters of my poor friend Taylor, and, coming into the room where he lay, began with the most perfect *sang froid* to rifle his portmanteau. Taylor stormed, and told them he was an English captain. "Major, 'tis very possible," said they; "but your money, your watch, and your linen are never the worse for that!"

"No; nor your bread, nor your wine!" added another; and with those words the ruthless savage swallowed the wine and pocketed the bread that had been portioned out to the languishing sufferer as his sustenance and comfort for that day. In short, in spite of his remonstrances, having obliged him to deliver up all the money he had—in search of which they ransacked the very bed and mattresses on which he was stretched—having taken his watch (which was of value) and all his linen (which was invaluable), and having devoured his daily bread, they left him, expressing the coolest contempt at his feeble menaces.

Feeling that such might be my case, still, even while Taylor continued to speak, I instantly took measures to conceal whatever was most valuable to me; and having deposited my money in a little earthen vessel, I sent it to be buried in the yard, and my watch and a great jar of wine to be otherwise concealed. Then, calling for my soup, which was at the fire, and hastily dispatching it, I poured into a large glass the last of General Sherbrooke's claret, and drank it with a sort of spiteful defiance, saying to myself, "You don't get this, my boys!"

Nothing that was at all less than the coil itself could be worse than the expectation of it into which Mr, Staniland's story threw me. Every object that I had been trying to consider a comfort in my distress, I no longer dare expect to be allowed the enjoyment of. The neatness and propriety that had been preserved about my bed now only served to mortify me, and to make the expected ransack the more cruel. The quiescence of spirit so desirable for one in my state was driven away. I took a mental leave of all that I could not hide, and began to consider how the money I had buried would renew that quiescence when the storm should have ceased.

When Mr. Staniland paid his visit next morning, he told us that the French infantry would arrive in an hour, and that the town was to be given up to pillage, because deserted by the inhabitants; "and," he added, "I am told that the general says it is impossible to put a guard over every British officer, and that they must take their chance with the rest. So I have had Captain Taylor removed to the hospital, where he will be safe."

The women consulted me on the propriety of locking the street door. "By all means," said I. "Make it as fast as you can, and don't show yourselves at the windows." The room where I lay looked into the street over the principal door, so that all parleys with the enemy must necessarily be held from my room.

Soon we heard the music playing before the infantry as it entered the town, and the women came flocking to the windows as if to see a raree-show, forgetting, in their eagerness for sights and songs, that these only announced the approach of the most wasteful ruin.

The soldiers marched close under my windows, passing through the town, to be encamped without the walls.

Soon after *thump! thump! thump!* sounded at the door. "Virgin of my soul!" said old Pollonia, tottering to the window. "There they are!" But, peeping out cautiously, she exclaimed, "No! 'tis but a neighbour. Open the door, Pepa."

"You had better," said I, "for the present, not suffer your door to be opened at all."

"No, no!" returned Pollonia; but Pepa pulled the string, and in came the neighbour.

"Well, neighbour, what news?"

"Jesus! Maria!" she exclaimed in a shrill tone. "The demons are breaking open every door, and plundering every house—all the goods—bales, chests—everything—dragged out into the street!"

"*Maria di mi alma! Señora!*"

"*Dios santissimo!*"

"Jesus!"

The crashing of doors, the tearing of windows, loud thumpings, knockings, and clatterings were now distinctly heard in every direction; and all outside seemed to boil in turmoil.

Ere long *thump! thump!* at our own door.

"Jesus! Maria! Jose!" the women screamed. But it was only another neighbour: so Pepa drew the string, and in the neighbour came, carrying the furniture of her house. Her head was piled up to a prodigious height with mattresses, blankets, quilts, and pillows. Under one arm were gowns, petticoats, caps, bonnets, and ribands, snatched up in the confusion of haste; her other hand held a child's chair, and strange articles of rude hardware seemingly but little worth the fervent anxiety which her countenance betrayed for their preservation. Add to all this that her figure was of a stunted and ludicrous character, and that she came in abruptly with a doleful crying face, under that cumbrous weight of household furniture, and beginning a dismal whine. All the grievances of my fellows in misfortune, heaped upon mine, could not suppress my laughter when that strange little figure burst upon my view.

"For the love of God, *señora!*" she said, "let me put these mattresses in your house."

"Woman," exclaimed Pollonia, "how is my house safer than your own?"

"O, *señora*, for the love of God! for the love of God!"

This pathetic adjuration was irresistible: they showed the good woman up into the garret.

Her example was followed by so many, that I feared the French would be enticed to the house. I told Doña Pollonia so; but she did not mind me. "Yes, yes, *señor*," she said, and then pulled the string again.

But soon there was a loud knocking at the door, accompanied by a volley of French oaths, that left me no doubt as to the nature of this disturbance. The door was assailed with such vehemence that it shook the house. Fearing that it could not resist much longer, I endeavoured to make a diversion from the window.

Summoning Pedro the Italian, who had a few words of barbarous French, "Tell them, Pedro," said I, "that this is the quarter of an English captain."

Pedro, who, when I took him at Coimbra, had totally lost his wits, and was naturally a poor, pusillanimous, miserable devil, had yet a little degree of Italian sharpness and education about him. He cautiously approached the window, and peeped out in breathless agitation.

"Gad so! there is but one," said he, somewhat assured, "and he has no arms. Hallo! *sair—la maison* for *Inglis captin!* Go to hell!"

Though much harassed and annoyed, this perfection in language, and the abrupt jabbering way in which it was delivered, forced the laughter out of me.

"*Ouvrez la porte—bête!*" vociferated the Frenchman, "I want some water," and again he banged the door.

"Holy Virgin!" said Pollonia. "We had better open the door!"

"No! no! no! "cried I. "Tell him, Pedro, that if he does not take himself off I shall send and report him to the general."

Pedro began in the same heterogeneous dialect to deliver my message; but he had not got half through it, when suddenly he ducked his head lower than his knees, and a great stone, whirling through the space he had vacated, struck the opposite wall.

"*Il demonio!*" muttered the women, as they ducked their heads.

Here, however, when the siege seemed most likely to prevail, it was unexpectedly raised; for the fellow, who was drunk, finding we would not open the door, and that he would get nothing but Pedro's jabber, just banged a stone at his head, and reeled off in search of some easier adventure.

Chapter 7

Pedro had hardly time to congratulate himself on his victory before the portal was again assailed.

"O!" said Pollonia, "it's only two officers' servants"; and she entered into conversation with them awhile, and then shut the window.

"Well," said I, "what did the officers' servants want."

"They wanted lodging for their masters; but I told them you were here, and that we had no room."

"And have you room?"

"Yes—but I didn't choose to say so."

"Run, Pedro," cried I,—"run and tell those servants that there is excellent accommodation here, both for their masters and for their horses. Persuade them to come if you possibly can! Don't you perceive, *señora*, that this is the only chance for preserving your house from pillage?"

But even this consideration could hardly reconcile the old lady to receive *los demonios* as lodgers in her house without having done her utmost to keep them out.

The two servants were far from unwilling to return. I sent for one of them—a Prussian lad of about thirteen. He spoke French very ill, but enough to tell me that he was servant to Captain de la Platière, who was *aide-de-camp* to the General of Division Villatte. The other lad, he said, was servant to his master's comrade, who held a similar situation under the same general.

I had seen enough of the French military to know that it was uncertain whether the falling into the hands of two French officers would be a mercy or a misfortune. A class so large must contain extremes of good and bad; and when education, habits, and example balanced the wrong way, it was evident on which side the scale must preponderate.

Notwithstanding all this, the hope that my fellow-lodgers would prove gentlemen encouraged a momentary feeling of security, and I anxiously wished for their arrival.

Meantime little Pedro observed the motions of the two servant lads with the eye of a lynx.

"*Signore*," said he, "those two *diavoli* are prying about into every hole and corner. I fear me they suspect something is hid."

Though I did not think there could be any truth in his conjecture, I sent Aaron to dig up my money, and bring my watch and the wine upstairs.

Soon after in came Pedro, strutting with a most consequential air.

"The French captain, sir!" said he.

There followed him a fine, military-looking figure, of a frank countenance, carried erect—with his hat on—armed *cap-à-pie*, and covered with martial dust.

He advanced to my bedside with a quick step, and a great air of frankness and anxiety.

"I have had the misfortune, sir, to lose a limb," said I, "and I claim your protection."

"My protection!" answered he, putting out his hand. "Command my devoted services! The name of an Englishman in distress is sufficient to call forth our most tender attention. Assuredly a wounded man can have no enemy; but the wounded of a nation so merciful to its fallen enemies have the most pressing claim upon our gentleness and friendship. 'Tis no favour—'tis our positive duty—to treat you with the same generosity and humanity which in our reverses we ever experience from you. We love and respect the English character, though our governments are always hostile. Compose yourself, my friend: you can receive nothing from the French but the alleviating care which your pitiable situation demands."

I was a good deal affected by the kindness of this speech. What he said was very true; but it was particularly delicate and acceptable to say it now. Kindness can never be thoroughly felt unless it be greatly wanted. Then it makes an indelible impression.

After sitting with me a few minutes (during which, in the most friendly manner, he inquired into all my wants), this gracious enemy prepared to leave me. Upon which I begged that occasionally, as he found leisure, he would pay me a visit, as I should consider a few moments' chat now and then a great relief.

"I will not only come myself," said he, "but I will bring my companion with me, who will be at least as solicitous as myself to soften a little the rigour of your situation."

So he left me, much more comfortable than he found me. My roast pigeon was served up in security: half of it, and a little bottle of wine, I sent to Taylor, who (poor fellow) was extremely well pleased with the present.

Senora Pollonia was charmed with the captain's kind manner to me; said he was very good, though a Frenchman, and that (she now remembered) he had lodged with her, when the French were last in the town, and had never offended her—but that the servants were sad *pigarones*.

Towards evening M. de la Platière brought in his companion. Captain Simon, whose appearance was still more prepossessing. He had the advantage of extreme youth, and was remarkably good-looking.

His manners could not be more kind than those of the other; but they were more soft and insinuating—his attention was more quiet and more delicate. He came and sat by my bed, and found many little things to say that might be consoling and inspiriting.

At the capture of the French at St. Domingo he was with Rochambaud, and might have been in England till now, but that he was befriended by Sir Thomas Duckworth, because he was high in the honours of freemasonry. The British merchants at Jamaica had treated him with hospitality fervid as their sun, and their generous presents had supplied him with a sumptuous sea stock for his voyage to England.

Thus he had received a most favourable impression of English character and English society. He knew some words of English, and with a tempered vivacity found means to make his conversation consolatory and agreeable.

Both offered to procure me dinner from their general's table. They went out on purpose to borrow books for me, and brought me some volumes, highly productive of resource for many weeks. They complimented me upon the valour and conduct of the British troops, and declared they had never witnessed a carnage so dreadful, or a battle so bravely contested.

In short, these officers did everything that men ought to do amid such circumstances; besides which, their personal qualifications and sprightly ease and candour of behaviour made me indebted to them for an alleviation which many with dispositions equally good would not have had it in their power to afford.

Thus was my situation for the moment even amended by captivity; and I regained the calm of spirit necessary to my recovery.

THE FELLOW I SAW ON THE SPIRE.

Chapter 8

It was not long that I was permitted to enjoy the alleviation which the society of those good-natured officers afforded me. On the 7th they apprised me that the division of Villatte was about to move, and that they must take their leave of me that night: before daybreak they must depart.

A rough cavalry officer bore them company in my room; he had long moustaches, was black, and looked a ruffian. They discoursed of England and France, and disputed on the present grandeur and future policy of the Emperor. Their opposite ideas bore no stamp of originality. It seemed as if they were reciting the current and popular language of the society in which they lived, rather than stating genuine opinions, the result of individual reflection.

It has been remarked that the French think less than other people, and that they are more liable than others to a contagion of sentiment, which, though it may render their conversation insipid to themselves, enables a foreigner the more readily to ascertain the general disposition. Conversing with one, you have the sentiments of a multitude! Yet these officers possessed a rapidity of utterance, propriety of language, and fire of gesture very like eloquence. Simon had a breadth in his cadence peculiar to the natives of Blois; that of de la Platière was impoverished by the refinement of Paris. Both spoke with a fluency and precision astonishing to an Englishman; and the Moustache interposed his barbarous sentiments with gruff and ferocious bluntness.

"The Emperor," said de la Platière, "may pretend to wish for peace, but it cannot be true. He is a warrior, and his element is a career of daring enterprise. His ambition is insatiate; he can't live beneath a serene heaven. It must be troubled with thunder and dark clouds, which he gilds and empurples by the glory of his achievements. I do not indeed believe that the conquest of England forms any part of his design—he knows too much to hope it. But, on the other hand, what has he to fear from her that he should wish for peace, notwithstanding his love of war?"

"*Mais, mon Dieu,*" exclaimed Simon, "after the feats he has performed—after having led the French through a track of conquest unprecedentedly splendid—after being to France a tutelary genius and an avenging deity—subjugating her enemies without—within replacing her laws, re-establishing her religion, multiplying her manufactures, beautifying her cities—and recalling the arts and sciences to their forsaken haunts—is it not most natural that the hero should at length incline to repose beneath the luxuriant shade of so many laurels; that he should now seek to consolidate and secure the vast dominion he has attained; to cure the populace of the disease of conscription; to nurse and recover the vigour of his finances, by stopping the vast flow from his widely-wasted treasures; and to reward the fidelity and bravery of his followers by conferring on them the blessings of property and peace? But he cannot attain these desirable objects any other way than by a strict alliance and treaty of commerce with England—with no other power! If Napoleon and George the Third would but say, '*Eh! soyons amis!* Let us divide the world between us—take you the seas, the islands, and the colonies, and I will take continental Europe'—no sooner said than done!"

"*Augh! C'est clair,*" exclaimed de la Platière; "and I wish with all my heart it was so! *Messieurs les Anglais* would then give us many things which we cannot do too well without, and we should send them wines of Bordeaux and Champagne. We should go to amuse ourselves in London, and they should return with us to Paris; and all the world could go and come at their ease."

"*Mais imaginez-vous, mon cher,*" continued Simon, "*la grandeur, la puissance alors de ces deux nations! Augh!* They are actually the only two nations upon earth! They contend without materially affecting the safety or the power of each other. The little states are not safe within the wind of such commotion; but the belligerents are too equally matched to gain anything by war. If serious hurt be done, it acts on both. Both may be weakened by loss of blood, but the superiority remains as undecided as ever."

"Those," interrupted Moustache, "are the speculations of politicians. All I know is that if I were the emperor I would burn every house and cut the throat of every human being on the continent of Spain! These miserable dogs of Spaniards, that murder and torture us whenever they can catch us straggling or sick! *Pardi!* I would make a fire in Spain of which the people in England should see the light, and know with what a signal vengeance we visit those who dare to maltreat the soldiers of France!"

"Well," said Simon, visibly shocked at this burst of tigerism, "let us talk no more of these matters, for I fear we fatigue this poor captain!"

"Ay," said de la Platière. "We had better leave him; it cannot be good for him to talk so much! [I had scarce spoken.] Goodnight, my friend. We shall soon return, and we hope to improve our acquaintance!"

"In the meantime," added Simon, "we have spoken of you in the most pressing manner to the officer who remains here as *Commandant de la Place*. His name is de Bon, and he is an excellent man. If you should want anything, and send to him, he will render you every service in his power. *Adieu!*"

I was truly sorry to part with these two officers, not only because they had interested me by their kindness, but also because, when they were gone, I should no longer have any security from the licentious visits of lounging soldiers; of which possibility they themselves were sensible, for they recommended me to conceal my money; and de la Platière wrote his name upon the door, in the hope that it might discourage those from entering whose purposes would not bear the scrutiny of their superiors.

Whether this frequent vicissitude of unquietness were the cause, or whether it arose from the natural progress of *curé*, I know not; but I now became subject to severe and almost incessant pain—the more harassing, as I could not seek to alleviate it by the slightest change of position, a relief which could not be attempted without risking serious consequences.

This, indeed, had been a harassing day. My fancied security had fallen from under me at a time when bodily pain began to tincture with discouragement the excursions of the mind; and I was vexed and disturbed by disagreeable reports of disasters to the British, and rigidly confined to one position, from the long continuance in which my whole frame had become irritable and uneasy.

To this apparently irremediable extremity the influence of opium applied a sweet and almost magical assuasive. I swallowed two little pills, and in half an hour how changed was my state! Every throb of anguish was profoundly stilled! Awake, I had only the consciousness of inviolable repose. Every sound was hushed. The voices in the room, or the noises in the street, though heard, were disarmed of all power to disturb my rest. The mind, still at liberty, and only disposed to range over the most peaceful and soothing scenes, restored me to my family, softly weeping with tender gladness at my return. So wondrous did it seem to be snatched from such wretchedness and placed in such measureless and enchanted repose, a line of Milton kept playing softly upon the ear of my understanding:

Yet with a pleasing sorcery could charm
Pain for awhile—and anguish . . .

Yet with a pleasing sorcery could charm pain for awhile! Then came the sweetly solemn, composed, and grave numbers of Milton, loosely floating on my mind with the gentlest recurrence:

The song was partial—but the harmony
(What could it less, when spirits immortal sing)
Suspended Hell, and took with ravishment
The thronged audience . . . .

Most grateful is the remembrance of these charmed moments—indelible their sweet impression.

I have written the account of them with a fidelity that to some will compensate for its seeming incoherency, and they who think I rave will find me brought to my senses in the next chapter.

Chapter 9

Thus entranced, and while conscious that the stillness of night had not yet given place to the busy hum of day, I was suddenly roused by the unwelcome accents of Moustache.

"*Eh, Capitaine, comment se va-t-il? se va mieux! Hah! bon!*"

When he had brought me down from the fairy voyage I was engaged in, he showed me that the blade of his sword was broken, and that it was no longer serviceable to give the soldiers the *coup plat de sabre*.

"As prisoner of war," said he, "you will have no use for a sword. Give me yours, and if you will, keep mine. 'Tis as good for you—as any! Where is your sword?"

"It stands," said I, "in yonder corner. Take it, by all means."

"Ha! bon!" returned he. "*Je vous laisserai la mienne.*"

So saying and so doing, he brushed off.

For my sword I did not care. He had said truly that I should have no use for it; but to be disturbed from a gentle rest was to one in my state a serious annoyance; and to be called from a rest whose soothing dream was Liberty by a hoarse voice croaking "Prisoner of War!" was exasperating. I am afraid I wished the sword in his gizzard; and from that moment my hopes of exemption from captivity were broken.

When dark Catalina came with my breakfast, she informed me that the bread I then saw was the last, and that the bakers were prohibited from selling any. Upon this I sent a note to the Commandant de la Place, requesting his assistance. He soon paid me a visit, and assured me that I should want nothing which he could supply. He was an elderly, respectable-looking man, and, sitting down by me, began to talk very rationally upon general subjects. I told him how much I was obliged to the kindness of the two officers who recommended me to him, and how much I deplored their absence.

"They are," said he, "two very amiable young men. You will soon see them again. They will probably be back Tomorrow. In the meantime, I shall endeavour to supply their place. Come, send your servant with me. I will find him some white bread."

Saying this, he left me, having relieved my dread of starving and of being plundered; for I learned from him that my two friends, in the expectation of immediate return, had left their servants, horses, and effects.

One anxiety made room for another, much more distressing—much nearer my heart—much more difficult to dismiss.

I remembered in what uncertainty as to my life the accounts that had been sent to my family would leave them, and that to this uncertainty would be added the horror of knowing that in so forlorn and helpless a condition I had been abandoned to an enemy made savage by a sanguinary war, and exasperated by recent defeat. Slender as the hope was that a letter would, amid such circumstances, reach its destination, my mind would, I thought, be easier after making the attempt.

Accordingly, I again applied to the commandant, who referred me to General Séméllé, chief of the staff.

It was then too late, I thought, to intrude on the general. So, having dined, and chatted with Catalina and Mr. Higgins, until my pains began to grow wearisome, I had recourse to the wondrous medicine, and tranquil repose soon held me in her soft embrace.

Next morning, after I had breakfasted, and the surgeon had performed his office, I called for pen, ink, and paper, and wrote to my father as follows:—

Talavera de la Regna, 9th August 1809.

My ever dearest Father,—I would give a great deal to know that this letter will reach you soon, for its purpose is to tell you that my recovery is proceeding fast. My dressing today gave me no pain. My appetite is good, and my spirits would be so if it were not from the fear of what you suffer.

The French officers have treated me with the most compassionate kindness, supplying me with books, or whatever else they thought might alleviate my situation.

As soon as I can travel, I shall go to Madrid, which is only four days' easy journey from hence; and then I have great hopes of being allowed to return to England on parole—for the French do not witness misfortune unmoved, any more than the English.

Let me think, my dearest Father, that the knowledge of my situation will be a relief to your anxiety. In this world, misfortunes must be borne; if borne with patience, they diminish; it is easier for us to bear them who believe that we shall all meet at last, in a world where they have no place!

We shall lessen the weight of actual misfortune by considering how naturally it might have been heavier. If, instead of the loss of a leg, the ball had taken any of the many frightful directions that make a man an object for life, and to which my body was equally exposed; or had it passed through my head, and debarred me from you forever, how much more need would you have had of your fortitude and resignation!

The operation promises the most favourable result. Consider then how capable I may hope to be of the enjoyment of my friends, and let me find amongst them a house of joy, not a house of mourning!

God bless you, my Mother and the rest! And believe me ever, yours, my dearest Father,   Charles.

Having finished this letter, I accompanied it by a note in French to General Séméllé, describing my situation and the motives which pressed upon me to give my friends some bulletin of my health.

In a very short time an officer, coming in and presenting a letter to me, announced himself as the *aide-de-camp* of General Séméllé. After thanking him for the honour he did me, I opened the letter and read as follows:—

A Monsieur Charles Boothby,
Capitaine du Génie, au service de S. M. Bque.

Talavera, le 9 août, 1809.

Monsieur le Capitaine,—J'ai reçu la lettre que vous m'avez fait l'honneur de m'adresser, et par laquelle vous me faites la demande d'envoyer à M. le Lieut.-Gal. Sherbrooke une dépêche qui a pour objet de l'instruire de l'état dans lequel vous vous trouvez, pour en donner avis à vos amis et parens en Angleterre.

Je vous assure, M. le Capitaine, que vos vœux à cet égard seront remplis, et dans l'instant même votre lettre va être envoyée aux avant-postes ennemis.

Si dans la position où vous vous trouvez, je puis vous être de quelqu'utilité, je vous prie de disposer de moi; je saisirai avec empressement l'occasion de vous prouver combien nous sommes reconnaissans des soins et des procédés que l'armee Anglaise a eu pour nos blessés et prisonniers.—J'ai l'honneur d'être, Monsieur le Capitaine, avec une parfaite considération, votre très humble serviteur, le Gal. Chef de État, Major-Gal. du 1er Corps,

Séméllé.

Translation

To Mr. Charles Boothby, Captain of Engineers in the Service of His Bic. Majesty.

Talavera, 9th August 1809.

Sir—I have received the letter which you have done me the honour to address to me, and by which you request me to send to Lieut.-General Sherbrooke a despatch which has for object to instruct him of the state in which you find yourself, in order to give advice of it to your friends and relations in England. I assure you, sir, that your wishes in this respect shall be fulfilled, and even now your letter is about to be sent to the advance posts of the enemy.

If in the situation in which you find yourself I can be at all useful to you, I beg you will command me; I shall seize with eagerness the opportunity of proving to you how much we are grateful for the consideration and care which the English army has had for our wounded and prisoners.—I have the honour to be, sir, with a perfect consideration, your very humble servant, the General Chief of the Gal. Staff of the 1st Corps,

Séméllé

The gracious manner of this letter was so pleasing, and its substance relieved me from such a weight, that after reading it I remained some moments overcome.

"And will you tell General Séméllé, sir," said I, turning my head towards the *aide-de-camp*—"will you express to him how sensibly I feel the kindness of his conduct—how much I am penetrated by the goodness of his letter? I am but an indifferent Frenchman—nor can I at present talk much in any language—but that so mild and so kind a man as your General will make allowance for!"

"My general," said the *aide-de-camp*, "has charged me to offer his services to any extent, and has desired me to assure you that he should think it a piece of good fortune to be able in the least degree to alleviate your suffering."

He then left me inexpressibly comforted.

I could now reasonably hope that my father would be apprised of my welfare subsequently to my being prisoner. This hope relieved me so much that I almost forgot I had any evils to contend with.

In the afternoon Pedro rushed in, in great agitation, and affirmed that the general himself was below, and begged to know if I would see him.

"Beg him to come up, Pedro," said I. And quickly he ushered in an officer of about the age of five-and-thirty. He was splendidly dressed, of an elegant person and a finely-formed countenance, beaming with good-nature and intelligence.

He came up to where I lay, and seeing that I received him with some emotion, without waiting for the form of salutation, instantly seated himself in a chair that was close to my pillow; and, laying his hand upon my arm, he said in a very mild and agreeable voice:

"*Ne vous dérangez, mon ami!* Solely I am come to see if I can possibly lighten a little the weight of your misfortune. Tell me, I beseech you! Can I be useful to you? Have you everything you want? Do you suffer much?"

For all these kind inquiries I expressed my gratitude more by manner than by words. I told the general, however, that since he had given me hopes of sending a letter to England, I really had nothing to ask—nothing to wish for—"unless, indeed," I added, "you could send me there too."

"Ah! if you were able to move," said he, "I would take it upon myself to exchange you—for just now I have the power; but by the time you will have gained strength enough to travel you will be at the disposal of the major-general of the army."

"Good Heavens!" I exclaimed. "Could not you make the arrangement now, to be executed afterwards? I cannot express the joy it would give me!"

"*Ah, non!*" he said; "but you have no cause for disquiet on that score. In your situation you will meet with no difficulty. Make yourself easy!"

Then, having again entreated that I would freely apply to him if I stood in need of his assistance, and repeating many expressions of kindness and protection, he left me. The comfort I had derived from his letter was much augmented by his charitable visit.

Chapter 10

In the evening de la Platière and Simon returned. We were already well acquainted, and our meeting was that of old friends. After inquiries as to how I had passed the time in their absence, de la Platière began to inform me that Sir Arthur Wellesley had met with disasters.

"*Taisez-vous, mon cher!*" interrupted Simon, in an under voice: "it may have a bad effect on his spirits!"

The other pulled up; and they would have given a sudden turn to the conversation, but that my anxiety was awakened, and I begged to be frankly informed of all that had happened.

"*Ce n'est rien, mon cher*," said Simon. "Your general—Wellesley—finding the roads impracticable, has been obliged to leave behind him his baggage and artillery. *Qu'est ce que cela lui fera? En Angleterre il en trouvera d'autres!*"

"*En Angleterre!*" I exclaimed. "*Comment donc?*"

"*Mais oui!* He is making forced marches upon Cadiz, where *plait au ciel* he will embark."

"Thank Heaven!" cried de la Platière. "*Messieurs les Anglais* once at sea, we will soon finish the campaign! *Sacré dieu! nous la finirons bientôt, allez!*"

"O!" said the other, "'tis the best you can do! Return to your happy island and leave us to quiet and restore this miserable country. Shed no more of your generous blood in the cause of a people unworthy of your friendship! See how they have treated you! When in their cause you have been fighting like gods, have they not tamely looked on and seen your brave soldiers fall by hundreds—nay, by thousands—without daring to make the smallest effort that might divert from your ranks the fury of the carnage? And now, when the bare thought of what you lose and what you suffer for them should tincture their valour with the noblest enthusiasm, how has this touching incentive worked on these barbarous Spaniards? They have butchered where they could their wounded enemies! And you—their wounded friends—in their cause wounded—have they not basely abandoned? They merit not what you do and what you feel for them. They are a nation of savages, who will be improved by being conquered. They are fit for nothing else."

"Poor Spaniards!" I ejaculated.

"I acknowledge," he added, "that they suffer grievous misfortunes, and I respect their determination to defend their country. But I detest them for their dark, bloody, assassinating ferocity. *Dieu du Ciel! c'est horrible!* I believe they would as soon murder you, their allies, if they found you alone and unprotected, as they would us."

"O pardon me," said I. "I have been all over the country alone. Every cottage—every palace—contained my friends and entertainers. So much were they impressed with gratitude for our conduct towards their country, that I received more the homage due to a superior being than the usual demonstrations of hospitality and goodwill."

I suppose the Frenchmen feared, from the animation with which I spoke this, that the subject might excite efforts beyond my strength; for with one accord, giving assent to what I had said, they begged they might not make me talk more than was good for me, and the conversation relapsed into that little easy chit-chat in which I might either join or not, or join sufficiently by a smile or a monosyllable.

I showed them the letter General Séméllé had written to me.

"*Il n'a fait que son devoir*," said they. "O! from our wounded we have heard innumerable instances where your generous countrymen have preserved them from the fury of the Spaniards. We will endeavour not to be behindhand with you. The king himself has declared that he will make the wounded we have taken here his peculiar care."

While we were talking in this manner, a French soldier walked quietly into the room, and, coming up to the foot of the bed, stood before the officers, astounded, petrified. When, after sternly eyeing him awhile, they sharply demanded his business, his faculties returned; and, stammering out that he took it for a shop, he made good his retreat. There seemed to be no doubt that his purpose was plunder, and I congratulated myself on the protection I enjoyed. I was still suffering, still immovable, oppressed by the excessive heat, and tormented by innumerable flies that blackened all the neighbourhood of my bed. Opium, patience, and lemonade assuaged some of these evils. Against the last, little Theresa, with a towel fastened to the end of a long cane, was very assiduous. Theresa was a very comical, arch little girl, and graced her occupation by many remarks of mingled simplicity and intelligence.

The day after my fellow-lodgers had returned, it was known that the corps of Victor was about to move towards the mountains of Toledo to repress the menacing attitude of General Venegas, who continued to threaten the Capital, and thereby to keep alive the ferment within it.

Victor was to be succeeded by Mortier in the occupancy of Talavera and its vicinity, while the united corps of Soult and Ney would show face to the allied army. My friends, in expressing their sorrow at again leaving me, assured me that the moment the troops destined to relieve them should arrive they would engage a particular friend of theirs to succeed them in their quarters. In pursuance of this promise, next day (the 11th) they brought with them a young officer of mild manners—fair in look, and strikingly gentleman-like. He said he regretted that he must decline taking the lodging proposed to him by his friends, but that should by no means impede his services to me; and he was convinced that he could with equal certainty offer those of General Girard, commanding in Talavera, to whom he had the honour to be *aide-de-camp*.

Recollecting the visit of the soldier who took the house for a shop, I asked if it would be possible to put a sentry in the house: the proposal was supported by my two friends, and readily assented to by the stranger. Then de la Platière and Simon took their leave, expressing the kindest wishes for my welfare; and I, as I returned them, added one that we might meet again under better auspices. This time my sorrow at their departure was unaccompanied by apprehension; nor did they leave me destitute of enlivening society.

The artillery surgeon was unremitting in his attendance, meeting Mr. Higgins at my quarters invariably at ten o'clock every morning; and their visit was usually repeated in the course of the day. As Mr. Higgins had of necessity intercourse with the French commanders, from him I used to hear all the news. His mind was of such a cheerful cast that it kept its tone amid all difficulties and all extremities. Never did I receive from his presence other than consolation. Since the battle he had never taken off his clothes—seldom, indeed, had rested—was ever in want of what could never be procured; and yet no whining—no complaining—no giving up!

Besides the occasional conversation of my medical attendants, I had that of the Spanish women, who, after the first emotions which patriotic feelings and domestic injuries had caused, soon regained a cheerful composure. I think that women are more excellent in this than men. We know that their feelings are more susceptible and more easily agitated; but when the blow, whatever it be, has fallen, and the inefficacy of lamentation has become evident, woman resumes her composure sooner than man. This was observable on both sides when poor Don Manoel re-entered his habitation. Gloomy and despairing was his sallow visage; his dark beard long and neglected. While his deep-folding cloak barely concealed the disorder of his dress, his hat, which he never removed (an old slouching cocked hat), rested on his eyebrows and flapped upon either shoulder. Forgetting all other consolation save that of shrouding himself in the tawny fumes of tobacco, dismal and breathing smoke he stalked about the house with the fearful gait of muttering melancholy madness.

Occasionally he would enter my room without noticing me or anyone else, so that I could only know of his presence by the waving of his long cloak, as he glided from the door to the window. At other times he would come to the foot of the bed, and, without seeming conscious that I observed him, would eye me with a look in which pity for me seemed to temper the extremest depth of sullen indignation. But if I spoke to him, instantly all moroseness or vindictiveness would drop from his countenance. He would listen with affectionate solicitude, and answer with an attention the most studiously gracious. By degrees his care found a refuge at my bedside. There he would sit, smoking and talking of his anger and his sorrow; glorying in having always defended and admired the political wisdom of Pitt; and listening with lively interest to my opinions about the persevering assistance that Spain might expect from Great Briton.

"O Don Carlos," he would exclaim, "if, with the assistance of God and of England, we could once sweep away these pestilent devils! If once we could plant the foot of our defence in the rugged defiles of the Pyrenees! Then, while our blood streamed there, poor Spain within might draw breath, and revive from her wounds, and be again herself. O Antonio, Antonio! how often, when thou hast eulogised the pacific wisdom of Fox—when thou hast demanded why England could not, like Spain, be at peace with Bonaparte—how often have I said to thee, 'Would to God the pacific wisdom of Spain may not peaceably resign her as a province to France! Would to God she could see, like Pitt, that for her there is no health but in exertion—no safety but in war!' And now, Don Carlos! What now can Antonio say to me? What, but that he was wrong! And with tears in his eyes does he now acknowledge it!"

At length Don Manoel, calmed by such expression of his trouble, would not refuse those little consoling attentions which the women of his country render to the dignity of man. He submitted his chin to the barber, and suffered his person to be tended as usual.

"CAPS OF THIS SORT ARE WORN BY THE WEALTHIER PEASANTRY—AS *ALCAL-DES* AND SUCH. THEY ARE MADE OF BROWN CLOTH STIFFENED IN THE CROWN, AND GARNISHED WITH BLACK VELVET RIBBONS AND TASSELS."

Chapter 11

I have not proceeded thus far in my narrative without many admonitions from that repugnance which all men, in the occasional remissions of vanity, must feel in giving a long history of them-selves. I struggle against this diffident reluctance, not because my vainer hours persuade me it is unfounded, but from a conviction that whenever I should hereafter perceive those impressive scenes of my life to fade and mingle in the retrospect as I left them farther, and still farther, behind me, I should feel incessant regret had idleness or ill-timed diffidence withheld me from fixing them beyond the transitory power of my memory. But, as I have no pleasure in writing anything that others are not to read, it behoves me to dress it in some degree for them, and to check myself in the diffuseness of egotism, that my narrative may not outlive the interest I wish it to excite.

As in this view it appeared unreasonable to have occupied so many pages in detailing the events of a fortnight. I have glanced back upon the matter they contain, and would unsparingly have curtailed it, but that my judgment, I confess, has acquitted it of prolixity. Peculiar circumstances attend this part of my history, which perhaps exempt it from the obligation of conciseness and dispatch which can seldom be well dispensed with in private memoirs; and I hope I am not misled by that purblind affection with which we are apt to look on our own works, when I conceive the causes of its bulk to furnish its apology. It is distended by the dialogues I have introduced; but, if I estimate rightly the curiosity of my readers, it will not be uninteresting to know how extraordinary circumstances acted upon foreigners respecting whose character and opinions the spirit of inquiry in this country has met with much contradictory information.

Faithfully and simply to narrate facts is to exclude the operation of prejudice; and it is giving my readers as fair an opportunity of judging as I possessed myself, if I state with truth what were the expressions of those people, when the nature of co-existent circumstances would naturally call forth the sentiments of the heart. This I have endeavoured to do. I have avoided drawing any inferences from the conversations I have related, and have written them from a careful effort of the memory—never of the invention. In translating the speeches of foreigners who spoke in their own language, I could always swear to the substance, and very often to the words.

The preceding pages are also distended by a minute attention to the effect of passing events upon my own feelings—in short, to the state of my mind during the pressure of an event which changed forever my corporeal frame, and cannot be supposed insignificant in its influence on my future life. While health and hope, in the effervescent fervour of youth, gave something of a magic colouring to the prospects before me—while, warm in heart and joyous in mind, the present seemed capable of but little improvement—one of those chance blows that are always impending over human enjoyment had fallen and wrought a change.

By dwelling upon that serious change, effected amid circumstances of exasperation and dismay, it is discovered that still much softness and mercy were suffered to mingle in the cup of calamity, not adventitiously found, but seemingly provided as the natural and innate shelter of a guiltless[1] mind; and in weighing the natural effects of a consciousness so delightful, it may be concluded that the influence of this change upon my future life will be beneficial. If so, I must consider laudable the greatest minuteness in giving detail which seem to authorise inferences so productive of confidence and courage.

Let not those who are untouched imagine that I clothe with undue importance an event that has happened to so many. It is not the less important because common. Death is common also; yet who, approaching his icy hand, has contemplated his stroke as less important because aimed alike against all mankind? Though of less magnitude than the change of death, of no trifling pressure is that alteration by which, from the buoyancy of adolescence, a transition is made to the slow and painful gait of irrecoverable lameness. Dear to me, and doubly dear because snatched away, is the free bound of exuberant youth. Dear the erect port, and the easy, deliberate, even pace of graver man-

---

1. The candour inspired by the tranquil gravity of my subject has betrayed me into an expression that sounds like the language of self-praise. By "guiltless mind" I mean no more than a clear conscience!

hood! Ever to be regretted, when lost, is the enviable power

To wander pensive through the silent groves,

or to range unfettered over the face of nature. Nor is there one movement, one sport, one exercise dependent on agility, but receives, as lost, a tenfold value in my mind.

These are regrets which follow my misfortune; nor perhaps are these the worst! But these and worse, had I no consolation but the blessings that remain, I trust I should bear without a murmur. The mind is still itself. There is health, and with it the spirit at least and the gaiety of heart that belong to youth; and if misfortune has deprived me of its activity, it is well to recollect that fortune enables me to move without it. The love of my friends is undiminished. It is they who have most lamented my distress. The social affections of life are mine! Nor is there any character, full of hope, to the feeling heart, that excludes me from its cheering promises.

And are not these enough? Ought I to deem the misfortune too severe which has left me the possession of these? No! The blessings that remain are enough to reconcile me to the blow. But if, while it has impaired the structure of my body, it may have improved the temper of my mind, if, imbibing under its pressure a great and momentous lesson, the mind may have learned to contemplate unappalled the extremes of misfortune in the instructed confidence that we are never abandoned; if, remembering the merciful softness with which its bitterness was tempered, I should own an enlivened gratitude to God (and even a better acquaintance with Him)—then who would wonder if not only I ceased to regret it, but, deeming it a blessing more than a misfortune, I would not even wish it to be recalled?

Chapter 12

After so long a digression, it may be necessary to remind the reader that my narrative has to be continued from the 11th of August, when my two friends, de la Platière and Simon, took their leave, having first brought to my acquaintance General Girard's *aide-de-camp*. Of this gentleman I have forgotten nothing but the name. His attentions to me were unremitting, delicate, and unobtrusive. Whatever he could discover I was in want of, he was industrious to procure; and came himself with plentiful supplies of coffee, sugar, and wine.

On the 14th I was informed that a British commissary who had fallen into the enemy's hands had just arrived at Talavera on his way to the English army, under a passport from King Joseph. A day or two before, Mr. Higgins had delivered to me a message from Colonel Bathurst, Sir Arthur Wellesley's secretary, most kindly offering his services, either in transmitting letters or messages to my friends or in any other way that I should point out. Taking advantage, therefore, of the opportunity which this commissary's arrival offered, I wrote to Colonel Bathurst as follows:—

Talavera de la Regna, 14th August 1809.
My dear Colonel,—I return you many thanks for your inquiries and offer, communicated to me by Mr. Higgins, the principal surgeon here.
My health continues very good, and my stump is going on very well: from what the surgeon says, I hope to be at Madrid in the course of two or three weeks.
I am sure you will be glad to give this information to my brother,—perhaps it would be more satisfactory to send him this letter.
Pray, if you can, advise him as to any exertions that may tend to enable me to return to England when recovered, either on pa-

role or by exchange. I should hope that, being (for the present at least) *hors de combat*, the thing might be managed. Pray tell General Sherbrooke, with my best regards, that I wrote to him on the 9th, enclosing a letter for my father, which General Séméllé *chef de état*, major to the corps commanded by Victor, kindly promised me should reach its destination.

We are treated very kindly by the French, and it is said that the king has interested himself about us.

Say everything kind from me to Colonel Fletcher, and believe me, with repeated thanks, my dear colonel, very truly yours,

Charles Boothby.

Lieut.-Col. Bathurst.

This letter, which Colonel Bathurst hastened to forward, reached my family before that of the 9th, and, being the first of my handwriting they saw after my misfortune, gave the first touch of joy to their sorrowing hearts.

About this time, my friend Taylor, having recovered sufficiently to move about with the help of a stick, paid me a visit. My soup was about to be served; so he seated himself by the bed, and we dined together. This unusual pleasure drew me into too much effort of conversation, and he left me fatigued and dejected.

About the 18th he wrote to me, complaining bitterly of the misery of his abode. "My sleep," he said, "is broken, and my uncertain appetite disgusted and driven away, by the deadly smell of a hospital and the groans of the dying. Make room for me if you can, and rescue me from this house of despair!"

I immediately consulted the good Pollonia, who, happy in the thought of obliging me and erecting a barrier against the French officers, delayed not her preparation. On the 19th, therefore, Taylor joined me; which, now that I began to regain my strength, was a great amendment in my way of life; for he was a kind, open-hearted fellow, full of spirit and entertainment.

We joined our establishments in the utmost harmony, except that his Englishman and my Italian used to amuse us by their petty disputes; the surly growling of the one and the pert chattering of the other, in languages as dissimilar as their manners, formed a remarkable contrast.

One day, however, their discordance took rather a more serious complexion. Pedro had passed some jest upon the Englishman, which, being delivered in Spanish, cut him off from all hope of retort, whilst he saw the Spanish women convulsed with laughter at his expense. The only answer which suggested itself to John was a thundering box on the grinning Italian's ear. Pedro, snatching up a large knife, with which he had been skinning eels, and swearing vehemently in every language he had ever heard, made John distinctly understand that his purpose was to stick it into him. Shocked beyond measure at so inhuman an idea, John rushed to his master pale and trembling, and began to utter the most grievous complaints.

"What the devil?" cried his master. "Can't you manage an Italian? If he runs his rigs upon you, can't you take and thump him?"

"I did thump him," John blubbered forth, "and he was going to stab me with a long knife!"

John in tears! Far from softening the heart of his warlike master, it served only to excite an alternation of ridicule and anger; and dismissing him with a volley of the most contemptuous reproaches, Taylor called upon me to join his mirth, which I could not help doing. Yet I apprised Pedro that if in his disputes he ever again dared to have recourse to a knife, the first use it should be put to would be to cut off his own ears—a threat at which he appeared less terrified than diverted.

The day after Taylor joined me, I had for the first time left my bed, and, seated in an elbow-chair, was carried to table in an outer room. This was at first a delightful change; but I was so much reduced and enfeebled that, the sitting posture soon becoming painful, in less than an hour I was glad to be laid again in the bed, and rest myself from this extraordinary fatigue.

Day by day, however, the difficulty diminished, and I was able to sit up longer, which restored to me the grateful change of occupation and rest.

While I had lain in bed there was no outward sign constantly before my eyes of the loss my frame had sustained; but when, refreshed with reviving strength, I had risen from the sick-bed, the deficiency was ever before me, to carry a pang to my heart; and it was now that I had to combat some feelings of regret, not perhaps unnatural, which I afterwards condemned as unmanly and ungrateful; and they fled before the reasoning supplied by calm reflection.

Meantime the progress of cure was not so favourable as had been expected. The disposition in the muscles to retract required a tightness of bandage which made me suffer extremely and broke my rest;

but as I became accustomed to it I bore it better. The perseverance of Mr. Higgins in this painful remedy warded off a predicament which in other cases was the cause of prolonged suffering, danger, or death. Taylor and myself lived very pleasantly and profitably together. Our breakfast consisted of tea, dry toast, and abundance of fresh eggs. After breakfast, I was replaced upon the bed with a book; and he used to walk out till dinner-time, and then return with all the current news, and perhaps with Higgins as our guest.

Then I, having been refreshed by quiet and composure, was very sprightly for the repast, and we generally attacked it with merriment and spirit; this more particularly when, by the arrival of a French sutler, we were enabled to heighten it with a bottle of claret. Pedro was an excellent cook, and made us eel pies and *stoffatos*; while as a standing dish the neat-handed Catalina prepared her incomparable *ollapodrida*.

The following letter is illustrative of our way of life at this time:—

Talavera de la Regna, 25th August 1809.

My ever dearest Father,—My limb, after a good deal of struggling, owing to a propensity in the muscles to retract, is now almost healed. I have quite recovered my appetite, and have got a friend to come and live with me, and we have very comfortable little dinners. I have great hopes that we shall get our liberty, as soon as able to undertake a long journey; at any rate, I feel confident that if I go to King Joseph's levy on my crutches and present my petition, it will not be refused.

I assure you, I could write in the gayest spirits, if I did not know that this letter would find you all in melancholy plight.

I wrote you a letter dated the 9th, to tell you how wrong it was to repine, and to scold you for your grief when you heard I had lost my leg. I assure you, the thoughts of the happy—many happy—days I shall spend in the midst of you, have lightened my sleepless nights, and have made me fed deeply grateful to God; not that I attribute to the Almighty any interference in the direction of the bullet, but I thank Him for so tempering the human mind as to enable it to draw consolation from itself at the very instant when the heaviest calamities assail the body. I shall, please God, return to you fresh, healthy, gay, and happy. Do not alter this by repining yourselves at that which now can-

not be remedied—but might have been so much, so very much worse. My kindest love to all. God bless thee, dearest Father!—
Yours ever the same, on one leg or two,   Charles.

Chapter 13

It was but a few days longer that I had the pleasure of Taylor's society. Hoping that the comfort of his situation, if not his prospect of exchange, would be improved by going to Madrid, he joined with other officers and accompanied a convoy proceeding to that capital. Before this period some British officers had removed thither. We had at first heard that the king made them his particular care. Afterwards a rumour circulated that some severity was resorted to, in consequence of an escape; but this rumour died away, and did not deter these officers from following.

Soon after Taylor's departure, my thoughts, as I began to promise myself ability to travel, turned towards my liberation. Marshal Victor had, on his own authority, exchanged several officers, and left with others their written freedom. Mortier might have the same power; and that he would not want the inclination I trusted from the accounts which Higgins had given me of his frankness and urbanity, to which, indeed, my friend now urged me to appeal. On the 29th of August, therefore, I wrote to Marshal Mortier (who is Duke of Treviso), stating my case and the anxiety that preyed upon my mind. I received his answer next day. It was as follows:—

> *M. Charles Boothby, Capitaine au Corps Royal du Génie, de l'armée Britannique, à Talavera.*
>
> *Au Q. Génal à Oropesa, le 30 Août 1809.*
>
> *Monsieur,—Je viens de recevoir la lettre que vous m'avez écrite hier. J'adresse à Madrid la demande de votre échange, et je prie S.E. le Major-Général d'avoir égard à la position où vous vous trouvez. Je m'empresserai de vous faire connaître sa réponse. En attendant, Monsieur, disposez de moi, ainsi que vos camarades, si je puis vous être utile à quelque chose.—J'ai l'honneur de vous saluer,*
>
> *Le Mal. Duc de Trevise.*

Translation
Headquarters, Oropesa, 30th August 1809.

Sir,—I have just received the letter which you wrote to me yesterday. I address to Madrid the demand of your exchange, and I beg His Excellency the Major-General to have regard to your particular situation. I shall hasten to let you know his answer. In the meantime, sir, make use of me—your comrades likewise—if I can be at all useful to you.—I have the honour to salute you.

The Marshal Duke of Treviso.

As I had indulged the hope that Mortier himself would have the power to let me go, his letter, kind as it was, disappointed me; yet I still hoped for a favourable answer from Jourdan, to whom he had referred my petition.

I think it was before this time that Colonel Donelan of the 48th Regiment died.

My own memoir promises to be so long that I do not profess to record in it the events which happened to my fellow-prisoners, however worthy of narration; but I should not be satisfied to omit the name of Colonel Donelan, who displayed yet more heroism in contemplating the sure approach of his last hour than when, glowing with glorious courage, and cheering his men in the thickest of the battle, he received the fatal wound. The French showed to his remains the greatest respect, and their superior officers joined our own in following them to the grave, wherein he was laid with military honours.

Early in September I had the pleasure to receive letters from the army—from Mulcaster, Colonel Bathurst, and General Sherbrooke. I copy the two last.—

From Colonel Bathurst
22nd August 1809.

My dear Sir,—I have sent home your letter to your brother, which, I hope, will give him pleasure, as it appeared to be written in good spirits. General Sherbrooke also wrote to your father by the same opportunity.

Sir Arthur has written to Mortier to request that such officers as are able to move may be allowed to return on their parole. I advise you to apply for this yourself to the French commander-in-chief, or direct to King Joseph, stating your situation; and I think you will succeed.

I have got a small quantity of tea, which I send to such as I know at Talavera; I am sorry it is not more—I have only two pounds. I wish you would divide one with Stanhope of the 29th, and the other between Major Popham, 24th, and Milman of the Guards. If I have any opportunity, I will try to send more.—Believe me, ever sincerely yours, James Bathurst. Captain Boothby.

From General Sherbrooke

24th August 1809.

My dear Boothby,—On the return of Mr. Commissary Dillon from Talavera, I immediately wrote to your father to inform him of the very favourable accounts which I had received of you, and of the very handsome manner in which, I understood, the whole of our prisoners had been treated by the French.

I hope that, when you acquire sufficient strength to be moved. Marshal Victor will allow you to come away upon parole; and should there be any French officer of your rank (about whom he may interest himself) a prisoner in England, I will use my utmost endeavours to have him sent back, in exchange for you.

I beg you will let me hear from you by every opportunity, as I not only am anxious to learn how you are coming on, but am particularly desirous to send information on so interesting a subject to your father and mother.

With every wish for the speedy and perfect re-establishment of your health, believe me, my dear Boothby, yours with great esteem and regard, J. C. Sherbrooke.

The kindness of these letters and of that from Mulcaster naturally gave me much pleasure. What they recommended, however, as a means of procuring my liberty, I had already done; and it was needless to communicate to Mortier General Sherbrooke's offer, since I had found that the discretion necessary to act on it did not rest in him.

The bed in which I slept was in a sort of recess, which might be separated from the rest of the room by drawing a curtain. On getting up, I had used to be carried to a window in the outer room, which, having a northern aspect, was cool and refreshing; but, though from this situation I could hear all that passed in the street, I could see nothing of it. About the 10th of September, I complained of this to Catalina, who instantly suggested that, if I would have myself carried into the passage and sit there, I should see all down the street. Accordingly, I was carried into the passage, and instantly found myself once more in the world.

The change which this trifling move wrought on my thoughts and feelings was incredible. I eyed everything with rapture; but chiefly a luxuriant fig-tree in full leaf, which, growing in the midst of the yard, thrust its broad fresh leaves over the balcony. Since my eyes had had nothing to dwell on but dirty white walls and the wretched images of Saints which hung thereon, they had become sadly weary. For more than six weeks I had seen no tree or growing thing; and I cannot express the delight with which I dwelt on every part of this fig-tree, curiously examining its manner of growth, from the substantial trunk through each twist of the branches to the consummate leaves:

First from the root springs lighter the green stalk.
And then the leaves more airy—last the bright
Consummate flower spirit odorous breathes!

I had never considered a fig-tree very wonderful before; but now it did indeed almost seem a miraculous thing.

On my right hand was a window, down to the ground, with a wooden balcony. Through this I surveyed the yard where the tree grew; where, also, the multiplied business of house and stable was by various hands proceeding. It seemed that I compared all that I now saw, not with like things which my eye had before been familiar with, but only with the pictures of such things. It seemed, in short, as if I were now viewing the reality of things, which I had hitherto seen only in picture! This was, I suppose, from my looking at everything with such avidity that no lineament of it escaped me, as we naturally do look at good pictures of common objects. For example, a man grooming a horse had not before seemed worthy of close observation; but any good drawing of it I had instinctively examined minutely. Now, long confinement caused me to examine the reality with equal minuteness; and, consequently, the mind compared what it now contemplated with the picture on which it had bestowed the like attention, not with the reality, which it had always viewed in a cursory manner.

In front of my chair was the staircase, by which all visitors were subject first to my inspection; and over the stairs was a window, through which the whole length of the great street was laid open to my view. It is worthy of remark, how much may often be done for comfort by little trouble. Just carrying my chair three yards farther had obtained for me a constant variety of interest and amusement; for now I could interrupt my reading by occasionally hearing the remarks of the women as they performed the business of the house. This would often draw us into conversation; thence came laughter, or gossiping anecdote; and time flew!

One morning, soon after this discovery, on my calling for Pedro, I found that he was gone out. As he did not come soon, I sent for Aaron, who, with a sleepy face, said that he believed Pedro had run away!

"Why do you think so?" said I, feeling sure that it was so.

"Because he has taken his things: I saw him packing them up last night."

The women now began to exclaim, and, coming to me, begged that I should instantly ascertain if he had robbed me.

"Far from it!" said I. "Yesterday he asked me for only half the wages due to him, which I gave him,—so that I am still in his debt."

They expressed great satisfaction at these tidings; and we presently acquitted little Pedro of all blame, and wished him a safe and prosperous journey.

He had stayed by me faithfully until I was becoming well, and able to do with little assistance, and then he had taken the liberty to think a little of himself. He might as easily have had from me the whole as the half of his wages. Perhaps this forbearance sprang from the fear of exciting my suspicion; but if from that of leaving me ill-provided, how very amiable was his moderation! Somebody met him on the day of his flight, near Naval Moral, by whom he sent his duty to me; and I have never heard of him since.

I had passed the expected time of my cure, which was retarded by unforeseen circumstances, prolonging my suffering and uncertainty. My strength, however, had rallied so effectually as to withstand the local relapse; and the progress of my health continued.

On the 14th of September I wrote letters to the army, enclosing one for my father to General Sherbrooke. These I sent to Mortier, with a request that he would forward them. I knew not yet how my family had borne the news of my disaster; and, judging from the fervent love I had ever experienced from them, I dreaded that their affliction would be unbounded. My chief anxiety, therefore, was to convince them that I myself was content, and to send them such pictures of my present state as to do away any despairing ones their sorrow might have painted. Such was the object of the following letter:—

Talavera de la Regna, 14th September 1809.

My ever dearest Father,—I enclose this to General Sherbrooke, and entreat the Duke of Treviso (Mal. Mortier) to forward it to him, which, unless there be any real difficulty, I am persuaded he will do; so that I have good hopes this letter will reach you. I have already told you that you are not to repine at the loss of my leg. I shall bounce upon you some day, expecting to find happiness and compensation among you. Think how I shall be disappointed to find you have all worn yourselves away in useless, pernicious pining!

In justice to me, and that you may be able to afford me the resources I shall seek, do not grieve for a loss that cannot be recalled. I dwell more on this subject than I should, from an expression which I remember my mother used when John Lumley lay ill. She thought, *to have a leg cut off was little better than dying.* I remember the observations of Philip Pierrepont equally well; they are more consoling: "He can ride, he can drive, he can walk, and at six o'clock he's as good a man as any!"

Look to the bright side, dearest Father, and be you as easy on the subject as I am, and it will soon be forgotten.

My cure has been retarded by an unexpected retrograde, but now it will probably be completed in a day or two.

I was very fortunately lodged in the house of a kind, good old woman, who was very much affected at my misfortune. Poor soul! she begged and entreated they would not take off the leg (for, owing to their want of skill, I believe they consider it a very hazardous operation). She came to me and proposed that some Saint or other should touch it, but I told her I wanted faith!

Now that I am up all day, and grown convivial, and make a deal of noise in the house, the old lady and I joke one another all day long! There is another dark, lively, dancing woman in the house who is entirely under my orders; and while she sits at work, I try to impede it by making her laugh.

The surgeon has forbade my mounting the crutches hitherto, but I sit in a situation whence I enfilade the principal street and see all that passes.

My companion is gone to Madrid, but I generally have somebody to dine with me, and am already no bad table companion!

I intended to cast over this letter a sort of decorous formality, as I must send it open; but I have been drawn out as it were, and there does not seem much restraint. The weather is less hot, which is a great delight.

My only restlessness is about you all; follow my advice, and this will not be such a blow as perhaps it has appeared to you. Give my kindest love! God for ever bless you, dearest Father!—Ever your most affectionate and dutiful son, Charles.

Peasants winding flax

Chapter 14

Though I have said much of the Spanish women, perhaps I have not made the reader acquainted with all the inhabitants of the house, every one of whom, in a greater or less degree, contributed to my comfort and entered into my acquaintance. By us, who keep such an impassable line between our own society and that of our servants, it cannot easily be conceived how freely, in the middle ranks of Spain, the two classes associate with each other. All the individuals under the same roof are treated as beings of equal natures. They have, indeed, different duties to perform—some to direct, others to obey—yet they are equally entitled to observance and consideration. Thus all contribute, according to their social talents, to furnish the family circle. Strange to say, this system, which should seem calculated to disturb the due subordination, appears to have an effect directly opposite. The submissive docility of the servants keeps pace with the urbanity and affability with which their masters treat them.

After these observations, the nature and variety of my domestic circle at Talavera will be the more easily understood. Don Manoel and Dona Pollonia have been already introduced to the reader; but these good people were not really entitled to such noble distinctions. Wherever I have been on the Continent of Europe, there has seemed to be a very lavish commerce with the titles of nobility. In Naples and Sicily every stranger not raggedly dressed was by the needy and expectant natives styled "Your Excellency" or "Your Lordship"; and every house, above a cottage, was by courtesy termed the Palace. I had a Sicilian groom who invariably used to say to me, "At what hour shall I bring Your Excellency's horse to the palace?"

So in Spain and Portugal the title of "Your Grace" is generally and indiscriminately used, and even passes between beggars. It was, I suppose, from this habit of bestowing liberally what may be so easily given that the inmates of the house called its mistress and her sons *Don* and *Doña*; and I naturally adopted it from them. Besides, they called me Don Carlos!

Don Antonio (a *Don* of the same description) was a lodger in the house, and much respected—a quiet, sensible, agreeable man. Next in consequence came Catalina—a tall, elegant woman of forty, whose dark complexion and jetty eyes gave great expression to agreeable features. She was more like a housekeeper than a common servant, and was held in the highest estimation by the *Señora*, who had known her from a child, and could not relish the *olla*, she told me, unless Catalina had put her hand to it. The inferior servants consisted of two old women, employed as charwomen, and a country wench as a house-lass. The old women were called Tia Maria and Tia Pepa; for, though the word *tia* means only aunt, it is commonly applied to such old women, even though their brothers and sisters should be childless. The name of the girl was Manoela—a lively, very simple, hardworking lass—plain, hale, and hardy, and capable of chastising with her fists any ill-mannered youth who gave her the least impertinence.

Each of the ladies allowed me to take a sketch of her person; and it was generally acknowledged (apart from the opinion of the subject) that each portrait was pretty successful.

But these were not all, nor yet the most agreeable, of my Spanish company. Soon after my feast of the fig-tree, which occasioned me to see so much more of what passed in the house, I was much struck with the appearance of a beautiful little creature playing in the yard. This, they told me, was la Marta, one of the daughters of Augustin, the carpenter. I soon became acquainted with this little beauty, and not long after with her sister, who had just grown into all the elegance and slender grace of a finely-formed damsel. Her face was not so beautiful, not so sparkling, as that of Martita; but it was more lovely, more replete with feminine charm.

Maria Dolores was in temper different from her little sister. She was pensive, tender, and, though not reluctant to laugh, did not herself move to mirth. That boneless simplicity of dress so advantageous to the female figure, when nature does not need constraint, gave its full lustre to the beauty of the young Maria. I remember the pliant stays, close grasping her thin waist, from the end of which a dark petticoat fell, not low enough to conceal how finely her legs and feet were made, nor how neatly they were clothed. Linen sleeves rolled up above her elbows exhibited smooth arms of alabaster.

A handkerchief, gathered about her throat in white but impervious folds, gave in modesty more beauty than it concealed. Her face, of an expression the most intellectual and a colouring the most pure and evanescent, blushed beneath the shade of her luxuriant hair, of a dark yet burnished brown, floating in broad artless curls from where it was attempted to restrain them. Such really was Maria Dolores. I am sensible that the description does not seem to suit a carpenter's daughter; but those who beheld her thought only of beauty in its sweetest prime and softest gentleness, "when unadorned, adorned the most."

These fair sisters, interested in my misfortune, and pleased with the kindness and openness of my manner, used to play about me with the familiarity and gentleness of kittens, and lightened many an hour. I was indebted for much of the society of Maria to those charms which made it so agreeable; for a French officer who lodged in the house of Augustin fell desperately in love with her and, because the parents wisely sent her to their neighbour's house, to keep her out of his way, used to be transported with fury.

The motions of the different corps, however, after a time took away this ungovernable lover and brought back my friend de la Platière. On the 19th of September, before I had done dressing, he brushed up with his wonted haste, and, suddenly embracing me, kissed each side of my face. Though somewhat disconcerted by this unusual mode of salutation, I was extremely glad to see him. He told me that Villatte's corps would enter the town in the course of the day. Marshal Mortier being destined to pursue the Spanish army.

He soon left me to finish my *toilette*.

When, having breakfasted, I had assumed my post in the passage, a French officer came to me, saying that General Séméllé had sent him to inquire how I did, and if I stood in need of his good offices. I was sitting in conversation with this officer when de la Platière returned, bringing me a letter from Mortier, of which the following is a copy:—

Oropesa, le 19 Septembre 1809.

Monsieur,—Son Excellence M. le Maréchal Jourdan, à qui je vous ai marqué que j'avois écrit relativement à la demande que vous faites de votre échange, vient de me répondre que S.M.C. lui avoit donné l'ordre de la soumettre au Ministre de la guerre à Paris.

Je désire, Monsieur, que la décision du Ministre réponds à votre attente, et que cette démarche ait tout le succès que vous pouvez souhaiter.

Je profiterai de l'occasion du premier Parlementaire pour envoyer au Général de l'armée Anglaise les lettres que vous m'adressez pour M. votre père.—J'ai l'honneur, Monsieur, de vous saluer.

Le Mal. Duc de Trevise.

Translation

Oropesa, 19th September 1809.

Sir,—His Excellency the Marshal Jourdan, to whom, as I have informed you, I had written relative to the demand you make for your exchange, now answers me that His Catholic Majesty had given him orders to submit it to the Minister of War at Paris.

I wish, sir, that the decision of the minister may answer your expectation, and that this proceeding may have all the success you yourself can wish,

I will avail myself of the opportunity of the first flag of truce in order to send to the general of the English army the letters which you send to me for your father.—I have the honour, sir, to salute you.   The Marshal Duke of Treviso.

I concealed, beneath as gay an air as I could summon, the. bitter disappointment which the perusal of this letter caused; but de la Platière, having read it, seemed rather disposed to congratulate me upon its contents.

After General Séméllé's *aide-de-camp* had departed, however, and I had been carried into my room, he said, "I perceive that the marshal's letter vexes you. You are wrong to let it. I can tell you exactly how all that will be managed. When you are well, you will go to Madrid. Refresh yourself there! See all that it contains! It is not Paris; but it does not want resource. You will be very well amused for a time. When you are tired, purchase a commodious carriage and travel quietly to France! Spend three delightful months in Paris (you cannot see it in less than that), and then you will be exchanged."

He said all this in such a flourishing manner that I was in doubt whether to be comforted or provoked,—a balance which enabled my good-humour to come forward, and I consented to be amused. But I would not acquiesce in the plan he had laid down as long as a hope remained that I should be allowed to go to Lisbon instead of to Madrid. General Séméllé, I remembered, said, when I first saw him, that he himself could exchange me but for my inability to travel. I was now able to travel. Did he still retain the power to release me? I thought it worth asking, and wrote to him for that purpose.

I was at dinner, enlivened by de la Platière's conversation, when, to answer my letter, and to satisfy his own good feelings. General Séméllé called upon me.

"*Ne vous dérangez pas*," he said, as he entered; and, quickly sitting down, added that it would give him great pleasure to see me finish my repast with a good appetite. Then, adverting to the letter I had just written to him, he informed me that he had forwarded to Madrid a list of such British officers as were mutilated, with such a strong recommendation as he hoped would effect their speedy release. He spoke of the battle, eulogised the English troops, and observed of Sir Arthur Wellesley, "*Assureéent c'est un homme de talent—oui! il a démontré un grand génie pour la guerre—il a beaucoup de talent!—beaucoup! il n'y a rien de plus sur!*" General Séméllé, had he commanded the French troops, would have attacked the Spaniards mainly, while he made a brisk reconnaissance upon our part of the line. Before he went away, he good-humouredly laid his commands on de la Platière to befriend me with zeal, and entreated me upon all occasions to command his own services without reserve.

This interview but little increased my prospect of liberty, and I began to think it so remote and uncertain that I indulged less in dreams of return. I was now almost constantly in the society of De la Platière, who, deeming solitude the most pitiable of evils, and especially, as he said, *quand on dine*, came to me invariably at dinner, in order (as he expressed himself) to make his court to me. But, unfortunately, either from a national or from an individual peculiarity, it is in some degree irksome to me to dine in the presence of a friend who is not dining.

Therefore I used to say to him, "Eat—I must insist upon you eating; for I cannot without horror sit devouring here while you do nothing."

It was to no purpose. Neither would he eat nor suffer me to dine alone. As now my health was more assured, and we knew one another better, we disputed freely. With an unusual degree of national vanity, even for a Frenchman, he possessed an immovable good-nature which ensured an amiable close to our debates. Among other things equally provoking, he said that if a single ship of France and another of England, each of equal force in all respects, were to come to close quarters at sea, there was no doubt that the French ship would gain the victory. Our admirals were better, he said; therefore our fleets prevailed; but, ship to ship, the French must beat, because they would rather sink than strike.

"And I believe," said I, "that wherever the experiment has been tried your ship has been obliged to do one or the other. These sentiments, my friend, are natural for you to encourage. I entertain those which I hope equally become me; but I should never have insisted on them in conversation with a Frenchman. I have never yet told you that I think our soldiers superior to yours; yet I feel as sure of it as that our fleets are so."

"*Non! non! non! non! non! Mon cher Capitaine !—ah! bah! bah!—par terre, vous ne pouvez plus lutter contre nous! non! non! par terre, notre supériorité est parfaitement décidé. C'est une chose qu'actuellement on ne peut plus disputer!*"

"By numbers you are superior—that indeed, cannot be disputed. You outnumber us so that we can but seldom look you in the face. When we do, I do not think we have your other superiority so very evident. *Mon cher ami*, you know I can bring an example, respecting which we can neither of us be misinformed. How have your 45,000 men been received here by 20,000 British?"

"You count for nothing, then," said he, "50,000 Spaniards?"

"Their amount, on paper, before the battle was 30,000. And recollect that it was only the other day that you yourself branded these Spaniards with ignominy for not firing a shot."

Facts were here so much against him that he could only account for them by the extraordinary skill of General Wellesley and the blunders of Victor—ending by a remark (with which perhaps he had better have begun) that on national subjects it was not to be expected we should come to an accordance of opinion.

But we agreed no better on points still more important. He said that he would rather die than suffer all I must have gone through. I answered that I must appear to him a much more forlorn and miserable object than I was disposed to think myself.

"*Ah, non!*" said he. "You have got through it; but I speak of when you received your wound, and, after a great deal of cutting and torturing proposed, life was to be very uncertain. That protracted suffering and being coolly carved with a great knife is intolerable. No: I had rather die. *On est tué—c'est fini! On meurt sur la champ de battaille—c'est en règle!—on y meurt avec gloire!* but to linger, and in cold blood to have one's best limbs severed from one in the flower of one's age! *Ah! Dieu! C'est terrible! Non, mon cher!* In such a case I have always a little store of opium to secure me from protracted torments!"

"How," said I, "do you know that opium would end them?"

"I would take enough to kill me!"

"You would die; but are you sure that dying would accomplish the view with which you would commit suicide?"

"*Ah, mon cher! si vous allez parler de l'autre monde*, it is what we can neither of us know anything about. No, no! I regard death as the end. If I am to live again, 'tis not my fault. I shall make the best of it!"

I am reluctant always to put forth to the storms of controversy opinions bereft of which I should seem such a bubble as de la Platière believed himself; and from a Frenchman I had an especial horror of drawing upon myself a tirade of modern philosophy, which truth's clearest voice would seek in vain to silence; for it is in the hope of drowning that clear voice that modem philosophy clamours. The sceptic, with all possible coolness, sits trifling with the Christian, who, on his side, shakes under the weight of the cause he defends. On the issue of the argument seems to depend the question whether he be an insect.

Born but to breathe, to suffer, and to end,

or an angel, for a while debased by a cumbrous, offensive body, but immortal, and capable, if he will, of becoming all, in grandeur, power, and knowledge, that his mind in her noblest flights has ever meditated. Anxious, alarmed, outraged, he is easily provoked by metaphysical substitutes which he wants the patience to examine; and the dispute ends, leaving him who has been arguing for more than life worsted and wounded; while he who has had nothing at stake but his ingenuity withdraws in triumph.

Yet with great reluctance I left de la Platière sunk where I found him!

"If," said I, "your own mind does not tell you there is another life, ailment is vain."

"*Il peut être,*" answered he,—"*il peut être que j'ai mes rêves de l'immortalité, aussi bien qu'un autre!*"

When reason, enchanted with her powers, gives herself up to her own conceit, and will not only go alone, but predetermines to leave the beaten path, what a fool she makes of herself! God and the Devil—without which the making of man, and man's too evident depravity, are unaccountable—she stupidly stigmatises as extravagant fables; and the noble aims of the misguided soul, instead of being gleams really divine, are only "*des rêves de l'immortalité!*"

Such is the steadiness of her incredulity against the clearest evidence, traditional and internal, when reason sets herself to make a belief after her own fashion, immeasurable are the absurdities she swallows!

Chapter 15

Some of the evenings which I passed in the society I have described were diversified by the *fandango*, in which both old women and girls, coming into my room, would join for the purpose of entertaining me. The graceful figure and the tender countenance of Dolores, her long flowing hair, free and disordered by the exercise, gave a lustre to this rustic pastime; while the beautiful Martita, acting the mischievous monkey, with an ivory grin and sparkling eyes, could do or say nothing that misbecame her. Contrasted with these were the stiff Tias, who, with stern visage and vehement gestures, seemed determined to show me that their youth had far surpassed the specimens I now beheld. Nay: so anxious were they that I should not be deceived in this particular, that the *Señora* herself solemnly assured me that her waist when a girl was not half so thick as that of the slender Dolores.

De la Platière sometimes sat with me to survey the dance, and the kind Spaniards, won by his attention to me, had lost the connection between his presence and their horror of all his nation. Mr. Higgins had stipulated with me that I should not attempt to walk until my wound had been three days healed; Augustin had made me a pair of crutches long ago; and, my surgeon's permission being at length obtained, on the 1st of October I prepared once more to go out of that house into which, nine weeks before, I had been carried with but little hope of life. Many were the feelings which thronged within me as, tottering and slow, I crawled along over the dirty, parched pavement! The sense of attracting general observation hurried me, and made more difficult a means of walking of which I had yet had no experience.

Neither the French soldiers nor the Spaniards refrained from observation as I passed. The former invariably expressed surprise at seeing the success of an amputation which in the hands of their field surgeons they knew to be almost always fatal. The Spaniards regarded me with the fondest compassion and the loudest sorrow, their affectionate sympathy touching their remarks with a colour of generous encomium.

"What a pity!" "Good God, what a pity!" "So young, too!" "Poor Englishman!" were pathetically passed along the street, and from one door to another.

Notwithstanding the difficulty with which I moved, I found such a pleasure in the glimpse of liberty that I managed to get as far as the square, where levies of officers were assembled, conversing. While resting in the shop of a *traiteur*, I had some conversation with Captain Christie of the Guards, who had been fortunate enough to get his exchange pre-arranged by Marshal Victor, and, being now able to travel, was to leave Talavera in a few days, for the British army. How I envied him! I returned fatigued with my walk; but it gave a value to repose and a zest to appetite which amply compensated for the labour.

I had met with General Séméllé in my walk, and the next day waited upon him to thank him for his kindness. That no time might be lost in preparation, if I should obtain my release, I put myself in treaty with a Spaniard who had just come from Madrid with a phaeton, in which he professed his readiness to take me to Lisbon; and, in order to ascertain how I could bear the motion of such a vehicle, at my request he brought it one evening to the door, drawn by two clever nags. I got up without much difficulty, and desired him to drive towards the field of battle.

Away we went at a great rate: it seemed to me now strange and enchanted, rapidly to cleave the fresh air streaming from the wild hills! The melancholy uniformity of a Spanish dwelling, the more melancholy dirt and disorder of a sacked town, had jaded my sight, which now flew with rapture to regain the scenes of nature that it loved—while all the events connected with those scenes passed over the mind in a wide current of thought. We could not get sufficiently upon the field to satisfy my curiosity. Fragments of red and blue dress peeping through the mounds of earth—and here and there a human form that had escaped the care of the buriers—brought back all that had passed. But my wish was to gain the hill where the British fought; there the mightiness of the carnage had repelled all thought of burial. This, my driver assured me, was impracticable; and I returned much refreshed, and well pleased to have found but little inconvenience from the motion of the carriage, from which the fair and gentle Maria helped me to descend, softly reproaching me for such indications of departure.

About the 4th of October, De la Platière finally took leave of me—Victor going from Talavera, and the headquarters of Mortier being established there in his room. I called upon this officer, the Marshal Duke of Treviso, the day after his arrival. He occupied the house which General Séméllé had left; it had also been the quarter of General Sherbrooke, who intended it for mine. The Duke, not having been at home when I waited on him in the morning, sent to beg I should dine with him. On presenting myself at his dinner-hour, I had to remain some time with his officers and French guests and Sir William Sheridan (who was now senior in rank of all the British prisoners remaining in Talavera, and was to go to Madrid the next day). The discourse turned upon some successes obtained by the marshal over the rear of the retreating Spaniards; the French officers claimed to have taken all the Spanish artillery.

The marshal soon entered from his private room. By his dress and figure he might have belonged to Frederick the Great—tall, thin, and upright, with good features, and a countenance so clearly marked with mild and simple honesty, combined with a look of direct intelligence and good sense, that whoever amid oppression had seen his head rising above the crowd, had confidently exclaimed, "O! that man will never suffer it! That man will surely help us." Towards me particularly he adopted a protecting manner at once the kindest and the least burdensome, being so easy as to make it seem a matter of course, and to keep the favour of it quite out of sight. For the good taste of such conduct did not appear to be the result of election, but the dictate of nature.

At dinner the Spaniards were much abused, the duke affecting not to pique himself on the mischief he had done them. Turning to me with a smile, he said, "We found them taking their *siesta* and were uncivil enough to wake them! They are like sheep—to beat them is to do nothing!" A *farouche chef d'escadron* at the other side of the table then applied to them every term of vile reproach which could be collected on so sudden an occasion. This induced me to state my opinion that the Spaniards individually were brave, as might be shown from many instances; but any military man, I said, would have no difficulty in understanding how an army might be coward collectively though composed of very brave individuals—under bad officers and a bad organisation.

The *chef d'escadron* cocked his hat, and seemed about to fire, when the duke exclaimed that my observation was perfectly just, and that bravery might certainly be unavailing where the usage of war was wanting. A shrug and a horrible grimace from the *chef d'escadron* notified his constrained acquiescence, and General Girard, Mortier's second in command, rallied him upon his furious hostility.

After dinner we went into another room to coffee, where the duke held a levee, and, while conversing with his officers as to the site of our battle, turned suddenly to me.

"Do you think," said he,—"do you in your own mind believe that General Wellesley would have manoeuvred in the same manner if our emperor had been before him instead of the King of Spain?"

Half laughing, I stated my conviction that, if the emperor's presence would have operated at all upon Sir Arthur, it would have been in the way of attraction.

"Then," said the duke emphatically, "without at all meaning to boast, I give you my word of honour, I have not the smallest doubt that, with the exact information which our emperor always has, and the measures which he would most surely have taken, not one man of your army could have escaped!"

Seeing me take snuff from the box of a French officer, he asked if I liked snuff, and, finding I did not like that to be met with in Spain, "I," said he, "have some excellent French snuff—and, sending for his *valet de chambre*, he ordered him to give me all he had, saying he could easily get more.

He spoke very good English when I addressed him in that language; but he generally spoke to me in French, and asked me why I wrote to him in English since I knew French.

"I write French very ill, sir," I said, "and I knew that your Excellency spoke English like an Englishman."

He seemed much pleased to have his skill in our language thus considered, but disclaimed the compliment, saying, "I could have spoken it tolerably—I resided in England a good while when I was very young. I went there only to spend money for my father!"

On returning home, highly pleased with the good marshal, I was met at my room door by Don Manoel, who was in great glee at the information, which had already reached him, that the marshal duke had treated me with much distinction at dinner.

By degrees I became more accustomed to my crutches, was less disconcerted by the remarks that were made on me, and felt independent; for after Don Manoel had told me of all that belonged to the place, and had shown me the shortest way to the river-side, I used to go there alone, and, seated on the bank, watch that current so swiftly flowing to Lisbon, carrying with it whatever fragments of timber or other floating substances accident had committed to its course. "Those," methought, "will go without hindrance to Lisbon. Why is man's body so cumbersome, so unaccommodating? What an easy method of journeying—to lay myself upon these waves, and let myself be floated along!"

About this time many of our men who had recovered found it no difficult matter to escape. I heard Mr. Higgins pressed upon this subject. He was perfectly master of his time and motions, not from having given any parole, but because those duties he so manfully undertook, which were hardly more beneficial to us than to the French, required that he should be unconfined. He was offered disguise and safe-conduct, and his success appeared to us both to be certain. The proposal was the more tempting because all the British surgeons, whose liberty one of the French commanders had guaranteed, were now declared prisoners as well as those for whose welfare they had suffered themselves to be taken.

Neither was Mr. Higgins ignorant that, all exchange of prisoners being impracticable, the liberty and prosperity of the best years of his life would probably be sacrificed. He felt, also, that every important part of his duty had been well performed. Almost all the soldiers had been removed to Madrid; his energy, his management, his mediation, were no longer wanted; and no one would now have suffered by his absence. But he rigidly considered that while one man remained sick at Talavera of those who had been committed to his charge, duty prescribed his stay; and all temptations to go were unavailing.

Since I had been able to go out of doors, I had become intimate with Charles Stanhope, a young officer of the 29th Regiment, who had been desperately wounded, and subsequently reduced to a shadow by illness. It was a great resource to me to meet with one so gentlemanlike and agreeable, and he, having long been debarred from any society he liked, seemed to forward our acquaintance with no less pleasure. He now, as well as Mr. Higgins, was often my companion at dinner, and occasionally there were one or two others.

Don Manoel enjoyed these parties. As Englishmen, he loved us all; and, with an expression of the darkest mystery, he would fasten the door as he entered, then look out of the window and all round the room, and when sure that all within hearing were honest and friendly, he used to talk in whispers of wonderful news of dangers past and hopes to come. One evening, when his heart was thus opened, the wine found an easy passage down his throat. His hat was removed, his cloak thrown back, and his dark visage was illumined by a smile but ill suited to his ghastly physiognomy. His mother came in and reproached him for his intemperance; but he had already drunk too much to be awed, even by the voice he was accustomed to honour. In the midst of her loud remonstrance, he regarded her with a satyr's grin, and filling a tumbler to the brim, swallowed it at a gulp; and immediately resuming the same grin, he gazed upon her again, till she was nearly beside herself with anger and apprehension.

"*Bestia! Lojo!*" she exclaimed; and then to me—"*Por l'amor de Dios!—Don Carlos!*"

"What can I do, *señora?* Can I refuse him the wine?"

Poor Manoel, however, unused to such excess, was soon glad to get out of the room, and did penance all next day.

Chapter 16

Having been so well pleased with the Duke of Treviso's first reception of me, I was not reluctant to comply with the following invitation:—

> *Au Quartier Général à Talavera,*
> *Le 9 Octobre* 1809.
> *Le Maréchal de l'Empire Mortier prie Monsieur le Capne. Boothby, de lui faire l'honneur de venir dîner chez lui aujourd'hui, à 5 heures.*
> Réponse s'il vous plait.

I took this opportunity of mentioning the subject upon which I had formerly addressed him by letter, desiring his opinion as to what would probably be the answer of the Minister of War, to whom my application had been referred.

"*Si vous voudrez suivre mon conseil, M. Boothby,*" said the Duke, "*ce serait d'aller à France tout de suite! Une fois en France, il n'y a pour vous plus de difficulté! Ou si, là, on vous détint pour quelque temps, au moins—ce serait en France! Si vous vous trouvez près de l'Empereur, M. Boothby, demandez le voir! Je suis sûr que si Sa Majesté vous voyait, Elle vous renverrsait chez vous. Je vous en reponds! Si j'étais à votre place, moi, je ne perdrais pas un moment de me rendre à Madrid. Là—vous pouvez faire très commodément vos préparations de voyage. Ici— on ne trouve rien—absolument rien! Madrid est une ville de ressource! Je vais y expédier un Convoi le 14—vous conviendrat'il de vous en profiter aussitôt?*"

Very far from pleased, I could not but be convinced that, whatever difficulty there might be in the way of my release, it could not be removed in Spain; and, accordingly, I did not hesitate (adopting the duke's friendly advice) to turn my face towards the Pyrenees.

I said I should be glad to go to Madrid with the convoy his Excellency had mentioned.

"But do not," said he, "let me send you away. Stay here, I beg of you, as long as you please!"

"I am aware, my Lord," I answered, "of your indulgence; but since I am to resign the hope of going to Lisbon, I consider Madrid as a stage on my way to Paris, and the sooner it is performed the better!"

"How will you go to Madrid, Mr. Boothby?" said the Duke. "I am sorry to say I have nothing but a waggon at my disposal: you must not go in that!"

I said I was in treaty for a conveyance which I had tried and found sufficiently commodious; at which he expressed his satisfaction.

The talk of my departure, particularly towards Madrid, gave the greatest disturbance to Maria Dolores and to the little Martita. They entreated my further stay, holding out as an inducement the hope there was that the English would return; and on the other hand, as a threat, the perpetual separation from my friends and country which would surely result, as they imagined, from my sufficing myself to be taken to France. "Once in France," they said, "you are a captive forever."

I was touched with their affectionate sorrow. Doña Pollonia, with a little air of festive allurement, painted to me the social comforts of their winter hearth. If I would pass the fireside season with them, "who knows but in that time," said she, "we may see better times? Staying here, you can't be worse; but going to that infernal France, and travelling such an endless distance by land, in such a plight as yours—Jesus! Maria! what will become of you, poor thing? Aye," said she (seeing me laugh), "aye! aye!—whatever I say, always laughing! When you lay as white as a sheet and almost in the agonies of death, and I wanted the Holy Saint to be brought to touch your mangled leg—even then" (turning to the rest)—"even then—the poor thing laughed. Well, thank God for all things! It's well you've the spirit to laugh. Poor Englishman! your heart has brought you through much. The commissary's wife said to me—the last word as she left the house—'Your poor young Englishman will die!' 'No! *señora*,' said I: 'it does not seem to me that he will die—*tien mucho coraçon!* Si, señor!—*esto dicheva Io!*" So the good old soul ran on, while the others chimed in, hoping to induce my stay.

On the 13th, in the morning, I received a kind note from the Duke of Treviso, accompanying sixteen letters, which he had taken the trouble to select from a great number sent to his outposts by Sir Arthur Wellesley. I did not know whether those from my friends in

England would have left them once their knowledge of my misfortune. The blood forsook my cheek—my forehead was cold and my heart laboured within me; but on opening a letter from my father, and seeing a picture of the misery which he and those with him were suffering, my passion burst forth in plentiful tears, which continued long and uninterrupted—relieving my breast, and perceptibly doing me a benefit my mind had languished for. This is what my poor father wrote:—

Edwinstowe, 17th August 1809.

O! my ever dearest Charles, how shall I find words to express all that we have suffered and shall suffer, till we hear the joyful tidings of your being quite out of danger? Thank the Almighty, all the accounts we have received confirm your dear letter, but still you know our hearts too well to suppose one moment of comfort can really possess us till every danger is passed. If anybody had told me you were to come home with the loss of a limb, it would have made me wretched. Now, it is all my hope and prayer—I see nothing dreadful in it. All the letters I have received from General Sherbrooke, from Stewart, and Colonel Fletcher give the most favourable accounts, and might content minds commonly affectionate.—I cannot proceed—may the God of all mercy send you safely to us. I have written to Mrs. Meynell to write to Admiral Berkeley; Lord Manvers has likewise written. God for ever bless and preserve you. With the most affectionate love of us all, I am, my ever dearest Charles, yours, with the truest love and affection,

W. Boothby.

Draw on me for what money you may have occasion for.

The next letter I opened, being directed by my father, was from his angelic neighbour. I copy it:—

Edwinstowe, 17th August 1809.

My dear Charles,—Your father is writing to you, and sends his letter to Lord William Bentinck, and I write this to send by another channel, through the Foreign Office. It is a great comfort to me to be able to give you a satisfactory account of your dear friends here; their anxiety about you is what you can easily conceive, but they look forward to seeing you return to us in good health, and their thankfulness that you have escaped with life keeps pace with their grief to hear of your sufferings.

They received your letter and General Sherbrooke's last night, since which we have scarcely left them; your dear mother and Louisa are now composed, and your father also. Louisa will write to you tomorrow; the kindness of your letter has been a balm to them all. We all join in prayers for your perfect recovery, and shall be most anxious for further accounts from you, and still more anxious to see you here. Milnes and myself feel for you as if you were one of our own children, and partake of the distress of your family. May God bless you, my dear Charles. Brooke was from home on the moors, but quite well, and they expect him as soon as he hears of this disastrous engagement.
We shall devote our time to the comfort of your friends, till they have further accounts from you.—Believe me, my dear Charles, with every kind wish, most affectionately yours,

Charlotte Milnes.

Lord Manvers has written to Admiral Berkeley about you, and a friend of mine will also write.

How comfortable was this considerate and benignant letter! At reading that which follows—from my brother—my tears fell in greater abundance:—

Isle of Wight, 18th August 1809.

My very dearest Charles,—Let this but find you recovering! I humbly pray to God that you may be restored to us. When I feel secure of that, I will endeavour not to repine at the loss you have sustained—at the terms upon which we get you back. Come to us, my ever dearest brother, and allow us to watch over and tend you! You can come to us without any land carriage; we have a room for you, and the best surgical attendance. It will gladden my heart and delight your sister to alleviate by our warmest attentions your present situation.

My kind friend Bathurst, in a letter dated the 31st July, has communicated all you have undergone, and has given an account of the general regret in the army at your misfortune, with a tribute to your worth as a soldier most grateful to me. I have written to our dear parents; therefore set your mind at ease, and only think of gladdening us all by your arrival. Let us have that dear recompense for the wretched anxiety we have within these few days undergone.

All belonging to you are well, and when you are restored to

them, will still be happy. With what joy, if it please the Almighty to permit it, shall I meet you at Portsmouth and convey you to our abode, where everything will be devoted to you! I think it fortunate to be so near the coast; the Isle of Wight will be the best place for you to recover in, and we have a carriage, when you are able, to drive you gently about in. Do come to us, my dear, dear Charles! Fanny and my children send affectionate love to you, and of the truest love of your brother I need hardly assure you. God send you a good passage to Portsmouth. *Adieu*, my dearest lad!—Yours ever most affectionately,

W. Boothby.

These letters made me feel again of some importance in the world, and seemed to establish the reality of my fond connection with it. My tears ceased not to flow. My mind could not suffer such a picture of my family's distress (which was too easily visible to it) without some pain; but, though totally subdued, my heart was much less affected than soothed and softened.

Had I needed a lesson on submission, the death of a young officer of the Guards which happened on the 30th of September might have read it to me impressively. Captain Bryan had only a mother; she only a son; and one of the fairest graces of his all-gracious nature was the fondness with which he loved that lonely parent. From the situation of his wound, which was in the thigh, amputation was impracticable. It was deemed a dangerous but not inevitably mortal wound. The hopes sent to his mother along with the first disastrous news were probably as great as those by which mine had been consoled. With what ardour had my parents clung to those hopes! But the widow—ah! what but Heaven shall pretend to support her when the bitter certainty comes? While she, with a heart sickly anxious, is looking for the accustomed letter, her noble son has mouldered in the ground. His only agony at leaving life thus in its dawn was that with him his mother's peace would sink forever.

"You see," he said to Higgins, "I don't mind about dying on my own account; but it's so dismal to think of my poor mother. I am the only being belonging to her—she is wholly wrapt up in me—and I much fear my death will be hers. But it is not so dreadful to me to think of her dead as at the moment when she finds I am gone—for I fear she does not expect it." This young officer, whose kindly nature was fully attested by the love, the respect, and the deep regret of all his brother officers, was only known to me by the intercourse of reciprocal kind messages and good offices since our common misfortune. When he died, I could not help congratulating myself that I had known him no more intimately; nor could I, when thinking of his mother, not be grateful that affliction had pressed with a lighter hand upon those I loved—that not only had hope been suffered to soften their bitterest tears, but that my life had been spared to wipe them quite away.

Mine, therefore, at reading their letters were sweet and salutary tears; though Higgins, who came to me ere they had dried, deemed them the indication of a mischievous sorrow. For he, I think, was the person upon whose information my kindest friend, General Sherbrooke, wrote to my father as follows:—

Badajos, 24th October 1809.

My dear Sir,—Enclosed is a letter from your son which came under cover to me, and was brought into the Spanish advanced post by a flag of truce. Captain Boothby sent me a few lines by the same conveyance, dated the 13th. He was then quite well, and expected to go to Madrid the day following.

It seems he has been very unhappy, at learning from you the misery which his misfortune has occasioned his friends. Permit me to recommend, when any of you write to him again, that this painful subject be touched upon as slightly as possible, and that you should rather signify the joy you feel at his recovery, and the very sanguine hopes you entertain of soon seeing him again in England. I am induced to trouble you with this piece of advice, having learnt from another person that Captain B. was particularly low-spirited after he received the last letters from his friends.

You will, I am sure, impute to its proper motive what I am now saying.—With best compliments to Mrs. Boothby, believe me, yours very truly—in haste,

J. C. Sherbooke.

I enclose also a letter for Lady Milnes.

On the day on which General Sherbrooke had written thus to England, my poor Mulcaster addressed himself to me. I did not get his letter until I had been some time at Madrid. I transcribe it with a heavy heart:—

24th October 1809.

My dear Boothby,—I had yesterday the pleasure of receiving yours of the 13th; I had before heard from Captain Christie of the Coldstream Guards of your recovery. I have been officious enough to write twice to your father, as good accounts of you reached us, when General Sherbrooke was absent—it could do no harm, and might be satisfactory. I am about to set off for Lisbon, where I shall probably remain some time. Pasley, who was dangerously wounded at Flushing, is fast recovering. There is no particular news, except that Mr. Canning and Lord Castlereagh, after having fought, and the former being slightly wounded, have vacated their places in the Ministry, which is not yet newly arranged. Fletcher is not with us at present; I shall send your letter on to him. We are all made happy by hearing of your complete recovery.

Burgoyne, Forster, and the little Scot join their best love to mine. That we may shortly see you, is the constant wish of your ever sincere and affectionate friend,

Ed. Rt. Mulcaster.

Chapter 17

Among the letters which I received on the 13th of October were two from General Sherbrooke, written at an interval of several weeks, although they now reached me together.

As they tended very much to shake the resolution which Mortier's advice had a few days ago established in my mind, I copy them both as the best elucidation of the doubt they threw me into:—

15th September 1809.

My dear Boothby,—Yours of the 9th of August I received, and I forwarded the letter therein enclosed to your father immediately. Send me any other letters for your family or for any other of your friends, and I will take great care that they are sent to them. I have received a letter from my brother dated the morning of the 17th of August; he had the night before received mine, informing him of your having been wounded, and he was then about to ride over to Edwinstowe to see your father. Your family were then all well; any information which may reach me respecting them I will forward to you. Pray let me know whether or no there is anything you want, or if you would wish me to remit you any cash. The Commander of the Forces (now Lord Viscount Wellington in the county of Somerset, and Baron Wellesley of the Douro) writes me word that he is sending money to the officers who are prisoners. Perhaps this supply may furnish you with less than you want; if so, and you wish any in addition, mention the sum when you write to me, and the next flag shall bring it to you.

The new titles of the Commander of the Forces have not yet been announced to the army; observe, therefore, that what I give you I take from the English papers, which may not be correct.

I hear that poor Colonel Donelan is dead. Of the other wounded officers we have good accounts. I conclude this will find you at Madrid, and that you will shortly obtain your parole. I don't know whether Generals Regnier or Maurice Mathieu may be with the French army in Spain; if they be, I daresay they will recollect the exertions I made, at their request, to recover the liberty of two officers, who had been sent by the Sicilian Government to Pantellaria last year, when I commanded in Sicily. One was a *chef de bataillon* named Laborie; the other, a *capitaine du génie*, whose name I do not now recollect.

But as I got them both released, and restored both these officers to the French army in Calabria, I make no doubt but, if either of those generals are at Madrid, they will, in return for the good office I was so fortunate as to have it in my power to render to these their countrymen, do me the favour to exert their influence to procure you your parole. Remember me most kindly to Major Coglan, Captains Blair, Geils, Milman, and to all my other friends with you, and believe me, with much esteem and regard, yours very faithfully and truly,

J. C. Sherbrooke.

Captain Boothby,
Royal British Engineers,
Prisoner of War.

I am not at all pleased at what you call "*the caprice of your detruncated limb,*" but recommend the greatest care and attention to getting it healed. Unless you can effect this, you will not be able to travel, even if you obtain your parole, which I shall hope soon to hear has been granted to you. The latest letter I have from Oxton is dated 28th August; your father and mother were then well, and had in some degree recovered their composure; for I need not conceal from you that they were at first very much afflicted, on hearing of your misfortune. Attend, therefore, to your recovery on their account as well as on your own.

J, C. S.

5th October 1809.

My dear Boothby,—Many thanks for your very friendly letter of the 14th of September, enclosing one for your father, which I shall have great pleasure indeed in forwarding to him by the mail which I understand is to be made up tomorrow morning.

I hope you received a letter I sent you about three weeks ago, in which, among other things, I informed you that Sir Arthur Wellesley was created Viscount Wellington. I will speak to his Lordship on the subject of your exchange, as you desire. He is already well acquainted with my desire to get this effected, but I doubt whether it can be accomplished in the way you propose. Be assured, however, that I will spare no pains or exertions to obtain your release.

In my last letter to you, I mentioned some claim I have upon the generals of the French army for attention to any friend of mine whom the fortune of war may throw into their hands, from having exerted myself, at the request of Generals Regnier and Maurice Mathieu, to get two French officers released from the Island of Pantellaria, and in which I succeeded with the Sicilian Government.

I am unknown to the Duke of Treviso, but if there be any officer of your rank, prisoner with us, about whom he or any other of the French generals feel interested, I beg you will send me his name, and that of the place he is supposed to be at, and I will use all the influence I have to effect an exchange between you. In the meantime, I make no doubt but, from your being incapacitated from serving by the loss of your leg, the French commander will be induced by motives of humanity to give you leave to return to your family in England on parole; and in the event of his granting you this indulgence, I shall ever look upon it as a personal obligation conferred upon me.

I inquired in my last whether you wanted money. If you do, let me know, and mention how much, as I shall have great pleasure in supplying you. Tell me also whenever you think I can be of any use to you, and in whatever way. I have not time to add more than to say I shall deliver your message to General Stewart and your other friends.

Write as often as you can, and believe me, with the most sincere regard and esteem, yours ever most truly,

J. C. Sherbrooke, Lt.-Gen.

Though, from what I understood of the tenor of my captivity, I did not now believe practicable the scheme of liberation thus zealously proposed to me, yet the proposal came in too authentic a form, and from too respectable an authority, either to be disused by me or slighted by the French commander. I determined to show him the last of these letters (containing a message to himself), and abide by the advice which, after perusing it, he should give me. I had just put it in my pocket for that purpose, when Higgins called upon me. He came to tell me that, as some cash had been forwarded by Lord Wellington for the use of the officers at Talavera, the marshal duke wished to see those who were about to leave it. Accordingly, I repaired to His Excellency's quarters, and found there many British officers, some of whom I now saw for the first time—Mortier, of a good-natured, friendly demeanour, with papers before him, towering up in the midst of them. The man with the *phaeton* having declined a trip to Madrid, I had made up my mind to go in the waggon, and Stanhope had determined to be my companion; accordingly, he was one of the group upon this occasion.

"Gentlemen," said Mortier, "Lord Wellesley has written to the Duke of Dalmatia forwarding to him a quantity of gold for the use of you and your brethren. But as the majority of the officers, prisoners of war, are at Madrid, I have thought it better to commit it to the charge of Captain Geils, who goes there tomorrow. He is, I suppose, aware of the manner in which it should be divided, and will leave for the officers remaining here the proportion . they may be entitled to. I am sorry to find that Captain Geils is still too much an invalid to come here himself. Is there anyone who will receive this money for him?"

Captain Stephens of the 66th came forward, as the senior officer present, and received it; Mortier comparing the money with Lord Wellington's letter very particularly, and then taking Captain Stephens's receipt.

The duke, first asking very kindly if I was in want of more money than was likely to come to my share, begged I would dine with him; then, desiring the names of the officers who would accompany the convoy to Madrid, upon Stanhope's name being mentioned, he asked if he were related to Lord Stanhope, and to an affirmative answer returned that he had been acquainted with two of the sons of that nobleman. Some letters too had been sent to him directed to Captain Howard of the 23rd Light Dragoons, who had gone to Madrid. In giving these to Captain Stephens, the marshal asked, "Is this Mr. Howard any relation to Duke Howard?" (I forget what his reason was for making the inquiry.)

There was among the English officers here assembled a very general feeling of attraction towards Mortier, because of the cordial manner of affability which he adopted towards them.

When all this was arranged, I opened to the duke the doubt which General Sherbrooke's letter had raised as to the expediency of proceeding to France, and, putting the letter into his hands, I pointed out the part referring to himself; which having read—

"With all my heart," said he, "I would do this if it were in my power. I wish you had made application to the Duke of Belluno, who took upon himself to arrange several exchanges which I have since suffered to be carried out. But now it is impossible. The business is transferred to Paris, and there you ought to be—or nothing will be done."

I was again satisfied, and, leaving his presence, I communicated with Captain Stephens (to whom I was a stranger) on our approaching journey. We settled that it would be best for me to join the waggon at Captain Geils's quarters at the appointed hour next morning, which to the best of my recollection was five o'clock. I then returned home, and employed the short time I had remaining in answering the various letters I had received. The impression of my father's was still warm upon my mind, and I wrote to him as follows:—

> Talavera de la Regna, 13th Oct, 1809.
> I shut the door and gave a full vent to my tears as I read your poor letter,—though I had been aware of all your sufferings, this document of them afflicted my heart most deeply, which relieved itself in copious tears. I consoled myself afterwards with the reflection that other letters have long ere this told you that all danger was over and that I was reconciled to my loss. Your having been kept in suspense for my life has (I thank God, who brings good out of evil) reconciled you also.
> The Duke of Treviso (who is one of the kindest-hearted men I ever met with, and who has treated me as if I had a right to his care and attention) having received money and papers for us, had the good-nature to pick out sixteen letters for me, so that no time might be lost in putting an end to my anxiety. Among these was a letter from William, which melted me again; a sweet and most consoling one from dear Lady Milnes; one from Lady Vernon, of old date, apprising me of Georgiana's approaching nuptials; one from Sir Brooke, offering a cork leg; and some most kind from General Sherbrooke and other officers,—they opened my heart, and I read them all with the greatest pleas-

ure. I go to Madrid tomorrow. It is now late, and I dine with Marshal Mortier at five o'clock, so that I cannot write a long letter, as I must take some notice of the many kind ones I have received.

My dearest, dearest Father! amidst whatever I have undergone, it has been your affliction that has lain heavy at my heart. Had I been alone in the world—or at least, loved only by such friends as surrounded my bed—my sufferings would have been light. But I knew that you could not bear to lose me, and therefore shrank from death, for I have no fear of hereafter—I thank the Great God, that I am full of confidence in His mercy, and think of appearing before Him without trembling; but I tremble at the thoughts of your grief; and when I was on the ground, expecting "to be trampled to death, the only exclamation I remember to have made was, "O! my poor friends!"

Don't show this letter; people may suppose I write for effect—*you* know I write from the heart and in the spirit of truth.

I never had better health in my life; my thigh has been long healed: I have some remains of pain, or rather disquiet, therein; but this I have no doubt will go off in time, and it is not now enough to interfere much with my comfort, or at all with my sleep. I tell you this, which you may not like, that you may believe all I say besides. I give you my honour that I conceal nothing from you respecting myself. If you were to stand at my door you would hear me laughing and talking just as usual, in spirits just as noisy—and as you will often again hear; for, to make the best of our bargain, we shall in all probability see much more of each other than we should have done had things not happened as they have.

If I ever have room to fancy that the loss of my leg has traced one furrow on the dear, dear faces of yourself and my mother, or has at all affected the happiness of any of us, then I myself shall cruelly regret it. But it will not be so! Surrounded by all that is most dear to my heart, I shall feel myself happy in having bought at such a price a life of tranquillity and social enjoyment, in exchange for one that I have found from the first but little suited to my disposition. God have us in His good care.

Charles.

I answered all the other letters, and then proceeded to dine with the Duke. He received me with the kindness of an old friend, placed me next to himself at table, and after dinner, finding on inquiry that I was unprovided with tea, took care to supply me with an article which he knew in England ranked among the necessaries of life. On taking leave, he gave me a letter addressed to Marshal Jourdan, in which he recommended me strongly to the good offices of that commander-in-chief; repeating his application for my exchange, or for my early and commodious conveyance to France, in order to further an object so desirable for my unfortunate situation. In short, though sensible of how much a noble mind deems due to the unfortunate, I was at a loss to conceive how I could have deserved such kindness and aid from the Marshal Duke of Treviso as would in all points have become the affection of a near relation.

At five o'clock on the morning of October 14, I took my leave of the kind Spaniards who had endeared themselves to me by such essential services and generous attachment. They were all in tears; those who had seen the sorrow of the good old Pollonia might well have supposed she was parting with a son. Was it possible I should leave them without emotion? I shall ever remember them with gratitude and affection, and wish it may be possible for me to befriend them.

On arriving at the place where the waggon was loading, I found that our baggage was all piled in the middle part of it, and that a little cell, capable of seating two persons, was reserved at each end. The cell over the hind wheels was occupied by Stanhope and myself. We made it as comfortable as we could, by sitting on the soft packages containing our beds. The first cell was arranged in a similar manner by Captains Geils and Stephens, whose wounds required a wheel conveyance. This which we were about to travel in, however, was but little calculated to soften to the wounded the rigours of the road. It had no springs, and was rather a large box or trunk placed upon wheels than a carriage for the transport of living animals. The lid of the trunk (if I may so call it) we were enabled to raise or close by a perforated bar, which could not, however, be changed in its position without much trouble and external aid.

Our friend Higgins, who was present to witness our departure, lamented the rudeness of the conveyance; but, recollecting that we had not more than eighty miles to go, we the more easily made up our minds to it. It was with some difficulty, and not without great suffering, that Captain Geils was got into his place. His pain was visible to us in the distended veins of his forehead and the tenseness of his features;

but he made no complaint. The waggon drove off.

I had been able to preserve a horse which remained with me at Talavera, and he now carried my servant.

Towers, an officer of the Guards who had been shot through both ankles, also was mounted. Several other English officers who had recovered from their wounds, and with them Mr. Staniland, the artillery surgeon, accompanied this convoy on foot; which was further increased by followers of all sorts belonging to the French army, who dared not travel a single mile without such powerful protection.

WAGGON CARRYING PRISONERS OF WAR.

Chapter 18

Though the road was excellent, our position immediately over the wheels without springs made the motion so rough that we could notice our passage over the smallest pebbles. If to Stephens and Stanhope it was fatiguing, and to me painful, to Geils it was extremity of pain. I have never seen more acute suffering than this journey inflicted on our unhappy fellow-traveller. When, from some extraordinary smoothness in the road, his quietness made us hope that some little re mission was allowed him, lively chat and laughter passed between Stanhope and myself. Either the country we were passing over was unattractive, or the nature of the waggon made external observation difficult: at any rate, we ignored the scenery.

Once, indeed, with a crowd of varying sensations that held me silent, I perceived we were crossing the Alverche. I remembered well how I had felt—how all-complete in the elastic power of youthful strength—when last, with an eye of the keenest interest, I surveyed this river; for it was when my general had desired me to seek upon its margin a position in which we might dispute its passage with the enemy. We travelled until after dark; and, that we might be more easily accommodated, our party, consisting of ten, was divided into two messes and lodged in two separate rooms.

This arrangement, adopted not so much for its obvious convenience to both divisions as in compassion to the nervous irritability of the suffering Geils (whom the clamour of ten wounded masters and the clatter of ten blundering servants would have certainly distracted), gave some umbrage, as if the captains of the party had thus arrogated to themselves a distinction incompatible with the good fellowship which we all owed equally to one another. But it was surely natural that our travelling together in the waggon should dispose us to live together, and that Towers should join the party of Geils, his brother-

Guardsman. Indeed, the unpleasant feeling excited by our separation was so unreasonable that I believe it soon subsided of itself.

From Talavera to Sta. Olalla, where we halted the first day, is six long leagues, not much less than thirty miles; and travelling foot's pace in such a conveyance during about fourteen hours we had found exceedingly wearisome. We were therefore most glad of any refreshment and rest within our reach, and quarrelled with neither the scantiness nor the rudeness of our lodging; for we had food and wine, and every man had space on the floor for his mattress. Geils, too, from the misery of the waggon now found comparative ease, and discovered a raciness of humour and kindliness of character that soon made the paroxysms of nervous agony by which his speech was often interrupted act more forcibly upon our nerves. He had a great fund of anecdote, strength of observation, and novelty of thought; and while, in the respites he could procure, he was engaging all our attention, a knife or a teaspoon dropt on the floor would break off his discourse by an access of temporary frenzy. His wounded leg being soundly healed, the surgeons attributed this extraordinary protraction of suffering and the entire loss of use in the limb to an injury done to the nerve, referring the patient to the softening hand of time as the only hope of relief.

As our journey for the morrow was to extend to Navalcarnero, a distance of eight or nine leagues, or at least forty miles, the appointed hour of departure was three o'clock in the morning, which made it very difficult for us to secure any breakfast; and the hurry attending that hot-water repast gave many a pang to poor Geils, who could not see the boiling fluid poured into the teapot without suffering as if it were falling on his leg. Yet the action of filling a vessel out of a pailful of cold water and pouring it back again, which he continued constantly, was the only remedy that seemed to have the least power over his pain.

The second day's journey was longer and more wearisome, and further carried into the night than the first. We rested twice during the day, and observed that the soldiers who accompanied us, or were stationed at the places we rested at, dare not forage in the vineyards under our view without a strong escort for their protection. They returned with long poles on their shoulders, loaded with grapes, a line of glancing bayonets moving along with them. The greater toil of the second day was borne with the more spirit from a sense that we had not much more to perform.

We figured to ourselves Madrid as the land of liberty, where we should naturally be under less restraint than even at Talavera. We quickened time in laying plans for the comfort and amusement of our residence in the metropolis, and were well assured that the *Dons*, into whose care we should probably fall, would be zealous to lighten our captivity and misfortunes by every resource of which their city was capable. We knew that its order had been but little disturbed by the events of the war; and Frenchmen of every rank and temper at Talavera, praising Madrid as *une ville de resource*, had urged us to hasten thither, as if it could not for a moment be doubted that we should be free to avail ourselves of all its advantages.

We were much provoked, therefore, with Stephens, who, though in other respects the most desirable of companions, whenever we were indulging ourselves on this topic, endeavoured to damn all our expectations by expressing his conviction that we should be closely confined. Not that he could in the least bring us to his way of thinking; on the contrary, the idea was too improbable to have been received, even on good information; but Stephens had none, and only gave us the gloomy speculations of his downright Antigallicism. We showed him no mercy. We could believe the French capable of the greatest cruelty where policy enjoined it; but here, as we apprehended, it would be perfectly wanton, and highly offensive to the Spaniards, whom it was their interest to tranquillise, to treat rigorously a handful of wounded officers who had suffered in the cause of Spain.

"Well," said Stephens,—"wait and see!"

"When we are jaunting about Madrid together, our arguments may be more persuasive!"

"I wish to God they may," he returned very drily.

"I suppose," said Stanhope, "there are plenty of hackney coaches in Madrid?"

"I hope so," said Geils.

"Of course there are," said I.

"Not," resumed Stanhope, "that I would give twopence for them for myself—except in wet weather."

"I don't imagine that our jaunts in Madrid will depend much upon the weather," said Stephens, with affected gravity.

"Why, you don't really think," remonstrated I—"you don't in your conscience believe, that they'll confine us to the house—do you, Stephens?"

"Perhaps," returned he, "we may have leave to take the air in the backyard and peep at Madrid through an iron rail!"

"Ha! ha! ha! What a croaker! We shall be about as much confined in Madrid as in London!"

"Thereabouts!" said Stanhope.

"Very little more!" murmured Geils.

"Well," said Stephens, "wait and see! I think I know these chaps!"

We were not so weak as to surrender our judgement to the influence of such national prejudice; yet the perpetual croaking of Stephens cast a damp upon our pleasing speculations, which prevented their so free communication.

On the third day, poor Geils's sufferings were greater than ever; and now come in sight of Madrid, he entreated of us that we would stop the waggon, have him left in a cottage by the roadside, and, having procured his billet, send his servant for him in a hackney coach. We saw that his torments blinded him to the impracticability of what he proposed; for, though all but Stephens fully expected to live in the city free and unmolested, we knew that it could only be after having given our parole to its military authorities. We therefore attempted to cheer our afflicted companion by urging the near conclusion of our journey, and the little while that his patience would be longer required.

But here the drivers, now come in sight of Madrid, and no longer needing protection, keeping the stony centre of the road, set off at a round trot, which carried his sufferings to a height that took from him the power of complaint. In spite of our loud remonstrances, they slackened not their pace until they reached the city, whose bounds are compact and defined, not, as in other capitals, blended into the country by interminable suburbs. As we drove slowly through the fine streets of the Spanish metropolis, we regaled ourselves with the view of populousness and plenty to which we had long been strangers.

The inhabitants and wealthy shopkeepers and mantled gentlemen, standing at their doors or passing along, gazed after us with the most evident anxiety, peering under the lid of the waggon, that, assured we were English, they might exchange a silent sympathy with our friendly countenances, and mark by the melancholy interest of their looks and gestures their compassion for our misfortunes, and their regret to see us enter their city in a manner so little consonant to their affection for our nation, and the hardships we had suffered for theirs.

This was the interpretation we made of their manners at the time, and my after-knowledge of those people enables me now to give it as matter of fact rather than conjecture.

Chapter 19

We passed quite through the town, and traversing an open space shadowed by avenues of tall trees, and beautified by sculptured fountains, we soon found that we were going through pallisades, sentries, and other symptoms of military guard. This appearance caused a sudden balance between our hopes and apprehensions, nor had either time to preponderate before, entering the quadrangle of the Retiro, we had drawn up to a door under the guard of a sentinel. The adjutant of the place was here ready to receive us, and showed us, ten in number, into three naked rooms opening into one another, all which, he informed us, were at our disposal.

They smelt like a French hospital recently evacuated; there was no chair, no table, no bed, no vestige of furniture to be seen; and poor Geils was writhing on his crutches, and asking piteously for a chair.

"Damnation!" said the adjutant, with the impetuosity of rage, raising to his head both hands, in one of which was a cane,—"damnation! have patience then! If you won't have patience, you shall have nothing!"

Geils was in too much real pain to be so sensible as we were of this officer's brutality. He only gathered that a chair was not to be had, and begged to be placed upon the floor.

But the rest of us, disdaining to converse with a clown who appeared to be as remote from common humanity as from the manners of a gentleman, demanded to speak with the commandant of the place.

A man of gentler manners and better aspect then appeared, and by his demeanour made us think that he was ashamed of the treatment we experienced.

"Whatever you may want, gentlemen," said he, "we will do what we can to provide."

"There is, sir," said I, "a sentry at the door: are we to consider ourselves confined to these rooms?"

Colonel la Fond bowed.

"We cannot then stir out of doors?"

"Not without the governor's permission."

"I am charged by the Marshal Duke of Treviso with a letter to Marshal Jourdan; how, under these circumstances, can I present it to His Excellency?"

"Give it to me, and I will send it to him."

"But I wish, sir, to deliver it in person, if I may be permitted to do so."

"If *monsieur* makes application to the governor, it is very possible permission may be given."

"Will you, sir, convey my application to the governor?"

"Assuredly."

I lost not a moment in writing to General Belliard, stating that the Duke of Treviso had committed to my care a letter for the major-general of the army, which I was particularly desirous of delivering to His Excellency in person; and I earnestly solicited the governor's permission to do so. I sent this letter to Colonel la Fond, whose residence was close by, claiming the performance of his promise.

Thus we found ourselves, like a few scattered and way-worn sheep, gathered into a strange fold—leaning against the wall in different parts of the room, or lying on the floor. The disappointment was complete and great to all but Stephens: he stood collected, in the sullen and unwelcome triumph of a prophet, who felt the pressure of the evils he had truly foretold. As we ruminated thus disconsolate—regretting even the waggon we had left—a stripling of a remarkably hand-some exterior and very gentle address, with a napkin under his arm and a clean white apron before him, came suddenly among us, and with all the ease of French self-possession made us a profound bow. We all stared at this unlooked-for apparition, and waited a while to see what it would signify. After a pause, and seeming to resolve what quarter of the room he might best address himself to, he told us that he belonged to the *restaurateur* who lived close by, and had taken the liberty to come to ask if he might have the honour of serving us.

Never was a restored prince received by his devoted subjects with a more undoubting welcome than we now gave this messenger.

"Can you give us some dinner?" said I.

"Whatever you may choose to have, *monsieur*, can be got ready in a quarter of an hour. Please you, I fetch the bill of fare?"

"But stay!" said I, "how can we dine without a chair or table."

"The *aubergiste*, for the pleasure of serving you, will do himself the honour to send chairs and tables immediately."

Away he flew.

This most convenient neighbour was indeed a very great consolation, and dinner was at least something we could look forward to with pleasure.

Wishing to discover (in order to remove) the cause which polluted these rooms with so dreadful a savour, we found that we had been preceded by Spanish prisoners, who, not permitted to pass the door, had left the attics in a most foul state, and it had not been thought needful in any manner to purify the building for the reception of British officers.

Jean—for that was the name of our Jove-sent Ganymede—soon reappeared, aiding others to carry in a vast pile of chairs and tables, which with a noiseless dexterity he soon bustled into form; and, as if possessed of the lamp of Aladdin, in a moment showed us a table covered with ample damask, porcelain, and silver, which gave to the apartment a very agreeable air of furniture and comfort.

Having received our order respecting dinner, the Slave of the Lamp vanished.

Our jailors brought in a supply of boards and tressels to lay our beds upon, and we quickly made our lodging arrangements. Our quarters consisted of a large room between two small ones. The small room at one end was occupied by Geils, Stephens, and Towers; the other by Stanhope and myself; the large central room by the rest of the party. Having done what was possible for the purification of our quarters, and the refreshment of our persons by water and clean apparel, we watched with some keenness for the return of our slave, who soon whisked in a well-dressed and most comfortable French dinner, with brisk and palatable wine.

The next morning, with equal facility and comfort, we were furnished with an English breakfast.

But so large a party soon became insupportable to poor Geils, who begged that the former division might be restored, when he found how ill we received his proposal to dine by himself. His wish was immediately complied with, and thereafter five of us dined in Geils's room—a step which might now with more reason displease the rest, since, from the specimen they had had of his good-humour and spirit, they had felt the value of his society.

The sentry having refused egress to our servants, and thus a difficulty having risen in procuring water, I was glad of the opportunity to write a laconic remonstrance to Colonel la Fond, simply stating that, to persons in our infirm state, to be debarred from supplying ourselves with water was peculiarly distressing. Colonel la Fond, as I intended, was alarmed to find himself formally petitioned for *water* by his wounded prisoners. He hastened to us and expressed his regret that we should have had room to impute such a barbarity to the French.

"You are sensible, I hope, *messieurs*, that the harshness with which you are treated does not proceed from any want of respect to you, but merely from policy with regard to the Spaniards, whom, you must know, we cannot trust."

"We have not been able, sir," answered I, "to comprehend the policy you speak of—perhaps that may be our fault—but if the policy be just, might it not have been thought essential to soften a little the rigour of captivity to officers on whom the misfortunes of war have already pressed somewhat heavily? Could no confinement less wretched than this have been found, wherein our recovery might have been promoted by the blessings of air and exercise? Surely, *monsieur*, policy did not make it necessary to show us, who with difficulty can either stand or walk, into naked rooms, destitute even of a chair, and noxious with the filth of former prisoners!"

"Whatever inconvenience you suffer here," said Colonel la Fond, "I sincerely regret—I only execute the orders I receive; but you will recollect that your situation here is only for the moment; you are considered to be on the march to France, and will proceed with the first convoy, unless, in consequence of stating your ill-health, you have previously been removed to the hospital. I beg to counsel you, *messieurs*, whose wounds will render so long a journey at present formidable, to represent without loss of time that your situation still demands medical care. You will then doubtless be removed to the hospital, where you will receive the most indulgent treatment."

We thanked Colonel la Fond for his gentle behaviour and kind advice, which we promised to reflect on. But we had been counselled to leave Talavera for Madrid, and had lost much liberty by the exchange.

The name *hospital* was not alluring, and perhaps, when there, we might wish ourselves back; yet the journey was indeed formidable, if to be performed in such a machine as had brought us hither, or perhaps in one still less enviable. For Geils it was out of the question; the wound of Stephens was still open, and inflamed by the journey from Talavera; and I, from the same cause, was now suffering so much that even opium could no longer procure me repose.

While we thus balanced as to the course we should pursue, who in a moment should appear to us but my social friend Taylor of the artillery, accompanied by Mr. Dormer of the 14th Dragoons!

The Commissary of War in charge of the hospital had made my friend suspect my arrival along with other English officers, and having, as a great indulgence, permitted a French soldier to conduct him to the Retiro, Dormer, remembering the vicinity of the *restaurateur*, got leave to accompany him, that he might give particular directions for a *perigord*-pie. That there might be no misunderstanding in this latter affair, the landlady herself paid us a visit, and talked about the seasoning and size of the pie with a manner of the most easy and lady-like civility.

During this dialogue, Taylor, taking me aside, advised me strongly to have myself removed to the hospital, where he and his party had been ever since their arrival; I should find myself as comfortable as could well be in a close prison; also I should have good medical attendance, and leisure to arrange my departure for France in the way I liked best.

I had scarcely time to thank Taylor for his friendly zeal, before, the sentry clamouring for his prisoners, they were obliged to hurry away, ere we could fully express how glad we were to see them, or ask them questions which crowded to our minds as soon as they were gone.

The advice of Taylor decided Geils, Stephens, Towers, Stanhope, and myself in favour of the hospital; the others were determined to proceed to France. One of them would, on Stanhope's account, have endeavoured to accompany us, had he not hoped to effect his escape. Afterwards, I believe, he succeeded. This was Lieutenant Wylde, the adjutant of the 29th Regiment, to which Stanhope also belonged; from which circumstance he was more with us than any of the other party, and showing a wish not to be separate from his brother officer, and having won Geils (to whom on that point we entirely deferred) by his most honest and frank, yet very peculiar, demeanour, we invited him to join our society, to which he became a very entertaining addition.

Except in gentleness of manner, he was a youthful Uncle Toby, all his ideas seeming to be conformed to some military pattern. Perfectly regardless of our laughter, and seemingly unconscious of it, he would sit with his eyes fixed on the ceiling, audibly, in gruff, blunt phrase, narrating or anticipating the manoeuvres of the negro tribes who spread their winged forces over that snowy tract. The tortuous cracks and their minor ramifications were rivers with tributary streams. The many discolorations of various shade were treated as mountains, fortresses, and woods; and he would very seriously discuss the strength of position favouring either army, and the probability of their effecting the passage of the great rivers which he considered to be meandering between them.

Nor was it always in the power of very substantial and corporeal evidence to dissolve his reverie. For at dinner, against which his own operations were far from imaginary, he was still the busy historian, and now and then the vigilant opponent, of the many foraging parties sent out from the insect armies above our heads.

"They've carried mustard-pot-hill though, I see!" he would say as he filled his mouth. "They mustn't keep that post, or they'll cut off our supplies!" and then putting the black squadron to the rout, he would gravely help himself to mustard.

Thus he went on, tracing their flying movements through the whole topography of the table, from the Tureen Mountain to Tablecloth Valley, and only carrying their positions where they seemed too much to straiten his own cantonments.

Several days had elapsed, leaving unnoticed a second letter which, in default of answer to the first, I had employed Jean to convey to the governor. And this determined disregard of all written petition decided me not lightly to part with Mortier's recommendation; hoping that some channel might shortly offer which I should have less reason to suspect than the two I had recently employed. I should have judged more wisely if I had reflected that a letter under the hand and seal of a Marshal of the Empire, addressed to the highest officer in Spain, was quite sure of finding its way. Yet, though I had become perhaps overwary, I had less doubt of the letter's reaching the hands of Jourdan than dread of its being forgotten and disregarded—unless I presented it myself, in which case some answer must be given in order to get rid of me.

Staying yet some days longer at the Retiro, our dislike to it abated. In the perfectly free and friendly intercourse of well-assorted minds, a flow of good spirits from one kindled the glee of the rest, and none could groan or sigh without the sustaining sympathy of several kindly hearts. There grows a bond amid such circumstances of friendship not often known to those associated only by the urbanity of good neighbourhood or the gaiety of pleasure.

The industry of our servants had purified our abode, and the aspect from our ample sash windows was living and various. The large square before us, bounded by the courtly façades and fane-twinkling minarets of the Retiro, enclosed a scene of ever-changing bustle, and that armed mouth was under our view which alternately swallowed and disgorged all the military expedience conceived in the headquarters of the kingdom.

Our *restaurateur* continued to supply us with excellent meals—at an extravagant price, it is true; yet, as we all had money, we drove away care, and, hoping for better times, were merry, in spite of our wounds, maims, and rigid confinement.

In truth, I look back to these days, of which it would not be difficult to make a melancholy picture, without much recollection of mental uneasiness; so greatly is calamity lessened by participation, and so disposed are we to cheer ourselves in actual distress by encouraging the hope of better times.

Chapter 20

The Convent of St. Francis, cleared of its monastic inhabitants, was used as a general hospital by the French in Madrid; and we who had avowed our present inability to travel were in a few days removed to that enormous building. We were out of conceit with our new abode before we had penetrated to it, for we passed to it by spacious floors covered with every shape of human suffering.

We would have glided quickly through this scene afflicting to all our senses, but that Geils—whose own sufferings were sharp enough to occupy all his thoughts—could with difficulty be got along, and the avenue between the feet of the wretched patients was too narrow for my crutches to be used without deliberate caution.

When we had gained that corridor appropriated to the use of the officers, we were greeted by Taylor and other fellow-prisoners, who were useful and kind in facilitating to us the manner of the place. For the most part, each officer had hitherto enjoyed a monk's cell to himself; but on our arrival it was no longer possible to give such liberal accommodation. Stanhope and myself, and I think Stephens and Towers, became fellow-lodgers, and we dined as heretofore in Geils's room. The cells or small apartments constructed on the exterior face of the building were very cheerful, looking west on a very pretty scene, which comprised a near view of the gorgeous palace and rural villa of the king, and at a distance the mountains and towers of the Escurial.

Under the end window which lighted the corridor came the garden paling of the Duke del Infantado, and looking to the south it commanded the great roads to Talavera and Toledo, the magnificent bridge over the disproportionate rivulet, and the stately avenue extending on its nearest bank which begins the highway to Aranjuez. These two aspects, therefore, were full of life and interest, and threw upon us the best beams of the sun. But there were cells also constructed on the interior face, whose windows, of course, opened to the dark and gloomy quadrangle, the area of which, like the bottom of a well, could from its depth receive no ray of direct light; nor could any fall upon that window in the first story through which both Stanhope and myself drew air.

Dank weeds concealed the pavement of the court, thickening round the mossy parapet of the well in its centre, and round the foot of those quadrangular walls, which, rising to a vast height above us, kept their dark hue until they reached the point where the sun's beams could overshoot the opposite side. Geils's room, in which we dined, looked the same way; and casting a thought almost of fondness on the cheerful scene we had left, we were soon almost regretting that we had not set forth on our journey, whatever might have been its evils, rather than suffer ourselves to be immured in so gloomy a prison, where on all sides we were surrounded by squalid misery and contagious disease.

On opening my eyes to the unwelcome gloom the morning after our arrival, I found I had been awakened by the entrance of a Spaniard, whose youthful age was almost concealed by a large cocked hat, and his cloak so worn as to conceal all but his eyes and nose.

He walked up to my bedside, followed by a troop of dirty Spanish menials, bearing burdens. Seeing that I was awake, he asked in stiff French, and with so careful an emphasis as seemed to demand a categorical answer, how I had slept; and perhaps supposing from my countenance that I was more inclined to ask why my sleep had been broken than to tell him if it had been sound, he announced himself as a Spanish physician, who had voluntarily come forward from motives of patriotism to attend upon the English prisoners.

Upon hearing this, I soon brushed away the sullen trace of regretted slumber, and with a manner of unfeigned welcome I expressed myself obliged to him and happy to see him.

I had nothing to complain of but a continuance of pain, which broke my rest, hardly ever leaving me, and not now, as at first, yielding to the effects of opium.

After some consideration, he said that I might hope much from camphor and time, an amalgam which he had hardly ever known to fail! Satisfied to end our conference with that pleasant conceit, he stepped up to Stanhope's bed, and, nothing discouraged by a very audible snore, mechanically began his inquiries.

"*Et vous, monsieur, avez-vous bien dormi?*"
"What!" said Stanhope, still asleep.
"*Je vous demands, monsieur! comment vous avez passé la nuit?*"
"What!"
"*C'est peut-être que la blessure de monsieur soit déjà guéri!*"
Still without stirring, Stanhope seemed to answer, "What!"

The phlegm of the Spaniard was moved neither by those unsatisfactory answers, nor by my laughter, which from the opening of the dialogue I could not restrain; and he gravely applied to me to interpret his object to my companion.

As soon as I could bring my jaws together, which laughter had kept apart, I shouted, "Stanhope! Stanhope!"

Waking now, and starting up in the utmost amazement, he fastened his widened eyes upon those of the immovable physician.

Not aware that he had hitherto slept, and having found French ineffectual, the doctor addressed him now in Spanish:

"*Onde sta usted herido?*"

Stanhope, through all his amazement hearing my laughter, could not restrain his own; and, keeping his eyes still fixed upon the doctor's, he cried out to me—

"What the devil does the fellow want?"

His mirth increased more than ever; then, finding it was at the expense of the physician, he became sensible of its impropriety; and when, to recover himself, he looked away from the grave character he feared he was offending, his eyes fell upon the greasy, grinning, gaping group by which he was followed. He was therefore obliged to hide his head and have his laugh out. Instead of being provoked, I was pleased to see that now the doctor began himself to be amused; and at last having ascertained the case of this most impracticable patient, with a face of perfect self-complacency, he swept away, with his oily train.

I had in the course of the day the mortification to find that one of the governor's *aides-de-camp* had a few days ago inquired for a British officer, who brought a letter for Marshal Jourdan; and now, in consequence (it seemed) of the mistake which prevented my being discovered, that minister had departed for France, without giving me an opportunity to benefit by Mortier's recommendation.

The party with which Taylor lived, contained, besides Dormer, whom I have mentioned before. Captain Howard of the 23rd Dragoons, who had been shot through the lungs; Sir William Sheridan of the Guards, badly wounded in the legs and still on crutches; and Major

Coglan of the 61st, who was wounded at the same time as myself, and was not less beloved as a companion than distinguished as an officer. These formed the leading set, and enjoyed the privilege of dining in a small refectory instead of a monk's cell; but they soon lost it.

The second night after our arrival Coglan effected his escape. He disguised himself as a servant, and, bearing a basket on his arm, walked unmolested through the French Guard; and the same evening, disguised in the same manner, several other officers successively found means to follow his example. Their flight was of course immediately known to those who remained, and though it was quite sure to entail on them a more rigorous, perhaps a vexatious confinement, they could only admit a common sentiment of exultation at the first success of the fugitives, and anxiety for its completion.

The expected storm was not tardy.

The Spanish physician went his morning rounds. He administered at those beds which contained patients, but regarded not those which were empty—held himself unconcerned; but Mr. Larreguay, the old French inspector, in silent trouble hastened to Mr. Commissary Perron, who, in utter dismay, made his report to the *commandant de la place*, who instantly repaired to the guilty spot.

The *commandant* was an old officer, whom the black feathers in his hat announced to us as a general, and he bore besides the most favourable form of French gentility. As his office made him responsible for the security of the prisoners, his countenance and manner expressed a severity excited by the governor's rebuke. But neither that irritation, nor the being assailed by one of us with uncourtly railing in language only intelligible enough to convey provocation, could make him forget that he had to do with persons whom their rank, their distress, and still more his power over them, entitled to more than ordinary politeness and consideration, as well as patience and forbearance; or provoke him to carry his new precautions further than seemed necessary to prevent the recurrence of evasion.

Another mark of high character in him was that though the innocent physician was examined and threatened, and all others who were connected with the hospital, no attempt was made to discover from us the manner in which our comrades had escaped; and the precautions taken convinced us it was not suspected. To narrow our range, and keep us under the survey of the sentries he placed in the corridor, the general deprived Taylor's party of the refectory; and, although he considered a loud remonstrance against this hardship with infinite patience, he at last decided that it was necessary. But though his manner to us admitted not the slightest disrespect to mingle with its displeasure, he spoke with reproach of the fugitives, and seemed to im- pute some dishonour to their escape.

This brought from Howard, who spoke French well, a spirited and very gentleman-like remonstrance:

"*Comment! mon Général!*" said he, "surrounded by your sentries, and forcibly confined to this narrow corridor, can you talk of dependence on our parole? Treat us like persons of honour! Leave us at large; and then our word shall be your security, which no temptation. General, could induce any one of us to break. But when we are in prison we think it appertains to you to look to us; to us, to regain our liberty if we can. Our brave companions have done no more; and surely it is not just to cast on their flight any dishonourable stain."

"Believe me, *Monsieur l'Officier*," returned the general, "I mean nothing disrespectful. I certainly did understand from one of your companions, who appeared to me to speak for the rest, that I might indulge my own wish to impose the least possible restraint upon you, relying that no advantage would be taken of my moderation; for it rested with me to answer for your persons, and without such an understanding I should naturally have made your escape more difficult. But if I misunderstood that officer, or if he did not speak the sentiments of the rest, I must now repair my former omission; and, whatever pain it gives me to aggravate the hardship of your condition, I must prevent your escape!"

And he repeated his orders to the sentinel to let no one pass into the refectory.

In answer to one of our complaints, "And can you think," said he, "that it is not harder for me to impose than for you to bear this little privation? Believe me, it is much harder; for no one can go beyond me in respect for the helplessness of a prisoner of war. We may do with him what we please. Can there be a stronger motive for treating him with kindness? He has a thousand claims upon all our charities! And, as far as personal aid can avail you, there is nothing within my individual power that I am not ready to do for all or any one of you. But in this case my duty is very narrow. It is thought advisable—and that such a thought was admitted you cannot regret more than I do—that you should not be at large.

"You are entrusted to me. The liberty of an equal number of my own friends and countrymen in England depends upon your safe custody. For every one of you who escapes by my lenity or negligence I lose an officer to France, and consign a brother to protracted captivity. Thus if you can give me no security in your forbearance, I must seek it elsewhere. I have already incurred the just reproaches of the governor; but those, I do assure you, did not give me half the vexation inflicted upon me by the hard necessity of coming down here to decrease the comforts of the unfortunate."

I could have taken this noble old general in my arms, so just were his sentiments, and his manner, though refined, yet so earnestly sincere; but no sounds my feelings could have dictated would have had a chance of prevailing over the torrent of rapid, incoherent, and unreasonable complaint which broke upon the general's mild discourse; who, perhaps, from the scarcely intelligible language in which it was conveyed, conceiving the speaker had not understood his expressions, gave a shrug of imposed forbearance, and having made his orders clear to the sentries, left us, followed by the audible thanks and praises of all who could understand his language, or appreciate his demeanour.

But, fearing he might again suppose that one had spoken for all, we entreated Mr. Larreguay (an old gentleman who executed his office of inspector with great kindness) to convey to the general an assurance of the pleasure and thankfulness with which we had recognised in his conduct all that could best distinguish a brave and highbred enemy.

Mr. Larreguay accepted this commission with great alacrity and some surprise, for it had quite, he said, oppressed him to see so good a man as that general put upon so ungracious an office. He assured us that the amiable old man had uttered nothing that was not amply supported by the general benevolence and nobleness of his life, which made him universally beloved.

This fracas was soon followed by the removal for France of a great many officers, including the party from which Coglan had withdrawn himself—an event which deprived us of much agreeable society, but at the same time greatly improved our comfort in point of accommodation. It was heavily impaired by the precautions which to the good general had appeared necessary, yet, in fact, answered no other purpose than to torment the prisoners, and tempt them to practise again that method of escape which he had failed to discover or suspect.

The sentries now placed at our doors, according to their several humours, vexed us by day with wanton restraints, such as forbidding us to look out of the window; and by night disturbed our rest by their shuffling march to and fro, and their whistling or singing, which our entreaties for silence commonly redoubled. But these soldiers, perpetually changed, could not soon acquire a personal cognisance of the officers under their guard, who, retaining the privilege of sending their servants into the town for provisions, could still, under disguise, substitute their own persons, at a hazard which they were now more willing to incur since to the hope of regaining their liberty was joined that of evading the present rigour of their confinement.

Thus more officers escaped, and the commandant, now assured that his measures had missed the evil they aimed at, ordered every officer whom it was possible to move to be instantly deposited in the Retiro, and thence put in march for France without delay. The removal immediately began. The lame and the infirm were invited to provide for themselves suitable means of conveyance, and several of us hired *berlins* or hackney coaches. Sir William Sheridan, still using crutches, had been for that reason suffered to remain when his former companions were removed; but now the plea of much heavier infirmity was not admitted, and he was already seated in the carriage which he had hired. Ours too was waiting. Those who could walk, the waggon for our baggage, and our servants,—all were assembled in front of the hospital, and only waiting our arrival.

We were all employed in assisting, cheering, and compassionating poor Geils, who was suffering inordinate pain. Hitherto time, to which he was referred for his chance of recovery, had only added to a morbid susceptibility which not only the slightest motions, but even sounds, could cruelly agitate. His sudden removal, joined to the notion that they would attempt to take him to France in his present state, had thrown his nerves into such irritation that his features, darkened and convulsed, exhibited an appearance of suffering really alarming. In this condition, sitting midway upon the great stair of the convent, he was observed with great concern by Mr. Larreguay, who heard us complain of the cruelty of moving our companion, and immediately desired he might proceed no farther. Then, going out to the place of assemblage, he discussed the matter with the commissary, and that officer being a good-natured man, whose anger had now subsided, selected from among us those who, in proportion as it would be cruel on account of their infirmity to move them, had it less in their power to escape. There was in consequence remanded to the hospital a considerable company, which included the whole party I had lived with.

Sir William Sheridan went with the others that evening to the Retiro, and shortly afterwards to France.

We now took undisputed possession of the best and most cheerful rooms. Stanhope and myself, accustomed to be together, liked better to share a cheerful cell than to have the sole command of a dark one, whose gloom solitude would deepen. The largest and best was allotted to Geils, and he still permitted us to assemble in it by day. Thus, after some annoyance (and to Geils, pain), our plight was greatly improved by this brisk affair.

The loss of so many fellow-prisoners brought us a great accession of quiet and repose; and less suspicion prevailing against us, the restraint upon us was slackened so as but little to trouble our retirement.

Chapter 21

The assemblage of British officers in the hospital, when first we joined it, was much too large to make acquaintance with each individual a consequence of our aggregation. Besides the party with which I found Taylor, and that to which I belonged, I remember rather names than persons, and of names not many. None appeared to want society. The community had divided itself into sets suited to the respective facility and comfort of all; and every cell, by the communication it held with others, seemed equally well placed with our own. All but one—on the gloomy side—near the door of which no officer was seen to loiter, and whence no sound of life came forth; yet there, in passing when the door for a moment opened, twice I caught a glimpse of a ghastly figure, at one time standing erect, at another stretched on a comfortless bed. The apparent misery would, I hope, have been sufficiently interesting, but extreme youth was also visible in this wretched object, clothed in the garb of a British officer!

On my asking why, amid circumstances so desolate, he should, as it seemed, be thus abandoned by his proper associates and by all the world, a story came out, which accounted for those appearances.

The inhabitant of the unfrequented cell was a young officer who, overpowered by his fears, had fled from the Battle of Talavera, and seemed now to be dying of disease as well as despair. By the policy of abhorring a coward in the army, flight is made more dreadful than death, and doubtless great military good results from it; therefore the sentiment is right and wholesome. But individual misery unmerited is its offspring, too; and though its adoption in a particular class may be defended upon particular principles, it would be difficult upon general ones to rescue it from a charge of injustice.

I shall not attempt to claim great praise or admiration for any character of man that is destitute of personal courage; without it no man can perform, or be ready to perform, his duty; and often I know the want of it proceeds from the prostration of a mind deserted by every worthy impulse. Yet it is not more certain that bravery may remain the only redemption of a character every way else detestable, than that virtue and ingenuous feeling worthy of being loved are sometimes united with timidity. Virtue predominant will carry the timid man through acts of valour. Fear may betray the man virtuously inclined into conduct that calls for general contempt. Is it said that, to the feeling mind, fear herself would present disgrace as the supreme danger? This is true, if the option were offered to the capable judgment; but in the breast of a timorous man, her guidance is naturally suspended by that sudden and overpowering danger from which then his loosened fears propel him; and not until clear of the gushing blood and roaring fire.

Which shook affrighted Reason from her throne,

can her return present to his agonised view the miserable choice he has made in her absence, which all too late he would die to revoke. A docile boy enters into the profession his friends have chosen for him, ignorant that he is less fit than other youths to brave its dangers, till a scene such as strong minds only bear unshaken suddenly bursts upon his feeble temper. Obeying, perhaps, an instinctive impulse to be relieved from the agony of his fears, the power of thought taken from him, he flies. Ever after, though innocent of crime, incapable of it, nay, perhaps an example of benevolence and virtue, he is turned from with looks of horror and excommunicating scorn! But many are the cases of suffering humanity which, unmerited and unmitigated, are beyond all remedy but the compassion of Heaven.

The soldier who exposes himself, as becomes him, may be doomed by his bravery to endless captivity, to slavery, to a lingering life of bodily pain, through which the voice of honour's applause would vainly seek him! Yet not more for these sad contingencies, which menace the brave, can man devise a remedy, than for the pitiless disgrace which awaits those estimable men who, unconscious of their want of courage to bestow the life they yet sincerely offer to their country, have adopted the profession of arms. The glory of that profession requires that scorn should wave behind the coward a scourge more terrible than the sword before him, and if blinded by fear he heed it not, that all may see she waves it not idly, let her merciless lashes pursue him to the grave!

Yet, so sensible that this should be that we suppress the sigh and disown the tear which rise for his sufferings, who would not seize every peculiarity which seemed to offer the boon of an exception? If quietly we may relieve him, unseen by those whom our lenity could mislead, shall we not fly with joy to do it? or if the circumstances of the victim point on us the commands of our Saviour in his behalf, shall we not eagerly plead the paramount obligation of religion?

Geils, Stephens, Towers, and Stanhope did not hesitate whether this unhappy youth were to be pitied and sustained, or left to perish, and they desired me to offer him the services of our little company.

Nothing could be more abandoned than the state in which I found him. As the noise of my crutches roused him from the posture in which he was lying, he presented to me but the shadow of a human being, so squalid and bloodless. His body so barely alive, and his spirit already so utterly crushed, that by the side of this hideous alternative death had seemed fair in the eyes of cowardice! His mind was the prey of shame and despair, his body of a wasting dysentery, and want of attendance (for even his servant but sparingly waited on a master left alone by his equals) aggravated that disorder by making it as loathsome as it was dangerous. Feeling how little desirable it was to cure the evils which afflicted the one, leaving the other but the more alive to those which were incurable, he seemed to have given up all interest in life.

Distrusting the unwonted voice of kindness and consideration with which he found himself addressed, and imputing it to my ignorance of his story, he hastened to remove it, perhaps expecting my indignant departure to follow his explanation. But when he found that our purpose of kindness and support had been consequent upon our knowledge of his disgrace, that we inquired with interest into the progress of his disorder, saw his medicines duly administered, provided with care whatever he might safely eat, by visiting him often, ourselves enforced the respect of his attendant, and engaged one of the women to provide for the fit comfort of his room, the poor youth soon discovered again some value in life; and seemed to hope that, if officers of character could regard him without abhorrence, perhaps, when out of the army, contempt might cease to pursue him.

Thus, his thoughts having assumed a more cheerful cast, he acknowledged our good offices with thankfulness; and now, careful of his own recovery, in due time got the better of his disorder. Thenceforward we invited him to come amongst us when he liked and freely associated with him, and so did all the brave officers who came to us afterwards from Talavera; all being soon persuaded that we need not in such a season, when mutual suffering had more recommended to us the temper of Christianity, adhere with rigour to those laws of military society, which were wholesome indeed for general observance, however unjust to individuals.

Had we not dared to dispense with them on the present occasion, perhaps ourselves had wanted courage, as well as common humanity. If any suppose, from my not mentioning the treatment this youth received from other officers whom I have named, that it was less kind, or, assenting to the propriety of *our* conduct, infer that *theirs*, if different, was less to be defended, their conclusions arc certainly very precipitate, and to the best of my belief entirely erroneous. I am ignorant whether much intercourse or none at any time obtained between the officers we found in the hospital and him in disgrace, but I think the circumstances under which he must have been first remarked by them would not have pleaded with us for the same indulgence as those into which he had sunk when we found him. He had made so little secret of his failure as to acknowledge it to Marshal Mortier. It was known even to the enemy, and his own desire of seduction was such that, carefully avoiding the sight of any officers belonging to his regiment, his choice was to be surrounded by those who knew of him nothing but his shame.

For to be deprived of the power of making new acquaintances, though solitary, amid numbers, was a mortification many degrees less than to meet at every turn the bleak eye of averted friends. If, then, complying with his own bent (which indeed best became one amid such circumstances), those strangers left him to himself unmolested, but unnoticed, I think they judged well, and acted not unkindly. And accustomed as they would thereby be never to see him, except just shutting himself into his cell whenever they entered the corridor, the ailments of his body might well—and I have no doubt did—advance unknown to any of them.

His disorder was at first slight. The physician visited him as well as the rest. He was in other respects not worse provided, and his pitiable state was, I believe, entirely unsuspected, until an accidental observation betrayed it to us. I find by the dates I have preserved that the events I have touched upon since our arrival at Madrid occurred in so few days, and that the officers we found in the hospital were so soon swept away, that I cannot wonder I know so little of the extent of their intercourse with this unhappy young man, or the information they had of his illness and despondency. But my thorough conviction of the manly kindness and generosity of their character, makes me feel perfectly sure that either they showed kindness to him, or that if they did not, when with propriety they might, the opportunity was never made known to them.

I have before observed that since the removal of the more active prisoners, being less suspected of a purpose to escape, we were less vexatiously observed by the sentries. But this amendment was perhaps more owing to the occasional presence of the officer on guard, who, if it happened that he had some gentleman-like feelings, gave us now a good deal of his company, and by that means expunged from the minds of the soldiers that tendency to insolence which their authority to control us had too readily excited. Unless he had been personally very disagreeable, his visit was sure to be welcome; for, having yet received no other, his throat was the only channel through which the town talk could reach us. On 25th October, however, a strange but very sharp-looking officer, most fancifully dressed in a sort of Mamlone garb, and smoking a long serpentine pipe, which hung dangling from his whiskered lips, came slashing up the corridor reiterating my name.

On my answering to that random call, he said he was desired by Marshal Mortier to wait upon me, to see if I were comfortably situated, and to offer me freely both the marshal's services and his own. I was greatly pleased with this mark of kind remembrance from one who by his former extraordinary goodness had commanded my affection, and I asked warmly after the health of the marshal duke, and if there was any chance of his coming to Madrid. Monsieur Galabert (for that was his name) answered that not only had he the satisfaction to assure me he had left him in perfect health, but also that His Excellency was daily expected in the capital, and in the meantime, he begged to reiterate his offers of service.

We learnt from this officer, who was very loquacious and self-confident, that Soult was appointed major-general of the army in the room of Jourdan, who only waited to give up the charge.

"I suppose, *messieurs*," added he, "you know that General Wellesley has embarked at Cadiz?"

"We knew no such thing" we said, "nor [laughing at him] did we believe it."

"*Eh! comme vous voulez, messieurs!—vous êtes les maîtres!*—but I solemnly assure you it is true! There is not at this moment a single Englishman upon the Peninsula, except as a prisoner, or perhaps in garrison at Cadiz. Your nation now confines its succour to advice and material; so that now our efforts are near their accomplishment, nor will the Marquis Wellesley, who is arrived at Seville, and it is believed will be named Regent, be able to retard it, however great his talents. That he has great talents few know better than I. I went to India to look after him, and in spite of his vigilance sent home the information desired! *Si! si! Je le connais bien!*"

"Then," said I, "you will be able to tell His Catholic Majesty what sort of a man he has to deal with!"

"Yes," returned he, with a sapient nod. "Yes, yes! I have already told them they must prepare to cope with a man of unbounded resources! But those are not enough without resources which are beyond his reach. Against French troops he must have at least an equal number of steady regulars. Spain cannot furnish them; and England has even recalled those she had furnished. For, indeed, you may rely upon the fact, gentlemen, that General Wellesley has embarked his army."

We told him, with something like a sneer, that people were apt too easily to believe what they would ardently desire; and that for our parts we confessed ourselves rather incredulous of news we disliked, and therefore trusted he would excuse us. Monsieur Galabert displayed a little national insolence and; but as he did not lose his good-humour on being rallied in turn, and rattled away in a style somewhat novel and entertaining, his visit was not only welcome to me from the kind messages he bore, but rather enlivening to all the party.

When he took leave, he mechanically discharged a profusion of gallant offers which he desired might be received, as they were made, *avec toute la franchise militaire*. His gold-bonneted head thrown back, his hands and whip thrust into the distended pouches of his immeasurable trousers, away he brushed at a five-mile lounge.

Chapter 22

The Duke of Treviso arrived at Madrid on the 26th of October. I wrote to him describing my situation and returning his own letter to Marshal Jourdan, which, I told him, I had not been allowed an opportunity to deliver.

He returned me a prompt answer, expressed as follows:—

26th October,
The Duke of Treviso has just received Captain Boothby's letter. He will see the governor this evening, and he hopes that tomorrow Mr. Boothby will have free egress; for the rest he may reckon on the endeavours of the Duke of Treviso to procure him all the indulgence his situation demands, and he will have the pleasure to see him tomorrow morning. It is to be wished that Mr. Boothby had sent direct to the Marshal Jourdan the letter addressed to him.

And it now seemed to me very odd that I had not done so. Nevertheless, my kind protector's note gave me no small satisfaction. It seemed even possible that he might now find some means of forwarding my return to England.

The next morning the officer of his guard arrived, and, asking for me, said he had the governor's orders to accompany me to the marshal. I apprehended, I said, His Excellency's residence might be at a greater distance than it would suit me to walk, and therefore begged the officer Would wait until a carriage was procured. As we were proceeding together, the officer adverted to the duke's disposition to befriend me, and the claim I derived from my misfortune.

"The duke's opinion," said I, "is that if I could obtain an interview with the emperor, he would immediately send me to England."

"He would," said the officer, "not because he would feel for your situation, but that he might seem to feel for it. It is thus that he has often done beautiful acts which narrate well; but he feels for no one!"

The duke received me as he had parted from me, and continued to give me proofs of the most generous interest.

"I am going," said he, "to dine with the king, "and I will ask him to grant you your parole to go to Paris. He will probably not refuse me this favour, and then I will take you in my *barouche* as far as Valladolid."

I had no words to express my sense of this kindness, nor have I now.

Although he was to dine with the king himself, he hoped I would dine with his officers. He could not, he said, interfere with the arrangements regarding the British prisoners in Madrid. He could not understand it. He had answered for me to the governor this day. And he hoped soon that the king's compliance with his request would relieve me from every restraint. I reminded him of Captain Geils and his continued affliction, and said that he had been recommended some prepared baths, whose efficiency his confinement prevented his trying. And I entreated the duke's good offices to have him lodged in the town. The excellent, the honest, the noble duke promised to mention his case to the Governor Monk.

During the absence of their chief, the officers of Mortier's staff were much more easy and babbling than in his presence. They talked of the Treaty of Vienna, which made France indisputably the great nation. Russia, said one with a most profound countenance, may have more territory; but it cannot be counted, it is so distant and so barbarous. "*Non! en Europe, c'est bien la France qui soit sans contredit la grande nation!*"

Seeing me smile, he immediately bowed and added—

"*Je ne parle pas de ces messieurs. Ces sont les dieux de la Mer. C'est toute autre chose!*"

I thought that a good trait in the man.

As the duke had not said when he was likely to go to Valladolid, I thought it best to prepare immediately for departure. I was in some difficulty about my servant, as my horse had been stolen, and I did not know how in so short a time to provide for his journey. At the worst, I thought it would not be difficult, with Mortier's assistance, to contrive that he should follow me.

Notwithstanding the brightened hope now offered to me, by performing so commodiously much the worse part of the journey to

France, and for the remainder having the aid of that powerful friend who would there be in command, it gave me much pain to think of parting with my companions, more especially when I saw the regret which gave a melancholy tone to their sincere congratulations.

Until the 30th of October I wondered what could prevent my hearing more of Mortier, but we then from the corridor window saw that chief, accompanied by his staff, proceeding over the bridge and retracing the road to Talavera. I readily supposed that some military charge had recalled him to that quarter instead of sending him to that of Valladolid, and at once conceived that to me he could not with propriety advert to any such change. While we were accounting for what we beheld, an officer arrived with the following note:—

29th October,

Sir,—His Catholic Majesty has been pleased to permit you to repair to Paris on parole, to take the orders of H.E. the Minister of War relating to your exchange. The Marshal Jourdan will send you the written authority Today or Tomorrow. I am charmed to have been able to be useful to you, and wish you, sir, a happy journey.   The Mar. Duc of Treviso.

IMPERATOR

Chapter 23

Madrid, Wednesday, January 10, 1810.—Having passed a turbulent evening in the midst of harness, turkeys, papers, hams, and pots of mustard, I sleep with the fear of not waking—call Delacourt, who reluctantly rises. We stir ourselves up with a long pole. At half-past six set off in my own chaise to the Retiro, having despatched a coach for Stephens and Morgan to the Franciscan goal; these arrive soon after me. Breakfast at the *restaurateur's* (our old friend) on *bœuf à la mode*, little birds, and *café au lait*. The place is filled with every description of French military, who, preparing for a long, painful, and perilous journey, have fortified their bodies with rude dresses, regardless of the grotesque appearance they make, wearing their cocked hats over red, blue, and green nightcaps. My friend, who talked English to me at Belliard's, comes up and most cordially greets me; he tells me that I have a charming equipage, and that as my party consists of three only, it happens extremely lucky, as he himself will be happy to take the fourth seat!

"There is not a fourth seat, my good sir."

"'Tis an unhappy misfortune, my dear," returns he, more disappointed than piqued.

It is very ill-judged of my young friend Pakko, who breakfasted with us, to insist upon going part of the way with us, though we are already full; I have much ado to prevent Morgan from convincing him how much he is *de trop*. Stephens exults much at the success of my arrangements, and is delighted with the carriage. We shall be more at ease in rear of the convoy than in front. As we wind along under old St. Francis, we shoulder forward to look at the well-known window, and discover the rest of our crippled brethren looking out for us. We wave our handkerchiefs, but they do not answer the signal, probably not supposing we could inhabit so smart a vehicle.

Travel through a disagreeable hilly country—few villages, those desolate. The convoy is conducted by a *chef de bataillon*, an active little savage. The bayonets are about 300, escorting English and Spanish prisoners; six or seven caissons, with sick French officers; bullock-carts with sick and maimed of all nations, and several coaches, *berlins*, and *cabriolets*, which have taken advantage of the convoy's protection, from fear of those predatory Spaniards whom the French call *brigands*—I believe they molest and rob French men only. About eight o'clock at night we bring in sight the village of our destination, Calapajar, five long leagues from Madrid. We know by the crashing and blazing in the village that the French are preparing for supper at the expense of the doors, windows, and furniture of the unfortunate Spaniards.

We enter the town, and are told that the orders are to lodge *militairement*. We are warm in the carriage and have victuals. As many of our comforts depend much on the outside passengers and horses, this lodging *militairement* we by no means approve of So getting out of the *chay*, and crutching through the turmoil, we find our way to the *commandant* of the place, and beg he will order us a lodging, saying that we are English officers. He begs us to come in, and desires the *alcaldy* to give a billet for three officers. The *alcaldy* turning to me says in Spanish, "For three officers, sir?"

I answer in his own tongue, "Yes, sir, for three English officers."

"English!" repeat the surrounding Spaniards (surprised and suddenly affected, as they look at my crutches and little Morgan's empty sleeve). "My God! they are English officers!" They say no more; a dead silence prevails, until the French officer asks me if I myself am not a Frenchman.

"No, I am an Englishman."

"That is," returns he, "you serve with the English, but you are French by birth!"

"Pardon me, sir; I am a legitimate Englishman."

We are sent to a miserable house, but some Spanish women follow us out of the commandant's house, and when we come to a place where no one can observe us, they stop us, burst into tears and lamentations, and, with all the frensical vehemence of long-smothered enthusiasm, clasp us in their arms and imprint our faces with kisses of agony and tenderness. Then, sobbing and wringing their hands with a poignancy of grief almost maternal, they suffer us to proceed, and give themselves to despair. Had the motive of this rare burst of virtuous sentiment been less sacred, the scene less impressive, or events we had witnessed less fresh upon our minds, perhaps this adventure had excited us to mirth. Far different are our feelings. Every tendency to compassion is moved within us.

Affected beyond measure, and struck with the highest admiration, far from forgiving any thought of levity, I should be angry with that man who, dry-eyed, could have beheld the surprising conduct of those patriotic women. On entering the house the billet indicated, we find it preoccupied by four French soldiers, and hardly have time to growl at this nuisance before the *alcaldy*, having despatched his business and then followed us, takes us with him to his own house, where all his humble means are put forth to entertain us.

Spreading our beds on the earthy floor of the inner cabin, we open our hampers, and having set out an admirable piece of spiced beef, a huge cold turkey, and a great leathern bottle of Madeira, we invite our rustic host to partake with us. In this honour he will suffer none of his household, not even his wife, to share; but carefully closing and securing the door, he sits down with us more from curiosity than appetite, and anxiously asks for all we know of the affairs of his unfortunate country, and whether there be any chance of freeing her from the legions of the devil.

Friday, January 26, 1810.—Rise by candlelight, contrive to get a little hot tea, and, thanking the good *alcaldy*, start. See, by the way, that our savage commanding is a most irascible animal. Pass over a not unpleasant country—weather beautiful. The road passing into the wild mountains that toss their rugged heads about the lordly Escurial becomes strewed with bloody skeletons and mangled carcases of men, murdered and buried by the roadside, but again raked up and half-devoured by the ravenous wolves that infest these mountains. No sight can be more revolting to humanity: it realises the bugbear of children, *raw-head and bloody bones*. The gaiety of the sunbeams glistening on the snowy mountains, and the courtly beauty of the Escurial, dissipate much of the horror.

The very steep mountain, which traverses this day's march, proves the mule a stout heart and the mare a *coquine*, unequal to her share of the draught. We fall into rear of the convoy. Stephens and Morgan walk on the edge of the precipice on the right hand. A bullock, rendered mad by being driven though lame, runs at them, and, as they turn to run, with his horns at Stephens's back precipitates him! I lose sight of Stephens; but, rising in the carriage, I see him lying at the bottom of the steep without the smallest motion or sign of life.

Soon, however, he comes to life, but not to recollection, and for more than a quarter of an hour after being put into the carriage exhibits the horror of a struggle with mental derangement. He mends, however, and soon is able to walk again, which refreshes him much. I am now obliged to walk too, to lighten the carriage, and we begin to be alarmed about getting up the hill. At length all our efforts are vain! The mare will stir no more. Just now a carter, with a convoy of hay drawn by bullocks, meets us. I invite him to help us up the hill; seeing the soldiers with us, he assents, and all his pairs of bullocks are pressed by them. I beg the soldiers that when they come to the top they will let him go. They say yes. He puts on his bullocks before our cattle, and so awkwardly that at the first start down comes the mare.

The oxen then draw us up very quietly—draw us up alone. Come to the top, he demands to go, but the soldiers are deaf. The peasant appeals to me; I intercede; but the Frenchmen oppose the order of their commander. I tell the man that I have no authority over them; he offers to take us to Otero if I will set the rest of the oxen free. I still plead want of power, and we proceed— down the steep descent, with a stupendous precipice without the slightest fence on the right hand. Suddenly one of the bullocks begins to kick with fury, and dart about in a terrible manner. In full expectation of dashing down the immeasurable steep, I hastily order the door to be opened, and the servants help me to jump out. I revile the peasant, who, we were all persuaded, had whispered to his animal to set a-madding, out of revenge. His beasts are unyoked, and down he goes in triumph; with difficulty we follow with our own, for frozen snow, forming an icy slope, makes the road most perilous. The road descends suddenly, and the scenery is greatly romantic.

At the foot of the mountain we meet the malicious old peasant returning with his bullocks, and he asks the reward I promised him. I shake my fist at him and give him nothing, while Morgan abuses him in very good English.

We find the rearguard with the bullock-carts at halt at a post consisting of a large building and a church, where the grand road, I believe, continues *right on*, and the road to Segovia, or the *route d'Étapes*, inclines to the right. It is getting dusk, and without much reflection we continue alone our way to Otero, now distant two leagues. It soon falls dark, and we observe the road, heavy and well-bushed, is very favourable for brigandage. We meet a man and ask the distance; he answers one league and a half; and, as we go at a brisk walk, we settle our arrival at an hour and a half. The moon rises. We dread the slightest hill on account of the mare. The time having elapsed, we look about for the village in vain, and see with consternation a most serious hill before us.

The road is very heavy. With utmost exertion, and all hands afoot, we get half-way up and there stick. As the town must be close by, we think it best that Stephens, who complains of the consequences of his fall, should mount his grey pigmy and, accompanied by his man Reynolds, proceed to the village and request assistance from the *chef de bataillon*. I write a note on a leaf of this book by the light of the moon that

> *Shadowy sets off the face of things.*

Stephens and his man start. Morgan and myself getting into the carriage, and drawing up the glasses, compose ourselves for a nap, while the warmth of gallantry for Reynold's bride prevents Aaron Delacourt, my man, and Moses Parnell, Morgan's, from minding the frost, the snow, and the keen wind; and I am willing to hope that the bright flame of chastity is equally serviceable to the Square Lady! No sooner is Stephens gone than I discover a league-stone, which tells me, by saying 10 *L. from Madrid*, that it wants yet a league to Otero; so that Morgan and myself make up our minds for a considerable time of perditage. Soon, by the sound of voices that cheerily break through the stillness of the night, we are apprised that the rear of the convoy, which we had passed at halt, is approaching.

When they come up to us and find us hopelessly sticking there, the French soldiers make very much a concern of our distress, and insist upon shouldering the wheel. This expedient failing, they leave us with regret and terror, one of them assuring me that he would speak to the Sergeant to send back a pair of oxen to drag us up the hill. So once more we are left alone among the robbers. We hand out a cup of Madeira to each of the outside passengers, and compose ourselves again to sleep. Let those who hold that distant dangers are less terrible say why, at Madrid, we felt enough of apprehension about the *brigands* to make us dislike the journey, and now in the midst of their haunts, and at the dead of night, alone, we feel no sort of alarm; for

> *Evils dreaded are ten times as great*
> *As when they press us with their actual weight.*

From the first, I never should have thought of dreading any intentional injury from these *brigands*; but as their mode of attack is naturally firing upon the convoy from their lurking places, as it passes through strong country, and never showing themselves till half are killed and the other half in flight, the goodwill of our friends might have come in action too late.

After waiting an hour in this situation, to our surprise a party of French soldiers appears with the promised bullocks. These good fellows express the utmost joy at finding us safe. They yoke-to the oxen, which immediately begin to dart about like mad bulls, whirling the carriage round and round. Morgan and I clamour lustily to get out, and in a pause descend. Now we hook the kindly mule in front, which obligingly undertakes to draw a full third, and up we get at last. At the top of the hill the sergeant says he would willingly give us the oxen on to the village, but cannot, as he has taken them from a cart occupied by wounded, whom it is impossible to leave upon the road. He may say that!

So once again we are left to our own beasts, who go on very well until just near the entrance of the town, where (having passed a wild of rocks rather than a road) the carriage obstinately sticks in a huge hole, and the mare will not even try to get us out; so I leave Morgan, and hobble cautiously on my crutches—difficult from the dark and roughness of the way—and seek the *commandant* of the place. The village is in good order. The *commandant* is very friendly, and sends his servant to find Stephens's lodging; and in the meantime we sit down to sup on cold mutton and salad. When the man comes with the direction for the billet of Stephens, whom I had greatly feared to be lost, I follow him. The streets consist of the untamed rock. "How the devil, thinks I, will the *berlin* get over all this?" But entering the premises I see a carriage in the yard: so I think, again, that where one has come another may. How is my satisfaction increased to recognise, on a closer inspection, my own venerable berlin!

From this point the luck seems to change; I find everything in clover. Morgan and Stephens sit by a rare kitchen fire preparing for supper. We sup lightly. The good people of the house are loving and characteristic. We are tired and ripe for sleep— hardly can I resolve to write another word. Thus well has ended this disastrous day, and the pleasures of a comfortable port are much enhanced in reflecting on the gales and buffetings at sea!

Otero is six long leagues from Calapajar.

BRIDGE OF ALCANTARA

AQUEDUCT OF SEGOVIA

Friday 1 January 12, 1810.—Get up, eat a good breakfast, get two bullocks to put before our mules, and set out walking—delightful morning. Pass the Palace of *Rio Trio.* It reminds us of Thoresby—a colossal statue of the House at Thoresby, in a barren plain. Immense steep hills, but the good, docile bullocks draw us up apparently without exertion. See a palace of the king at the foot of mountains on the right, where he was wont to repair to cool himself in summer. 'Tis the Palace of St. Ildefonso.

Arrive at Segovia at half-past two An old wretched town in a bare, rugged country, has old turreted walls, no good buildings, but a beautiful, venerable aqueduct, consisting of two tiers of arches in the style of the bridge of Alcantara, but indeed less grand and striking. This only is worth seeing in the place. Here we buy another mule, which we hope will smooth our difficulties. In answer to an application from me for assistance of bullocks comes, when I am in bed, an answer from the *chef de bataillon,* couched as follows:—

À Monsieur Ch. Boothby,
Capitaine Anglais, à Segovia.
  Séjour demain.

Monsieur le Capitaine,—*J'ai reçu votre lettre et vous préviens que vous pouvez être tranquilles sur la demande que vous me faites; du reste, je vous engage à vouloir bien recommander à vos soldats prisonniers de rester tranquilles, et de suivre avec ordre le convoy; s'il en était autrement, je cesserais d'avoir les égards qui sont dus à votre rang.—J'ai l'honneur de vous saluer,*

Le Chef de Bataillon.

From the *Séjour demain* we are happy to find tomorrow is a halting day. I read the letter to Stephens and Morgan; and then, dismissing the orderly and putting out the light, we confer on the contents from our several kingdoms. We think by any counsel of ours to impede the escape of our brother prisoners would be unworthy conduct, and therefore at once determine against it; but, on the other hand, we know ourselves to be at the disposal of this *farouche* colonel, and that it is well in his power to harass and torment us. To take no notice of the observation, as it does not demand an answer, might be best. But then he will suppose we admit the reasonableness of his expectation, and in case of any escapes, he would be emboldened to treat us with vigour and disrespect. It is best, therefore, to protest at once against the idea, and in a tone which, though respectful, shall give him to understand we will not be put upon. Here the council breaks up.

Saturday, January 13, 1810.—Write to the *chef de bataillon* as follows:—

Segovia, le 13 Janvier 1810.

Monsieur le Commandant,—J'ai reçu hier au soir la lettre que vous m'avez fait l'honneur de m'écrire, et je vous rends les remercimens des officiers Anglais pour vos assurances des secours. Mais, je suis fâché, monsieur, qu'au même temps vous exigiez d'eux ce qu'ils croient ne pouvoir pas hire.

Il est peu nécessaire de vous dire que quand les soldats prisonniers sont tenté par l'espérance de retrouver leur liberté tout conseil que nous les donnassions ne les empêcherait de se sauver tous les fois qu'ils en trouvassent l'occasion, et qu'il ne soit pas possible de les empêcher qu'en les gardant, ce que ne tient qu'à vous.

Quant à nous, j'espère que vous nous feriez la justice de croire que l'engagement que nous vous ayons donné ne soit la garde la plus forte dont vous pussiez vous server.

Nous sommes bien persuadés que vous. Monsieur le Commandant, ne cesseriez pas d'avoir les égards qui sont dus à notre rang que quand nous aurions fait quelque chose qui en soit indigne.—J'ai l'honneur d'être. Monsieur le Commandant, votre très humble et tres obéissant serviteur, Charles Boothby,
Capitaine au Corps de Génie de S.M.B.

We walk about the town and dislike it more and more. The 28th Regiment enter from Astorga. Meet a fellow in one of Joseph's Spanish regiments, a Dutchman who, having served fourteen years in our 10th Hussars, was wounded in the Affair of Cavalry at Benaverte under Lord Paget, and had been taken at the hospital. Dine snugly, and drive away care—but with sobriety. Segovia three leagues from Otero.

Sunday, January 14, 1810.—Rise at half-past six. Breakfast. Start at eight. Weather very fine. Our unicorn answers perfectly. The worst of Segovia is the interior. Round the town there is an air of courtly antiquity, a curious wall with a tower, and an abrupt, rocky broken boldness of ground that renders the scene highly attractive. The antique towered wall, dilapidated by time, following the crest of a red precipitous rock, surmounted again by fretted towers and glittering spires that, with unequal loftiness, add variety to grandeur. This *coup d'oeil* prepares disappointment for the expecting traveller. The redness of the stone adds much to the warmth of the scene.

Opposite the crest of the town rocks is another crest, and between the two runs a clear and plentiful stream, traversed by elegant bridges, and bordered by crowding trees and happy-looking cottages—they really were happy, till abominable war had hither stretched his iron hand! We soon come up with the convoy. 'Tis a corn country. The stream is a mllowy stream, with sand-banks. Bare hills bound the view contiguous, strewed with good-looking villages. Mountains clad with snow are in the distant prospect. Over these hang flocks of cloud resembling birds. Road very bad. Pass a river by a bridge, and then through a pine-wood and divers villages, and arrive at half-past four at Sta. Maria de Meve, five leagues.

Are met in the square by an officer, who gives us our billet, which is on the schoolmaster. We walk about the village, which is considerable, but offers nothing worthy of remark. We steer towards the *chef*, who gives us a wide berth. We repair to our quarters, a snug little room, with a good pan of fire. Beefsteaks, turkey, drumsticks grilled, and potatoes getting ready below. We have Muscadel, Madeira, and red Paxarate: so propose to dine well. Goodnight, my little red book: I must talk to my companions.

Monday, January 15, 1810.—Rise at six. Breakfast, and start prosperously. Weather fine, dry and cold. In the prospect are very remarkable heights not much above the horizon, cut off in the prospective semicircle as with a scythe, and forming an apparent table, without the slightest perceptible deviation from the dead level. Road heavy sand—very open—wine and corn country, clouded with spacious woods and considerable villages, in one of which I am now writing, and see from the carriage windows women dressed with red gowns, turned over their heads, displaying a bright yellow petticoat, which is short enough to discover their scarlet stockings. So that, grouped together to see the convoy, they resemble a flock of huge birds of gaudy plumage, running about one after the other, and then stopping with undecided motion. Road execrable.

On the brow of a hill overhanging a stream stands a beautiful rich old castle, strikingly charming, well contrasted with a lean, high watch-tower. We ascend a terrific hill, then traverse large pine-woods. Shoot ahead of the convoy, and at seven o'clock arrive at Olmedo—six leagues, a considerable town. The French have taken here barricading precautions for their security. We get a good billet, and prepare as usual to be comfortable. The Table Mountains, which diversify this wide country, are very remarkable.

Tuesday, January 16, 1810.—Signora Nicolosa and her household are very unpleasant people. She puts on the courtesy of fear, but, finding us harmless, soon evinces her discontent and narrowness. At seven o'clock we start for Valdestilias. The river Eresma somewhat relieves the sameness of the country. The *chef* comes up to the carriage and affects civility, telling us how admirably the English behaved to the French in Portugal. "Ay, ay" (swears), says he, "you are very snug (swears)—in a comfortable carriage (swears), although prisoners. Well—well—it ought to be so (swears); you behave to your prisoners magnificently (swears); I have good reason to say so (swears horribly). Had it not been for the exertions of *Messieurs les Anglais*, we should have been assassinated by hundreds—after the Convention."

Dead bodies, half-devoured, are again seen. Arrive at Valdestilias—deserted and destroyed! In searching about for some house that may not infect or defile us (for here the convoy halts), we find a venerable assembly, consisting of the clergy of Salamanca, mounted on asses, led by the venerable Dr. Curtis, whom I well remember, supposed to be bound for France. Dr. Curtis is a learned, respectable old man, who for thirty years has been rector of the Irish College at Salamanca, which office is united to that of rector of the university, and now the French are dragging him and his brother clergy, God knows where or why! The French soldiers hoot them as they pass. The doctor, however, preserves a manly dignified spirit.

Some little time ago the Spaniards, under, I think, the Duque del Parque, snatched Salamanca from the hands of their enemies. But obliged again to retire, the French visit the joy, and perhaps the aid, evinced by the clergy on that occasion by this act of severity on their re-entry. Our search for lodgement being fruitless, we request of the colonel that we may go on four leagues more to Valladolid, which is granted. *Mais soyez sages!* says the *chef*. After baiting the beasts, we set forward. Immediately below the village a noble bridge leads us over the Eresma, a smiling copious river. Road still sandy. The swift part of our convoy and the one from Salamanca have set forward, and are a mile ahead. We wish to rejoin them on account of the patriot *banditti*, which by daylight we do not fear, but by night we do.

The road dreadfully heavy sand—slow—slow—slow! Reach at length the Douro, here a rapid, considerable, sea-green stream. "In different and in distant places have I beheld thee, fair stream," say I to myself; "foaming under the frown of rocky Toro, or swiftly laving the vine-clad luxuriance that adorns thy track from Lamego to Oporto." We have for some time seen Valladolid away to the right, and to the left a town with a castle on the site much resembling Toro. Now we pass a half-eaten cadaver. This bridge over the Douro is called the Puente del Douro. It is suspiciously barricaded, and the village on the other side displays the terror of the little garrison. Here we lose sight of the convoy we did wish to reach.

We are overtaken by some Franco-Spanish *grandee*, escorted by twenty-six *cuirassiers*, with brazen helmets, as we are entering the awful pine-wood that stretches between us and Valladolid. Night is falling. The sand returns no sound as these fellows trot—trot—trot away, leaving us ploughing the sand. Their brazen *casques*, long, flowing, black horse-hair plumes floating on their white cloaks, their passing as if they saw us not, with steady onward attention, and riding into the awful gloom which overhangs the depths of the wood, and the still silence which swallows the faint echoes of their paces, altogether make the appearance spectral and imposing.

The sand is so grievously heavy that Stephens and Morgan are obliged to get out and walk all the way. And I, as I sit, inwardly revile the folly that has thus a second time committed us by night in the midst of these sanguinary scenes. For seven miles the heavy sand and deep wood continue, and perfect darkness closes round us.

Very glad to get out of the wood! Meet a French officer on horseback with two soldiers, one with and one without arms. I let down the glass and ask him how far it is to Valladolid. "*Mais, mon dieu, monsieur*," said he in great agitation. "We have been lost in the fields these two hours—have you never left the great road?"

"No."

"Thank God," exclaimed he, and the soldier slammed his musket with great vehemence. We reach the suburbs of Valladolid.

From the gate the sergeant of the guard sends a soldier with us to the commandant of the town, who gives us what they call an invitation to the municipality,—that is to say, "The *commandant de la place* invite *la municipalise* to lodge," etc. The head of the municipality gives us a billet upon the English College. He calls me to the window to point out the way, and says in an under voice, "I wish it were possible for me to lodge you in a palace! Indeed, sir, the will (laying his hand on his breast and looking mournful) is not wanting!"

The moon having risen, sets off the square to great advantage. The streets knee-deep in sludge. We are well received at the college by the rector, Mr. Colborne, a mild honest man. He puts us into a comfortable room, and makes a blazing fire. We dine at ten o'clock. Go to bed at twelve, and fall fast asleep. Olmedo is six leagues from Valladolid.

Wednesday, January 17, 1810.—Finish breakfast by half-past one. The rector invites us to dinner. I carry Marshal Mortier's letter to General Kellermann; not at home, leave it, go to the square. Though well sized, the houses are miserable and entirely deceived us last night. There is nothing in this huge town worth noting: nothing rises above mediocrity, and the much greater part of 8000 houses are old and wretched. The streets are flowing with mud, the squares heaped with filth, and the main sewers are open. Never such an assemblage of buildings offered so little attraction. Never so populous a city exhibited such marks of neglect and depopulation.

At five o'clock the rector arrives, and tells us that the Salamanca clergy, having applied for their parole, had been offered it upon condition that they should be mutually responsible for one another; and that, on the failure of any one of them, twelve of their number should be shot! These hard conditions Dr. Curtis refused. We descend to dinner; much hospitality, and but little that we can eat. Of the three English collegiates at this college, one is a youth named Challenor who comes from Worksop. He has a large nose, but is otherwise agreeable.

Thursday, January 18, 1810.—At nine go to the *chef*; he is not at home. We leave our names; receive the following invitation from General Kellermann:—

Printed.
Le Général de Division Kellermann prie M. le Capitaine Chas. Boothby de lui faire l'honneur de venir dîner chez lui. Aujourd'hui 18 Janvier à 5 heures.
R.S.V.P.

Yesterday the air was ice and promised snow, but today, though frosty, it is shiny and fine. Dine with Kellermann, who speaks English and is very gentleman-like and attentive. Gives me letters from Burgos, Vittoria, and Bayonne. Very good cookery, but bad wine. Kellermann talks of the Convention of Cintra and his trip to England. He laughs when he says that the English would not let him come to London; we wondering why they should not. He praises the Isle of Wight, where he was suffered to set foot on shore. He is in great distress for one of his *aides-de-camp*, whom the *brigands* have got hold of; and sent an English officer to propose an exchange in vain. His English servant lights me back to the college at night, and we talk by the way. This man had fallen sick four miles (leagues, I would say) from Corunna. He was in the 5th Regiment during the retreat of Sir John Moore. The Spaniards, he says, took their arms, loaded them, and would have immediately killed them, had it not been for the French. The Gallicans even stripped to the skin the poor Englishwomen, who sat fatigued or ill by the roadside.

"General Kellermann," says he, "is a fine man for everybody. But O Lord! sir, he behaved shocking cruel to the Spaniards at Alba di Tormes. Ever such a sight of 'em laid down their arms, fell on their knees and cried, 'Prisoners! prisoners!' But the general, the first man, rode in amongst them, lulling some with his pistol, then drawing his sword and cutting and slashing with his own hand. The dragoons followed at a gallop, rode in amongst them and cut them all to pieces. Their arms and heads flew about! Oh! it was shocking!"

He also dwells with much horror on the behaviour of the French to their Spanish prisoners. "Lord!" says he, "when the poor devils be tired or sick and can't come on, they'll take 'em behind a house and put a couple of balls through 'em in a minute!" This fact, which one fondly would hope incredible, but which all the inhabitants have unceasingly affirmed, is but too well corroborated by the carcases of Spanish soldiers on the road, upon whose bodies the uniform declares their nation, and the wounds the manner of their death.

That the Spaniards, a people at once patriotic and ferocious, should commit atrocious barbarities on such invaders as the French, and that the French should be disposed to retaliate amidst the tumult of battle or the inebriation of conquest, cannot raise our wonder, though it fills us with disgust But we must see with amazement, as well as horror, that the French soldiers have attained that pitch of human butchery, which enables them to murder without emotion, amidst the easy cheerful fellowship of a peaceable journey, numbers of wretches, whose only crime is to be sinking under disease, nakedness, hunger, and fatigue. I may safely affirm that in the present state of our army the officers would order such acts in vain. The reason of policy alleged for these monstrous massacres is, that if those wretches were left sick on the road they would only serve to strengthen the *brigands*. "But as for the English soldiers," say the inhabitants, "they feed 'em and treat 'em well!" The clergy of Salamanca are let out of prison.

Friday, January 19, 1810.—We procure a cart and two mules from the *chef*, which make us more simple arrangements. Start at nine; leave our fire with regret. Before we go, I write to Captain Walsh, General Belliard's *aide-de-camp*, and beg General Kellermann to forward it, hoping that through old Geils our safe arrival at Valladolid may make its way to England. In starting, we thank Mr. Colborne for much hospitality, whilst deploring the hardships and contributions to which the French subject them. He admits that, by comparison with other religious houses, he has no reason to complain.

The road is beautiful, the country open, but at distance broken by mountains. Some that approach the road have been anciently occupied as military posts. The country has a great appearance of richness, intersected by considerable rivers, traversed by handsome bridges. The largest of these streams, which flows on our left, is the Pisuerga, and waters extensive vineyards. The weather is bright, but freezing intensely, with a high wind. Luckily the road is so grand that the carriage runs lightly, as our new mule is lamed in the shoulder. At five o'clock arrive at Duenas, six short leagues from Valladolid. It is a large place, stationed like a ship in a rough sea, near the confluence of the Pisuerga and Carrion. Not liking our first billet, get a second; not liking that, ask the woman servant of a large house next door if they will take us in. "*Non tenemos camas, señor*" (We have no beds, sir).

"*Las tenemos nos otros Muchacha querida*" (We have them ourselves, dear wench). So she consents, but slips slyly over to the next house to abuse the man who (she supposes) has advised us to trouble her, and this mistake makes the street ring again. I have much difficulty to still this storm, and then all goes well. Intensely cold.

Saturday, January 20, 1810.—Freezing—bright and dear—the road superb. The country rich, open, beautified by a considerable frozen river, superbly bridged, and broken by mountains. Seven large glittering villages in sight at once. On the roadside lies the body of a Spanish soldier, with blood on his bosom. We are reconnoitred by sixteen brigands on horseback, and being much in rear of the convoy I wonder they did not attempt us. At two o'clock we arrive at Torrequemada, a large village half-burnt, sited on a hill overlooking a twenty-three-arched bridge, which in a zigzag crosses the river Pisuerga, large and swift, completely frozen and reflecting the sun—it adds a brilliant gaiety to the scene. Torrequemada is four fur leagues from Duenas, and here but for a meeting convoy we should have halted. As it is, we proceed.

Meet a large convoy and the 26th Regiment, almost all boys; leave the great road and steer four points from it to a village on the left. At half-past five arrive at Herrera, six long leagues. Lodge in a poor house, but pretty well for such a poor village. The people, however, are very cordial; and our host tells exciting stories of brigands, and dwells with the greatest delight on the destruction of a detachment that was effected, three days gone, in this very village, an officer and thirty men. Says he: "Ay, that Valentian was a proper fellow. The officer came up joining his hands and crying, 'Prisoner! prisoner!' but the Valentian plunged a sword into his breast, and it came out half a yard behind! Ha! ha! ha!" This he repeats, and measures on his arm the length it came out.

Mrs. Reynolds falls very ill. I get the good woman to put her to bed. A charming, pretty, elegant woman comes into the smoky kitchen, where I am sitting by the fire surrounded by Spaniards (Stephens and Morgan are upstairs). This bewitching woman, in her light blue gown, puts her laughing twinkling eyes into mine, and asks me what I say. "That you are very pretty," say I, although I had not spoken.

"*Mas guappo es Usted,*" returns she.

"Pray tell me who you are?" I ask.

"The surgeoness," she answers.

"O! then you must go and see a poor English woman that lies sick."

"O yes, indeed," exclaims the hostess; "the poor thing is very bad."

"But," rejoin I, "do you yourself profess chirurgical skill, or are you only the surgeon's wife?"

"Only the surgeon's wife," returns she, with a disclaiming shake of the head.

"Then, pray, go and fetch your husband instantly!"

Mine host now tells of a great battle in Valentia, and that Spaniards, English, and Portuguese made up 100,000 men, "Your authority, good mine host?"

"Our surgeon," says he, "went to shave the commandant."

"Shave the *commandant!*"

"*Si senhor es Barbero tambien.*"—"Yes, sir, he's a barber also; and so the *commandant* told him this news." (Enter Chirurgio-barber.) He greets us with ceremonious courtesy, and immediately asks for the lady. Hear our dialogue:—

Chi. (pointing to me) "Is this her husband?"
Beo. "You are come to prescribe for the woman. What have you to do with her husband?"
Chu (laughing heartily) "You say well! you say well! Ha! ha! ha! ha! Come along, then! come along! Where is the lady? But (stopping short), does she speak Castilian?"
Beo. "Not a word!"
Chi. (in despair) "Purest Virgin! how then shall I tell what ails her?"
Beo. "Look at her and touch her."
Chi. "Ay, that I can do!"
Boo. "She has the headache, a stiff neck, and pains in her bones."
Chi. (going out) "O! then we shall get on wondrously!"

He soon returns, declaring she has a severe cold, for which he prescribes a dish of chocolate and a decoction of sauce flowers; both which being soon administered, the patient betters. Reynolds bears his wife's indisposition with wonderful fortitude. We dine very well; at dinner drink brandy-and-water, and crack a bottle of claret after. As we go to bed, the floor gives great indications of a capacity to lower us into the stable, it having settled in the shape of a punch-bowl.

Sunday, January 21, 1810.—We are hurried and bothered by a French officer, who is ordered to wait with the rearguard to see us off, for it seems these parts are full of *brigands.* "*Sacré bleu,*" says the officer with rapid repetition; while sleepy Dilly, lazy Reynolds, and feeble Nelly Par, walk over each other and dawdle into the harness in such a lackadaisical manner that he naturally loses all patience. When ready to start we offer him a place in the carriage, which immediately gives him back his good-humour, and he very courteously declines our civility. We soon come up with the rear of the convoy, which is at halt. A musket goes off in front! "It's finished," cries a French soldier, laughing.

Again!—two!—three! four!—five!—six!—seven! I let down the glass and say to Stephens, who is walking, "What the deuce is all that? Are we in action with the *brigands?*"

"No!" says he, with a black look, "they're shooting Spanish prisoners!"

Again!—eight!—nine! "Holy God, pardon us!" cries a French soldier.

"O, cursed *commandant!*" exclaims a French woman. We are penetrated with horror, but hang on the hope that bullocks have been the victims, not men. Moving on, however, we pass the lifeless bodies of two unhappy wretches, who have thus required so many bullets to despatch them. Close to the scene of action is the murderous director. I look out of the opposite window. Stephens looks at him without acknowledgment. Now he rides up to the window, bowing and complimenting. Answer his questions categorically. He says, "I have just been shooting two rascals! (swears). Thirty of the Spanish prisoners have hid themselves in the wine-caves, where the devil himself could not find them (swears). I caught these two (swears), and have made them an example to the rest (swears). Thirty have got away (swears a great oath). It's just so many *brigands!*"

This explanation, though far from satisfactory, takes away the idea of wanton blood-spilling. We look right on, gloomily grave, and he rides off.

Although not entirely without excuse, this act is clearly unjustifiable! If a prisoner runs away, and the guard shoots him in the act, he does no more than he ought, because when the prisoner runs he is no longer surrendered, and is an enemy, the capture of whom is doubtful. But when he is retaken, you may put him in irons, not to punish, but to secure him, for he has committed no crime *and to kill him is murder.*

The carriage overturns in a ditch and wakes Dilly. With the assistance of the French soldiers, we are presently righted without damage. At half a league on our way we come to a little shivering village, in which a party of French are barricaded, and now enter again the great road, which is superb. Ascend the spur of a mountain, and an interesting scene stretches below us. A wide plain bound in by broken mountains, which are skirted by towered villages half-buried in woods. The Arlanza and Arlanzon, two copious streams, intersect with majestic sweeps the fertile plain, and make their confluence close to the road. Their frozen currents, reflecting the gold sun, streak the prospect as it were with flashes of glorious diamond; while the sun and frost and snow light up the whole with magic touches. Meet a battalion of the 1st Swiss and the 66th with convoy. Arrive at a poor village half-destroyed, where a captain, three subalterns, and fifty Germans are barricaded. We ask one of the officers, a Dutchman, to eat bread and cheese. He declines, but entering into conversation expresses himself after the following manner.

"Unhappy are we, condemned to serve in this miserable country; above all, unhappy the emperor's foreign troops, who are invariably employed upon every disagreeable and unprofitable duty! On our return to Madrid after the Battle of Oceana, nothing was heard of but the bravery and good conduct of the *German troops,* and how much they merited *reward. Behold our reward!* to be barricaded in this ruined village, surrounded by hordes of robbers, whose character excludes from one the consolation which, with other enemies, one might find in the hope of an honourable death! What is danger in the field of battle? If I die there, I die at once and die like a soldier. But to be taken by a band of barbarous, incensed thieves, who, after loading me with indignities, will torture me to death! What possible consolation can I find, impressed with the expectation of such an end?

But three days ago, this village not being capable of sheltering a detachment, an officer and twenty-two men were sent on to Herrera. The brigands, fifty in number, entered the village, lulled the officer and most of his men, taking the rest prisoners. This sort of thing happens every day, and may happen to me tomorrow! Every courier that arrives we are obliged to escort (for we have no cavalry), and the danger is so great that no money could tempt me to take a turn for a comrade. You can have no idea of the number of men we lose. When our regiment entered this country, it was 3400 strong, and now we have but 600. We have been constantly in action, and lost 600 men at Talavera alone."

The officer having finished his complaint, I get into the carriage and wish him good-day. I could not but hear him with more pleasure than sympathy. As an individual, I wish him a better plight; but as a part of Napoleon's horrid instrument of wasting oppression, may dangers and horrors complicate, multiply, and blacken round him. Shall I not feel more, unhappy Spain, for thy bleeding bosom and lacerated heart! Land where, whatever the errors of ignorance and superstition, the real God was reverenced. The social hearth was decently maintained, and the dues of hospitality and honesty reacted, and had in honour. Too easily with all thy fire and intrepidity, too quietly didst thou adhere to the love of order and legal government. Thy king, though despicable as man, thou didst honour in his crown; and by thy very loyalty wert thou betrayed. Where, then, is the country whose sufferings shall find a greater interest in my heart? My right leg lies in thy fields. If it has served thee, thou art welcome!

It appears from this German officer's complaint that the predatory system of warfare adopted by the Spaniards grows terrible and important. It is no wonder that to prevent the increase of this species of force the French should adopt cruel and unjustifiable measures. At four leagues turn off the road, and proceeding 500 yards arrive at Villa-Topeque, a miserable, desolate collection of forty poor houses. Pampliega, a considerable place, not half a mile off, sited on midmountain, would naturally have lodged us, but it is, they say, occupied by reinforcements from France. One officer tells 3000 Polish lancers, and another 1500. The latter more probable.

We get a billet with the Spanish officers' prisoners, consisting of two brigadier-generals and three colonels taken at Oceana. They joined our convoy from Valladolid in an old stage-coach drawn by four mules, which equipage General Kellermann, with a delicacy not much practised by either party towards the other, had provided in respect to their rank. They seem to be very agreeable, good-humoured old codgers. One of the colonels belonged to Romana's army, Ildefonso Roxas. He was with Romana in the North, and was embarked by Admiral Keats at Nyebourg. He wears a sort of pendant star given by the King of England, inscribed *La Patria es mi Norte*. On his arm is embroidered in two places, *Se distingue en Medelin*. He was brought to King Joseph at Oceana, who offered to make him a general if he would serve him; but O'Farrel interposing observed that he was from the North. Upon which the king in a rage told him he should be shot. But O'Farrel, interceding, begged the king to spare his life, which His Majesty mercifully accorded, but reproached him with deserting France and loving the English. "Sir," replied the Spaniard, "Spain has made peace with England, and so have I."

"Take him away," cried the offended monarch.

I have great difficulty in getting upstairs, but, animated by the excessive cold, I overcome all obstacles; have much greater difficulty in getting down, but, rendered desperate by the dread of suffocation from the smoke, I succeed, and issue from the house, weeping with smarting eyes, and panting with the laboured respiration of resuscitation. The Spanish *grandees* get another house. While Stephens and Morgan endeavour to ameliorate our tenement, I stroll to a huge bonfire, which the soldiers have made in the little *Place* of the village. Here I warm, and there comes to me the poor French officer who would fain have had the fourth place in our vehicle. He talks English with deliberate confidence. "How do you do, my dear?"

"Ah! for me I go from bad to worse. One of my legs is quite—quite—*forlorn!*"

"Ha! ha! ha! poor fellow! forlorn—ha! ha! ha!" says Morgan, as he comes to fetch me to our cabin. It is a little dark cave with black beams. Notwithstanding, we eat the back of a roast turkey broiled, a good mutton-chop, and hot potatoes, moistening the repast with our remaining brandy and two bottles of claret. When I would turn into the hole in which my bed is crammed it is too short, but I prefer lying crooked to defiling my bed by a contact with the floor, which is like a hardened dunghill.

Monday, January 22, 1810.—Rise at half-past five; breakfast in peace—ready in time! Morning intensely cold and threatens snow. The mighty coach of our Spanish friends leads off, and we follow. One of them, Colonel Ramon Salvador, is a wondrous, dirty, blackguard-looking little fellow, and talks exquisite English very fast; swearing tremendously, with a laughing face. These good Spaniards take me for a general, and call me *el General Ingles,* and say *"buenas dias el Senhor General."* This tickles me so much, that I have not yet found in my heart to undeceive them. We enter the magnificent great road. It begins to snow like blazes. In the midst of it we meet the Polish lancers, fine savage-looking dogs! They seem to wag their whiskers in the snow. The flags to their lances give them a very striking appearance. Other cavalry are with them amounting to about 1000. 2000 infantry also are with them belonging to Loison's division coming from Vittoria; so that it appears no reinforcements, at least of infantry, have reached thus far.

The snow ceases after an hour's feathering and it becomes fine. View, streams of willows like the Fens of Lincolnshire; road charming, moderate mountains, corn and wine. Celada di Camino, two leagues, a better sort of village; pass other villages, too, by the same sort of road. Evening falls, and we discover the towers and spires of Burgos. For the last three leagues the road has passed through an avenue of stately trees, and the entry into Burgos is thickly wooded by them. At seven o'clock arrive at Burgos; snowing again. Get out of the carriage and walk to the municipality. They see at once we are English; talk a good deal of patriotism, and give us a wretched billet up two hundred stairs.

Disagreeable people with much palaver; a filthy room, stinking like an Augean stable! I find poor Mrs. Reynolds almost senseless in the kitchen, and not one of the inhuman women offering her the least assistance. I reproach them, and a man who sits profoundly idle in the chimney-corner proves to be a physician. Ask his advice. The tinker colonel enters and disputes with him, maintaining cathartic against emetic. I assist the physician, and drive the colonel from the field, who makes submission, does Ramon Salvador. Eat with appetite; but palpable stink mixes with our food.

Tuesday, January 23, 1810.—Excellent butter by way of rarity. Wait on General Solignac with the letter General Kellermann had given me. Wait an hour and a half, the premier *aide-de-camp* insisting on my stay. Said *aide-de-camp* a remarkably mild gentleman-like man who, as well as his general, served in Portugal with Junot; speaks well of Admiral Cotton. The general at length descends in a dirty greatcoat, woollen stockings about his heels, unshaved, his manners not prepossessing. Refuse to breakfast with him *à la fourchette,* but accept his invitation to dinner. Go with Stephens and Morgan to see the cathedral, which is eminently beautiful—a great assemblage of fretted, shelly spires seen from every point. In the middle a tower, not enough mounted.

Next we go shopping; weather inclined to snow, cold and raw. A Franco-German surgeon is very attentive to Mrs. Reynolds. Repair to dine with General Solignac. A noble fire irradiates the room. The general's manners are very pleasing on proof. His enunciation, slow and deliberate, gives a pleasing novelty to the French tongue; his conversation pointed and entertaining. He has no use of his left hand, which is covered by a glove. He had a shot through it at the Battle of Vimiera. He thinks that had he been taken prisoner the English surgeons would have cut it off; complains that they are addicted to excessive amputation, and had an idea they were specially paid for it.

At dinner sit next to the *chef*, who makes the capable. The general discourses much of his gambling adventures in different parts of the world. At Milan a famous *charlatane* cheated him, "*Je me jettais sur lui comme un coup de foudre*. 'Robber!' said I, 'restore me the money you have stolen'—*ce qu'il me faisait de suite!*"—that sort of man.

After dinner the crowd disperses, and the general asks me amongst a few others to go upstairs to coffee. Upstairs we find a luminous, vigorous fire. The general puts me in an armchair and extends himself in another, and lets the rest provide for themselves. He speaks with the most lively indignation of the financial chicanery of Joseph's Government.

"I have staked my *cent mille francs* on the stability of their Government," says he; "had it been overthrown, my *cent mille francs* went with it. But now that I would not scruple to place my fortune—the inheritance of my son—at the foot of Gibraltar, what pretence in the world have they for giving me their paper at a depreciation of two-thirds? It's robbery, gross robbery, and no other thing. I give you my word of honour [lays his hand on his breast], I give you my solemn word of honour, that the very next public money that comes this way I will stop and pay myself my *cent mille francs! nets! C'est ce que je ferai, ou diable m'emporte, bien sur! précisément ça! allez!*"

The French officers stand aghast, which provokes the general to renew his asservation with additional solemnity. He asks me to dine again tomorrow, which I decline on account of my companions. Find Stephens and Morgan asleep in the persuasion that we march tomorrow. Have what the French term a *nuit blanche*.

Wednesday, January 24, 1810.—Morgan wakes us at four o'clock and wonders we don't get up, till, having awakened Stephens three times, who would fain sleep, he is obliged in his own defence to tell him we do not march. We stroll about the town, which is very good. The gateway bears a full-length *basso-relievo* of Charles V. The river looks stylish and commercial, and the row of fine houses along its right bank resembles the Marinas of the Mediterranean. Though less than Valladolid, it is ten times, nay, twenty times, better. Write to the colonel to relieve our baggage-cart. He begins "My dear captain," and gives an evasive answer. Write to the general, who instantly complies. Beg him to forward to Madrid a letter for Geils. There is here a very elevated and pre-eminent citadel, in the fortifications of which recent pairs are visible. On that eminence the cathedral should have been built. Mercy on us, how grand it had been! As it is, it is much obscured.

Thursday, January 25, 1810.—Mrs. Reynolds worse. Write to the *chef* to beg he will put her in some covered conveyance; he gives no answer. Make up as well as we can with our beds. Weather improved; snows now and then. Road still superb through an avenue of trees; corn country. Meet about 1000 cavalry, ill-mounted, of the 10th, 22nd, and 26th Regiments. At four leagues is the village of Monasterio, where a group of men, women, and children, standing on a bank that overhangs the roads, throw quantities of huge biscuits to their unhappy countrymen. 'Tis a very moving sight. The country, the prospect, the road, the culture, the soil visibly improving as we get on; the road, straight as a dart, loses the sight amidst the bordering trees. At nightfall turn off a little to the left and proceed to Vriviesca, a considerable town.

Are lodged at the house of the *Padre Cura*, a Spaniard! a Schedoni in figure. Comfortable house, good people. This town famous for valour and true principles. Send for the physician to Mrs. Reynolds. On account of his general talents and sagacity, he goes by the name of *Mrs. Pitt*. 'Tis a little humpy, crook-legged, hook-nosed, sharp, funny-looking mortal. Wen on forehead, cocked hat, square to the front; has been prisoner in Ireland, never so happy in his life. The *captinis and milord*s took him to coffee-houses and gave him *iggs, melk, bride, botto* (all pronounced with the most laboured articulation); and then took him home to dinner, where they made him drunk with punch and put him to bed. "O!" he exclaims, "what fine times! When I had dressed myself in the morning my work was done for day!" (a type of the Spanish idleness).

Mrs. Reynolds may travel without danger, and is not very bad. He refuses his fee, saying that he had a fever in Ireland, and that the faculty would not take anything from him, but gave him many *shelligs* and *pekkies*. A short time ago he was summoned to Burgos and charged with animating the *brigands*,—a mighty, droll, honest little fellow! Several valiant women come to see us. One, a fruit-seller, had, with her fist, knocked down three Frenchmen in the market-place in presence of Murat, who applauded her. As an instance of the incredulity of the Spaniards to the reports of the French, the curate tells us that Buonaparte was at Madrid some time before the *Priviescars* were convinced that he had passed through their town! They are in a greater degree credulous on the other side of the question. That 200,000 *Moorish cavalry* had come over from Barbary to their assistance was perhaps not the most incredible thing firmly believed by all ranks of Madrid. The *Padre Cura* sleeps in the same room with us, and snores all night like a bassoon.

Friday, January 26, 1810.—Pass the convoy before daylight and join the coaches; road elegant; rains pretty heavily. Go off at a round trot, which lasts until four leagues from Vriviesca. We approach the romantic scenery of Pancorvo, where a rock like Gibraltar traverses the way. How we can pass it we know not. For colours, boldness of outline, harmony and keeping, this rock surpasses any that I have seen. The road wriggles through it with majestic breadth, great design, and beautiful contrivance, sloping with gentleness, now cut through the rock, and now built over the dell. The rocks, with a natural scarp of 300 feet plumb down upon the road, form for half a mile a continued pass, never to be forced, and as little to be turned. I would trust the security of my kingdom on its strength, if occupied with judgement.

Issuing from this defile, which looks like the den of a giant, we stretch our eyes over a beautiful and very changed country, and the road, forming a noble avenue as straight as a dart for many miles, stretches through a luxuriant tract, finely varied with mountains, woods, and villages, laughing amidst the fertility of a rich black soil. Arrive in very good time and some hours before the convoy at Miranda del Ebro, a little tiled town. Pass the Ebro by a pretty light bridge to get to the *commandant* of the place, as the river severs the town in twain.

Get a billet upon the apothecary, who shows us into a large and perfectly naked room, whence I could drop an egg into the Ebro, which is here a struggling stream, sundered by islands, maybe seventy yards across; bottom shelvy rock, probably fordable in many parts hereabouts; banks open soil, current not rapid. Miranda is twenty leagues from its source. The weather is very mild. The cursed woman refuses to admit Mrs. Reynolds on account of her illness, and in the midst of the abuse we bestow on each other Stephens announces the elopement of the muleteer with his car and mules. I brush off to the *commandant* over the bridge again, and hasten into the levee-room. A French officer, proud to display his acquirements, comes up and says in a quick, offhand style, "*What do you believe?*" I have the good fortune not to let my countenance go, but answer gravely in French, as if he had said "*What do you want?*" in the best English in the world. His reputation in languages thus confirmed to the admiring auditors, he orders us another car with the greatest alacrity.

Repass the Ebro; return to the naked room, now cheered by some crackling faggots. Mrs. Reynolds is better lodged in a less inhospitable dwelling. Stephens superintends the mutton-chops, Morgan the potatoes, whilst I, more ambitious, undertake an omelet and the melted butter; these with the redundant addition of pork chops, and enlivened by two bottles of pure claret,—what should we do but lay aside our cares with our greatcoats, and refresh ourselves merrily?

Saturday, January 27, 1810.—Mrs. Reynolds much better yesterday and today. Our cart today is a leetle wee carty, with two leetle wee bullocks. Set forward at daylight; road bad, heavy and hilly. A German, deserted from the French and become an officer of *brigands*, hangs on a bran-new post by the roadside. In front of us a curious church forms the pinnacle of a high mountain. A pretty river of *verdigris* forms graceful cascades of green silk with white fringe. Pass the confine of Old Castile and enter Alava, of which Vittoria is the capital; but before we reach the green river see on a rock close to the road a frozen waterfall, which has a most beautiful and surprising appearance. Traverse an irrigated plain. The soil black. In the boundary of the prospect plenty of gay villages, goodly towered, picturally coloured, in clusters of trees, at the foot of wooded or castle-topped mountains.

Road still an avenue, but heavy with sludge; weather not sunny, but serene and freshly soft. Halt to refresh at Puebla de Arraganzan, a miserably dirty and resourceless town. Morgan eats a quantity of garlic in the shape of a sausage; Stephens and myself divide a black pudding, which, by way of guarantee, the filthiest hag we ever saw assures us she made with *her own hands*—*such* hands! On leaving this place enter into enchanting scenery, where the beautiful green river bottoms in large basins and busy cascades. The richly-clothed, broken and fantastic mountains impend over the road with awful grandeur; on the shaggy top of one of these is an old mouldering turret. This romantic scene soon changes for one but little remarkable.

At dusk arrive at Vittoria, five long leagues from Miranda. It is situated advantageously on an eminence, has the appearance of a fine town, which it supports on proof. The square is not very large, but perfectly uniform, noble, and finished. The French never lost their hold of this town, which therefore has never been subjected to those rude vicissitudes which have spoiled the other Spanish cities. No very gorgeous building insists upon instant notice; but the liberality of the houses generally, the breadth and perfect pavement of the streets, give it a metropolitan air unmixed with meanness, seldom observable even in the very first-rate towns of Spain.

Vittoria was a very rich trading city, giving chiefly iron in exchange for the commodities of England and France. The former branch of her trade the unceasing protection of France has, of course, strangled. And in respect to the latter she is not left in very advantageous circumstances, from the contributionary system under which she labours, and the embarrassment which the incessant transit of the military machines throws upon land carriage. Dark, dark, before we get lodged in the house of a physician, a comfortable house, but cold reception, except from his daughters, who seem very glad to see us. The second is very pretty, but fourteen years old, graceful hair and laughing eyes, very good-humoured and agreeable.

A MOUNTAIN CHURCH IN OLD CASTILLE

Sunday, January 28, 1810.—We bustle up betimes, long ere the day breaks, and despatch Dilly to the Forum to procure a baggage-cart from him who distributes the means of transport. The *chef* keeps poor Dilly till every soldier's servant is provided for and the whole convoy in motion; and at last, on going myself into the square, I am fortunate enough to get a slow bullock-cart, and not till eight o'clock we start in rear of everything. *So* disagreeable! road execrable! Country fully peopled, and cultivated. Serene soft weather. Though of fine frame, the road is hideous for want of repair, in great holes, etc.

Being in rear of the shrieking, creaking, *cree-cree* carts, added to the sudden change in the road, ruffles the surface of our minds, and prevents our enjoying the fineness of the weather or the prettiness of the scenery. Our only hope is to be able to shoot ahead when the convoy halts. It halts at a village two leagues from Vittoria, in such a way that we find ourselves stuck on a narrow bridge where, *ne* backwards, *ne* forwards, *ne* on one side—no, no! here we are fast enough! Get out and walk, to my knee in sludge, through the town, and get on a bank a quarter of a mile on. Here will I wait for the vehicle. My spirit plumes herself and looks abroad, uninterrupted and no longer deafened with the noise, nor shaken by the long prospect of the slow-trailing convoy.

Some boy-regiments pass upwards, and are bantered *en passant* by the old blood-spillers going down—106-120—not Frenchmen. There is a sleepy, half-sulky carelessness about Dilly that moves me from the little moderation I possess. Forever he leaves the horses by themselves on the sides of precipices where the difference of a hair would dash us to atoms. Am more fidgety than a woman, and swear like a trooper. Without having made any very remarkable ascent, lo! a wonderful scene suddenly opens on our view. Looking out of the right-hand window, the eye falls 10,000 fathoms down and gazes with rapture on the luxuriant and indescribable beauties of Nature, admirably mingled with the works and dwellings of men, scattered with the most lavish and fantastic variety.

Plumb down! as if soaring with the wings of yon eagle that animates the scene, we gaze with insatiate pleasure and ever-growing admiration at the luxuriant abundance and vivid colouring of vegetation; and as the swain gazes on the face of his beloved, contemplating separately and at once the fascinating beauty of her features, so our eyes dwell with rapture on those wild, graceful, ever-changing forms which the wonder-working waters have impressed upon the earth, and which now lie spread before us in countless variety, clothed in all the splendid, glowing, but ever chaste colouring of Nature. As the road obtains upon the rugged steep on whose side it is formed, more and more wonderful features rise up in prospect and snatch us from the preceding objects of admiration.

The vast but softly-moulded mountains in the foreground, richly clothed with woods, with verdure, and with rushing waters, shoot towards each other their mossy slopes with hasty swiftness or majestic deliberation, while herds and flocks ramble over their awful steeps with native familiarity. Underneath, the splendid vales, or rather mighty ravines, are adorned by cascading rivers, that with a beautiful inconstancy wind amongst the villages, orchards, and gardens which everywhere emboss this luxuriant land. Numerous bridges over-span the trembling streams, contrived with a rudeness whose simplicity is elegance, and some so overgrown with ivy as that they seem but arching bowers for the light tread of aerial beings. White gulls floating over the dark ground seem flashes of light.

Over the aspiring tops of these amazing high mountains in foreground, still higher and horrid uplift their dun, sleet-covered heads, boldly tracing in the horizon, with a rocky line, overhanging steeps and highly-pointing spires. The road, in majestic breadth descending the steep side of the mountain, takes us to Nasconaza, a comfortable village three leagues off—it is a league farther to Escoriessa, a good town. The people know and salute us. Again half a league to Achavaleza, a good town. Scenery still kept up. About dark descend to Mondragon, five long leagues of excessive bad road, but soft weather all day. We are billeted at the house of a good old woman, who looks to be at least four hundred years old; she does not know how old she is now, but knows that in six years she shall be fourscore.

Am surprised at my own ignorance that the language of Biscay, called by the speakers of it Basco or Bascuenza, is not more Spanish than Welsh or Erse is English. Those who have not studied Spanish do not understand one word spoken by a Castillian. An interesting, funny little girl is of the greatest use to us; she makes herself understood in very odd French, and busies herself mightily for us, reproaching the people, astounding the dull, and then laughing at their astonishment, throwing herself into all the energetic attitudes of impatience. Reynolds in walking across the street from the carriage to the house loses his master's case, containing a *couvert* of silver. This troubles Stephens exceedingly. How the devil *he could lose it* in that little space!

Monday, January 29, 1810.—Have great difficulty in getting a cart for our baggage, but with the help of my little girl Bustle I get one. The *chef*, in a fury because the carts escape, gives most savagely the *coup plat de sabre* to the first wretch, that meets him. A sweet pretty Biscayenna comes into the room and asks if we have lost anything, at the very instant that Stephens is offering a reward to Bustle if she will find *his couvert*. The Biscayenna found it in the street, and says she does not choose to profit by any accident at the expense of a stranger and an Englishman. Pretty Biscayenna, the reward you obtain thus honestly will give you more pleasure than the most costly findings!

More than any other part of Spain that I have seen by a great many degrees, is the Province of Biscay flourishing and populous. The most avaricious and precise cultivation, added to the irrigated fertility of the soil, ensures a luxuriant produce. The tillage extends to the very tops of the highest mountains where there is soil, and this Province supplies all the neighbouring ones with butter and cheese. The cattle are very small and nicely proportioned. Beef and mutton both very good. But the disproportioned population and industry of this part of Spain is attributed to another cause besides the natural advantages of the *terrene*, and that is the state of liberty which, until lately, its inhabitants had been happy enough to preserve; for they maintained extraordinary and essential privileges, which put them far above any part of the Peninsula subjected to the Crown of Spain.

They paid no duties whatever to the king, being taxable only by their particular *juntas*, to which His Catholic Majesty applied occasionally for pecuniary assistance, which was granted or denied as the junta thought fit. Biscay was equally exempt from any tribute of soldiers, nor could any troops be quartered on the people except by permission of their Provincial Government. If a Biscayan, say they, committed a capital crime in any other province, or even in the metropolis, capital punishment could not be inflicted unless the criminal was sent to be judged in his own province.

Thus these people, allowed the advantages of their soil and mercantile situation, are industrious, and by consequence rich. In other countries equally fertile, as in Sicily for instance, rich land lies neglected, because tyranny, stupidly greedy, lays on taxation with an ignorant hand, and mars the prosperity of the land-owner. The Biscayans are the most sensible, cleanly, civilised, and amiable class of Spaniards I have seen, and not only from patriotism dislike the French, but because King Jo is equalising them with the rest of his subjects. Start at nine o'clock alone. It begins to rain, soon ceases, and now is beautifully soft and fresh. Road rather better.

Meet, in separate battalions, 1800 *cuirassiers*, fine men, well mounted and appointed. The officers' helmets richly gilt and ornated with silver. From the crest descends, glossy and with free silky fluency, the copious horse-hair. We come to a village, and turning a corner come upon the convoy at halt This is about half-journey, where the great road to Bilbao turns off on the left. About 7000 Infantry file by us here; very many boys. An officer of the Irish Legion accosts us, and walks with us a good way—a fine active young fellow—and exerts himself much to prevent plunder. I take him to be a West Indian. 36,000 men, he says, have been embarked at Portsmouth for Spain— doubt not! He presses us to stop at some wine-house and drink at his expense. This we disincline, and therefore decline to do.

Leaving this village, which is considerable, we wind steeply to an immense height; leaving an enchanting scene behind us, laughing to be cheered in January by the beams of the illustrious sun, wind down the mountain, and open upon scenery less inviting. A spiral mountain is remarkable ahead. At half-past three arrive at Villareal, a small town. We are billeted in the same house with our friends the Spanish generals, and in our room is a fine fire. Hear various political reports from a rich and obliging Biscayan—Archduke Charles declared Emperor, renewal of the Austrian war, and so forth; don't believe one word! Four leagues we have come today.

Tuesday, January 30, 1810.—Start at eight. File in rear of the coaches; meet 2000 horse-hair cavalry, and 9000 infantry of a better description than yesterday, newly equipped. They pelt Nelly Par with turnips. We arrive at Villafranca, two and a half leagues; enter the *château* of a marquis, from the back of which we have a most enchanting view of the spiral mountain, from which the French country lies open to the eye. Admirable gardens, orchards, rivers, woods, and green fields—a, paradise! a paradise!

This mountain is in a range which branches from the Pyrenees and runs in a direction parallel to the coast of Biscay at about thirty miles' distance from it. It was this range we passed when the scenery delighted us so about Mondragon, and, having traversed it, we now behold it on the right hand and on the starboard bow. Villafranca, a very good but small town; walking out of it and looking back, I see it in a beautiful posture backed by fertile mountains. A lovely Biscayan, whose open smile is like the sunshine, and who steps over the earth as if it were no bar to her progress, accompanies the convoy as it approaches Tolosa. Old Brigadier Domingo is instantly captivated, but she rejects his suit with frankness and good-nature, unaccompanied by the slightest embarrassment. At dusk we bring in sight Tolosa, with milk-white houses, under circumstances of the most enchanting beauty—in a bottom enveloped by rich and fantastic mountains and watered by the river Oriia.

Tolosa is a good, populous town. We are sent to the inn with the Spanish *brigadieros*—a very good house. This day's journey has been five long leagues through the most glowing and romantically-beautiful country I ever saw, all the way winding through the vales, whereof there is none that does not speak prosperity and abundance—shining single houses, gardens, orchards, large villages, strew the land as thick as hail. And the most rigid cultivation clothes it with inconceivable splendour. The day has been heavenly, and the beams of the sun, piercing the mist of the mountains, sparkled in the frequent cascades which the charmed eye was ever catching through the leaf-less woods or auburn foliage. Some of the horse-hair cavalry tarry here tonight. Tolosa five long leagues from Villareal—ay, long ones!

SPIRAL MOUNTAIN AT VILLAFRANCA FROM WHICH FRANCE IS SEEN

Wednesday, January 31, 1810.—Start at eight o'clock, meet 2000 horse-hair cavalry—a heavy-shouldered, labouring horse hard worked. The officers" helmets seem solid gold, gorgeously embossed; the most graceful and complete warrior's head-dress I ever saw. The men uncommonly fine. Meet a troop of Horse Artillery—four 6-pounders, two 5½-howitzers, twenty tumbrels, sixty caissons or thereabouts. Meet 5000 infantry—grown, but not fine men—newly equipped. Charming weather. Road, mending apace, goes by the side of the river Oriia, which, receiving the Elzain at the good village of Andoarn, becomes a fine-looking river, and one would think in some degree navigable.

It empties itself into the Bay of Biscay about two leagues west of

St. Sebastian. Andoarn is two leagues from Tolosa. At Unheta, two and three quarter leagues, a small but good village (good, for all the houses are town houses; no such thing as a cottage), the road resumes its excellence. Country beautiful, but less exquisite than elsewhere. The air is cooler than yesterday. At ten o'clock the sun appeared in splendour. It is not twelve, and Hernani peeps above a steep hill most attractively, a quarter of a mile off, backed by noble mountains that reach the clouds and glory in the sun. See a child drawing a vegetable-cart, the body the shell of a gourd, and the wheels two flat turnips.

Arrive at Hernani at quarter-past twelve, a nice little town, three leagues. Take *café au lait* at a dirty French coffee-house. The scene behind this house, glistening in the sun, with a river running past, is superb. Start at one o'clock in precedence of the convoy. Scenery on leaving the town, Elysium! Where are the terms of sufficient praise? I am forced perpetually to use the same, yet are the scenes the same? O no! ever varying, ever changing, yet ever lovely! Submit, dull mortal, to your trammels, and describe things as you may. What a sweet trout river! How *populous* the country is! Have I mentioned before that the Biscayan women universally have enormous flat queues that descend considerably below the waist? In some of the towns two queues hang from the back of the head straight down, or sometimes tucked under the zone.

The men dress in all sorts of gaudy colours and flowered jackets, flannel leggings stripped black and white, and red sashes. Before

BISCAYAN PEASANT

we came to Hernani we met what the Austrian bulletins termed an armour-equipped cavalier—a *cuirassier*. His whole body and head was in steel, which looked beautiful, and must be a marvellous protection. Raven horse-hair flowed glossy down his *casque* abundant. The scenery is always in bursts of laughter. Away on the pinnacle of a mountain to the right a huge obelisk points upwards. Mountains in front broken and grand; road hilly. Meet Artillery—ten 9-pounders, four 8-inch howitzers, seventy-three tumbrels, four of which are saddled and slung for men to ride on, eight spare carriages, sixteen open waggons, five caissons, three forge carts. Now infantry; 6000 fine lads, newly equipped.

In ascending the hill to Ollarsu, met seventy-eight covered waggons or caissons, and two with Engineers' stores. All the artillery and equipage we meet is new. Ollarsu is a small good town, five leagues from Tolosa. The coaches, which we join here, set off before us. They are better horsed than we, and soon leave us. It grows dusk, and we have a long hilly league to Irun. Our friends the Spanish brigadiers call a council of war. We declare our intention to proceed; they fear to go without the convoy. *Con dios, ustedes!* Meet a French officer. "*Messieurs,*" says he, "this road is much infested with *brigands*, and you risk yourselves much, being so few in number. At this time of evening especially no distinctions of nation will avail. I met about quarter of a league on a number of carriages, which I recommend you by all means to join. You will soon do it if you push on. It is but a few minutes since I myself was fired at."

Merci, monsieur, merci bien! We disbelieve *monsieur* and proceed. Very heavy hills and deep woods. It gets dark. A shot fired behind us! Begin to believe *monsieur! Another shot! Diable!* I hope they'll hail the carriage before they fire at it! Ho! ho! here we are! Irun! It is not yet seven o'clock. Seek the *commandant de la place*; find at his house our *chef*. He takes his leave of us desiring us to present ourselves to the *commandant de la place à Bayonne*—glad to have done with him. After providing ourselves, etc., meet one of the Spanish *brigadieros* on horseback. They had spoken to the same officer who told us he had been fired at, and soon after, hearing the shots we also heard, they thought it prudent to go back to Ollarsu, where meeting the *chef* he desired them to come on, and here they are at nine o'clock, sorry they did not follow our example. Take leave of these Spaniards.

These were they—(1st) Brigadier-General Domingo Lasala, colonel of the African regiment which at Talavera behaved so well, sharp shooting on the right of the British, where he was himself severely wounded in the arm. A good, honest, loyal, brave, jolly, comely old fat Spaniard! (2nd) Brigadier-General Marmillotti, a mild, thin, squeaking, tall, pale, genteel old woman! (3rd) Lieutenant-Colonel Jose Rivas, colonel of Cavalry of the North, a stout-hearted, loyal, cut-and-thrust hussar, covered with wounds and medals; believes all good news! I pleased him greatly by giving him the king's arms in silver fretwork which I took from Towers's gorget. (4th) Colonel Ildefonso Roseas, captain of a frigate, a good-looking gentleman, quiet and good-humoured. (5th and last) Lieutenant-Colonel Ramon Salvador, surnamed the tinker, a little, queer-built, punch-faced, olive-coloured, laughing, dirty, smutched-artificer-looking, honest, friendly, intelligent, up-to-snuff Timothy. He speaks in English which cannot be understood.

What I have commonly comprehended under the name of Biscay contains three provinces which have nothing in common, but have laws, customs, and languages totally distinct. The first which joins Castile is Alava, of which Vittoria is the capital; next Biscaya, of which Bilbao is the capital; and then Guipuscoa, of which St. Sebastian is the capital. Seven leagues today. We are lodged in a schoolroom and sleep on the copy-books.

Thursday, February 1, 1810.—Start at ten o'clock a.m.; a nasty little uninviting town, this *Irun,* marshy and cold going out. At one mile arrive at the river Bidasoa, which here divides Spain and France. The wooden bridge which crosses it is occupied by the transit of 5000 infantry. These dogs jeer as they pass us. Now the wooden bridge is clear; on this side is a Custom-House lodge. The officers make some demonstration of searching our baggage, which being understood as a hint for some silver, we pass the bridge without further let and enter France!

The frontiers of the two countries have nothing remarkable on either side, but are strikingly unamiable contrasted with the gorgeous beauties of Guipuscoa. But as we penetrate, a striking and general difference from Spain obtains. The scenery and enclosures are of great beauty and have a very English aspect. The style of cultivation, too, is English. The snow-clad Pyrenees mount the sky on the right; on the left the sea—the sea, our proper domain—breaks upon our view through a heavy mist. It will be difficult for those who have never seen it under similar circumstances to conceive the fondness and softened recollections with which we gaze upon it.

It holds us long in silence. Its waves, noiseless from the distance, flow gently to the land, and seem to welcome us and offer us liberty and protection, and tell us they surround our darling island, and keep from her the calamities and horrors we have witnessed. *May they ever!* May England's happiness and high favour continue long after we have ceased to breathe! The road is very fine, continuing over the tops of the hills. At two leagues arrive at Ouronne, the first French town, a small place; the people speak a miserable patois unintelligible to a Frenchman. We catch a glimpse of the sea now and then, and we could throw a stone into the last dip. Arrive at St. Jean de Luz, a considerable seaport town, pier, harbour; two rivers enter the sea here. The view up the river is enchanting; leave the sea somewhat and arrive at Bayonne, six leagues at half-past six.

Chapter 24

Bordeaux, 11th February 1810.

My dear Mulcaster,—I send this letter *via* England, and hope it will reach you. Having lost all hope of exchange in Spain, and conceiving strong hopes of effecting it in France from my being disabled, and assisted by the influence of Marshal Mortier, I at last determined to undertake the journey, particularly as in France, if I were obliged to live there for some time, my life would pass more agreeably, I should hear more of what was going on in the world, feel altogether nearer home, and get rid of the horrors incident to feeling myself in the midst of a vast uncivilised dispirited country. I bought a comfortable light post-chaise at Madrid, and two other officers, my friends, promised a pair of beasts, that is to say, a mare and a mare mule.

The roads being unsafe, we were obliged to travel with a convoy escorted by infantry—some of our halts were in miserable villages. We were obliged to carry everything with us, beds and provisions, etc., although creeping after bullock-carts for twenty-five days. The distance of about 400 miles was tedious and very disagreeable, added to the bad lodgings and the constraint of a convoy; yet, upon consideration, sitting all day in a comfortable carriage, and sure of cover, victuals, and a bed at night, with two agreeable companions,' being well recommended to the generals in the cities, who were ready to lend occasional assistance, although I look back with great satisfaction on this Spanish journey as a thing over, I cannot boast to have endured any of the real evils of life.

On the contrary, comparing experience with expectation, I find myself obliged to congratulate myself on my good fortune. Travelling in the depth of winter, we only found a little severity about Burgos, before it was fine, and afterwards up to this day it has been heavenly. One of my companions, precipitated from a 20-foot rock by the horns of a furious ox, lay without motion at the bottom; he might well have been dead, or at least have a limb or two broken. He came to himself, and the cloud passed over without bad consequences. The carriage overturned by Aaron Delacourt in a ditch, but neither we nor it were disabled nor broken. Biscay and Guipuscon a perfect paradise, set off by the most brilliant weather. I was a good deal surprised to find all my Spanish unserviceable here, the people only understanding what they call Basque, which I have no doubt resembles Hindustani more than it does Spanish by a great deal.

Valladolid, a nasty old town; Burgos, a very fine town, with an exquisite cathedral; Vittoria, a fine town, surrounded with such profuse and romantic beauty as beggars all description. We blessed God for all things on arriving at Bayonne, where we passed two or three days. My letters procured us leave to take Versailles in our way to Verdun and to stay there some days, and the General (Hedonville) explained to me that during the stay I might urge any claims or make use of any interest I could to effect my exchange, or, if I wished, in case of failure, to reside near Paris. He did not think that, in my position, it would be refused me to remain at Versailles, which I shall certainly endeavour to do, if I find it impossible to get away.

Marshal Mortier, not content with his efforts to procure me my liberty, has recommended me to his friends in Paris, supplied me with cash at Madrid to prepare for my journey, and gave me besides a letter of credit for Paris to an unlimited amount. He told me he had not the smallest doubt of my procuring leave to return to England until my exchange could be effected. If I find that I cannot do this, I am confident he will make use of every means in his power, that the hopes he has given me may not be disappointed. We found everybody amiable and agreeable on our entry into France, where people seem to consider us with a sort of friendly distinction.

We found no difficulties, were immediately left in the full enjoyment of our liberty, have put ourselves at our ease, consider ourselves travellers in France, and prepare to trace with a sort of triumph our considerable routes on the map of Europe. The contrast between being in unhappy Spain and in France, you will easily believe, is sufficiently remarkable—cheerful fires, palatable food, obliging manners, excellent inns, capital posting, claret and champagne, English scenery, burst upon us with all the graces of novelty, or rather of return after a long privation. As the carriage I had bought was not worse for wear, and was light and convenient for posting, we determined to travel as far as Bordeaux, and to continue it, if it did not prove too expensive. We find it as cheap as any other way, and so shall keep on to Versailles in the same agreeable way.

We have nothing before us but good roads; that between Bayonne and this is very heavy. The post is extremely well regulated, and travellers are protected from imposition or difficulty by purchasing the book of orders on that subject. We arrived here the day before yesterday at ten o'clock at night, and the next day again set forward. This city with its harbour is so superb and the town-plan so gigantic as completely to astonish us. If its wealth and prosperity were to go on and be promoted by peace and security of commerce, it would soon surpass in stately beauty London or any town that I have ever seen. Its grand theatre, erected with the highest architectural magnificence, shamed the dusky clay-built pile which, fortunately burnt, enclosed in such a metropolis as London one of the finest theatres in Europe—shamed the dusky clay-built pile of the Haymarket, that does enclose perhaps the most splendid assembly in the world.

We dined yesterday with a wealthy merchant, to whom we were recommended by one of Bayonne, who took us by the hand, befriended us, and entertained us with his intelligent conversation merely to please himself. We went to the play in the evening, the performance was mediocre, and the audience thin and not remarkable. We go to the play again tonight, and dine with the wealthy merchant again tomorrow. When I get to England again, you must make a point of writing to me very often, you and Gos; I cannot bear the thoughts of being forgotten by you.

Tell my chum Mudge not to forget me, for I am much attached to him. I wrote to him from Talavera, but by some accident I lost sight of the letter when I was making up my packet before leaving that place. Remember me very kindly to all brother-officers and friends. Make a point of going to General Sherbrooke and telling him that every anxiety for his welfare which his nearest and dearest friends can feel, I feel also. Tell him . . . I still have hopes of exchange. You will not forget to tell General Stewart that you have heard from me and General H. Campbell. I am still upon crutches; but if my stay in France is to be prolonged, I shall consult the Faculty at Paris respecting a wooden leg. May God bless and prosper you, my dear Mulcaster; and allow me always a high place in your affection, and do you always class me among the warmest, the most attached, the most grateful of your friends,

Charles Boothby.

Paris, 2nd March 1810.

My dearest Father,—The first step is to procure permission to remain in Paris, which, although I have not yet received officially, I am given to understand will be granted. I shall then turn my attention with all my powers to procure either my exchange, or permission to go to England to endeavour to effect it there. I do not wish to raise hopes which perhaps might be disappointed, but I cannot persuade myself that I am doomed to a very long separation from you and all that I love. I am so well that I can enjoy all the sights of Paris.

We are treated with the utmost liberality, even with distinction; and if I get amongst you soon I shall not regret the being captured, which has given me an opportunity of seeing things which perhaps may never offer again. Would to God I could hear something from you, three words would be sufficient; do try if you cannot just let me know that you are all well. Captain Stephens is very well, and I fancy will get leave to remain in Paris some time.—Ever, my dearest Father, your most devotedly affectionate son, Charles.

Paris, 10th March 1810.

My dearest Father,—I have made application, grounded upon my infirmity, to be allowed to come to England for a limited time, for the purpose of effecting my exchange, with the obligation to return in case of failure.

The success of this application is uncertain; I therefore would recommend your casting about to discover whether it is impossible to forward it by any arrangement on your side the water. More exchanges between individuals have been effected by interest there than here.

The Abbé Dillon found me out the other day, and has made me acquainted with his sister, niece, etc., which is a great resource, as they are very agreeable and friendly people. I am perfectly well. In writing to me confine yourself simply to private and essential subjects, which would not be stopped or opened.—
Yours,   Charles.

P.S.—My petition has not yet received any answer—which is so far in its favour, for those answers that come quick are generally negative. If you can find out any interest sufficient to draw out such a paper as I have mentioned, take care that I am not put down 2nd Captain, which is a regimental distinction and does not interfere with army rank—mine being the same as that of all other captains according to date. Nothing is so dangerous as a *hitch* upon these occasions; and if the French Minister thought that they wanted to underrate me in order to get me cheaper, he might stop all proceedings.

                                      Paris, 26th March 1810.
My dearest Father,—When I tell you that I have no letter from home of a later date than the 14th September 1809, you will conceive that my anxiety to hear of you is painful. Write to me and address it to Messrs. Mallet Frères and Company, Bankers, Paris, and write "Mr. Boothby" at one corner of the direction; then enclose it to Jos. Casenove and Company, Old Pay Office, Broad Street, London. You may seal your letter and talk to me at your ease on family affairs, but always so as that you would not mind if it were to be opened.

I gave a letter for you in charge two days ago to Major L'Estrange, who has got leave to effect his exchange. In that I told you that my hopes of coming to England shortly were increased, but that still I could not bid you to be sanguine; the case remains as it was. An officer of rank, who was interested about my exchange, told me some days ago that it appeared my affair could be managed by means of the officer whom I, in my petition, had proposed to get sent for myself. I shall know more shortly. I had the satisfaction of seeing the emperor last Sunday at his chapel—a sight for which I had been very curious. I had an opportunity to observe him well for half an hour.

With my kindest love to all, I am ever, my dearest Father,
                                                                       Charles.

Paris, Friday 13th April 1810.

My dearest Lou,[1]—I take every opportunity of writing to you, but the grievous silence in which you have all been enveloped since the 14th September 1809 is not yet broken. I hope, however, that you receive my letters, although some sour devil evidently makes yours to me miscarry. I have seen all that was desirable in these vast *fêtes* which have celebrated the union between Napoleon and the Archduchess, and have seen them very close. I shall, I hope, be able to tell you all about these things before they are forgotten.

I cannot tell you how pleasant I find the society into which Arthur Dillon introduced me at the house of Madame de Boigne, his niece, who is a sweet, pretty little creature. Her mother, Madame d'Osmond, Monsieur d'Osmond, and Mr. Ernulf d'Osmond,—all these and many more are very choice people, and extend a familiar kindness to me, which makes my residence here much more agreeable. I am in a most enviable lodgings and see from my windows an old powdered gentleman, his lady, and their daughters, working in a very pretty tasty garden, that cheers me and puts me in mind of Edwinstowe. To be sure, there are some "tops"[2] in sight also, such as made Mamsey cry at Nottingham.

My health and spirits are just the same as they always have been. I go out less, but am forever "cheerful and merry," never finding the day long enough for what I have to do and not do. The pain which I mentioned a long while ago as still remaining I cannot say is quite gone, but I am sensible that it is going, because at Madrid it used to plague me and break my sleep, whereas here I very seldom think of it, sleep all night, and never feel it in bed. I should not care twopence if it were always to remain as it is, but as I think it will go entirely, to be sure I make no objection. I talk of myself more than anything else, because I believe the subject interests you more than any other, thank thee.

Madame d'Osmond talks of dear Lady Milnes; give my best love to her and Sir Robert and every Nottinghamshire thing. Tell Jasper that I have been apprised that the Minister of War has received my petition favourably, and has laid it before the

---

1. Louisa Rafela Boothby, sister of Captain Boothby.
2. Chimney-pots, called "tops" by his mother before she could speak. English perfectly.

emperor, for whose decision the affair waits. H.M. may say "no," but in truth I cannot think he will.

All doubt is at an end. My petition is assented to by the emperor; but from some vacation in the offices I am told that it will be yet a month before I shall receive my passport, perhaps more, so that I should place my arrival somewhere about the middle of June at latest. My mind is now easy, if I could but get letters from you. God bless thee, my lass,   Charles.

Paris, 24th April 1810.

My ever dearest Father,—I cannot express to you the load that your letters of the 1st February and 9th April have taken off my mind; the latter I received last night, so that nothing can do better than the mode of communication I have pointed out, and as it came sealed, you may write with more freedom about ourselves, not considering it as at all likely to be opened, but avoiding all subjects of a political nature to guard against a possibility. I hope to get amongst you time enough to see the garden dressed in the beauties of summer. Nobody loves that garden so much as Rafela[3] and myself. I wrote to Billy[4] the other day to desire that he would find out the commissioners for the Transport Board, to ascertain and if possible obviate any objections to the liberation of Captain Meseure, against whom the emperor, at my own request, has authorised my exchange.

I was advised to make my petition as definite as possible, and therefore proposed the French officer above mentioned as of the same rank and the corresponding branch of service. The proposal, I know, has been made by the French government, and I have no doubt I should be immediately liberated if the British government would certify its acceptance of it.

I wish Billy to find out if there be any hesitation about it, and if there be, to give in immediately a written statement representing that the nomination of Captain Meseure was made by me in my petition to the Minister of War, and did not proceed from any suggestion from the French War Office, but merely from my inquiring if there was any captain of Engineers in England against whom I could propose myself in exchange; but if there will not be any hesitation let nothing be said about it. In the

---

3. His mother.
4. His brother.

meantime I have written to ask permission to depart immediately, and am not at all certain that it will be refused.—Your ever dutiful and affectionate   Charles.

P.S.—26th April I have not got any answer to my request to be allowed to come to England on parole.

Letter from Major William Boothby to his son Captain Charles Boothby

Edwinstowe, 20th May.
(Received in Paris, 29th May.)

My dearest Charles,—I send you a copy of a letter I have just received from Lord Newark in answer to one I wrote to him on receiving yours of the 20th April.

> On the receipt of your last letter I lost not a moment in sending it to Mr. Douglas, fearing, however, at the same time, that although definitive as to its object, it might be thought indefinite as to the means by which that object was to be obtained. The event has proved me in the right, as Mr. Douglas, whom I saw yesterday morning, informs me that it is impossible for the Transport Board to release the officer mentioned in Charles's letter, unless they receive some official intimation from the French government that your son's liberation shall immediately follow, and no such intimation, either private or public, has yet been received.
>
> The steps that have been already taken by the Transport Board are as follows. They sent several weeks since two certificates to Paris. By the one they engaged to release an officer of equal rank upon Charles being permitted to come home to England; by the other, that they would immediately release any officer of equal rank, upon an assurance that Boothby should be released upon the appearance of that officer in France. But to neither of these propositions have they received an answer.

Mr. Douglas belongs to the Transport Board. I hope amid these circumstances there can be no doubt that you will soon be able to avail yourself of the kindness you have received on both sides of the water. Your letter gave us much delight by telling us you had at last received intelligence from us. All your friends are

well, and desire their kindest love to you, my dearest Charles.—
Your ever truly affectionate, W. Boothbv.

Letter from Duchesse de Fitz-James to Madame d'Osmond

Paris, le 15 Juin.
Je vous envois, ma chère, la lettre que je reçois du Ministre de la Guerre.
Je pense que déjà vous savez peut-être ce qu'elle m'annonce, mais dans l'incertitude je vous l'adresse toujours, heureuse si je pouvais croire avoir un peu contribué à la réussite d'une chose que vous désirez.

Paris, le 18 Juin 1810.
Le Ministre de la Guerre présente ses hommages respectueux à Madame de Fitz-James, et a l'honneur de lui annoncer que M. le Capitaine Anglais Boothby auquel elle veut bien s'intéresser recevra un passeport pour retourner sur sa parole dans sa patrie, dès qu'il se présentera dans les Bureaux du Ministre.

Letter from Madame d'Osmond to Captain Charles Boothby

Beauregard, le 16 Juin 1810.
C'est avec une grande joie, mon cher Monsieur Boothby, que je vous adresse les incluses—retournez, retournez dans votre heureuse patrie, que je regrette tous les jours de ma vie; vous y trouverez le bonheur que vous méritez, mes voeux et mon tendre intérêt vous y accompagneront.—
Je suis bien fâchée que vous n'avez pas donné quelques jours à Beauregard avant votre départ. Si vous rencontrez mon frère Edouard, parlez lui de nous tous et de notre tendre amitié pour lui et pour toute sa famille. J'espère que la robe que vous portez à Georgina ne vous causera pas d'embarras. Monsieur d'Osmond et F.-J. partagent tous mes sentiments pour vous. Mademoiselle de Boigne est à Paris.

Letter from Captain Charles Boothby to his Father and Mother

July 1810.
This letter will be a little satisfaction for my beloved Father and Mother.

Madame d'Osmond, engaging in my behalf the *ci-devant* Duchess de Fitz-James, succeeded at last in getting me permission to come home on parole, engaging myself to return at the expiration of three months, if I failed in procuring the release of Monsieur Meseure, in which I suppose there will be no difficulty from Lord Newark's letter which you sent me. I confess, my dear old Dad, I have some little uneasiness at the thoughts of our meeting, arising from a feeling which perhaps does you injustice. If, like me, you have trained your ideas rather to be rejoiced at blessings which still remain to me, and promise to make my life happy, than to repine at the blow my youth has sustained, then, indeed, our joy at meeting will be unalloyed; and I will hope for this triumph of your philosophy over your tenderness.

I have told you that I am still on crutches, which gives me an appearance of helplessness that does not at all belong to my health and strength. The remedy I shall find in London will, I anxiously hope, do away almost entirely with this appearance. If I thought less of your piety and temper to make the best of things, I would recommend you to defer our meeting until after I can walk, but as it is, if I find my apprenticeship will be very long, I will certainly take a trip to Notts to satisfy our mutual impatience. But write to tell me all your feelings on this head, Mamsey's and Lou's. I am not afraid of the brothers and sisters so much as the fathers and mothers; but, my crutches apart, I believe you will not find the slightest alteration. But in your joy at my return keep in mind that you are to see me on crutches.

If you don't see me in high spirits, which are natural to me, you may be sure that it is because I see you not reconciled to my misfortune. After all, my darlings of Edwinstowe, there is no use in saying anything more about it. I doubt not we shall pull through, and shall be guided by the letter which I shall find from you at the Blenheim.—Yours ever, Charles.

Letter from Captain Charles Boothby to the Maréchal Duc de Trevise [5]

Morlaix, 2nd July 1810.

My Lord,—In the very hour which precedes my embarkation, I sit down to take my leave of Your Excellency in a manner which, though hurried, carries with it a strong appearance of sincerity, and I beseech you to forgive whatever may be wanting in form, and believe at least that my intention is to express every sense of gratitude and regard which your uncommon

---

5. *Le Maréchal de l'Empire* Mortier.

goodness to me ought naturally to call forth. I address Your Excellency no longer as a prisoner who may derive benefit from your protection, or freedom from your influence. Before this reaches you I shall be in my own country beyond the reach of your extensive benevolence; and although I do not doubt but the candour of your character always gave credit to my expressions of gratitude, yet I cannot but be pleased with the moment in which I can offer thanks that cannot be suspected of design, or as the inviter of further favours.

My Lord, I can never forget the voice of kindness that, in moments of desolation, penetrated the abode of sickness and infirmity. It had a cheering sound, whose impression is at this moment fresh upon my heart and revives that series of unlimited favours, which my unfortunate situation afterwards moved you to heap upon me, not one particular of which is it possible for me to forget. They have terminated in restoring me to my own country, whither I am now going on parole for the purpose of effecting my exchange.

It is scarcely permitted to me to hope that I can ever make any other return, as in my own country I am devoid of that rank and influence which has enabled Your Excellency to be so essentially my protector; but should the good fortune of any such occasion present itself, in executing your wishes I shall ever consider myself as performing the most agreeable of duties. I should not omit to mention that Colonel Montfort's attachment to Your Excellency has led him to assist me with the most good-natured zeal.

I have the honour to be, my Lord, with the most distinguished respect and attachment. Your Grace's most obedient, humble servant,　　　　　　　　　　　　　　　　　Charles Boothby,
Capitaine du Génie.

LETTER FROM CAPTAIN CHARLES BOOTHBY TO THE MARÉCHAL DUC DE TREVISE

Newcastle-on-Tyne, 11th May 1814.

My Lord Duke,—A British officer, who, having lost a leg at the battle of Talavera, had the good fortune to fall into your gracious hands, begs permission to recall himself to Your Excellency as a person bound to you by gratitude and affection. During the reign of the Emperor Napoleon, I would not allow myself the liberty of addressing you, lest any communication from England might by possibility subject to suspicion a character, which its great elevation made so obvious to remark. But now that all the world seems to reclaim the voice of confidence and joy, I cannot longer deny to my heart the relief of breaking its long silence, to beg that Your Excellency will not, after having listened so indelibly upon my memory the impression of your benevolence, yourself forget that I have a right to hear and to repeat your name with interest and pleasure.

That I have never heard or repeated it with opposite sensations (though often indeed with anxiety), I count amongst the things for which I ought most to be thankful

It would have seemed too much to hope that I should never in *this country* hear one of the most conspicuous officers of Napoleon mentioned with dislike. Yet more than this has been accorded to my feelings, for throughout this free-speaking country the name of Mortier is repeated with affection; and never, amidst all the tremendous scenes in which it has been so eminent, since it became interesting to me, have I had to vindicate it from the censures of my countrymen, or to lament that the part which circumstances had imposed on my illustrious protector was unsuited to the nobleness of his nature. On the contrary, after seeing him conduct his share of the war, always in its most generous character, it has been to me a triumph that he was the last to quit the side of his fallen master, and the first to be honoured with the confidence of him newly risen.

Would it seem, my Lord, by the freedom of my language that I am forgetting the rank of the person I address, let your goodness attribute it rather to my remembering so well the reasons I have to rejoice in all that may redound to his fame and honour.

Indeed, I cannot much fear to offend him, while conscious that my pen is guided by nothing worse than the most unfeigned respect for his character, and the purest gratitude for an unmeasured kindness towards my misfortunes, the recollection of which can even persuade me that he will not deem impertinent some mention of that humble individual, for whose welfare he so effectually exerted his powerful means.

Before I quitted France I addressed to Your Excellency a letter from Morlaix, which I hope you received, as it would not only assure you of my gratitude, but also give your kind heart the satisfaction of knowing that your protection had been complete and effectual in my behalf. It secured me from every difficulty arising from a want of communication with England, to which (my country) it soon effected my return to dry the tears of my father and mother, and to restore their happiness by showing them that mine was not destroyed. By habit, and by the ingenuity of our mechanics, I have recovered much bodily activity. On horseback I am perfectly at ease. I walk with facility without a stick, and am grateful to find how little I have lost of life's enjoyments.

That *all her enjoyments,* my good Lord Duke, may very long be continued to you; and that, when at last those cease, better and more perfect may await you, is the sincere and earnest wish of Your Excellency's most faithful and gratefully attached servant,

Charles Boothby,
Captain Royal Engineers.

Letter from the Maréchal Duc de Trevise to Captain Charles Boothby

Au Château du Plessis Lalande,
Le 22 Juin 1814.

Monsieur,—J'ai reçu avec un véritable plaisir votre lettre du 11 mai; celle que vous m'avez écrite de Morlaix, en quittant la France, ne m'est jamais parvenue. Il ne m'a point été indifférent d'apprendre que malgré vos longues souffrances, et la nature d'une blessure aussi grave, vous étiez parvenu au point de faire avec facilité tous les exercices du corps; vous ne pouviez rien m'apprendre qui me fut plus agréable, car jamais je ne vous ai perdu de vue; et l'intérêt bien senti que vous m'avez inspiré m'a constamment porté à demander de vos nouvelles toutes les fois que j'en ai trouvé l'occasion. J'appris donc avec une vive satisfaction d'un officier Anglais, avec lequel je dînais il y a environs deux mois chez Lord Castlereagh, que vous jouïssiez d'une bonne santé; puisse le ciel vous accorder une série de jours heureux au sein de votre respectable famille. Je me figure tout le bonheur que doivent maintenant éprouver Madame votre mère et M. votre père; je me le figure par celui que j'éprouve moi-même près de ma femme et de mes enfans, après une aussi longue et une aussi pénible séparation.

J'espère que vous n'avez pas renoncé au désir de revoir le continent: il me serait alors bien agréable de vous voir chez moi; j'aurais beaucoup de plaisir à vous présenter à ma famille.

Veuillez, mon cher Monsieur Charles, agréer l'assurance de ma considération distinguée et de mon attachement.

Mal Duc de Trévise.

PASSE-PORT À L'ÉTRANGER.

Police Générale de l'Empire

Département —

Délivré par les Soins de S.M. pour l'homme de la
Majesté Impériale un Royale, au Parte Du nom errit
aux Ministres des Rel.

Soit à Paris

le 16 juin 1810

Le Ministre de la Guerre,
[signature]

Le Bn. Jg. Ministre
[signature]

AVIS ESSENTIEL

Dans les villes et lieux où il existe un Commissariat de police, le Porteur est tenu de se présenter, dans les 24h pour faire viser son Passeport.

ALSO FROM LEONAUR
AVAILABLE IN SOFTCOVER OR HARDCOVER WITH DUST JACKET

NAPOLEONIC WAR STORIES *by Sir Arthur Quiller-Couch*—Tales of soldiers, spies, battles & sieges from the Peninsular & Waterloo campaigns.

CAPTAIN OF THE 95TH (RIFLES) *by Jonathan Leach*—An officer of Wellington's sharpshooters during the Peninsular, South of France and Waterloo campaigns of the Napoleonic wars.

RIFLEMAN COSTELLO *by Edward Costello*—The adventures of a soldier of the 95th (Rifles) in the Peninsular & Waterloo Campaigns of the Napoleonic wars.

SMITH-DORRIEN *by Horace Smith-Dorrien*—Isandlwhana to the Great War.

1914 *by Sir John French*—The Early Campaigns of the Great War by the British Commander.

CAVALRY AT WATERLOO *by Sir Evelyn Wood*—British Mounted Troops During the Campaign of 1815.

THE SUBALTERN *by George Robert Gleig*—The Experiences of an Officer of the 85th Light Infantry During the Peninsular War.

DIGGERS AT WAR *by R. Hugh Knyvett & G. P. Cuttriss*—"Over There" With the Australians by R. Hugh Knyvett and Over the Top With the Third Australian Division by G. P. Cuttriss. Accounts of Australians During the Great War in the Middle East, at Gallipoli and on the Western Front.

THE LIGHT INFANTRY OFFICER *by John H. Cooke*—The Experiences of an Officer of the 43rd Light Infantry in America During the War of 1812.

THE CAMELIERS *by Oliver Hogue*—A Classic Account of the Australians of the Imperial Camel Corps During the First World War in the Middle East.

RED DUST *by Donald Black*—A Classic Account of Australian Light Horsemen in Palestine During the First World War.

NAPOLEON AT BAY, 1814 *by F. Loraine Petre*—The Campaigns to the Fall of the First Empire.

NAPOLEON AND THE CAMPAIGN OF 1806 *by Colonel Vachée*—The Napoleonic Method of Organisation and Command to the Battles of Jena & Auerstädt.

THE COMPLETE ADVENTURES IN THE CONNAUGHT RANGERS *by William Grattan*—The 88th Regiment during the Napoleonic Wars by a Serving Officer.

AVAILABLE ONLINE AT **www.leonaur.com**
AND FROM ALL GOOD BOOK STORES

www.ingramcontent.com/pod-product-compliance
Lightning Source LLC
Chambersburg PA
CBHW030216170426
43201CB00006B/107